PSYCHOLOGICAL DEVELOPMENT IN HEALTH AND DISEASE

GEORGE L. ENGEL, M.D.

Professor of Psychiatry and Professor
of Medicine, The University of Rochester
School of Medicine and Dentistry

W. B. SAUNDERS COMPANY

PHILADELPHIA AND LONDON

Reprinted February, 1963, July, 1964, and July, 1966

Psychological Development in Health and Disease

FOREWORD

I WONDER IF there has been any period previous to ours in the history of medical education, including the exciting two decades which followed the Flexner report, in which there has been as much change and growth. Challenges to existing and traditional concepts and practices have come from prodigious increases in knowledge and techniques and from the changing needs of the society in which we live. In my view, we are experiencing a major reorientation in medical science and practice. This may be as great as or greater than those associated with the beginnings of bedside clinical instruction in the sixteenth century or with the application of physics and chemistry and the quantitative method to biology in the mid-nineteenth century.

Tomorrow's physician must be better informed than was his predecessor about medicine in human as well as in infrahuman terms. He must learn many things, in substance and in method, about the psychology and sociology of his patient and his family. He must learn methods necessary to obtain relevant data about the social and psychological determinants of his patient's illness. He must gain understanding about man's thoughts and emotions and their effects on his body. He must learn about man's relations with other men. Tomorrow's physician can no longer depend solely on his personal idiosyncratic sample of human experience. No longer can he be content to perpetuate the dichotomy of a systematic and scientific approach to man's body

v

and one of intuitive artistry in dealing with man's mind and his emotions. Without proper skills and knowledge, the physician of tomorrow will indeed be found to be wanting.

This, in essence, is what has been and continues to be the central and pervasive concern of this university department's teaching to undergraduate medical students. As a member of our faculty, George Engel has devoted himself fully and generously to these objectives. His contributions have been original, outstanding and significant, as the readers of this book will learn for themselves. The book has evolved out of many years of his teaching psychological concepts to medical students and house officers in the University of Rochester. Its major theme is that of human psychological development and its relation to health and disease. I can attest personally to the appreciation and admiration of many classes of medical students and house officers for Dr. Engel's unusual skill and devotion as a clinician, as a medical scientist and, most particularly, as a teacher.

JOHN ROMANO, M.D.

Professor and Chairman, Department of Psychiatry,
University of Rochester School of Medicine and Dentistry,
and Psychiatrist-in-Chief,
Strong Memorial and Rochester Municipal Hospitals,
Rochester, New York

ACKNOWLEDGMENTS

THIS BOOK represents a synthesis of my understanding of human behavior in health and disease as it has evolved over some twenty years.
These views are still very much in flux, as any discerning reader will
quickly detect from the inconsistencies between early and later chapters, even though these are separated by only eight months of writing.
As a book, it has developed mainly in the course of my teaching of
medical students and it has been in the process of being written for
some fifteen years as four successive editions of a mimeographed
syllabus distributed to students and house officers. It has now reached
a point of sufficient stability that I am at last willing to have it published, something which I have resisted for many years in spite of the
urging of some of my colleagues and students. I still feel some lingering
reluctance, for with each revision over the years I have soon found
myself disenchanted with what I had so recently written, even though
at the time of writing it seemed to me almost like revealed knowledge.

The orientation of this work reflects my background and long
interest in biology and my continued teaching and investigation in the
field of internal medicine, activities which I have not relinquished as I
have pursued further education in clinical psychiatry and psychoanalysis. Indeed, even today much of my clinical teaching and experience continues to be on the wards of a medical service rather than on
the psychiatric service per se. But this does not mean that I have been
disinterested or detached from involvement with the more traditional

areas of clinical psychiatry. On the contrary, I have been actively engaged for many years in the educational and administrative activities of the Department of Psychiatry, conducting teaching exercises and staff conferences for students and house officers and supervising residents. My private practice has involved mainly consultative and short- and long-term psychotherapeutic endeavors (including formal psychoanalysis) with a wide range of psychiatric and psychosomatic patients, while the clinical material used in my research has known no administrative boundaries, involving patients from all the clinical services of the hospital, including the pediatric service. In my efforts to understand human behavior better, I have not let myself be restricted in access to clinical material. Nonetheless, the fact remains that I cannot lay claim to as intensive or extensive experience in certain areas of clinical psychiatry as can the traditionally trained and experienced clinical psychiatrists. On the other hand, I believe I have had a richer experience with sick people hospitalized in other clinical divisions than have most psychiatrists. This background will be clearly reflected in this book, which, as its title indicates, is concerned with health and disease in a broad sense and with psychological development in relationship to medicine as a whole, rather than to psychiatry alone. It is not and was not intended to be a textbook of psychiatry, in the strict denotative meaning of the word psychiatry.

I record this information here so that the reader may be aware of what types of experiences and influences have contributed to the views developed herein. Obviously, not all such influences can be identified; many, of course, are unknown to me. These views reflect my own development as an internist, psychiatrist and psychoanalyst and the current status of my understanding of human behavior. I have called upon the full range of my experience and knowledge and with this background have used, modified or rejected such theoretical frameworks as I have mastered, and where they were lacking, I have advanced theoretical notions of my own. It is not easy in a work of this sort adequately to document the data upon which such theoretical notions are based, and in many instances I am acutely aware of the deficiencies in this regard. Nonetheless, I have used or devised such theoretical formulations as I have found the most useful to explain the behavior under consideration. But the "most useful" is not necessarily entirely satisfactory or even correct. All I can say is that at the moment and with the information available to me, "This is what makes the most sense." In taking this position, I make no apology to those who will say that my views are too biological, or too psychoanalytic, or not sufficiently encompassing of social determinants, or whatever. I can say this with confidence, for through experience with earlier versions of this book I too have repeatedly arrived at just such conclusions. And it should go without saying that, although I play a large role in the undergraduate and graduate teaching program of the Department of Psychiatry, my views as organized in this volume by no means represent a frame of reference acceptable to all members of the department. Indeed, the opportunity to engage in vigorous discussions of differing viewpoints has been one of the most important influences in helping me to evolve and clarify my own views and has sustained in me the necessity for a highly critical attitude toward my own ideas.

In a work that has been in process for more than fifteen years it is impossible to acknowledge, much less identify, all the individuals who have contributed to its final form. Some readers will no doubt discover ideas or formulations for which, with considerable justification, they may claim not only priority but even the responsibility for my knowledge and understanding thereof. To all such persons whose contributions I have incorporated as my own so thoroughly as to lose sight of their origins, I offer my apologies and plead innocent of any willful intent to deprive them of proper recognition. Such a risk of inadequately acknowledging the contributions of others is increased by the fact that I have limited the references to those that I feel will be of most use to students and residents. I am fully aware that I have not provided a complete bibliography; accordingly, I should welcome having my attention drawn to any serious omissions or inaccuracies so that corrections may be made in future editions, should there be any.

To certain persons I am especially in debt, and to them I wish particularly to make acknowledgment.

First and foremost is John Romano, friend, colleague and mentor for more than twenty years. When in May, 1941, I went to the Peter Bent Brigham Hospital as a Dazian Foundation Fellow in Medicine, the late Soma Weiss, then Hersey Professor of Medicine at Harvard and Physician-in-Chief at the Brigham, somehow detected an incipient interest in the psychological aspects of medicine which was hardly yet conscious to me. He therefore suggested that I work with John Romano, a move which proved to be a turning point in my professional career, for it has been primarily through Romano's influence and guidance that my interest in and knowledge of this aspect of medicine have evolved and matured. It has been largely through his support, encouragement, inspiration and guidance that I have had the opportunities to learn, to work and to teach in this field and to develop thereby. A superb model of the critical scholar and teacher, he has inspired similar standards in my own work. And as a vigorous advocate and supporter of new ventures in medical education, he has encouraged me in my efforts to explore untried paths of teaching. Perhaps no small part of the gratification that I feel in finally bringing this book to completion is the opportunity it affords me publicly to acknowledge my gratitude and affection for the man who has been most responsible for my professional satisfactions and achievements over the past twenty years.

In the Cincinnati period (1942–46) Milton Rosenbaum, now Professor of Psychiatry at the Albert Einstein School of Medicine of Yeshiva University in New York, and I. Arthur Mirsky, now Professor of Clinical Science, School of Medicine, University of Pittsburgh, were the two figures most influential in furthering my interest in psychological concepts. Rosenbaum encouraged me in my first tentative excursions into the study of the psychiatrically sick, an area which I had tended to skirt while attempting to maintain my identity as an internist. Mirsky's brilliant research and conceptualization of psychosomatic interrelationships, the subject of endless rewarding discussions, left a lasting impression.

Sandor S. Feldman, wise clinician, scholar and psychoanalyst, shepherded me through a rewarding analysis when I first came to Rochester. Through him I learned about myself and then first came to understand and appreciate the contributions of psychoanalysis to the understanding of human behavior and to medicine.

At the Institute for Psychoanalysis in Chicago (1950–55) the stimulating scientific spirit of Franz Alexander was all pervasive, and for the atmosphere of scholarly inquiry he created at that Institute I am most grateful. There the most germinal and stimulating influence on me was Therese Benedek, to whom I am indebted for many hours of fruitful and illuminating discussion of psychoanalytic concepts. Control hours well spent!

My close colleagues of the Medical-Psychiatric Liaison Group of the Departments of Psychiatry and Medicine of the University of Rochester, William Greene, Franz Reichsman and Arthur Schmale, can claim responsibility for many of the ideas formulated in this book. Week after week, as a group, in our weekly Separation-Depression Conferences, and as individuals, we have discussed and shared our ideas over many years. If in this book they find much that is familiar because it is theirs, I trust they will accept it as a tribute, even though I may at times be remiss in identifying certain individual contributions. So extensive and so extended have been our discussions that priority no longer can be established. Many other colleagues of the Department of Psychiatry and of its division of Psychology have also at one time or another shared in many of these discussions, and I am deeply indebted to them as well.

Fifteen classes of medical students have contributed to this work. The challenge of teaching critical students is the greatest incentive to careful, clear thinking.

And finally I must express appreciation to those who had to put up with some of the drudgery and hard work of this enterprise and who did so with a degree of loyalty, cheerfulness, conscientiousness and efficiency that is nothing short of phenomenal. I refer to my secretaries, who have worked over the final revisions during the past several years, Evelyn Stingle Ledyard, Sara Evens Herrmann, and Cynthia Stober Warshaw.

My colleague Dr. Sanford Meyerowitz has been good enough to proofread both manuscript and page proof, and I am indebted to him for helpful suggestions concerning content and form as well as for catching errors that escaped my jaded eye.

During the years that I have worked on this book I have received generous financial support from the Commonwealth Fund, the Foundations Fund for Research in Psychiatry, the Ford Foundation, and the National Institute of Mental Health. I am deeply grateful for the opportunities this support has provided me to pursue both research and teaching.

Last, but not least, I must acknowledge the patience and good humor of my family as they put up with my prolonged periods of detachment and preoccupation while I labored to bring the work to completion.

GEORGE L. ENGEL, M.D.

Rochester, New York

CONTENTS

Part Two.   Health and Disease

Chapter XXXIII

Chapter XXXIV

INTRODUCTION

ON THE USE OF THIS BOOK

I HAVE PREPARED this work mainly for medical students and psychiatric residents, though of course I hope it will prove useful to other professional persons as well. The span from beginning medical students to psychiatric residents is a broad one, and one may question whether it is feasible to address oneself to as heterogeneous a group as this. I believe that it is if proper attention is given to the role of the teacher. This book is not intended to stand by itself. Nor is it conceived of as an elementary text, to be read once before going on to a more advanced work. On the contrary, I have made no effort to avoid the inherent complexities of the material under consideration, even though I am aware that much of it can become meaningful only after some clinical experience. Therefore, I have written with the expectation that the book will be used and reused through the preclinical and clinical years of the undergraduate medical curriculum and returned to again during residency training, each time with a further increment in understanding. Only in this way will the reader acquire the data to examine the validity of the concepts and will the concepts provide some framework within which to organize clinical observations.

Such a view as to how the book is to be used has evolved out of more than fifteen years of teaching psychological concepts to medical students and house officers at the University of Rochester. It originated in 1947 when I began the course in psychiatry for second year medical students, which I continue to teach to this day. It quickly became apparent that there was not available any reasonably concise and systematic presentation of the concepts considered basic to the general subject of the psychological development of man in health and disease to which students could be referred. To meet the need of the students for some written material, I began in 1948 to supply them with mimeographed copies of my own lecture notes. In subsequent years these notes were bound together and distributed to each new group of first year students, who began using them in the first year course and continued to use them throughout the four years. These notes went through three revisions, in 1951, 1954 and 1958, and now have finally been completely rewritten to become this book. This syllabus has constituted the core of the reading material for the students throughout their four years, and it is also supplied to all new psychiatric residents as well. Many graduates not continuing on into psychiatry have attested to its value in their internship and residency years. But most consistent has been the testimony of students and graduates that its usefulness increases as they acquire clinical experience. Repeatedly heard has been the statement, "I thought I understood it in the second year, but it only really began to make sense when I saw more patients."

As this syllabus has developed and become more complete, it has broadened the scope of my own teaching in the second year, permitting me greatly to reduce the time spent in the exposition of the basic concepts and to concentrate instead on developing techniques whereby the students and the teacher could share in the examination of some of the data underlying such concepts. Such a transition in teaching approach has evolved quite naturally in response to the greater engagement of the students in the material and their obviously better grasp of the concepts being considered.

From this experience I have come to the conclusion that the main function this book should serve is to free the teacher to teach. The book develops and organizes basic concepts in such a way that the student can at least begin to evolve some kind of framework of theoretical knowledge, but such knowledge is of relatively little value unless it is supported by active engagement and experience with the data and clinical material from which the concepts have been developed in the first place. To provide such support is the responsibility of the teacher. The book, therefore, does not represent simply a handy compendium of what the well-prepared student should know by the end of the year (nor what the teacher should teach), and any student who imagines that he can meet the requirements of the preclinical education in this field simply by reading the book will find himself sadly deficient. Similarly, the teacher who merely lectures on the content of the book should not be surprised to find his students bored and inattentive, if they come to class at all. Under such conditions, the student, if he comes away with anything, will merely have learned by rote certain abstract concepts, and he will have gained little comprehension of their meaning and application.

On the other hand, if the teacher is successful in his undertaking—and it is by no means a simple one—the student will, through reading, gain some grasp of concepts, he will achieve some degree of clarification of these concepts through classroom discussion and exposure to the primary data through which the concepts can better be examined, and he will then reread the textbook material for further clarification and elaboration. As we have learned over the years from the use of the mimeographed syllabus, this only begins the learning process for the student.

Because this book first of all is directed to the beginning medical student, a question arises as to the aims of undergraduate education in psychiatry, for clearly the focus of the book should reflect such objectives. This has been a matter of intense interest to the members of the Department of Psychiatry and especially to its Chairman, John Romano, who in a recent address summarized these objectives as follows:*

What are our objectives in the teaching of psychiatry to medical students? Is the teaching to be principally a preparation for those who will become psychiatrists? Is it to point especially to the family doctor of tomorrow—to the exclusion of the surgeon, the internist, the radiologist, and others? Neither of these has been, nor is, the primary purpose. Regardless of the eventual destinies of the students in the many fields of medicine, we try to meet certain needs they have in common.

First and foremost, we do all we can to encourage the student's curiosity and to foster his capacity for critical perceptiveness. By this we mean his need to question, to be sceptical, to subject data to his own inquiry, to examine the method and evidence of others—in short, for him to become critically informed.

Second is the need to understand the sequence of growth and decline in our society with attention to genic and experiential factors as determinants. In this he may learn about the emergence of man from early parasitic dependence to increasing capacities for interdependent human behaviour, and about the multiple-person field, the family, and other groups.

Third is the need to understand how the concepts of health and disease have developed from primitive animistic and more recent single-cause ideas to modern views of biological systems, of dynamic steady states rather than fixed immutable equilibria. In this we also draw attention to the frequent emotional crises in human family life, which by themselves do not constitute disease, but if neglected or mishandled may lead to disability.

Fourth is the need to understand the unique reciprocal relationships between patient and physician, and the latter's reciprocal relations with nurses, social workers, the clergy, health visitors, technicians, and others with whom he is associated in the care of the sick.

---

* Romano, J.: Teaching of Psychiatry to Medical Students. Lancet, 2:93–95, July 8, 1961. Quoted by permission.

Fifth is the need to understand the psychology and sociology of the patient and his family in acute illness, chronic illness, convalescence, and disability; and the special problems of elective and urgent surgical intervention and of other episodes needing medical attention.

Sixth is the need to learn to recognise emotionally and mentally sick persons who express their distress in physical, psychological, or social symptoms. Traditionally this comes under the heading of psychopathology; but latterly there has been a tendency to extend it beyond classical descriptive psychopathology, in an attempt to learn more of the variations of normal development and behaviour—i.e., to learn more about the adaptive devices used at successive stages of life to meet the stresses, challenges, and rewards he may encounter. This implies reasonable mastery of methods of physical examination and of clinical psychiatric examination, and the judicious and critical use of accessory methods, such as physical and chemical tests and psychological examinations. It also implies the need to learn more about the zones of healthy and sick behaviour in our society, and the ability to distinguish between normal, neurotic, psychopathic, psychotic, and intellectually defective behaviour.

Seventh is the need, implied in the above, to learn how to listen to the patient's story and how to record it. The ability to interview properly is of the utmost importance in all branches of medical practice, and our teaching is directed to basic principles of interviewing patients, regardless of the nature of their presenting complaints. Implicit in the learning process is familiarity with the dynamics of the patient-physician relationship.

Eighth is the need for the doctor to understand what he can and should do:

1. In the management and treatment of emotionally healthy people who become sick.

2. In the management and treatment of the patient in whose family certain common emotional crises are being experienced.

3. In the first-aid management of disturbed patients—the anxious and panicky, the delirious, the suicidal, the depressed, the grief-stricken, the excited, the aged, and the demented.

Ninth is the need for the doctor who is not a psychiatrist to understand what he cannot do and should not attempt. He must learn the limits of his own knowledge and skills, and how to make intelligent referrals to specialists, clinics, and hospitals. Here, too, he should learn the most effective ways of working with the psychiatrist and with the psychologist, social caseworker, nurse, occupational therapist, and others. He should be well informed, and capable of realistic appraisal of methods used in the treatment of the mentally sick.

Tenth, and last, is the need to know about the community resources which can be extensions of the doctor's care of his patient. The student should learn about the assistance to be obtained from social, welfare, and legal agencies and from the clergy, and about the existence and operations of special institutions for the chronically ill.

This statement spans the over-all objectives of undergraduate psychiatric education, which obviously are not to be achieved through the medium of a textbook, this or any other. If one examines the table of contents of this book, one sees that it provides only the skeleton around which may grow the student's understanding of psychological development and its relation to health and disease. For the most part it stresses concepts, much of the supporting data for which must be supplied by the instructor or diligently acquired by students in the course of clinical demonstrations and experience. The book provides a framework around which the student may begin to systematize his knowledge, gained in the course of observing and taking care of other human beings, sick and well. It does not deal with method per se and it places upon the instructor the responsibility both to develop in the students the necessary skills in observation and to provide them with the appropriate clinical material for study and examination.

I have deliberately excluded from this book the traditional illustrative case histories and vignettes because I believe such data are best provided through classroom exercises. Besides, I have serious question as to the value of such material in this kind of textbook. For one thing, it appears to me that no written description, no matter with what skill and in what detail it is prepared, can adequately communicate to a beginning student the relevant data. Not only are too much condensation and predigestion required of the author to fit the material into the confines of a book, but also any instructor other than the author is placed in the unsatisfactory position of not being in possession of the many unrecorded facts which are essential if he is intelligently to respond to students' questions and misinterpretations. It is only *after* one has had appreciable clinical experience of one's own that one can successfully read the case reports of others. Beginning students are hardly in this position.

Another reason for excluding such material is, from a pedagogical point of view, more important. Case summaries give the beginning student a false sense of what the primary data really are, since it is not possible accurately to describe how the information recorded in a case report actually was obtained, not to mention how and why it was edited and organized as it was. Although admittedly more difficult, it is better, in my opinion, for the student himself to be exposed to the behavior itself and thereby to learn how to make the observations and how to categorize, relate and record them. To guide the student in this achievement is one of the most important tasks—if not the most important—of the instructor. No textbook has been written—or is likely to be written—which will accomplish this end.

Admittedly this emphasis on the student's own developing capacities to make observations carries with it the risk that he will not be exposed to certain data or that he will not have certain experiences and hence that important areas or concepts cannot be adequately taught. It is obvious, for example, that the data upon which depend certain premises concerning unconscious mental mechanisms or the role of remote developmental factors simply are not accessible to exploration through the observational skills of a beginning student. In my opinion, the omission of such data is of lesser importance for the student's education than is the acquisition of observational skills and critical perception. It is, after all, quite unnecessary that the student be exposed to and grasp all that is "important" (as if one really knows!), and we must also forever remind ourselves that this is only the very beginning of his education. He has ample time ahead of him to fill in the details. We have achieved success in our educational undertaking if the student gains enough of both method and content to enable him both to make accurate observations and then to make sense out of what he observes. Thereafter he is in a better position to use the data of his own experience to test and examine critically and to add to what he has learned in the past and to what he will hear or read of in the future. Without skill in observing other human beings, as well as oneself, the whole process of learning is seriously hampered, for the data reported by others remain relatively sterile unless they can also be related to one's own observations.

This emphasis on the importance for the medical student to acquire skill in the observation of human behavior might also be seen as a more general objective of medical education over and above the more limited goal of learning how to obtain the data specifically relevant to understanding the concepts developed in this book. Indeed, clinical observation is the most fundamental technique of the physician, who first and foremost remains dependent upon his own senses for the information upon which his clinical, diagnostic and therapeutic judgments are based. Hence, the development of observational skills among medical students is one of the basic tasks of medical education, and nowhere in the preclinical years is there provided a better opportunity for student and teacher to begin this education than in a course in human behavior. To watch and listen to children and adults, to observe their spontaneous behavior and their interaction with an interviewing physician, to hear their accounts of their lives and their experiences with illness, to see people short and tall, thin and fat, sick and well, anguished and happy, perplexed and confident, febrile, dyspneic, jaundiced, cyanotic, sweating, comatose—in short, to encounter the whole range of phenomena common to clinical medicine and to do so under the guidance of an experienced clinical teacher constitutes an important preparation for the student's subsequent clinical career. To fail to use such opportunities to aid the student in developing his own observational skills would be a regrettable omission.

Now, let us examine some of the problems involved in the teaching of psychological concepts and methods. These are numerous and it is well to be aware of them. In the first place, students come with very varied backgrounds, not only in respect to their formal educational experiences in biology and the behavioral sciences but also in respect to their individual life experiences. This variability in preparation makes for great unevenness among the students, though in my experience I have not found it in the long run to be a crucial matter. For most students the medical orientation, with its emphasis on health and disease and the role of the physician as healer, is new and at the same time comes to be the unifying perspective around which their interest and knowledge develop.

More important is the range of personal experience characteristic of each student and the age typical of medical students. Students do not come with a tabula rasa, and they differ not only in respect to what they must unlearn in order to learn but also in respect to the kinds of personal life experiences upon which they can draw in their efforts to appreciate the experiences of others and to comprehend basic psychological concepts. Further, most medical students simply have not lived long enough and are not experienced enough in life. They are barely out of adolescence and are still too close to their recently gained achievement of independence from their parents to be able to appreciate more than intellectually the psychology of either children or parents. Only a few have begun roles as husbands or wives and still fewer as parents. A very small number have paid more than fleeting attention to babies or small children, and only a few of these have been intimately concerned with their care. Yet how vital for an understanding of the development of mind is familiarity with the range of behavior of infants and small children! Few as yet have had a brush with serious illness, with death, with a major loss or with the host of life experiences to which psychological adjustment is necessary.

Yet such deficiencies among students in the breadth of their life experiences do not constitute insuperable barriers to their ability to grasp psychological data and concepts any more than does a full rich life assure such an ability. The instructor, however, is well advised not to make gratuitous assumptions about the range of the students' experience. It is patent nonsense, for example, for an instructor to imagine that he can speak about infant behavior to a group of students who have only the vaguest familiarity with babies without first adequately exposing them to the behavior under discussion. Again, the reflective instructor will appreciate to what extent his own added years of life experience have contributed to his ability to grasp and comprehend psychological data and he will not have unrealistic expectations of his students. Indeed, he will anticipate with confidence that future life experiences will be as useful for the student as they have been for him.

A more familiar obstacle to teaching and learning and one which has been widely discussed is the fact that because much of what is dealt with exists at an unconscious level only derivatives can be demonstrated and the intervening links cannot always be proved. Other sciences, too, deal with derivatives, from which deductions are drawn about the behavior of such elements as atoms, molecules, genes, hormones, etc. But these lend themselves more readily to experimental manipulation and therefore at least give an illusion of reality that is comforting. In psychology the observing instrument, the mind, is the same as the system which is being observed. Introspection is a necessary, valuable, but sometimes misleading tool. When confronted with an alleged fact, it is natural to explore one's own mind for corroborative evidence. If this fact concerns a mental process it is natural to expect to find evidence in one's own mind, and when this is not forthcoming scepticism is justified. Yet we know, and the student will learn, that certain mental content remains unconscious and is accessible to consciousness only with difficulty, if at all. This is especially so of much that concerns early development. The student will also learn why it is a psychological necessity that such content remain submerged, and yet he will be asked to accept the existence of phenomena which he himself cannot recapture from his own memory and for which evidence is not easily forthcoming.

In practice the fact that much with which we deal concerns unconscious processes proves not to be as formidable an obstacle as one might imagine. In the first place, to demonstrate the existence and operation of unconscious mental mechanisms is not as difficult as it may seem. The resourceful instructor will find many opportunities to do so in his work with the students. Second, individual students differ greatly in what each has subjected most intensely to repression or denial. Hence, it is common among a group of students that some will have little difficulty in seeing the evidence for one category of unconscious processes while others will have great difficulty; in relation to some other set of unconscious processes still a different group of students will prove free to grasp it while the group who understood some other set will not be. Most students, therefore, sooner or later will have the experience of observing classmates who are unable to see or recognize what they themselves can see clearly. At this point, the camel need only get his head into the tent. With further clinical and life experience and with further maturation most students gradually succeed in extending their knowledge of the unconscious to the point where it becomes pragmatically useful. It is, after all, neither necessary nor desirable that all the resistances of individual students be resolved. Only the principle and fact of unconscious mental mechanisms need be grasped.

Additional difficulties are encountered in the development of observational skills. Some of these are related to idiosyncratic unconscious mental blocks which render it impossible for individual students to recognize certain processes in others because to do so would jeopardize their own psychological adjustment. In my opinion, such individual difficulties are of less importance from the point of view of teaching than is the fact that this kind of observing of other humans requires a change from the manner in which the student is accustomed to deal with the communications and behavior of others. Up to this point the student has listened to, looked at and spoken to others primarily as a means of establishing and maintaining some kind of relationship or of getting some information from the other person, not as a means of "figuring out" what is going on in the other person. The latter has generally been prompted by a need for more information in order to guide his own behavior, to protect himself or to maintain or modify the relationship. Now he is being asked to become a dispassionate observer and analyst of the behavior of others, and at the same time to assume a role new to him, namely, that of physician or healer. Most students find their first attempts at dispassionate observation difficult and frustrating, especially when they are expected at the same time to establish and maintain a relationship and achieve for themselves a new role. Many feel that it is not only impossible, but outrageous, that it does violence to their human sensibilities to try to observe and analyze the delicate nuances of the behavior of their fellow human beings.

Further, they discover to their dismay that much of their observational activity and many of their judgments are based on cues and on mental operations of which they are unconscious (a discovery which the resourceful teacher can also put to good use). They discover that much of what they had thought were observations are already interpretations ("I think he's angry" or "He's anxious"). Further, they note that their peers, observing the same person, may come to quite different conclusions. When they attempt to analyze what aspects of behavior led to such conclusions they become aware of the degree and frequency with which their own judgments are based not on generally valid principles but on cues learned from their own earlier idiosyncratic experience and relationships and how these are being used unconsciously. For example, a student's judgment that a patient is angry may be based on a fragment of a facial expression or on a gesture characteristic of that student's parent, a cue from which he unwittingly generalizes. It may not be possible for the particular student to recognize this, but other students may and will comment thereon. Thus, individual differences begin to be exposed, and painstakingly the student begins to learn some of the ways in which behavior, verbal and nonverbal, can be analyzed so as to yield the data upon which accurate judgments can be made. The working over of behavioral observations shared with an instructor by a group of students is an active learning experience in which students not only enhance their ability to make observations on patients but they also learn a great deal about mental mechanisms in the course of resolving disagreements among themselves as to what they saw and what it means. This is all grist for the educational mill, especially in respect to the ever-present task of demonstrating the operation of unconscious mental mechanisms.

TEACHING AIDS IN PRECLINICAL INSTRUCTION

The resourceful teacher will find no end of devices useful in rendering accessible to students data relevant to the concepts under consideration while at the same time developing their skill in observation. What follows is merely an account of some devices that I have found useful in teaching second year students and I offer them with the hope that they may prove useful to other teachers. Clearly, such factors as the personality and style of teaching of the instructor, the size of the group, the frequency, number and duration of the teaching sessions, the nature of the classroom facilities, the nature and variety of patients available for demonstration, and many others will be crucial in determining what will prove practical for any particular teaching situation. For orientation, let me specify that I meet twice weekly throughout the year for two-hour sessions with 70 second year students who have already been through a first year course consisting of a weekly two-hour session, also throughout the academic year. In the first year course the student is provided with a general historical and social perspective of the development of medicine and psychiatry and the concepts of mind and body; he is introduced to some of the issues of medical care and medical education as they bear on understanding of health and disease and on mental health and mental disease in particular; and he hears something of the background of biological and psychological principles bearing on the brain-mind problem. In addition, some of the basic concepts of the operation of the mental apparatus are touched upon and psychological development is sketched in broad outline. Much of the latter material is re-examined in greater depth in the second year and with the advantage of the students' greater knowledge of biochemistry and physiology. More detailed consideration of concepts of health and disease and of pathological processes becomes feasible only in the second year, after the student has had some exposure to microbiology and pathology. Demonstrations with patients become increasingly meaningful in the latter half of the second year.

Though much of what I discuss in terms of method evolves from my experience with second year students, it is likely that some of the methods would be equally appropriate in first year teaching as well. Not having taught in the first year, I cannot base such a statement on any personal experience. My teaching experience must also be seen in the framework of the over-all teaching program in psychiatry at the University of Rochester. (See Romano, op. cit.)

The Use of Motion Pictures

Motion pictures have their greatest usefulness in dealing with the material of infancy and early childhood, when verbal production is scanty. They may also be used to focus attention on the nonverbal behavior of adults, but this has been of less value in my experience. I have found it instructive to interrupt the film frequently and to have class members describe the behavior demonstrated. This is especially valuable in demonstrating infant behavior, which for the most part is strange and unfamiliar to students and the details of which are crucial for understanding the ontogenesis of mental functioning. Some of the difficulties in making and reporting observations quickly emerge and an opportunity is thereby provided to assist the student to organize his technique of observation and reporting. Differences of opinion among the students as to what they see are common, but these can be reconciled by rerunning the sequences in question. Such variance in the reports of behavior, incidentally, provides an excellent opportunity for class discussion of the reasons why individuals differ in their perception and reporting of the same data.

A wide variety of excellent motion pictures is available for purchase or rental, and their usefulness is enhanced if the instructor does not feel constrained to use them only for the specific purpose for which they were intended by their producer. Indeed, too much direction and structuring on the part of the film maker may at times interfere with the students' learning experience, which tends to become too passive. For this reason I generally prefer not to use the sound track commentary of a film, for I find that students are more often distracted than instructed by it. It is better for the instructor to be thoroughly familiar with the film and to have clear in his own mind what he hopes to demonstrate thereby. After the group have worked out as much as they can with the instructor, it may then be worth while to run the film through again with the sound track. An arrangement whereby students may observe the film by themselves during their free time is conducive to further learning and scholarship.

What are some of the areas of infant behavior most effectively taught with motion pictures? In my experience they include birth and neonatal behavior; patterns of infant-mother relationships; motor and cognitive development; affect, motility and expressive behavior; patterns of object relating; and the behavioral aspects of personality development.

In addition to their usefulness for further understanding of infant and child behavior, some films may also be used as means of developing an understanding of affective responses. For example, in demonstrating affective patterns among infants and small children, it is easy to call to the attention of the students their own affective reactions to what they are observing and from this to provoke a discussion of nonverbal communication. An instructive exercise is to have the members of the class record both their own affective response to the child's behavior as well as their interpretation of the child's affect. The power of affective behavior to elicit affect in the observer is thereby clearly demonstrated, as are some of the factors determining the variety of affective responses so evoked among the students. These may then be collected and analyzed for class discussion.

Among the films we have found useful in our teaching are the following.* They are listed roughly in order of developmental sequences.

Birth and the First Fifteen Minutes of Life. (Film Studies of the Psychoanalytic Research Project on Problems in Infancy Series. Producer: René A. Spitz, M.D.)

Some Basic Differences in Newborn Infants During the Lying-in Period. (Film Studies on Integrated Development Series. Producers: Margaret E. Fries, M.D., and Paul J. Wolfe, M.S.)

Some Observations Concerning the Phenomenology of Oral Behavior in Small Infants. (Infant Psychology Series. Producers: Sibylle Escalona, Ph.D., and Mary Leitch, M.D.)

Eight Infants: Tension Manifestations in Response to Perceptual Stimulation. (Infant Psychology Series. Producers: Sibylle Escalona, Ph.D., and Mary Leitch, M.D.)

Expressive Movements (Affectomotor Patterns) in Infancy. (Producer: Bela Mittelman, M.D., in collaboration with Laura Malkenson and Ruth L. Munroe, Ph.D.)

Motility in Parent-Child Relationships. (Producer: Bela Mittelman, M.D., with Laura Malkenson and Ruth L. Monroe, Ph.D. Technical assistance on photography: Burgess Meredith.)

Nature and the Development of Affection. (University of Wisconsin, Department of Psychology Primate Laboratory. Producers: Harry F. Harlow and R. R. Zimmerman.)

The Smile of the Baby. (Film Studies of the Psychoanalytic Research Project on Problems in Infancy Series. Producer: René A. Spitz, M.D.)

Shaping the Personality: The Role of Mother-Child Relations in Infancy. (Film Studies of the Psychoanalytic Research Project on Problems in Infancy Series. Producer: René A. Spitz, M.D.)

* With few exceptions noted these are more fully described in the catalogue of the New York University Film Library and in the Psychological Cinema Register of the Pennsylvania State University, University Park, Pennsylvania.

Mother Love. (Film Studies of the Psychoanalytic Research Project on Problems in Infancy Series. Producer: René A. Spitz, M.D.)

Anxiety: Its Phenomenology in the First Year of Life. (Film Studies of the Psychoanalytic Research Project on Problems in Infancy. Producer: René A. Spitz, M.D.)

Genesis of Emotions. (Film Studies of the Psychoanalytic Research Project on Problems in Infancy Series. Producer: René A. Spitz, M.D.)

A Balinese Family. (Character Formation in Different Cultures Series. Producers: Gregory Bateson and Margaret Mead.)

Bathing Babies in Three Cultures. (Character Formation in Different Culture Series. Producers: Gregory Bateson and Margaret Mead.)

Life Begins. (Yale University Clinic of Child Development. Producer: Arnold Gesell.)

Somatic Consequences of Emotional Starvation in Infants. (Film Studies of the Psychoanalytic Research Project on Problems in Infancy Series. Producer: René A. Spitz, M.D.)

Grief. (Film Studies of the Psychoanalytic Research Project on Problems in Infancy Series. Producer: René A. Spitz, M.D.)

Monica, an Infant with Gastric Fistula and Depression. (G. L. Engel and F. Reichsman, University of Rochester Medical Center.)

Food and Maternal Deprivation. (Producer: l'Association pour la Santé Mentale de l'Enfance, Paris, France, under the direction of Dr. Jenny Aubry, President.)

Maternal Deprivation in Young Children. (Institute National d'Hygiene. Producers: Jenny Aubry and Genevieve Appell.)

A Two-Year-Old Goes to Hospital. "The Effects on Personality Development of Separation from Mother in Early Childhood." (Producer: James Robertson, Tavistock Clinic.)

Two Children: Contrasting Aspects of Personality Development. (Film Studies on Integrated Development Series. Producers: Margaret E. Fries, M.D., and Paul J. Wolfe, M.S.)

Anna N. Life History from Birth to Fifteen Years. The Development of Emotional Problems in a Child Reared in a Neurotic Environment. (Film Studies on Integrated Development Series. Producers: Margaret E. Fries, M.D.,and Paul J. Wolfe, M.S.)

A Character Neurosis with Depressive and Compulsive Trends in the Making: Life History of Mary from Birth to Fifteen Years. (Film Studies on Integrated Development Series. Producers: Margaret E. Fries, M.D., and Paul J. Wolfe, M.S.)

The Use of Tape Recordings

There is a decided advantage in introducing students to verbal material through the use of tape recordings in that it permits the instructor to limit the material to what beginning students can cope with. The student must learn something of the many aspects of spoken communication, including the nonverbal components of speaking as well as verbal communication per se. This can effectively be accomplished by making up a tape of excerpts illustrating the various components and aspects of spoken communication as well as the nonverbal sounds. By playing and replaying short segments, the student's attention can be drawn to such features as intonation, rate, intensity, pauses and mannerisms of speaking, as well as to some of the subtleties and significance of nonverbal sounds such as laughter, sobbing, sighing, guttural sounds, etc. The use of the tape also makes it possible to keep the amount of material within the range of the student's attention and to check on his success in hearing what is to be heard. In this way the student is assisted in developing more systematic ways of listening, and his attention is called to elements of which he may otherwise be unaware.

Similarly, selected tape recordings are of value as means of illustrating the various mental mechanisms as well as the phenomena of mental disorder, e.g., delusions, hallucinations, obsessive ideas, etc.

A tape recorded interview provides a good means of checking the student's capacity to listen to and record data accurately. For example, I have had students listen to the recording of a patient's response to the question, "Tell me about your mother?" and then have them answer the question, "How does the patient describe his mother?" Their answers provide much valuable material for classroom discussion, not the least of which are the disparate views of the same material held by different students. Much clarification comes from replaying the tape.

Needless to say, like all teaching aids, the use of tape recordings can also be abused, especially by overemphasizing minutiae at the expense of the over-all material. The optimal setting for observation of humans is to listen and to watch simultaneously. Hence something is lost by excluding visible nonverbal behavior. Tapes are useful mainly to focus attention on audible elements of which the student might otherwise be unaware.

Presentation of Patients

Interviewing a patient before the class is still the most valuable teaching device available. The main drawback of the patient interview in the preclinical years is that the student too often is confronted with a quantity and complexity of material far in excess of what he is capable of coping with. He has to watch and listen to a complex two-person exchange and to a story, both in terms of the process and behavior and in terms of content. Under such circumstances and with his limited background, the student all too often has no idea on what to focus his attention and he readily becomes lost. To circumvent this problem, I make it a practice also to tape record the interview. This tape may then be used in two ways. In the discussion that follows the patient interview, I may replay parts of the tape in order to focus attention on particular features of the interview imperfectly recalled by the class. It does not do to rely on the students' memory, for all too often they have failed to attend to the important issues. Discussion proceeds much more productively if all the students as well as the instructor have a clear understanding of exactly which data are under consideration.

Another way in which such taped interviews may be used is to assign a group of students the exercise of replaying the tape and then writing a brief essay on some assigned topic relevant to the interview. The students are encouraged to listen to the tape in a group, playing and replaying certain segments as often as they wish, and discussing among themselves what they hear. I cannot answer whether it would be more productive to do this under the guidance of an instructor, since this has not been my practice.

The nature of the clinical material selected for class presentation is a matter of considerable importance. My personal preference is to begin with and to use a great number of patients from services other than the psychiatric, in keeping with the unified concept of disease that is formulated in this book. The primary objective is to expose the students to illness in all its multifarious expression. All patients with organic disturbances manifest psychological phenomena as well. The reverse is not true, so that the tendency of the student to dichotomize is increased if he deals first or largely with psychiatric patients. This is especially true in the preclinical years when it is likely that the only live patients the students see may be those presented in the course in psychiatry.

A device which has proved most effective in my hands is to concentrate on patients who all suffer from the same organic disease process. Diabetes mellitus serves this purpose splendidly, though no doubt other disorders would do as well. Diabetes is widely distributed in the population and is encountered at all ages, from childhood to old age. It involves a great number of complications and may also exist concurrently with many other disease states. Hence diabetic patients are found on all clinical services of the general hospital, including the psychiatric. The students are asked to read up on the subject of diabetes in a textbook of medicine. Then as one diabetic patient after another is interviewed, they become familiar with the hard core of symptoms which are manifestations of the specific biochemical and physiological disturbances of diabetes and which are found in all patients, with the various manifestations related to the complications of diabetes, and finally with the many ways in which different patients speak of and experience the same disease process. Further, they begin to glimpse the great range of manifestations, many of them psychological in origin, and the variety of life histories demonstrated by these people who have only diabetes in common.

Another advantage of utilizing patients from the medical, surgical or other services is that it leaves no question in the students' minds as to the frequency with which psychological problems are encountered among such patients. Indeed, most of the varieties of psychopathology may be demonstrated among these patients, and recourse need be had to patients on the psychiatric service mainly to demonstrate certain grossly psychotic syndromes. Psychiatric entities as such and the problems of clinical psychiatry are best taken up during the clerkship and out-patient experiences in the third and fourth years.

The problem of teaching human behavior in the preclinical years is a complex one and we have much to learn about how this may be done. The suggestions I have offered reflect my personal experience, for what it may be worth to others. I, in turn, should welcome learning of the experiences of others in this difficult area.

Part One

PSYCHOLOGICAL DEVELOPMENT

CHAPTER I

BIOLOGICAL CONSIDERATIONS

This work is concerned primarily with the phenomena of growth, development and adaptation, with how man as a biological and social organism develops and adjusts in a physical and social environment. Beginning with a consideration of the general properties of living organisms, from the most primitive to the most complex, we shall gain some perspective of the biological antecedents of psychological processes. Examination of the changes wrought during evolution will throw light on the increasing complexity of the adjustments of living organisms and will reveal some of the phylogenetic background. We shall then consider man from the viewpoint of his phylogenetically determined endowment and potential; the factors which bear on his growth and development; the nature of the adaptive devices, physical, biological, psychological and social, which he develops and utilizes in adjustment; and the failures of adjustment. We shall be especially concerned with the development of the psychic apparatus and of psychological adaptations and their interrelations with other life processes in health and disease.

It is manifestly impossible in a work of this sort to give more than superficial attention to the basic biological processes concerned in the development and function of a mental apparatus. Yet, as inadequate as any such discussion will be, it seems important at least to indicate some of these relevant areas, with the hope that the student already knows something about them or will extend his knowledge thereof by independent reading.

We may start with the broad statement that our concern is with the phenomena of life, with how man survives, grows, develops, adjusts, functions and maintains himself and his kind. This is biology, human biology, if you will. We shall be especially occupied with *behavior*. Behavior includes not only overt behavior, what the person as a whole does and how he acts or conducts himself, but also psychological processes, that is, all manner of activity of mind, conscious and unconscious, as learning, perception, thinking, symbolization, self-awareness, abstraction, planning, fantasy, dreams, feelings, moods, affects, etc. All these properly are the domain of psychology.

In any consideration of behavior and of the theories or concepts constructed to explain behavior, it is necessary at the outset to emphasize certain points (see Rapaport[6]). In the first place, behavior is integrated and indivisible. Various concepts that are constructed to explain behavior may refer to different components of behavior (e.g., the conscious, unconscious, instinctual, etc.), but not to different behaviors. Second, no behavior stands in isolation, all behavior being that of the total organism and an indivisible personality. Third, all behavior is part of a developmental (genetic) series, a consequence of temporal sequences bringing about the current form of the personality, implying regulation by inherent (biological) laws of the organism *and* by cumulative experience. It is an *epigenetic* product (Erikson[4]). Finally, all behavior is multidetermined, being influenced by biological factors, reality factors and social factors. How these factors relate to each other will be a major concern in this book (see Chapter XXIII).

We begin by looking at some of the biological determinants of behavior, as revealed phylogenetically and ontogenetically. To what degree are the overt behavior and the mental activity of an organism determined and circumscribed by the nature and capacity of the body? Whether we view the development of mind from a phylogenetic or an ontogenetic perspective, the fact is inescapable that prior to some point in development it is impossible to identify psychological activity, even though one can always describe manifest behavior. Further, it is obvious not only that the appearance of psychological phenomena parallels the development of a nervous system, but also that there is a hierarchy of development of both. Thus, what we designate as psychological includes phenomena which the living organism acquires relatively late in phylogenetic and ontogenetic development. They constitute a new and different category of biological activity. As such they require tools and techniques for their study and investigation and systems of notation for their categorization and theory building which are unique and appropriate for such processes and not simply borrowed from other fields. One cannot apply the terminology or techniques of biochemistry or anatomy to psychological phenomena. But, at the same time, a comprehensive knowledge of biology and the biological sciences in the broadest sense is indispensable for the elucidation of the psychological and behavioral. The problem of dealing simultaneously or sequentially in multiple frames of reference is forbidding but inescapable, and the burden becomes more difficult as one deals with successively higher levels of organization of living systems. If those concerned with behavior and psychology are to develop any comprehensive theory, they must take into account not only the total biological framework and background of the organism with which they are concerned, but also the social and cultural setting in which the organism operates. And certainly the physician, who is at all times engaged with human beings, sick and well, rarely can enjoy the luxury of splendid isolation, ignoring one or another aspect of living processes, at least not without grave restriction of his effectiveness and knowledge. It is an illusion to believe that the problems of mind will be solved by concentration exclusively on biochemical phenomena. To establish the nature of the relationship between biochemical processes in the brain and psychological phenomena requires as precise definition and formulation of the latter as of the former, yet some scientists speak as if the development of psychological science will be rendered superfluous by the advances of biochemistry. Similarly illusory are the views that psychological knowledge and theory can develop independent of biology. I hope this volume will help clarify why this cannot be so.

With these general remarks on the relationship of the biological and psychological, let us touch lightly on some of the biological issues that have most bearing on our understanding of psychological development. As already implied, we assume an essential unity of all living matter and regard that which is psychological as one aspect of life increasingly manifest in higher organisms. Nonetheless, the psychological has its biological anlage, and we might now explore some biological predecessors of the processes which will become psychological by a consideration of properties common to all living organisms, including very simple, primitive organisms which can hardly be considered to manifest psychological activity.

1. All organisms manifest spontaneous activity, which is apparent in growth, development and various physiological processes. The limits of these activities are initially genically determined; the character of the growth, the intracellular enzyme composition, the development and the movement of an amoeba as well as of a man are circumscribed by the original genic* constitution. The available energy

---

* The word "genic" is used here to refer to the characteristics of an organism determined by the action of genes. Although the noun "genetics" is conventionally used to refer to that branch of biology dealing with the phenomena of inheritance, the adjective "genetic" has a broader meaning, referring to development and mode of originating, not necessarily restricted to what is determined by gene action. The use of the word "genetic" in its broader sense long antedates its more specialized usage as referring to gene action. In this book we shall continue to utilize "genetic" in its less specific sense and we shall use "genic" when we wish explicitly to refer to processes determined by the action of genes. Accordingly, "genetic" may be considered as encompassing all developmental factors, both genic and environmental.

for such activity is presumably finite, each organism having a life cycle, a period of rapid growth and development, a relatively stable period and a period of decline.

2. All organisms have a limiting membrane, the intactness of which is essential for the maintenance of relative constancy of the internal environment. It is sensitive to many modalities of change in the physical environment. It keeps out, within limits, much which is noxious and permits a continuous exchange of substances between the two environments, assuring the continuation and replenishment of the internal energy sources determining life activity. As we shall see, this relative independence of the internal environment from its surroundings is in itself a prime determinant of what we are calling behavior.

3. All organisms have the capacity, within limits, to adjust to environmental changes and to obtain from the environment what they need for survival, growth and development. This is genically (as well as phylogenetically) circumscribed and experientially modified. The enzymic constitution, the physicochemical composition and the morphology determine, as well as limit, the capacity of an organism to deal with an environmental process. To paraphrase H. S. Jennings,[5] a cornered amoeba cannot escape by flying. Some of the basic types of behavioral adjustment, as seen even in unicellular organisms, are as follows: The organism may accomplish an internal metabolic rearrangement or develop an adaptive enzyme so that a noxious substance becomes harmless or even useful. The antibody-antigen reaction is one example. The organism may utilize motility, moving away from a harmful agent, or toward it if it has special organs of attack, or it may move toward a useful or assimilable object. The organism has the capacity to retain and ingest as well as to eject substances. The organism may insulate itself against unfavorable environment by changing the character of its membrane (i.e., spore or cyst formation). As we shall see later, these are the biological anlage of corresponding psychological processes in higher organisms.

4. All living organisms have the capacity to reproduce and thereby to continue the species. Implicit in this fact is that some behavior is both self-regulatory and species- or group-regulatory. Behavior in the service of reproduction and continuation of the species also has internal sources and external stimuli and is of profound importance in determining interanimal relationships. As will be demonstrated later, interanimal relations are important for growth and survival as well as for the continuation of the species.

EVOLUTIONARY ASPECTS

Having noted some of the basic biological functions common to all living organisms, we shall now consider briefly the changes brought about through the evolutionary process. Evolution provides a record of the successful and unsuccessful efforts at development of organismic organization to adapt to a changing cosmic environment.[8] How activity is expressed is determined by the particular stage of evolutionary development achieved by the organism, and it is only in the higher organisms, notably man, that we see the representation of the basic driving forces in psychological form. The spectrum from the purely biological to the psychological can be sensed by tracing development from the most primitive organisms to complex man.

The unicellular organism incorporates all functions within its one structural unit and the basic modes of behavior concerned in survival, and reproduction as found in the higher organism have their anlage in such relatively primitive organisms. The higher organisms, however, manifest these activities at more complex biological and psychological levels.

The development of multicellular organisms requires specialization of function in cells and organs, the development of systems of internal communication and coordination, and systems of external and internal perception. Coordination in the multicellular and multiorgan animal is achieved through the nervous and endocrine systems. With the development of a nervous system, a delay can be interposed between stimulus and response. Beginning with relatively fixed and circumscribed responses, the progressive phylogenesis of the central nervous system allows for an increasing variety and complexity of response. Further, as the organism becomes increasingly independent of the environment, reactions and processes which originally occurred in transaction with the external environment now occur within the body, and the central nervous system becomes the locus where the outer world, as experienced through the senses, becomes internalized as an inner world. It is from these developments that a psychic apparatus evolves, but we must not lose sight of its primary biological derivation. The psychological adaptive devices have sources in biological anlage. Awareness of the self and of one's behavior as an individual among individuals comes with the development of the psychic apparatus, but action and process long antedate such awareness.[3, 5] Thus, both the invertebrate and the newborn human infant have all the necessary organization for the ingestion of food, but the concept of feeding, its recognition as a form of behavior and the ability to distinguish the self from food and from the sources of food are all later psychological developments.

In the service of continuation of the species, three important developments occur during evolution. First, the reproductive potential is concentrated in the germ plasm, which alone retains the capacity to reproduce the whole organism. Second, two sexes are differentiated, although the original basic bisexuality is never entirely lost. This includes a differentiation of function between the sexes and the development of specific sexual organs. The survival value gained from new gene combinations is self-evident. Equally important is that this establishes the necessity for interanimal relationships to continue the species, for in order to mate, the male and the female must come together in some sort of social relationship. There are, of course, biological influences other than those having to do with reproduction which also lead animals to aggregate.

The third evolutionary change has to do with the forms of reproduction and the status of the young. The over-all change is in the direction of a wider developmental span between the young and the adult forms. Two important consequences stem from this. First, the young have much greater possibility of experiential and environmental influence as compared to the more fixed, genically determined patterns of lower organisms. As a result, they not only have greater flexibility in development, but at the same time they may be more vulnerable to injury before full development is achieved. The second consequence is a social one, namely, that if the species is to survive, the young must be cared for, thus adding a new component to interanimal relations. Also, in this prolonged dependency of the young is the genesis of family and other more complex social units which distinguish the higher organisms, and especially man. The biological and physiological aspects of these interanimal transactions are as yet unexplored, but there is increasing evidence that interference with the orderly development of such relationships may have profound influences on bodily processes as well as on psychological and behavioral processes, in man as well as in animals. Not only is the maintenance of certain patterns and varieties of relationship between animals important in determining how they develop, but it also appears that interruptions of such relationships may have significant and, at times, harmful effects. This will be discussed further.

Man, as the most highly developed living organism, enjoys the advantages as well as suffers from the complications of these evolutionary advances. Born adequately preadapted to his particular human environment, he is able to survive and develop, if the environment provides the conditions necessary for survival and growth. His phylogenetic heritage provides for this preadaptation and for the particular manner in which it is manifest (i.e., all the primary modes of functioning of the infant). But it is also necessary that the infant's presence and behavior elicit the appropriate succoring, nurturing and stimulating responses from the environment. Though biologically helpless, the human infant is still provided with the basic sets of apparatuses essential to initiate postnatal living. But by virtue of the paucity of established behavior patterns in the nervous system he enjoys an unparalleled capacity to internalize the external environment and create from the samples afforded by sensory input the means and the tools not only for survival and growth, but also to change, mold and manipulate the environment and to create new environments. This achievement of the biological capacity to integrate and synthesize internally (intrapsychically) in the forms characteristically human (including spoken and written language) shifts evolutionary developments into the social sphere. The inheritance from the past becomes extrabiological, accessible for transmission at will from generation to generation. Man thus extends the span from the biological to the psychological to the social, thereby also extending the range of the environment in which he grows and develops. The successive phases of biological development of the human infant and child elicit not only phase specific biological responses, but also psychological and social responses from the environment (e.g., nursing the hungry infant, toilet training, teaching the child to read, etc.). These in turn provide means and stimulation for further psychological and social growth. The external environment, in its physical, biological and social contexts, thus constitutes a matrix in transaction with which development takes place. The process involves a high degree of mutuality in adaptations and adjustments. The concept that life consists primarily of a struggle for survival against a basically hostile environment is not in keeping with the facts (see Erikson[4]).

REFERENCES

1. Bertalanffy, L.: Problems of Life. New York, John Wiley & Sons, 1952.
2. Bertalanffy, L.: The Theory of Open Systems in Physics and Biology. Science, *111*:23, 1950.
3. Engel, G. L.: Homeostasis, Behavioral Adjustment, and the Concept of Health and Disease. *In:* Grinker, R. (ed.): Mid-Century Psychiatry. Springfield, Illinois, Charles C Thomas, 1953, pp. 33–46.
4. Erikson, E. H.: Childhood and Society. New York, W. W. Norton & Co., 1950.
4a. Fuller, J. L. and Thompson, W. R.: Behavior Genetics. New York, John Wiley & Sons, 1960.
5. Jennings, H. S.: Behavior of the Lower Organisms. New York, Columbia University Press, 1906, pp. 177–179, 231, 261–264, 296–297, 299, 310, 312–313, 345, 349–350.
6. Rapaport, D.: The Structure of Psychoanalytic Theory. II. The Structure of the System. Psychologic Issues, *2*(2):39–71, 1960.

7. Schrodinger, E.: What Is Life? The Physical Aspect of the Living Cell. New York, The Macmillan Co., 1947.

8. Simpson, G.: The Meaning of Evolution. New Haven, Yale University Press, 1949.

9. Sinnott, E. W.: Cell and Psyche: The Biology of Purpose. Chapel Hill, University of North Carolina Press, 1950.

10. Weiss, P.: The Biological Basis of Adaptation. *In:* Romano, J.: Adaptation. Ithaca, New York, Cornell University Press, 1949.

CHAPTER II

INSTINCTS, DRIVES
AND HOMEOSTASIS

Having touched on some of the general biological properties of all living organisms and on the implications of evolutionary developments, we may next consider some of the regulatory processes involved in the maintenance of life and in growth and development. The living organism maintains itself in an environment which in some respects shows great variability and in other respects is relatively consistent. Yet, as Claude Bernard[1] first pointed out, the living system has the capacity to maintain its internal environment within fairly constant limits and thus to have some degree of autonomy with respect to the physical environment. To accomplish this, not only must there be systems of regulation whereby what enters and leaves the organism is controlled and the internal milieu is maintained constant, but there must also be systems whereby the energy necessary to carry out such work is rendered specifically available for such ends. Such regulatory systems obviously are concerned not only with processes inside the body, such as circulation, metabolism, etc., but also with behavior in relationship to the environment necessary for the maintenance and continuation of life processes, such as seeking for food and its consumption, courting and mating behavior, care of the young, etc. Processes within the body are usually considered to belong to the domain of physiology and those related to the external environment to the field of behavior, but clearly these are only convenient differences of perspective of the same processes. Indeed, it is one thesis of this work that from both the phylogenetic and the ontogenetic perspectives, the primary determinants of behavior and psychology are embedded in the biological characteristics of the particular species and organism. This is essentially the same view as origi-

11

nally put forth by Freud,[6, 7, 8] and the intervening years have provided much support. This chapter will therefore indicate in a sketchy fashion some of the present knowledge and concepts of the interrelationships between physiological and behavioral processes, the nature and organization of the internal regulatory system in relationship to autonomous behavior patterns, and the structuring and channeling of energy for such purposes. As has already been pointed out, the central nervous system is the critical system in this development in higher animals and man, being the system which ultimately regulates the constancy of the internal milieu, total behavior and psychic processes. By the same token, it must be the system which regulates the intake of energy and its further disposition (see Chapter III).

The ultimate sources of energy are, of course, in the external environment. The living organism, as an open system in transaction with the external environment, "captures" energy within its organization.[2] This is the energy available for the maintenance of structure, for growth and development, and for the work of maintaining life. Increasing independence from the external world is achieved by the performance of work against the environment to maintain the constancy of the internal environment and to achieve growth. From the point of view of the observer, this maintenance of *relative* independence from the external environment justifies the concept of directing (as contrasted to random) unlearned forces within the organism. The organization of the living system channels the utilization of energy in such a way that it appears (to the observer) to be purposive, even if only in the broad sense of maintaining life. Later it will prove useful to categorize the various ways in which forces in the living system are expressed and to indicate how they are represented at the psychological level. It is one of the undeniable features of behavior and psychic activity that they include the quality of a pressure from within which must be responded to in some way. The terms used to refer to such forces, namely instinct and drives, will be discussed later.

To the self-regulatory tendencies of the organism, the term *homeostasis* is applied (Cannon[4]). Homeostasis refers to the processes whereby the internal environment fluctuates within fairly narrow limits as the result of reactions to disturbances induced from within or without—in essence, a closed information system. There are many different processes going on within the organism and between the organism and the environment. Each process influences other processes so that there is a continuous transaction simultaneously disrupting and restoring. But, by virtue of a continuous feedback, the degree of variance from the normal within the internal environment is kept at a minimum and relative constancy is maintained in spite of great changes in the external environment.

How do such basic biological processes as are concerned with the maintenance of the constancy of the internal milieu, growth, development and continuation of the species influence behavior and psychic activity and development? The following examples are intended only to illustrate principles, not to document in full detail, and therefore are manifestly oversimplified.

1. The metabolism of the cells of the body is aerobic, requiring a sustained supply of oxygen. This is accomplished through the activity of respiratory and circulatory apparatuses, which in turn are controlled through a highly efficient regulatory system located within the central nervous system. Under ordinary circumstances this is an entirely automatic, self-regulating process in which changes in regional peripheral needs are responded to efficiently and silently through feedback systems, both neural and chemical and both central and peripheral. Thus, a tissue need for more oxygen may be satisfied both by a locally and by a centrally mediated increase in local blood flow, the first in response to the local chemical changes of increased metabolic activity, the second through neural or chemical messages reaching the central nervous system and evoking reflex vasodilatation in the tissue in question. Let us suppose, however, that some change takes place which cannot be compensated for by such internal (physiological) processes alone, but requires some behavior as well, as might occur if the supply of oxygen were to become inadequate for some reason. At some point the falling oxygen tension would be detected by the sensitive receptors of the central regulating system, through which would then be initiated activities to correct the situation. Such activities might involve not only physiological changes in the body designed to maintain the oxygen supply where it is most needed, especially in the brain and the heart, but also more complex behavioral, psychological and social processes, such as (1) motor activity to leave the scene of the low O_2 supply; (2) the seeking and enlisting of help from other individuals; (3) the arousal of impulses to overcome or destroy responsible agents, real or imagined; (4) the revival of memories of past experiences and the induction of anticipatory behaviors which in some individuals might stimulate the kind of psychic activity which eventuates in such solutions as the development of ventilating systems, gas masks, etc., as well as in the curiosity to investigate the effects of O_2 lack on living systems. Thus, the reaction and adjustment to O_2 lack in man is not only achieved at a variety of levels, chemical, physiological, psychological and social, but also may initiate behavior and psychic processes remote from the immediate specific requirements of the moment. Here are illustrated the immediate and delayed consequences of biological processes on psychological and social activities. This is but another way of emphasizing the interrelatedness of biological needs on the one hand and the conditions

of the physical environment on the other as circumscribing as well as stimulating influences on behavior, psychological processes and social-cultural developments. To make a ridiculous contrast, no physiological, psychological or social systems are needed by man to assure an intake of gaseous nitrogen, which is metabolically inert.

2. Oxygen, water, electrolytes, food and the various substances that are necessary for the metabolic integrity of the cells, tissues and organism as a whole are what may be called *imperative* needs, imperative in the sense that other materials in the environment cannot be substituted for them and the organism cannot provide them from within itself. They are imperative also in that in their absence only a limited time is available before irreversible changes or death will ensue. Survival in the absence of oxygen is a matter of a few minutes. Water lack is tolerated for a few days. Total starvation is tolerated not more than a few weeks. All such needs evoke not only behavior in relationship to the external environment which is intended to procure that which is lacking, but also internal readjustments which, within the capacity of the organism, compensate for the deficiency (e.g., utilization of body fat and protein stores). Such dependence on the external environment for certain supplies is in itself a determinant of the evident drive quality of certain behavior, giving the impression of an inner pressure or urgency to perform or function in certain ways. Even lower organisms acquire the capacity not only to anticipate such needs long before states of cellular depletion have been reached but also to initiate patterns of behavior designed to satisfy the needs. In higher organisms such functions become organized as special systems within the central nervous system, such as those concerned with the regulation of respiration, eating, drinking, etc. Such a central organization concerned with a function like the assurance of adequate food intake must, if it is to serve its purpose, mediate a whole sequence of activities, including perception of the need for food, search for and obtaining of the food (appetitive behaviors) and all the activities involved in its consumption and assimilation (consummatory behaviors). In addition, highly specific behavioral patterns may be so mediated, such as the appearance of specific taste preferences among rats deprived of particular food elements (Richter[9]) or the salt appetite of the patient with adrenal insufficiency and the sugar appetite of the diabetic. How such central neural organizations influence behavior and psychic processes will occupy much of our attention in subsequent chapters.

3. Although certain needs must be satisfied if the organism is to survive, it is important to note that the organism is not necessarily at all times competent to satisfy such needs by its own independent actions. Comparatively, the supply of oxygen is more autonomously regulated than the supply of food and water, for which the young of higher species

are variably dependent upon the presence and specific activity of the adults of the species. This dependence increases with progressive evolutionary development so that the very survival of young birds and mammals rests upon a highly specific interaction between the infants and their mothers, the reciprocal feeding-nurturing pattern. This means in essence that certain qualities of interanimal relating, especially during infancy, are so closely linked with the satisfaction of imperative physical needs that relating itself also acquires the driving quality of the imperative. Indeed, among higher animals the interposition of the feeding parent as a requirement for survival becomes so prominent that the process of physically relating comes to assume dominance as a determinant of behavior and psychological development. Contributing to this dominance is the fact that the feeding parent usually anticipates by a considerable margin the biological need of the infant. In the service of survival the central nervous system organization concerned with feeding therefore includes for both mother and infant the mediating of behavior concerned with relating in ways which will facilitate and assure feeding. This biologically determined "fit" between mother and infant is of great importance and will be the subject of much further attention. We see here, then, the biological beginnings of systems which will influence certain subsequent psychological developments.

4. The biological importance for survival of interanimal relationships is further extended by the necessity for specific types of relationships between animals for the purpose of continuation of the species. Here we can identify a continuum including the activities necessary to assure care of the young, activities concerned with the security and supplies of the group, and activities concerned with mating. Here again it is evident that well defined biological patterns underlie these activities and that they have a mediating structural organization within the nervous system assuring a certain consistency in their basic aspects. Again, we can identify phylogenetic and ontogenetic biological anlage of what eventually become manifest as psychological processes in higher animals. The systems of communication between animals, the patterns of pleasurable animal-to-animal contact, of courtship, of mating, of care of the young, all have basic biological determinants, including intrinsic rhythms and timetables of development which exist before, as well as during their elaboration in psychological terms.

ENDOGENOUS BEHAVIOR PATTERNS

Behavioral observations of animals, especially the newborn, justify the concept of "innate" or "endogenous" behavior patterns.

These are patterns that (1) are manifested at the appropriate stage of development in the appropriate situation by all members of the species (or of the same sex of the species) and (2) do not require either instruction from another member of the species or previous conditioning by means of externally provided reward or punishment (cf. Ewer[5]). Such "endogenous" behavior patterns are self-differentiating, meaning that they come into being as part of the normal development of each individual, *as long as the environment permits of their development and provides the necessary stimulation ("nutriment") for their evocation.* The existence of the "endogenous" behavior patterns provides the necessary fit with the environment to assure satisfaction of the needs of the body for survival, growth and development. As the animal grows there is progressive evolution of further endogenous behavior patterns, first permitting the animal to become progressively more self-supporting and later to engage in courtship, reproduction and care of the young. The fact that such patterns develop in a relatively orderly sequence indicates that certain intrinsic developmental processes are either time-bound or require certain antecedent steps before they can evolve. In either case, they serve to identify that which is more or less consistent about the behavior of a species, regardless of environmental variations. Patterns of feeding, locomotion, sexual behavior, etc., are essentially similar and develop in essentially the same sequence in each species. This must correspond as well to the maturation of particular organizations within the nervous system.

Although such behavior patterns have been described as "endogenous," this does not mean that they evolve spontaneously, regardless of circumstances. Indeed, an appropriate response from the environment may be necessary before the behavioral pattern can be completed, and in its absence the pattern may weaken or fail to evolve normally. Thus, the gaping behavior of nestlings or the suckling activity of newborn mammals requires feeding activity from the environment for consummation. On the other hand, successful consummation of the behavior tends to reinforce the pattern, extend it in relationship to other experiences taking place at the same time, and facilitate the development to the next phase. Once the pattern becomes smoothly operating, the animal can go on to learn to the limit of its capacity. Thus, once the pattern of locomotion has been established, the animal can learn a further wide range of activities for which agile locomotion is necessary. Later we shall illustrate this principle in humans (see Chapter IX).

Endogenous behavior patterns seem to operate as if they have their own source of energy, the accumulation of which facilitates the response and which is dissipated by the performance of the appropriate behavior. Thus, at certain times or under certain circumstances, pressure seems to build up to carry out such patterns as feeding, courting, nest building, mating, etc. At such times, the behavior pattern is readily released by certain external stimuli, some of which are unlearned (or innate) and some of which are learned. On the other hand, upon consummation of the act, and for some time thereafter, the animal may be relatively unresponsive to the same external stimuli or even to the actual objects (e.g., food, sexual object, etc.) ordinarily required for the consummation. Further, the particular behavior pattern that evolves may, in lower animals, be changed experimentally by such means as the injection of hormones: for example, prolactin initiating nesting behavior and gonadotropin courting behavior in the stickleback (a fish).[10, 11] But even more noteworthy is the fact that when the external object necessary for the consummation of the act is not present, searching or appetitive behavior is initiated. Thus, for example, when the internal changes in the body indicating a need for food develop, the animal initiates appropriate behavior to secure food; it does not wait for the presentation of the food or a signal thereof, though it is ready to respond to such when presented. The same, of course, holds true for other periodic patterns of behavior, as already described.

An analysis of all such patterns of behavior reveals that they all occur in situations in which something in the environment is needed for the continuation or completion of some internal biological process. We shall apply the term "objects" to such needed things in the environment and emphasize here that the concept of objects is first of all a biological one. Later we shall develop their psychological significance. Central nervous system organizations operate to initiate appropriate behavior to assure that "objects" are found and are incorporated into the organism and in this sense define certain behavioral tendencies as obligatory.

INSTINCTS AND DRIVES

Terms such as "instincts" or "drives" have been used to refer to the internal forces which impel behavior, essentially concepts of energy. The problem of energy as it applies to living systems is highly complex and cannot be dealt with properly in this volume. Living organisms, as open systems, take in from the environment materials which are assimilated and converted into energy-yielding systems within the body. Such systems provide the energy whereby the organism maintains itself, grows and reproduces. To this general pool of energy within the body the term *instinctual energy* may be applied. It may be regarded as limited both by the availability of external supplies for input and by the innate capacity of the organism to capture and store sources of energy for growth and development, the latter capacity perhaps being genically determined. Such energy may be regarded as freely available for use by any system of the body. Such a proposition implies a single instinct theory, meaning that such energy serves the purpose of maintaining life and continuing the species. For the organism as a whole the supply is finite; only the germ plasm has the capacity to renew the system through the reproduction of new organisms.

However, we have also seen how organizations have developed within the nervous system which are concerned with the mediation of particular patterns of behavior. Such organizations may be seen as channeling the utilization of energy along certain pathways important for survival, growth and reproduction and in this sense may be thought of as binding energy. These are primary biological systems with phylogenetic and ontogenetic determinants which have come to be located within the central nervous system as the central integrating and controlling system. As such they have a driving influence on both behavior and psychic activity. Classic psychoanalytical theory takes note of the fact that some of the behavior and psychic activity so induced have as their aim some variety of contact, union or relationship with objects in the environment and that this is experienced ultimately as body pleasure, especially in certain so-called erotogenic zones, e.g., mouth, skin, anus, genitals; other behavior and psychic activity seem to have as their aim the destruction of objects. This suggests a dual instinct theory, differentiating life (or libidinal) instincts and death (or aggressive) instincts.[7] Although there can be no question that such categories of behavior and psychic activity exist and that they have a driving, compelling quality, it seems less reasonable to postulate independent sources of energy underlying each. Instead, the contributions of biology and ethology emphasize that the maintenance of the life of the individual as well as of the species is indivisibly dependent on a range of physical contacts with other animals as well as on behavior which may happen to be destructive to objects, including other animals. The latter may be manifest in efforts to control the environment to assure needs as well as in defense against environmental dangers.

As already discussed, it is possible to identify endogenous behavior patterns and their sequences of self-differentiation which form the core patterns for both overt behavior and psychic activity. These constitute the biological basis for the so-called libidinal stages proposed by early psychoanalytic theory and indicate certain modes of bodily and mental activity characteristic of successive phases of development (oral, anal, phallic and genital). Such a perspective has heuristic value and is helpful in emphasizing certain biological aspects of psychic development. Similarly, it is useful to retain the phenomenological distinction between libidinal and aggressive drive activity (while questioning primary energy sources for each) since each has different psychological implications and consequences and is served through different organizations in the central nervous system.

Further consideration of the development of a mental apparatus will help to clarify the use and place of such concepts.

REFERENCES

1. Bernard, C.: An Introduction to the Study of Experimental Medicine (1865). New York, The Macmillan Co., 1927.
2. Bertalanffy, L.: The Theory of Open Systems in Physics and Biology. Science, *111:*23, 1950.
3. Blauvelt, H.: Dynamics of the Mother-Newborn Relationship in Goats. *In:* Schaffner, B. (ed.): Group Processes. New York, Josiah Macy, Jr., Foundation, 1954, p. 221.
4. Cannon, W.: The Wisdom of the Body. New York, W. W. Norton & Co., 1932.
5. Ewer, R. F.: Ethological Concepts. Science, *126:*599, 1957.
6. Freud, S.: Instincts and Their Viscissitudes (1915). *In:* Standard Edition of the Complete Psychological Works of Sigmund Freud, vol. XIV. London, The Hogarth Press, 1957, pp. 111–140.
7. Freud, S.: Beyond the Pleasure Principle (1920). *In:* Standard Edition of the Complete Psychological Works of Sigmund Freud, vol. XVIII. London, The Hogarth Press, 1955, pp. 3–64.
8. Freud, S.: The Theory of Instincts. Chapter II in An Outline of Psychoanalysis. New York, W. W. Norton & Co., 1949, pp. 19–24.
8a. Harlow, H. F. and Zimmerman, R. R.: Affectional Responses in the Infant Monkey. Science, *130:*421, 1959.
9. Richter, C.: Total Self-regulatory Functions in Animals and Human Beings. Harvey Lectures, *38:*63, 1942.
10. Tinbergen, N.: Social Behavior in Animals. New York, John Wiley & Sons, 1953.
11. Tinbergen, N.: Psychology and Ethology as Supplementary Parts of a Science of Behavior. *In:* Schaffner, B. (ed.): Group Processes. New York, Josiah Macy, Jr., Foundation, 1955, p. 75.

CHAPTER III

THE NERVOUS SYSTEM AND THE MENTAL APPARATUS

Discussion so far has revolved about the basic biological fact that living organisms are preeminently characterized by a capacity to maintain themselves in and relate with the environment, to resist actively forces which would damage or destroy them, to grow and to reproduce. Among higher organisms we identified the central nervous system as the organ in which is centered the systems concerned with the management and control of such activities. The impelling or drive characteristics of these activities were pointed out, as was the presence within the nervous system of specific organizations concerned with the basic behavioral patterns necessary for survival, growth and reproduction, the so-called endogenous behavior patterns. As an open system, the living organism maintains constancy of the internal milieu and achieves growth and development through relationships with external objects, ranging from actual physical incorporation and assimilation (e.g., nutrition) to experience in and with the external environment (e.g., learning). Such, then, are some of the biological "constants" of all living organisms. Now it is necessary to consider further the functions of the central nervous system and its relation to a mental or psychic apparatus in man and higher animals.

THE FUNCTIONS OF THE CENTRAL NERVOUS SYSTEM

The functions of the brain will be examined in terms of the organism operating within the environment rather than in terms of the anatomy and physiology of the brain itself. In this way, the central nervous system may be seen as an organ which regulates the relationships not only between the external and internal environments but also between different parts of the internal environment. In terms of the behavior and function of the organism as a whole we can identify a number of systems concerned with such activities, and we shall note, without going into detail, that all are represented at many different levels of the nervous system, indicating the acquisition during phylogeny of new or more varied means of carrying out these same functions. These systems may be categorized as follows:

1. SYSTEMS FOR INTERNAL REGULATION. The nervous system receives through afferent nerves and through chemical receptors continuous information on the status of the many compartments of the internal milieu and initiates nervous activity, acting directly on the periphery or through the endocrine system, serving to maintain the constancy of the internal milieu, the conditions for growth, etc. Such systems are mainly concentrated in the phylogenetically older parts of the brain with a final common pathway through the hypothalamus and medulla, but they also have connections with neocortex.

2. SYSTEMS FOR TRANSACTIONS WITH THE ENVIRONMENT TO MAINTAIN THE BODY'S DYNAMIC STEADY STATE, GROWTH AND REPRODUCTION. These include all the systems underlying what have been described as the endogenous behavior patterns and have the purpose of assuring the supplies from the external environment needed for vital activities. These include appetitive behavior patterns, namely, those concerned with seeking out and securing the object (external supply), as well as consummatory behavior patterns, namely, those concerned with the consummation of the act and incorporation of the object. Among these are the patterns of behavior concerned with the securing of oxygen, water and food, sexual activity, parental activity, etc. Such activities obviously involve very diverse functions of the nervous system, including systems of internal perception indicating changing metabolic or endocrine conditions, systems of external perception needed for the detection of the needed objects in the environment, motor systems innervating the musculature responsible for the activity concerned in the search and consummation of the act, and integrating and feedback systems to relate all these processes. As already discussed, these may be regarded as relatively primitive, yet highly efficient, basic systems necessary for vital functions, with a developmental timetable probably determined in part by the rate of growth and maturation of the nervous system itself and in part by the experience of repeated successful consummations of the act, which in turn also contributes to the growth and maturation of the nervous system, as will be noted later. Although some vital systems, such as that underlying breathing and control of respiration, are largely mature at birth, others, such as that

concerned with feeding, have a long developmental sequence requiring other neural and behavioral developments before the full range of function is achieved, as indicated in the spread between suckling and hunting or foraging. Other systems, such as those concerned with procreation or rearing of the young, although evolving progressively from early infancy, do not become fully operative until adulthood.

3. SYSTEMS FOR RESPONDING TO CHANGES IN THE EXTERNAL ENVIRONMENT. These include the various systems of sense perception, sensing environmental changes both as they impinge on the surfaces of the body and at a distance; the motor system concerned with motility within or in relation to the external environment; and systems which correlate such information with the status of the internal environment. Important here are the sense modalities that warn of damage to the body, notably pain, as well as any intense sense stimulation. These form the basis for the development of another motivational system, the avoidance of physical pain and damage to the body. Here again we note the presence of primitive emergency systems which serve to alert the animal to prepare the body for damage and to mediate flight from or resistance to threatening or damaging agents, signals for some of which are innate, as the monkey's reaction of terror on first sight of a snake. Such an emergency system obviously is integrated with the systems concerned with the stability of the internal milieu.

4. SYSTEMS CONCERNED WITH LEARNING AND THE STORAGE OF INFORMATION. The three systems so far described may be regarded as the primary systems necessary for survival and self-regulation in the relatively limited environment of the fetus and neonate. Through further self-differentiation they also constitute the basis for the characteristic modes of patterned behavior typical of the species. Beyond that, however, the nervous system has the function of relating changes and events in the external environment with the state of the internal environment, especially in regard to the satisfaction of needs and the avoidance of injury. This means learning—the acquisition of bits of information and the establishment of meaningful relationships between such bits of information to provide new means of regulating and controlling behavior. Further, it includes systems for the storage of information in such a manner as to make it readily available for use when the occasion demands. In the long-term developmental perspective we can regard these processes as constituting a device whereby the external environment, past and present, becomes internalized through its organic representation in the nervous system. The brain, particularly the newer parts, may thus be seen as providing a third environment, representing and relating the external physical and social environment with the internal physiological and biochemical environment. Learning takes place through the linkage of events occurring simultaneously in different

parts of the brain and is facilitated when such simultaneous experiences also involve either the satisfaction of a need or the avoidance of pain (John[8]). Exploration of the brain with micro-electrodes has revealed areas the stimulation of which apparently yields highly pleasurable sensations (Olds[9]). Animals readily learn to depress a lever or carry out other behavior if it results in stimulation of such a pleasure area and will do so for long periods of time and at extraordinary rates, at times even giving this priority to vital needs, as for food or water. There are other areas stimulation of which yields pain or some unpleasant sensation, and animals so stimulated rapidly learn avoidance behaviors. The association of learning with reward and punishment has long been known, but the studies just mentioned provide information on the neural systems mediating the experiencing of pleasure and pain in relation to vital activities and to learning. We shall later see the significance of pleasure-pain as a regulator of psychic life.

In addition to learning which takes place, so to speak, under the impact of the more basic drives, there is much evidence that the nervous system itself requires and seeks stimulation as a necessary condition for its functioning and development. Such a "stimulus hunger' 'or "stimulus need" is revealed in the functional and developmental defects that occur when a sensory modality is eliminated experimentally, as when animals are deprived of vision from birth until early maturity; in the disturbances evoked by so-called sensory deprivation or isolation; and in the spontaneous seeking of activity and stimulation over and above that concerned with vital needs that especially characterizes higher animals. This is of the greatest importance in learning, for it underlies the tendency of the animal to explore, sample and test the environment purely for the sake of continuing and completing certain experiences no longer directly or even closely connected with the more basic biological needs. That some of such behavior may prove to have value in terms of survival, growth and development does not mean that it necessarily originated from such needs. This property of the nervous system, that it seeks nutriment in the form of sensory input, is an extension of the more primitive biological need system and greatly enhances the variety of means whereby needs can be fulfilled, but it is not always in a direct relationship to it. Indeed, it is most active when the vital needs are least pressing. Thus, a hungry dog will be highly motivated to learn if food is the reward. The fed dog, on the other hand, will engage in a wide range of exploratory and other activity in the course of which he maintains a high level of input from the environment and feedback from his own activity and thereby adds to his store of information about the environment and his operation in it. Such learning takes place best when he is not hungry. The relevance to human development will be discussed in Chapter VIII.

THE MENTAL APPARATUS

The higher developments of the nervous system result in the new
dimension known as psychological, and we postulate a psychic apparatus
to designate the system whereby psychic activity is mediated. Obviously,
this is a function of the central nervous system, but it concerns phenomena that must be studied, observed and analyzed in psychological
and behavioral terms (see Chapter I). We shall see, however, how the
biological and physical characteristics of the body as a whole and of the
brain in particular constitute both molding and limiting factors in
determining the nature and range of possible behavioral and psychic
activities of each species. At what point in the course of the development
of the brain, during either phylogeny or ontogeny, it can be said that
psychic activity begins is impossible to say. This is a matter partly of
definition and partly of the inaccessibility to the observer of psychological data when verbal communication is not possible. Although this
question cannot be answered satisfactorily, it is clear that the development of psychic activity is a distinctive feature of the development
from embryonic life to adulthood of man, if not of all higher animals.
The nature of this developmental process whereby a psychic apparatus
evolves and matures will occupy most of this book. At this point, however, it is worth while to summarize the major characteristics and functions of the developed psychic apparatus, with particular reference to
the functions of the central nervous system as just outlined.

1. ATTENTION TO AND AWARENESS OF INTERNAL AND EXTERNAL
ENVIRONMENTS. The sensing of the condition of the internal environment as a function of the central nervous system has already been
discussed. As a psychological process this is represented in the form of
feeling states, comfort or discomfort, need or satisfaction, pleasure or
unpleasure, which, later in development, include as well more complex
verbal or other types of imagery as further means of experiencing and
representing awareness of the status of the internal milieu. These
processes are known as *affects* and are of great importance in the regulation of behavior and psychic activity. They will be considered in greater
detail in subsequent chapters. (See Chapters XIV, XVIII, XXII.)

The sensing of the external environment and its subsequent representation in terms of categories, symbols, abstractions, words, etc., in
relationship to internal events constitutes the distinctive activity of the
psychic apparatus whereby the person learns to function within and
cope with the external environment while maintaining the constancy of
the internal milieu. This includes such processes as learning, thinking,
imagination, problem solving, creative activity, etc., and makes possible a delay between a biologically (internally) or environmentally
(externally) determined pressure and the behavioral response to it. To

paraphrase Freud,[3] psychic activity thereby provides the opportunity for trial action before one is committed to a particular course of action. There is, accordingly, the possibility to relate and integrate in terms of past experience the present, real, external situation with the psychic and biological needs of the moment. The highest and most effectively developed psychic apparatus is thus characterized by a considerable degree of *autonomy* from both internal and external pressures, prolonging the period during which such pressures can be tolerated while solutions are being reached.

The functions of attention and awareness of internal and external environments also include *awareness of the self as an individual differentiated from other individuals*, including an image of the body as well as of the self as a thinking, feeling, sentient being with needs, fears, hopes and wishes and with relationships to other individuals as well as with status and roles in a physical and social environment. The capacity to experience a sense of personal identity and individuality is an essential function of the psychic apparatus.

2. THE SATISFACTION OF NEEDS. The autonomy of psychic apparatus is only relative since ultimately the vital needs must be satisfied if the individual is to survive, grow and reproduce. It is in this area that we see the greatest influence on the psychic process of the primary biological organizations as represented in the central nervous system. These have already been discussed under the heading of instincts and drives in Chapter II. These biological forces exert an influence not only on what is experienced as pleasurable but also on the form and nature of psychic activity. As will be spelled out later, these biological requirements influence certain ways of looking at, experiencing and conceptualizing the world, evident in the character of fantasies, dreams, myths and the psychic productions of children, primitive peoples and psychotics, as well as of adults when under the influence of certain drugs, extreme fatigue or sensory deprivation. These psychic modes of representation of the primary biological processes are not necessarily concordant with external reality, being the expressions of the needs of the body without regard for the concurrent conditions or needs of the environment. It is this possibility of disparity between the biological needs and their psychic representation on the one hand and the real conditions and requirements of the external interpersonal and social environment on the other which makes for conflict with environment, while the form in which the environment becomes incorporated in psychic apparatus makes for *intrapsychic conflict*. This vulnerability to conflict is another characteristic of the psychic apparatus, leading to the necessity for psychic systems concerned with the resolution or avoidance of conflict.

We have already identified the two major categories of drive activity as *libidinal* and *aggressive* and pointed out that these are operational distinctions based on the character of the behavior and psychic activity manifest in relation to each and not implying that each has a separate source of energy. The *libidinal drives* reflect the biological need, beginning in infancy, for relationship and for certain types of body contact and experience with other humans for survival and growth and, later on, for reproduction. The *aggressive drives* reflect the biological needs both to incorporate and assimilate objects in the external environment for survival and growth and to resist or overcome forces in the environment which are injurious or which interfere with the securing of vital supplies. The distinctive biological features of each of these types of activities form an important determinant of how they are experienced in the mental terms of fantasy, wish or dream. During the course of development from infancy to maturity it will be noted that these two categories of drive activity have close interrelationships, thereby introducing another possibility of intrapsychic conflict, namely between libidinal and aggressive impulses. This fact in itself justifies on heuristic grounds the retention of this differentiation between the two major drive categories.

3. THE AVOIDANCE OF INJURY. The psychic apparatus assumes the task of organizing perception and information in the service of anticipating and warding off injury which may threaten from the external environment or from the pressure or urgency of drives originating within. This function includes the elaboration of an alerting and emergency system, partially represented in affects, to anticipate or deal with crises, as well as psychological mechanisms of defense that serve to monitor, control, modify, relate, integrate or synthesize the input from the external environment, the internal (body) environment and the data of past experience so that the conditions for living can be assured with due regard for external and internal reality. The resolution of conflict, intrapsychic and interpersonal, is an important aspect of this activity. It is through the defensive activities of the psychic apparatus that adaptation is achieved and motility in relation to the external environment is controlled.

4. CONSCIOUS AND UNCONSCIOUS PSYCHIC ACTIVITY. It is a characteristic of the psychic apparatus that it operates silently as well as with awareness. Actually, consciousness may be thought of as the sense organ of the mind, meaning that through attention one can focus on the feelings and on the mental content present at the moment. This is a selective process. Although one can voluntarily turn attention to or away from certain mental activities, other mental content or feelings may force themselves upon the attention of the individual against his will, and still others may become or remain inaccessible to consciousness or be so changed as to become not understandable. Such psychic

processes which remain unconscious may continue to exert an influence on mental activity and behavior. The disposition of mental processes as conscious and unconscious is in the service both of economical mental operation and of the intrapsychic defense mechanism to maintain comfort and stability. Psychic activity, of course, continues during sleep, as evidenced by dreams.

5. THE MOTIVATING FORCES OF THE PSYCHIC APPARATUS. These may be summarized in a hierarchical fashion from the most primitive to the most refined, as follows: (a) the drives, rooted in the biology of the organism, with "pleasure" as the aim; (b) the primitive systems to protect against bodily damage or injury, with avoidance of pain as the aim; (c) affects, as psychic signal and scanning activities evolving in the course of development; (d) learned signals, symbolically or otherwise represented, which provide information about the environment relevant to basic needs and to dangers; (e) highly derivative psychic processes related to all of the preceding but operating with relatively less urgency in the service of self-realization, productivity, creativity, play, work, etc. These last operate with the greatest degree of autonomy and are the most accessible to control by will.

6. COMMUNICATION, NONVERBAL AND VERBAL. The psychic apparatus is preeminently the organ mediating communication, both to the self and with the environment and the objects in it. Communication begins with nonverbal modes, including sounds, facial expressions, gestures, movements, etc., and evolves into the use of the spoken or written word and many varieties of symbolic and plastic representation, ranging from the symbols of mathematics to artistic productions. It is, of course, through these modes of communication that the data of psychology are available to us.

In subsequent chapters the development of these various functions of the psychic apparatus will be considered in terms of the more traditional tripartite structural theory of psychoanalysis: ego, Id and superego. What have just been listed as functions of the mental apparatus are essentially the functions of ego; the drives belong to the Id and the internalized standards and controls derived from the environment belong to the superego. (See Chapter XXII.)

REFERENCES

1. Cannon, W.: Bodily Changes in Pain, Hunger, Fear and Rage. New York, D. Appleton-Century Co., 1939.
2. Engel, G. L.: Homeostasis, Behavioral Adjustment, and the Concept of Health and Disease. *In:* Grinker, R. (ed.): Mid-Century Psychiatry. Springfield, Illinois, Charles C Thomas, 1953, pp. 33–46.

3. Freud, S.: Formulations Regarding Two Principles in Mental Functioning (1911). *In:* Standard Edition of the Complete Psychological Works of Sigmund Freud, vol. XII. London, The Hogarth Press, 1958, pp. 213–227.
4. Freud, S.: The Unconscious (1915), *Ibid.*, vol. XIV, 1957, pp. 159–217.
5. Freud, S.: Instincts and Their Vicissitudes (1915). *Ibid.*, vol. XIV, 1957, pp. 109–140.
6. Freud, S.: A Note on the Mystic Writing Pad (1925). *Ibid.*, vol. XIX, 1961, pp. 227–234.
7. Hebb, D.: Drives and the C.N.S. (Conceptual Nervous System). Psychol. Rev., *62:*243, 1955.
8. John, E. R.: Some Speculations on the Psychophysiology of Mind. *In:* Scher, J. (ed.): Toward a Definition of Mind. Chicago, The Free Press of Glencoe, 1962.
9. Olds, J.: Self-Stimulation of the Brain. Science, *127:*315, 1958.
10. Riesen, A. H.: The Development of Visual Perception in Man and Chimpanzee. Science, *106:*107, 1947.

CHAPTER IV

STAGE OF DEPENDENCY: I. BIRTH AND NEONATAL PERIOD

In the first stage of existence of the human, the fetal stage, there is tremendous internal activity in the direction of growth and development along certain more or less predetermined lines, but extremely limited relationship to the outside world. The fetus exists as a symbiont. The various needs generated by its drive toward growth and development are satisfied through the exchange of the necessary materials across the placental membrane. The mother relates to the outside world for the fetus, so to speak, the needs of the fetus being experienced by the mother as her own needs, as indeed they are, since the fetus draws on and depletes the supplies of the maternal organism. It is only toward the end of gestation that there develop some sort of limited motor responses on the part of the fetus to forces originating outside the mother, such as trunk or limb movements in response to external pressure on the abdomen. What other processes within the mother are experienced by the primitive developing nervous system of the fetus as input are unknown. They may include chemical substances which cross the placental barrier, as well as physiological rhythms of the mother, such as the maternal pulse, respiration, voice and body movements, which may be experienced by the fetus as some type of rhythmic or intermittent stimulation. It has been suggested that such rhythmic stimuli during fetal life might come to constitute fetal experience learned as "background noise," the absence of which after birth leads to "discomfort," which is generally relieved by corresponding stimulation. Some evidence in support of such a notion is found in the fact that crying infants may be quieted by certain rhythms of patting, rocking, and walking reminiscent of rhythms that may have existed antenatally (Greene[3]).

PHYSIOLOGICAL CHANGES AT BIRTH

If development proceeds properly, we may assume a certain readiness for birth, a point beyond which the uterus becomes no longer a suitable environment.* Nonetheless, the birth process itself represents an abrupt change in physical environment of the infant, requiring new adjustments for survival, including the following:

1. A new circulatory and respiratory system is inaugurated, involving the opening up of the pulmonary circulation, aeration of the lungs and the closure of the bypass channels, such as the ductus arteriosus. These changes begin immediately upon birth and are completed within a matter of minutes. The act of breathing constitutes the first major rhythmic exchange with the environment after birth.

2. Oral alimentation replaces transplacental nourishment. This necessitates the continuation of an obligatory relationship with a feeding adult, usually, but not necessarily, the biological mother. The importance of this continuing need for a relationship will be discussed at length.

3. The necessity to maintain body temperature in the face of much wider ranges of environmental temperature fluctuation demands both increased efficiency of temperature regulation by the neonate as well as assistance from adults.

4. Exposure to a variety of new physical forces which impinge on the surface of the body, including the sense receptors, provides the first bits of information about the external environment. Following birth there is also cessation or diminution of certain kinds of input to which the fetus had been accustomed, including more or less constant surface contact and support, weightlessness, the rhythmic stimulation of maternal heart and respiratory activity, and others not yet identified.

In addition to such physiological changes it is also necessary that behavior evolve to continue the biological symbiosis with the mother in the new state. Not only must the mother be ready, physiologically and psychologically, to accept, nurture and respond to the baby, but also

---

* Oliver Wendell Holmes described this developmental push thus:
"So the stout fetus, kicking and alive,
Leaps from the fundus for his final dive.
Tired of the prison where his legs were curled,
He pants, like Rasselas, for a wider world.
No more to him their wonted joys afford
The fringed placenta and the knotted cord."

the baby must have the primitive equipment to initiate and sustain the relationship. To see the new baby and to hear its first cry act as stimuli to evoke a nurturing response in the mother, and the ability of the baby to suckle makes possible the first mutual contact between mother and baby and assures that feeding can be initiated. The newborn thus begins its extrauterine life preadapted in respect to initiating and sustaining those processes necessary for survival and growth. These include both processes for which no external aid is necessary, such as breathing, excretion, digestion, metabolism, and so forth, and systems whereby the biological symbiosis of fetal life can be sustained in the new environment. The latter include the sensori-motor apparatus necessary for nursing as well as all the modalities of pleasurable physical contact with the adult and a variety of means of eliciting responses from the adult.

THE PRIMARY SLEEP-WAKING CYCLES[6]

The usual state of the newborn infant in the first days of life is one of fairly regular cycles of sleep and activity. Sleep ranges from a *deep, regular sleep*, during which breathing is smooth and even, through an *irregular sleep*, associated with irregular breathing patterns and a variety of movements, to *drowsiness*, during which the infant lies quietly, intermittently opening and closing the eyes. The awake and active states include an *alert but inactive state*, an *alert and active state*, and *crying*. In the *alert inactive* state the infant is motionless, but "bright-eyed," the eyes wide open and appearing to focus. Indeed even within the first day of life auditory and visual pursuit movements to appropriate stimuli may be demonstrated in this state. In the *alert active* state the infant is actively moving its limbs and trunk, with eyes open but not fixed or focused. The baby must, of course, be awake in order to nurse and if not awake, is awakened. The alert state and the crying state typically lead to nursing, which now constitutes a new condition in which mother and infant re-establish a biological relationship.

The typical cycle of the neonate is from stages of sleep to stages of alertness and finally to crying. In general, the awake periods last longer before feedings than after, and they are accompanied by much more kicking, mouthing, hand-to-mouth contact and crying. Crying before meals is rhythmical and associated with tandem kicking. Feeding characteristically terminates this type of crying and is followed by drowsiness, sleep and then resumption of the cycle. However, hunger is not the only factor which evokes crying, and feeding does not always suffice to terminate the crying. Some episodes of crying stop spontaneously, without any intervention, whereas others stop only with holding, rocking, stroking, patting, use of a pacifier or hand-to-mouth contact. These modes of relieving the crying state indicate an inherent receptivity, if not need, for certain kinds of sensory experience, whereby a state of discomfort or "unpleasure" is changed to one of comfort or "pleasure." The term "stimulus hunger" has been used to designate this apparent need and seeking for certain kinds of stimulation.

In most infants a finger or pacifier in the mouth is much more effective in stopping crying in the period before feeding than after. Some infants, however, seem to require something to suck on even after adequate feeding. Not only will they cry and be unable to sleep without a finger or pacifier in the mouth, but they will awaken if it is removed before deep sleep is achieved. This indicates that sucking needs and feeding needs do not necessarily correspond in intensity. The need for food may be satisfied without satisfying the need to suck. Such need for stimulation of the buccal mucous membrane may be another example of stimulus hunger.

The responsiveness of the infant to different types of external stimulation differs in the various states of the sleep-waking cycle. Most stimuli, such as noises, jarring, pressure, air blast, etc., if intense enough and presented suddenly, evoke a startle response under all conditions except vigorous crying. The actively nursing infant in the mother's arms is also a little less likely to startle upon such extraneous stimulation if the act of nursing is not interrupted. Individual newborns differ in the vigor of the startle response, some having only a slight startle, while others startle vigorously and begin to cry (Fries[2]).

When the external stimulus is of insufficient intensity to produce startle, the newborn may respond by either increasing or decreasing activity. Such responses are most likely when the infant is *awake, alert* and *inactive* and least likely when he is in *deep, regular sleep* or is crying vigorously.

In general, the same stimulus tends to increase the infant's activity when he is relatively inactive and to decrease it when he is more active, but to have little influence when the infant is actively nursing or vigorously crying. Heart rate shows a similar response to sensory stimulation, also tending to slow if rapid and accelerate if slow ("Law of Initial Values"), but to be little influenced when the infant is crying or is nursing (Bridger[1]).

These varying states presumably reflect intrinsic rhythms of the central nervous system and constitute the matrix around which the earliest psychic processes evolve. During deeper sleep the infant is most withdrawn or detached from external environmental influences and the motor system is least implimented for interaction with the environment. Spontaneous startle reactions are common during this phase, and as sleep lightens, responsiveness to environmental stimuli increases. We can only speculate as to what influences are involved in the spontaneous lightening of sleep, but presumably a need for food (hunger) is one. Sucking and other activity preparatory for feeding appear as the infant begins to awaken. Here we postulate that internal processes bring about changes in behavior (restlessness and crying) that not only elicit a response from the mother but also prepare for a particular activity (e.g., nursing). The infant thus has one cycle in which it moves from a state of relative unresponsiveness to the external environment to one in which a very specific interaction with the environment is called for, whether it be feeding, being rocked, patted, etc. In this latter state the infant exists in a mutual relationship with the adult whose appropriate behavior constitutes the basic environment to which he is responsive. During such mutually satisfying transactions between mother and infant, not only is the infant less responsive to extraneous stimulation, but also he resists interruption of the mutual state. Thus, withdrawing the nipple during nursing while the infant is still actively sucking is not only resisted but evokes a reaction of distress. Some infants respond with vigorous crying and diffuse motor activity, whereas others become limp and hypotonic and pass quickly into a withdrawn sleep state (Fries[2]). (These contrasting patterns of response to a stressful situation —protest and increased activity among some, withdrawal and inactivity among others—represent two basic reactions which will be discussed further.) Resistance to interruption and the higher threshold to extraneous stimulation when needs are being satisfied through active interrelation with the mother highlight the degree to which this constitutes the environment of the baby at such times. The biological unity of mother and child is re-established, and we shall see in subsequent chapters how the experience of repeated interruption and re-establishment of this unity results in the development of a psychological relationship from the original biological relationship which began in utero.

In addition to the awake state in which the infant is actively relating to the mother for satisfaction of a need (drive), there is another state in which, in contrast, the infant apparently is more reactive to external stimuli, internal pressures presumably being at lower ebb. This is the condition described by Wolff as *awake, alert, inactive* and *awake, alert, active.*[6] In the inactive state we clearly see the beginnings of a nonspecific attention to the environment through ears, eyes and other sense modalities, whereas in the active state we see what might be regarded as "practice" motor activities, which in themselves undoubtedly also provide a source of sensory input from the infant's own movements as

well. This identifies another condition under which interaction with
the external environment is taking place and through which a process
of internalization of the external environment is beginning. In this
state, however, the infant is not operating under the pressure of a drive
which for its satisfaction demands a particular type of interaction with
and response from the mother (or other adult). On the contrary, such
drive pressure must be at a low level in the neonate before this type of
more random responsiveness to the external environment can develop.
The importance of developments in this sphere for cognitive and other
processes will receive particular attention in Chapter VIII.

These two modes of interacting with the environment are by no
means independent. Under ordinary circumstances the largest part of
stimulation during the alert, awake state (other than feedback from
the baby's own spontaneous movements) undoubtedly takes place in
response to the activities of an adult in the environment. Hence, in
respect both to satisfaction of a more pressing need, as with feeding,
rocking, patting, etc., and to the more random contacts during the
awake, alert states, the activity of another person is the crucial intervening element. Further, the alert, awake phase typically occurs in
two periods—before the drive tension (of hunger?) reaches threshold
and culminates in crying, and in the course of achieving satisfaction
(e.g., during or after nursing). Brief in the first days of life, these periods
of alertness become longer and more frequent as the weeks pass by.
The significance of this will be discussed further.

Another condition linking these two states is the development of
other modes of expression on the part of the infant which evoke responses on the part of mother or other adults and vice versa. For
example, the precursor of a smile, restricted to a gentle, sideward,
upward pull of the mouth without other facial movements, occurs
spontaneously in the first days of life during irregular sleep, drowsiness
and alert inactivity, and especially just after feeding (Wolff[6]). But soon
this can also be elicited by certain high pitched sounds, particularly
the mother's voice. By the third week of life a fuller smile appears and
this has an irresistible quality, almost invariably evoking in the adult
not only pleasure but a desire to reproduce the conditions under which
the smile appeared. The mother coos or baby-talks to her baby, who not
only smiles in return but also looks to the source of the sound. In the
next two to three weeks a variety of interactions between mother and
child, including mother's voice, looking into each other's eyes, and the
game of patty-cake regularly evoke smiling on the part of the baby
and pleasure in the mother. Through this medium the pleasurable
interactions between infant and mother (and other adults) are extended
and intensified. Wolff[6] notes that mothers sharply increase the time
spent playing with their babies when the smiling response is established.

THE MENTAL APPARATUS OF THE NEWBORN

From the foregoing behavioral observations certain inferences can be drawn about the operation of the primitive mental apparatus of the newborn infant. In the first place, the behavior of the infant is predominantly determined by internal conditions and is relatively much less influenced by external factors. An intrinsically established cycle of sleep-wakefulness constitutes the background against which limited patterns of response may be evoked from the outside. Probably of greatest importance in this cycle are the processes concerned with nutrition and metabolism, in which ingestion requires alertness and interaction with the environment (specifically with the mother) whereas digestion, anabolism, and cellular growth proceed optimally during quiescence. Accordingly, we note that need for food is associated with three processes, alerting, preparation for use of the feeding apparatus, and activities which communicate the need for food to the environment (restlessness, kicking, crying). Thus the primitive mental apparatus is geared to respond to a rising need with behavior which will lead to the satisfaction of the need. But since satisfaction depends on the participation of a nurturing figure in the environment (mother), this process constitutes a major medium whereby a relationship with another human is established. This process will be discussed later in terms of objects and object relationships.

It is characteristic of this aspect of early behavior that the changing internal conditions which require the activity of an environmental figure have a demanding, insistent quality. This reflects the activity of basic drive, which, since it cannot be satisfied from within, brooks no delay or substitute. Only a specific sequence of interactions with the external figure will end the crying. The term *pleasure principle* is used to define this property of mental functioning in which a drive reaching threshold leads at once to action in relation to the external environment (see also Chapter XXII).

There is also evident some behavior which is not directly a response to a mounting drive, yet which also initiates further interaction with the environment. This system thus operates under different conditions, thereby enlarging the scope of potential contact with the environment. But as already pointed out, it is not unrelated to the system more explicitly operating under the pressure of drive.

Finally, we emphasize the degree to which the operation of the mental apparatus of the neonate is geared to a specific fit with the nurturing adult, the mother, so that infant behavior tends to elicit complementary maternal behavior. In subsequent chapters the importance of this for the development of the concept of objects and object relations will be considered.

REFERENCES

1. Bridger, W. H. and Reiser, M. F.: Psychophysiologic Studies of the Neonate. An Approach toward the Methodological and Theoretical Problems Involved. Psychosom. Med., *21*:265, 1959.
2. Fries, M.: Psychosomatic Relationships between Mother and Infant. Psychosom. Med., *6*:159, 1944.
3. Greene, W.: Early Object Relations, Somatic, Affective, Personal. An Inquiry into the Physiology of the Mother-Child Unit. J. Nerv. & Ment. Dis., *126*:225, 1958.
4. Ribble, M.: The Rights of Infants. New York, Columbia University Press, 1946.
5. Smith, C. A.: The Physiology of the Newborn Infant. Springfield, Illinois, Charles C Thomas, 1951.
6. Wolff, P. H.: Observations on Newborn Infants. Psychosom. Med., *21*:110, 1959.

CHAPTER V

STAGE OF DEPENDENCY: II. BEGINNINGS OF MENTAL FUNCTIONING AND OBJECT RELATIONSHIP

In the preceding chapter we discussed the earliest stages of infancy, which might be called premental or prepsychic in that psychological processes, as we know them as adults, do not exist; or, at least if they do exist, they are not demonstrable by any technique which is available to us. Let us focus our attention now on what we can imagine the mental apparatus of the infant to be like at this point. I say "imagine" because there is no direct way that we can approach this problem. We can approach it only by drawing certain inferences from overt behavior as we see it, by certain types of retrospective reconstructions, by interpretation of psychoanalytic data from older children and adults.

We know that the infant, soon after birth, passes through *cycles of relative quiescence and activity*. For the purposes of this discussion of developing mental activity, we shall begin by conjecturing only in terms of the feeding needs of the baby, and we shall exclude for the moment other varieties of needs, such as touching, clinging, stroking, rocking, etc., for which a similar cycle may also be imagined or which may be integrated with the feeding cycle. If we view the infant organism in terms of its metabolism, we note that the baby rapidly consumes energy in activity and growth. It has relatively limited stores of nutriment in the body as contrasted to the adult, e.g., the amounts of glycogen in the liver and of adipose tissue are relatively small. Hence, the baby is dependent on external supplies of food at frequent intervals, as compared to the adult, who can, for a limited time, draw on his own resources. We can postulate that soon after birth, as the supply of nutriment stored up during fetal life approaches exhaustion, a cycle is established in relationship to hunger and thirst. We cannot yet speak correctly of hunger or thirst as psychological experiences, but the newborn must have some neural systems to warn that energy sources are becoming depleted and other systems to initiate a change from the resting, quiescent state to a state of preparation or readiness for feeding. As described in the preceding chapter, the baby during sleep gradually changes from a motionless, quiescent state to a restless state in which sucking movements appear. Soon the level of awareness rises, the movements increase, and the baby awakens and eventually begins to cry. If the mother now picks up the baby, he may quiet down, but if the main need is for food, he will continue to cry and will not be soothed by any maneuver other than feeding. In such a case, he will orient himself toward the mother's breast. As the mother holds the baby in her arms, the contact of the baby's cheek with the mother's breast or clothes will lead the baby to turn his mouth toward the breast. With some help from the mother, the baby will find the nipple. There may be an interval of a few seconds or a minute or so during which the baby may continue to cry and be unable to get hold of the nipple, but as he secures the nipple, he will initiate sucking and quiet down. He may suck quite actively for a while, but soon the sucking begins to diminish and finally stops as the baby achieves satiation. He again becomes relatively quiescent. Sometimes before this stage is reached, the baby may close its eyes and may actually fall asleep at the breast. Or there may be a brief period of alert inactivity before drowsing. As the baby becomes a little older, there is an increasing interval of wakefulness between the satisfaction of hunger and falling asleep, during which the baby, lying in the mother's arms, may look at her face, perhaps grasping her finger, before finally falling asleep again.

How can we conceptualize this feeding cycle in terms of the *primitive mental apparatus?* To begin with, we identify *primary autonomous apparatuses* that are specifically directed toward the consummation of these activities. These involve a specific organization of the central nervous system serving the feeding pattern, including the responsivity to the specific types of internal stimuli that elicit it and the preferential innervation of the specific types of motor activity leading to the achievement of the feeding. A *system of perception* is also involved which, at this stage of development, is mainly interoceptive. The perception is directed toward some kind of change within the body related to the need for food, perhaps including certain kinds of sensations in the mouth. This might also be conceptualized in terms of a disturbance in the dynamic steady state, resulting from a lack or a need, or provoked by a signal anticipating such a lack or need. The disturbance in the dynamic steady state (or "unpleasure") leads eventually to activation of the feeding pattern, which includes not only the actual motor processes involved in the feeding but also the communicative aspects, namely, the crying. The baby's cry evokes a complementary response in the mother, which is a complex one because it is influenced by the whole range of her previous life experiences. Ideally, it includes a basic maternal pattern of wishing to go to the baby, to quiet the baby's crying, to nurse the baby, to hold the baby, and to gratify the baby. If successful, this response provides pleasure for the mother. There is a *reciprocal relationship between mother and child* in that mother experiences pleasure in the baby's quieting down and the baby experiences the primitive equivalent of pleasure in being nursed and in being satisfied.

In respect to the *neonate's mental apparatus*, we only postulate at this time two poles of feeling. One is a state of relative balance or comfort, the dynamic steady state, in which the supplies are adequate and needs are relatively fulfilled; the other is a state of discomfort or "unpleasure," which initiates some type of behavior which leads to restoration of a dynamic steady state. In terms of what exists in the baby's "mind," there is nothing comparable or equivalent to thoughts or ideas but perhaps something comparable to what we know as feelings or affects, unconnected yet with words or symbols.

Further, all this is experienced by the baby as within. For the infant, that which is outside does not yet have an independent existence in the sense of something separate from himself. What impinges on the baby from the external environment during the earliest weeks of life, such as the nipple in his mouth or the arms of the mother around him, is apparently experienced by the baby in bodily terms with no distinction yet between the thing producing the sensation and himself as the one experiencing it. For the baby, the nipple exists only when it is in his mouth, and then it is part of a mouth sensation. When the nipple is withdrawn, the baby may experience a sensation of discomfort in the mouth, as evidenced by crying or restlessness, which is relieved only by restoring the nipple—or something like it—to the mouth. The baby does not yet have the systems of either perception or analysis to conceive of the nipple as a thing which was taken away.

The modalities of contact with mother and other adults are not restricted to the feeding situation. As described in the last chapter, the evolution of the smiling response becomes a potent catalyst for pleasurable transactions. The full smile is readily evoked by two modalities of stimulation in particular, the human (female more than male) voice and the human face. In these first weeks it is the configuration of the face in movement, especially the hairline, mouth and the eyes looking into the baby's eyes, which constitutes the eliciting stimulus. Even a moving mask will be effective. The face arrests the baby's attention, he explores it, and finally stares into the eyes, at which point the smile breaks out. If the face (or mask) is turned to the side so that only a profile presents, the baby stops smiling and may look blank or puzzled, but the smile will return when the full face again is presented. Ordinarily vocal and visual stimulation are combined by the mother, further facilitating the smiling reaction. At this age the voice and the face configuration evoking the smile are nonspecific; the smile therefore is a nonspecific pleasure and social response, not a sign of recognition of a particular person (Spitz,[9] Wolff[10]).

Once the smiling reaction has developed, usually at around four to six weeks, there are increasing periods when baby and mother are relating to each other through the smile, a *reciprocal communication*, evoking pleasure in both. Because it evokes pleasure, it is reciprocally reinforcing. The mother, who experiences great pleasure from her baby's smile, attempts to stimulate more smiling, and the baby derives pleasure from the mother's activity. The smiling response is most readily evoked when the baby is gratified and comfortable, and least when he is hungry or fatigued. Once established, smiling (and laughing) begins to appear in response to the sudden appearance of familiar things or stimuli which have previously given pleasure as well as to certain new configurations of stimulation. There is now a generalization of the smiling response to indicate pleasure even when the infant is alone. Later it will signal the anticipation of pleasure.

We also soon observe that the sight of the face and the sound of the voice themselves may quiet even a crying, hungry baby, at least for a brief period. There may be a pause now—perhaps only half a minute, perhaps one or two minutes—during which the baby will look at the mother's face and smile and delay taking the bottle. A significant change has now taken place; the baby now reveals the beginnings of what can be called *primitive recognition* and *anticipation*. The predominantly interoceptive organization, in which what the baby feels are the two poles of "pleasure" and "unpleasure" or "comfort" and "discomfort" in which everything is experienced as coming from within, now develops an associative link with certain *exteroceptive* processes. An association is developing in the primitive mental apparatus between the feeling state of pleasure on the one hand and an image of the human face and the sound of the human voice on the other. No doubt this association includes considerably more than the face and voice; it is probably further reinforced by whatever the mother does in relationship to nursing, how she holds, rocks and pats the baby, how she smells, how her breathing and heart beat are felt by the baby. All of these will gradually become a part of this associative gestalt in relation to satisfaction of needs.

We introduce another concept here, *the ability to wait.* The baby does not have to have immediate satisfaction of the needs to suck, to swallow and to have food in order to stop crying. He can now wait. Clearly, *one of the functions of the mental apparatus is to interpose a delay between the development of a need and acting upon the need.* This delay is achieved by a system of signals; later on, symbols. The signals and the symbols are made up from a combination of interoceptive and exteroceptive stimuli. They are sensations arising from within as well as from outside the body. The baby's mental apparatus has reached the stage at which a particular gestalt which actually has nothing directly to do with feeding, nursing, nutrition, calories, proteins, carbohydrates, vitamins, etc., becomes an adequate anticipatory signal indicating that satisfaction *will* take place. In other words, we have now introduced the concept of future. Something will happen, and as the experience is repeatedly reinforced, *confidence* is established in the baby that the "signal" means "discomfort will be followed by satisfaction."[1]

By such steps does a central, organizing, anticipating system develop. This is a further step in ego development. But here we must appreciate the vast potentiality of *individual differences.* The kind of signals that one mother will provide for her baby may be quite different from the kinds of signals that another mother would provide. As we go a little further on in development, we shall find there are more signals and that the signals become more specific. By around six to eight months of age, the face that evokes a smile has become a specific face. It is no longer just a face—it is mother's face, the face of the person who nurtures. Further, there is a multiplication of signals. The baby will now stop crying when he hears the mother's voice, the mother's movements, the bottles rattling and a host of other cues which in the past have repeatedly preceded the satisfaction of needs.

A similar formulation may be considered around the satisfaction of other drives, including the need for stimulation of other sense modalities, all of which require something from or some interaction with the environment. The satisfactions of a number of needs are often experienced together and hence become linked. In the course of associating outside processes with need satisfaction there begins to develop in the baby the possibility of identifying or recognizing that there is something outside him as compared to something just inside. (See Chapter VIII.)

Now, if we retrace our steps and consider these same processes in terms of *object relationships,* we have to say that if the mother is to be an effective instrument for sustaining the life, growth and development of a small baby, certain qualities and aspects of her features, behavior, etc., somehow or other become incorporated into the baby's mind. This process takes place in relationship to the feeding experience and to other modalities of need gratification. All those attributes of the mother which serve the function of relieving tension, of satisfying needs, become incorporated into the structure and function of the baby's mind. Because much of this occurs in relationship to the feeding experience, one of the earliest perceptions that the baby develops about the external world is an intaking one, meaning that that which is good, that which is desirable, that which is tension-relieving in the outside world comes inside. This is the classic *oral concept* of psychoanalysis, which should be understood as a vector or directional concept, in which the oral cavity, as the organ of sucking and the avenue for feeding, plays a major, but not an exclusive, role in the development of the mental mechanism. Things in the external world are also "brought in" through the eyes, the ears and other receptors as well. The fact that the "inside," as the site of pleasure-unpleasure, exists before "outside" is distinguished determines that the first orientation to things in the outside will have this intaking vector quality. And it is in the mental apparatus that representations of the external world are being established.

REFERENCES

1. Benedek, T.: The Psychosomatic Implications of the Primary Unit: Mother-Child. Am. J. Orthopsychiat., *19:*642, 1949.
2. Brody, S.: Patterns of Mothering; Maternal Influences during Infancy. New York, International Universities Press, 1956.
3. Erikson, E. H.: Childhood and Society. New York, W. W. Norton & Co., 1950, pp. 67–76.
4. Escalona, S.: Emotional Development in the First Year of Life. *In:* Problems of Infancy and Childhood. Transactions of the Sixth Macy Conference, 1953, pp. 11–27, 32–47, 51–59.
5. Leitch, M. and Escalona, S.: The Reaction of Infants to Stress. A Report on Clinical Findings. *In:* Greenacre, P. et al. (eds.): The Psychoanalytic Study of the Child, vol. III/IV. New York, International Universities Press, 1949, p. 121.
6. Levy, D. M.: Experiments on the Sucking Reflex and Social Behavior of Dogs. Am. J. Orthopsychiat., 4:203, 1934.
7. Ross, S.: Sucking Behavior in Neonate Dogs. J. Abnorm. & Social Psychol., *46:* No. 2, 1951.
8. Seitz, P. F. D.: Psychocutaneous Conditioning during the First Two Weeks of Life. Psychosom. Med., *12:*187, 1950.
9. Spitz, R. A.: The Smiling Response: A Contribution to the Ontogenesis of Social Relations. Genet. Psychol. Monogr., *34:*57, 1946.
10. Wolff, P.: To be published (Ciba Symposium).

CHAPTER VI

STAGE OF DEPENDENCY: III. ORAL DEVELOPMENT; INTROJECTION AND PROJECTION

We have carried the development of the infant to the point where he has achieved the capacity to interpose a delay between stimulus and response and to anticipate a satisfaction. The mental apparatus now includes representations of perceptions from the environment combined with internal pleasurable feelings that enable the infant to anticipate satisfaction or relief of tension. We have seen also that the mother, as the person who has had the most to do with the care of the baby, is a major source of these experiences.

The mother and the external environment are not the only determinants, however. The process is still circumscribed by the biological developmental schedule of the infant. Direct observation of infants in the first year clearly reveals that their predominant organization is first and foremost an oral and a clinging one. The first neural organization of the infant equips it to nurse and to cling to the mother, as evidenced by the sucking and grasp reflexes and the Moro reflex, all of which are present at birth. That sucking has the quality of a need is well established; less well known is the need to cling. As we shall see, both of these have drive qualities, and as such influence the nature of psychic development.

As vision and hearing develop, perception at a distance becomes possible, and the baby tends to respond by attempting to grasp and to bring to its mouth what it perceives at a distance. As the eyes fix on the object, the total bodily response becomes one of reaching, grasping and bringing to the mouth. Whatever is presented when the baby is attentive and receptive is dealt with in this manner, and the baby actively perseveres until the object is in his mouth, when he may quiet down. As compared to that of the neonatal period, however, the mouth behavior is now different. The mouth is now also used as a testing organ. The baby "feels" the object with his mouth. If it feels "good," he sucks it, licks it, bites it and rolls it about in his mouth. If it feels "bad," he spits it out, screwing up his face into an expression that we call "disgust." In this behavior we see an elaboration and an accentuation of the oral behavior originally associated with the feeding and sucking experiences. The baby's oral and clinging orientation to the environment becomes the predominant one. Not only is it in the service of relief of tension arising from within, but it is also a means of dealing with many stimuli from the outside. A first concept of judgment is developing, for the "good" is kept in the mouth or swallowed and the "bad" is spat out. This lays the basis for a psychological concept that what is "good" is to be taken into the mouth and what is "bad" is to be kept out or spat out. This behavior the baby begins to regulate himself. He brings to his mouth what he wants; he closes his lips firmly, shakes his head, or spits out what he doesn't want. It must be emphasized that this is first of all a built-in or endogenous developmental pattern of infancy and that secondarily this mode of behavior achieves psychic representation and comes to contribute to the baby's characteristic way of looking at the world and the objects in it.

This development is an important one also in that it means the achievement of some independence of the external world. Not only is the baby now able to anticipate satisfaction through the memory traces of past satisfactions, but he is also able to provide himself with some satisfaction by putting his finger or other things in his mouth. This is true of all infants, and for varying periods of time it persists as one of the chief means of consoling and comforting oneself. The finger in the mouth becomes the substitute for the mother who is not available. It satisfies both the need for something in the mouth and the need to cling and is one of the earliest expressions of developing autonomy.

Later, chiefly in the second year, we see different infants adding other modalities of stimulation which are reminiscent of mother as object, such as stroking with a piece of cloth, a pillow, a cuddly toy, rocking, etc. Here again the elements of clinging and rhythmic stimulation, usually accompanied by simultaneous sucking, reflect transitional activities between an actual physical contact with an object and the purely psychic experience of remembering and imagining the mother.[4] It is noteworthy that such possessions are highly valued by the child, who is manifestly distressed if they are taken away or changed, as when the soiled blanket is replaced or cleaned. The varieties of stimulation include odor, taste, sucking, touch or tickling with a particular texture of cloth, grasping, cuddling, clinging and probably others, all of which were earlier experienced by the baby while being held or nursed by the mother or other important caring persons.

We are now in a position to explore further how the mental apparatus has developed. By the end of the first year, the baby has gained some mastery over his neuromuscular system: He can sit and perhaps stand, he can fix his eyes, he can grasp and he can bring his hand and objects in it to his mouth and face. He can recognize his mother and he can communicate both pleasure and unpleasure in a nonverbal but, nonetheless, highly meaningful way. His periods of wakefulness are longer and he can achieve many types of gratification from his own body. As great as these advances are, he still remains largely dependent on the adults in the environment for ultimate satisfaction of needs.

These changes, however, reflect the development of the mental apparatus. The pressure for immediate satisfaction of needs has now been modulated. The ego now includes some control over the motor system, which now can be put to the service of need gratification in a limited way. Through memory traces of past satisfactions, the baby can "imagine" satisfactions to come and can even reduplicate for himself some modes of gratification for which he was previously totally dependent on the environment (e.g., finger sucking or rocking). The memory traces are internalized samples of the external world which make possible partial gratification and anticipation of further gratification. Since these memory traces must be most intimately connected with the person (mother) most involved in need gratification, we can postulate an internalized image of a "good mother" connected with the "good" feelings of need gratification. Thus, the mother, who in the outside world has been functioning for the baby's not yet developed ego, now, through this process of internalization, is becoming part of the baby's developing ego. One might postulate that as the tension of an ungratified need rises, whether it be hunger, a sucking need or any other, the baby can for a short period, at least, reduce the tension by "imagining" the "good mother" and by doing what the "good mother" does, i.e., providing something (e.g., a finger) to suck. Needless to say, the effectiveness of such a self-contained psychic mechanism is limited; the rising tension eventually overcomes the mental mechanism of imagined or hallucinatory gratification and the baby must summon the mother or be overwhelmed again by the pressure of the instinctual drive. Successful development into adulthood is marked by increasing capacity to regulate intrapsychically the gratification of needs in terms of reality. (See Chapter XXII.)

The developing communication between infant and mother is

another reflection of the changes in mental apparatus. The mutual stimulation of pleasure in infant and in mother invites repetition and helps to establish preferred patterns of behavior on the part of the infant, since the pleased mother pleases her infant. Behavior which pleases the mother may become associated by the infant with feeling "good" and behavior which displeases the mother with "bad." We see here the germ of future conflict.[1]

The biologically determined oral organization contributes to an intaking orientation to the environment. The baby's developing recognition of objects in the environment involves the concept that what provides gratification is to be taken in, retained and clung to, whereas that which is unsatisfying and associated with bad feelings is to be ejected or kept out or pushed away. For the corresponding mental mechanisms we can use the term *introjection* to refer to the first process and *projection* to refer to the second. These become fundamental attitudes which continue to operate in modified forms throughout life, but they constitute basic mental mechanisms in the first year of life.

At the end of the first year we may visualize the neonatal cycles of tension and quiescence as taking the following course:

1. As a need—let us say, hunger—rises, the sleeping baby may become restless and suck.

2. He awakens, sucks his finger, moves about. Here we postulate reduction of tension by mental imagery anticipating satisfaction on the basis of past satisfaction while the infant at the same time is stimulating himself. In so doing, he utilizes an introjected image, the memory traces of past satisfactions.

3. As hunger becomes more insistent, he in some way calls the mother. Again, the sound or sight of his mother reduces tension, evokes pleasure, and for a short period delays the need for food. He responds to the mother in an introjective manner, as though to take her in as food is taken in. Her real presence reinforces the previous introject of "the mother who will gratify." But, in addition, he may try, literally, to put her hand or finger in his mouth, cling to her, grasp her and mouth her as he does other things. He may also put his hand to her mouth.

4. If the mother now feeds the baby, the tension is relieved and pleasure is secured. If the mother fails to come or fails to feed, the baby finally will begin to cry. The pressure of the unsatisfied need is now experienced as a "bad" feeling. If this develops into a full-blown crying fit, we see a striking loss of previously acquired capabilities and a return to behavior reminiscent of much earlier infancy. Now the mother's efforts to quiet the baby may be much less successful and the baby may have difficulty in accomplishing the nursing. Here we postulate that the baby attempts to get rid of the "bad" feeling by projection, by

seeing mother as "bad," i.e., as the source of his own "bad" feelings. As the mother succeeds in quieting the baby, he again introjects. In this process of calming down, since the "bad" feelings have been projected to the outside, to mother, the reintrojection now includes a "bad" image of mother. This is the beginning of a psychic concept of mother as "bad" as well as "good," possibly experienced as two quite separate images. We shall return to this in the next chapter.[1]

5. With the alleviation of hunger, the year-old baby has sufficient surplus energy and sufficient mastery of his body now to remain alert and active, playing with and exploring his body and his environment and making and retaining contact with the mother. Important developmental strides take place during such periods when drive tensions are relatively low, as the work of Piaget shows and as will be discussed in Chapter VIII.

6. Eventually the need for stimulation begins to subside; the baby becomes fatigued and again falls asleep.

The oral concept is well established by direct observation of infant behavior and by analysis of adults as well as by the study of myths and legends of primitive people. Study of Monica,[2] an infant with a gastric fistula, has revealed that the stomach also functions in a fashion consistent with such a concept. In other words, when Monica was outgoing and relating to persons in the environment either affectionately or aggressively, her stomach secreted actively. When she withdrew or fell asleep, her gastric secretion diminished. As she became more active in sleep, her gastric secretion rose. The most active secretion was noted upon reunion with a loved person from whom she had been separated. Such findings do not prove the validity of the "oral" concept, which is based on psychological data, but they do indicate that the behavior of the stomach is consistent with such a concept.

REFERENCES

1. Benedek, T.: Toward the Biology of Depressive Constellation. J. Am. Psychoanalyt. A., 4:389, 1956.
2. Engel, G. L., Reichsman, F. and Segal, H. L.: A Study of an Infant with a Gastric Fistula. I. Behavior and the Rate of Total HCl Secretion. Psychosom. Med., 18:374, 1956.
3. Escalona, S.: Emotional Development in the First Year of Life. In: Problems of Infancy and Childhood. Transactions of the Sixth Macy Conference, 1953.
4. Winnicott, D. W.: Transitional Objects and Transitional Phenomena. Internat. J. Psychoanal., 34:89, 1953.

CHAPTER VII

STAGE OF DEPENDENCY: IV. EARLY OBJECT RELATIONS; ANXIETY AND DEPRESSION-WITHDRAWAL

In the last chapter we saw that the baby's development in the first year follows certain predetermined biological pathways and that the mental apparatus develops concordantly. Thus, the original primitive sucking and clinging organization is progressively integrated with improving motor and perceptual coordination, enabling the infant to direct attention to and to grasp, to cling to, and to bring to the mouth what it wishes. The mental apparatus now includes not only the systems concerned with these activities (the "autonomous ego" or "conflict-free sphere of the ego") but also mental representations of experiences and perceptions which, when linked with the primary feeling states of pleasure and unpleasure, allow for delay, anticipation and confidence in respect to future gratifications or frustrations (beginning integrating functions of ego). In addition, mechanisms of ego are developing to assure what is pleasurable and to avoid what is unpleasurable. The first such defense mechanisms of ego are *introjection, projection* and *rejection*. Rejection, which involves ignoring or turning away from an unpleasant stimulus, the erection of some sort of barrier against its admission to consciousness, will later be represented in the two basic mechanisms of *repression* and *denial*.

Mental apparatus is thus developing out of transactions between basic biological processes within the growing infant organism and the external environment. Regulating, coordinating and integrating processes are developing within the central nervous system, which, so to speak, is "taking in" samples of both environments for future reference. In a way, we can think of the mental apparatus as a third environment, providing an historical record of all that has reached it from the rest of the body and from the outside. The most important "outside" experiences for the infant come through the persons concerned with the baby's care, notably the mother.

We shall now consider in more detail what role such persons play in the development of the mental apparatus of the infant. We have already described how these persons begin to assume an identity for the infant; we have also indicated that they have an essential role in need gratification. To persons who come to acquire this kind of identity and role, we apply the term *objects*.*

The information bearing on objects and the development of mental apparatus may be summarized as follows:

1. The biological necessity of a mother for the survival of the helpless infant prescribes the mother figure as the first object. Some of the varieties of perception involved in the earliest development of object relationship have already been described.

2. The smile in response to specific individuals and not to others is an early point at which an observer can recognize that the adult is acquiring for the infant some sort of identity separate from the self. This takes place in the latter part of the first year and indicates that such persons are achieving distinctive status as objects and have become represented in the baby's psychic apparatus in ways which permit the baby to identify them as sources of pleasurable feelings. Now when the familiar adult comes into view the baby will immediately break into a smile of greeting. It will be noted, however, that if the adult does not respond or breaks off the contact before the baby is satisfied, the baby may then react with signs of disappointment or crying until the adult reappears, and he quiets down quickly as contact is reestablished. Further, the baby, when alone, may spontaneously begin to fuss and cry, yet be appeased only when a particular person appears, rejecting all others. In this behavior he reveals the capacity to imagine and wish for a particular person and to differentiate him from all others. His

---

* Later we shall learn that this definition of objects is much too narrow. In addition to persons, the term may apply to things, functions, ideas or modalities which have the characteristics that they once existed apart from the self but have now become, in a psychic sense, a part of the self and play a necessary role in the satisfaction of needs. From the operational point of view, objects cannot disappear or be taken away without the person experiencing this as a loss in some sense. Thus, objects may include persons, pets, possessions, parts or functions of one's own body, one's job, home, and even abstractions like one's country or one's beliefs. They have a real existence in the external world as well as a psychic representation within the mind and they play an essential role in the satisfaction of needs.

internal state, as determined by current needs and the memory of past modes of gratification and the persons involved, establishes the basis upon which this choice is made. Pleasure when the "right" person appears, disappointment when he leaves prematurely, and rejection of the "wrong" person all speak for the development of some kind of intrapsychic representation of the gratifying object and the capacity to differentiate such an object from one not gratifying or strange.

3. Spitz[6] has observed that when a baby of 8 to 12 months is confronted by a stranger, he may respond with a look of bewilderment, may cry, may turn away and may attempt to crawl to the mother. He refers to this as *"eighth month anxiety."* He postulates that by this age the infant has built up a gestalt of perceptions from the familiar objects, something that might be called psychic *object representations* of the real persons in the environment who have had some kind of caring contact with the baby. Such psychic representations are associated with confidence that needs will be satisfied and therefore enable the infant to tolerate delay. However, they require repeated reinforcement from the real objects in order for them to serve this function successfully. At this point in development, the baby cannot tolerate seeing a strange face; the psychic representation of the familiar person cannot yet be maintained in the presence of a strange percept. The baby deals with this by turning away (rejection of the unfamiliar perception) or by going to the familiar person, to whom he clings. If the stranger persists, the baby cries. The crying and other expressions of distress reflect the loss of the confidence-supplying mental or intrapsychic representation of the good object and the consequent regression to an earlier state of dysequilibrium in which needs were not satisfied. The reaction may be overcome if the mother holds and comforts the baby while relating to the stranger, or if the stranger first presents his back rather than his face so that the baby has time to relate first to the back, which has fewer distinctive features than the face. These techniques of overcoming anxiety in the presence of strangers indicate that if the baby's psychic representation of the good object can be maintained, then percepts of strange faces can be tolerated without significant distress. This is well illustrated in motion pictures by Spitz* and by Engel and Reichsman.†

4. Infants who are brought up with a minimum of human contacts, such as the foundling home infants studied by Spitz, may show a profound general retardation of development as well as an inability to establish relationships with adults.[4] Spitz studied a group of infants in a foundling home who had been separated at four months from their

---

* Spitz, R.: Anxiety. Its Phenomenology in the First Year of Life.

† Engel, G. L. and Reichsman, F.: Monica, an Infant with Gastric Fistula and Depression.

prison inmate mothers and who were kept thereafter in an hygienically isolated environment with no contact with each other and only the barest contact with adults. One nurse was assigned to eight infants and was occupied chiefly with feeding and essential body care. (This was the well-meant policy of the foundling home, designed to avoid infections, without realization of the serious consequences. Spitz was an outside observer who chanced upon this situation and simply reported what he found.) By the end of the first year, these babies showed retardation of both physical and psychological development. They were unable to sit or stand, had no beginnings of speech, showed no smiling response and had prolonged periods of crying. Eventually they became very apathetic and unresponsive (except for crying) and manifested a variety of disturbances in motor function. In spite of the hygienic conditions, there were high morbidity and mortality rates, chiefly due to infections.

5. When infants between 3 and 7 months are separated from the familiar figures and are placed in a strange environment, they may exhibit a disturbance in behavior characterized by extreme preoccupation with searching and scanning the environment while at the same time being relatively detached from and unresponsive to the persons in it. The facial expression is blank, except for fleeting bewildered or frightened looks, and the infant may spend hours craning his neck, scanning his surroundings without apparently focusing on any particular feature, letting his eyes sweep over all objects without fixing on any one. Sometimes there is first staring, with relative immobility, and the use of toys or other attempts to interest the baby are ignored. There is no response to familiar figures, who may be stared at or through blankly or passed by in the persistent scanning of the environment. Disturbances in eating and sleeping, including excessive sleep, are commonplace. This syndrome has been called the *global syndrome* because it appears to be related to the total environment and to involve the total organism (Schaffer[3]).

6. After the baby has reached the point of recognizing and responding to the mother figure as a specific individual (usually from the eighth month on), separation from this person may lead to a profound grief response.[5] This is most likely to occur when the mother has been most satisfying and when the separation is abrupt and complete and an unfamiliar person takes over the care. When the mother figure has been less successful or when there have been multiple figures, the consequences of separation may be less profound and less apparent.

Such babies, after an initial protesting, searching and crying reaction, show apathy, hypotonia, inactivity and sad facies. They sit or lie motionlessly, crying noiselessly or staring into space. They present a picture of profound sadness. When an adult approaches, they cry sadly and if held may cling desperately. They cannot easily be consoled. The condition is cured by reunion with the mother, although sometimes not without a brief period during which the baby appears not to recognize the mother. Following reunion there may be a relatively prolonged period of increased dependence, with clinging, great intolerance of even very brief or minor separations and intensified anxiety in the presence of strangers.

Such depressed babies are frequently observed on any pediatric ward. This reaction is illustrated in the motion picture by Spitz: Grief, a Peril in Infancy.

Sometimes similar disturbances are observed among infants not physically separated from the mother when the mother is unsuccessful in relating as a person responding to and satisfying needs. Engel and Reichsman[2] studied an infant (Monica) with a congenital atresia of the esophagus and a surgically produced gastric fistula whose mother felt unable to hold and cuddle her baby because of her fear that she would disturb the tube through which the baby was fed. After age 6 months, the baby was left for long periods to cry fruitlessly because the mother knew no way to relieve the distress. In spite of a more than adequate caloric intake through the gastric tube, this baby thereafter failed to grow and by 15 months weighed only ten pounds and showed a profound state of fretful withdrawal, essentially a depression. The depression was alleviated in the hospital in a few months when a nurse and doctor spent a great deal of time with the baby. In other words, this baby showed physical and mental retardation and depression when with a mother who was unable to satisfy many basic needs, but when there was established in the hospital a sustained relationship with two adults, the baby was able to resume both psychic and somatic development. She remained, however, vulnerable to depressive responses. (These data are illustrated in motion pictures by Engel and Reichsman.)

Such observations of the reactions of infants subject to various degrees and varieties of separation and isolation serve to emphasize the important role of human contacts and relationships for the normal physical and psychological development of the infant. Once aware of these more gross disturbances, one can easily observe more subtle evidences of how the developing mental apparatus depends on and is molded by sustained contact with the persons caring for the baby. Very easily one can note the tendency of the infant to repeat with pleasure what evokes pleasure in the mother and to respond with distress when the mother is displeased. When the baby is performing well, as in nursing or sitting or just being responsive, the mother experiences pleasure which she communicates to the baby by her facial expression, movements and behavioral response, and this in turn is experienced pleasurably by the baby. Conversely, when the baby cries or is fretful, the mother feels distress and initiates behavior to relieve her own distress, sometimes by relieving the baby's distress, sometimes by leaving the scene. Thus, there are situations in which the baby's behavior in one way or another is so distressing to the mother that she responds mainly in terms of the distress she experiences, prolonging or intensifying the distress of the baby. In such ways the baby begins to learn what disturbs the mother and to try to avoid it. Since the baby's pleasure and unpleasure and the mother's pleasure and unpleasure tend to coincide and to reinforce each other, we see that there is a reinforcement within the mental apparatus of percepts and pathways which lead to mutual pleasure and which avoid mutual unpleasure. Further, the baby comes to anticipate and expect these specific ways of relating of the mother and other familiar figures and is not able to respond to persons who behave differently or even look different, at least not without an intervening period to "get used" to the new person. The baby seeks the familiar object, misses the familiar object, and avoids the stranger. This learning of how to secure pleasure and to avoid unpleasure takes place through transactions between mother and infant, and these learned patterns constitute further steps in the development of the mental apparatus. The object representation within the mental apparatus becomes part of the developing ego. It must be emphasized that this is a transactional process; both baby and mother influence each other and change in its course. But the baby's developmental timetable is biologically determined; he can relate to the mother only through those modalities which are adequately developed at a particular time. No matter what the mother's wishes may be, the baby will not sit, stand, talk or control its sphincters until the appropriate degree of bodily maturation is achieved. The baby's relationship with the mother will stimulate his development and influence its course, but it will not determine it.

The data summarized above indicate how the original biological dependence of the infant on the mother develops into a psychological dependence as well. Through the relationships with mother and mother surrogates, the baby develops the psychic functions which enable him to anticipate and assure satisfaction of needs and to avoid some measure of distress. The baby's ego has developed by acquiring memory traces of mother which mean "good" mother who satisfies needs, but such memory traces are effective in maintaining balance only if they are repeatedly reinforced by a mother who really does satisfy needs. The psychic dependence is revealed by the reactions which occur when the real object is missing or is replaced by a strange person. Under such circumstances the baby seems to lose much of what he had achieved in the course of development and to go back to much earlier behavioral patterns. More specifically, with loss of the object and of the psychic representations of the object, the ego's capacity to maintain balance and to tolerate frustration is greatly reduced. The psychic object representation cannot be retained without repeated reinforcement through transaction with the real object in the environment. Effective ego function is regained upon reunion with the mother; the baby is comforted and happy when the mother returns and is able to go about its business of growing and developing.

By the same processes whereby the mother figure achieves a measure of identity for the baby, so too must the baby be beginning to achieve an identity of self, separate from the mother. But at this early stage the psychic representation of the mother must also be an integral part of the self image, for without the mother the baby quickly regresses to the undifferentiated stage at which the difference between inside and outside and self and object did not exist. In subsequent chapters we shall trace further the development of the child's concept of self as distinguished from his concept of object, but it is important to appreciate that at this stage the baby's image of self must also be fused with his image of mother.

Earlier we spoke of the primal feeling states of "good" (satisfied, comfortable, etc.) and "bad" (unsatisfied, uncomfortable, etc.). We can now say that the "good" feeling state becomes linked with psychic representations of "good self–good mother" and the "bad" feeling state with representations of "bad self–bad mother." These refer to the memory traces of all the associated perceptions, experiences, etc., with the object which led to comfort and satisfaction of needs on the one hand, and those which were accompanied by feelings of unsatisfaction, discomfort and unpleasure, etc., on the other hand. This is the beginning of *ambivalence*, and we shall later see how this acquires specific mental content allowing one to think of an object and of one's self as both good and bad.

Having established the importance of object relationships and psychic object representations for the development and function of the mental apparatus and the necessity for relationships with the real objects to be sustained and satisfying for this process to continue, we must now examine how object loss affects the mental apparatus. Obviously, in the course of ordinary events, the baby is repeatedly subject to minor separations, but since these are brief, he eventually develops confidence that the separation will be overcome. Such repeated minor separations followed by reunion are of cardinal importance in enabling the infant to develop the capacity to function in the absence of the object. We have already described some of the steps involved in this process. Very early in life the baby manifests a diffuse, undifferentiated crying fit in response to unsatisfied needs; later it occurs on separation, even briefly, from the mother who is satisfying or who is needed, and the baby comes to anticipate the consequences of separation just as he comes to anticipate the consequences of reunion. For this anticipation of unpleasure, we postulate now a *warning function* of ego. The crying fit is the model of one kind of response to such an anticipated state of unpleasure, and it serves the function of an active attempt to call to and achieve reunion with the (absent) mother. As motor development progresses, the baby becomes able to move away from or avoid something strange or threatening and to move toward the mother, essentially *fleeing from a situation of unpleasure (danger) to the good object* who relieves the unpleasure. This basic state of ego is called *anxiety,* and it comes to include both the warning mechanism, anticipating the impending state of unpleasure, and the flight response, which is a primitive device to avoid the uncomfortable state.

What happens if the crying fit does not bring mother and relief? Eventually the baby becomes exhausted, gives up crying and falls asleep. With repeated failure of the anxiety mechanism, we now discover a second line of defense, indications of which were noted earlier (Chapter IV). This warns of impending exhaustion. To this signal the primitive response is to reduce activity, to turn away, to insulate against outside stimulation. This combination of warning signal and conserving response constitutes a second basic ego mechanism, *depression-withdrawal.* Its operation is well illustrated in the infant Monica, mentioned earlier, whose mother was unable to relate to her because of the baby's physical defect.[2] After prolonged fruitless crying, she developed a severe depression. Upon recovery in the hospital, she revealed an unusual susceptibility to recurrence of a depression-withdrawal response whenever she was separated from the good object (the doctor or nurse who cared for her) *and* was confronted by a stranger. The reaction of depression-withdrawal promptly ensued and persisted as long as the stranger remained. The baby remained motionless and hypotonic, not looking at the stranger, eventually falling asleep. Upon reunion with the good object she immediately recovered. Of interest is the fact that gastric secretion and oral behavior were greatly reduced during the depression-withdrawal reaction and were very much increased upon reunion with the good object. In essence, this baby averted the exhaustion of fruitless crying by responding at once to the warning mechanism of ego and effecting both a massive withdrawal from contact with the unsatisfying environment and a reduction of activity in the interest of conservation of energy. This pattern is illustrated in the motion picture referred to previously.

Biologically, these two patterns of *anxiety* and *depression-withdrawal* have their anlagen in the activity and conservative patterns of living systems. Living systems may respond to internal or external changes by activity designed to restore the dynamic steady state through internal rearrangements or through alterations in relation to environment. Such a reaction is dependent on ample available energy. This is the biological anlage of anxiety. But when energy supplies are depleted, are threatened with depletion, or for some reason are unavailable, the biological system may respond with a reduction of activity, a husbanding of energy, and this may include metabolic rearrangements or structural changes which insulate against the environment (e.g., spore formation) or reduce metabolic requirements (e.g., hibernation). This is the biological anlage of depression-withdrawal. With the development of a central nervous system and a psychic apparatus, general regulation of such responses becomes concentrated here and they are then experienced and manifested psychologically and behaviorally as *affects*. (See Chapters XIV, XVIII and XXXIII.)

REFERENCES

1. Bowlby, J.: Grief and Mourning in Infancy and Early Childhood. *In:* The Psychoanalytic Study of the Child, vol. 15. New York, International Universities Press, 1960, p. 9.
2. Engel, G. L. and Reichsman, F.: Spontaneous and Experimentally Induced Depressions in an Infant with a Gastric Fistula. A Contribution to the Problem of Depression. J. Am. Psychoanalyt. A., *4:*428, 1956.
3. Schaffer, H. R.: Objective Observations of Personality Development in Early Infancy. Brit. J. Med. Psychol., *31:*174, 1958.
4. Spitz, R. A.: Hospitalism. *In:* Freud, A. et al. (eds.): The Psychoanalytic Study of the Child, vol. 1. New York, International Universities Press, 1945, p. 53.
5. Spitz, R. A.: Anaclitic Depression. *In:* Freud, A. et al. (eds.): The Psychoanalytic Study of the Child, vol. 2. New York, International Universities Press, 1946, p. 313.
6. Spitz, R. A.: Anxiety in Infancy. Internat. J. Psychoanal., *31:*138, 1950.

CHAPTER VIII

THE DEVELOPMENT OF INTELLIGENCE AND REALITY SENSE IN THE INFANT

In preceding chapters we have shown how the infant's dependence on the mother becomes progressively transformed from a biological to a psychological dependence in the course of the infant's becoming capable of differentiating his mother as an object separate from himself. This means that thereafter the relationship is increasingly mediated through psychological processes, the development of which is dependent upon continuing transactions between the familiar adults and the infant. Gratification of needs is assured by the availability of the nurturing adult, whose effectiveness for the infant is no longer dependent on actual physical contact. As the infant enjoys repeated success in overcoming distress and satisfying needs, he gains greater confidence that the adult *will* come when needed. In brief, the adult begins to become for the infant an object that has separate existence in the environment and is represented in the mind as well. The baby can tolerate brief separations because he can imagine his mother and have confidence that she will come back.

So far, these phenomena have been described in rather general terms, and the main emphasis has been on the role of drive mechanisms and the pleasure-pain principle as the major determinants. Although a description of infant development based on "crises" serves to highlight the role of the basic biological requirements for survival and growth, it pays insufficient attention to other processes which also play a role in the development of the capacity to conceptualize the reality of the environment as separate from the self. Further, it overlooks important

57

aspects of the development of intelligence in the infant. We shall now examine some of these processes and, in so doing, we shall follow closely the observations and views of Piaget.

Primitive intelligence may be regarded as an extension, through the operation of the central nervous system and mental mechanisms, of the biological processes whereby the organism takes in from the environment what it needs for survival and growth and adjusts itself within the environment. Piaget uses the terms *assimilation** and *accommodation†* to refer to these two aspects of the biological processes as they apply to the development of intelligence and reality testing. Beginning with a biological organization tuned to respond (in a more or less reflex manner) to certain internal and external changes, a stepwise development takes place, culminating in the second year of life with the clear-cut capacity not only to distinguish objects from self in respect to space, time and form and to have mental representations thereof, but also to be able to manipulate intrapsychically symbolic representations and schemata (see below) in order to solve problems and operate within the environment. In contrast to the behavior which occurs in response to the pressure of more urgent biological needs, these developments take place optimally when such needs are relatively satisfied. The baby who is hungry, thirsty, cold, wet or in pain or who is missing the satisfaction of certain physical contacts is primarily occupied in a form of behavior which will bring about satisfaction of his needs. In the first weeks of life this is indeed the dominant pattern, but as repeated success in need gratification is experienced, favorable conditions are created for the kinds of interactions with the environment necessary for the development of intelligence and reality testing. It is for this reason that the first strivings of the infant are so much concerned with processes involved in establishing and maintaining a relationship with the mother, for without it survival and further development could not take place. For the same reason the success of the mother figure in assuring basic gratifications becomes a major facilitating factor for the intellectual growth of the infant. When the baby is free of the more insistent instinctual demands, a condition assured when he is in a

---

* Piaget uses *assimilation* to refer at the biological level to the physico-chemical incorporation of substances into the organic structures of the body; at the primitive psychological level, to the tendency of the organism to incorporate sensory and motor components of a behavior into an endogenous or reflex schema they have activated; and at a later psychological level, to the tendency of the mind to incorporate ideas about the external environment and the products of mental activity into preexisting schemata of thought.

† *Accommodation* is the term used by Piaget to describe the processes whereby what is assimilated is changed or utilized to bring about adjustment within the environment. What is *assimilated* provides experience; *accommodation* modifies this appropriately to new stimuli or conditions.

satisfying relationship with the adult figures who supply needs, he is also free to engage in the kinds of examination, exploration and experimentation through which the real environment is discovered and learned. When relationships are unsatisfactory or seriously interrupted, as described in the last chapter, intellectual growth and reality testing are interfered with or crippled. Clearly, then, intellectual development is not a thing apart from emotional and interpersonal development as so far described.

Piaget identifies six stages in the development of primitive intelligence. At the risk of some repetition of material already covered, we shall adhere rather faithfully to his sequence of presentation. It will, of course, be possible to present the Piaget material only in sketchy outline. For more detail the reader is referred to the original works.[1,2]

THE FIRST STAGE: "THE USE OF REFLEXES" (BIRTH TO END OF ONE MONTH)

This stage is characterized by the use of what Piaget calls "reflexes" serving earliest survival needs. (We discussed these previously in terms of "endogenous behavior patterns.") Sucking and grasping are examples of two reflex patterns established at birth which rapidly become stabilized and more efficient with utilization. Further, they tend to repeat without apparent external stimulation, e.g., when the baby manifests sucking without anything in the mouth as well as during nursing. Once it is established, there is a tendency toward generalization of the behavior in response to less specific stimuli, as when the baby mouths the coverlet or his fingers as well as the nipple. Further, it is noted that after a few trials the hungry nursling can find and differentiate the nipple yielding milk from other things, indicating the development of a primitive type of recognition. This is not recognition of an object in the environment, but rather only a recognition of a previously satisfactory (or unsatisfactory) action; sucking on the nipple satisfies hunger, sucking on the covelet does not. In earlier pages we have conceptualized this in terms of awareness of internal changes or feelings of pleasure or unpleasure. Piaget extends this concept to include the idea that patterns of behavior involved in the utilization of external things become assimilated in the neural apparatus in the course of successful repetition. He uses the term *schemata* to refer to such assimilated patterns of behavior. In other words, by repetitive and successful action on the thing in the environment, this complex or schema is not only crystallized as mental experience (assimilated) but is also used in furthering adjustment to and learning about the environment (accommodation). This process does not yet involve mental images, but only a familiar pattern of action and reaction evoked reflexly and on contact by something in the environment which itself does not yet have existence in the infant's mind. It is necessary to emphasize that these primitive patterns are mediated through nervous system organizations already present and designed for just such purposes, to nurse, to cling, etc. For this end, recognition of objects as objects, and of spatial, causal and temporal relations plays no part and, indeed, is not necessary. These are merely the earliest reflex systems necessary for survival and the beginnings of development.

THE SECOND STAGE: "THE FIRST ACQUIRED ADAPTATIONS' AND "THE PRIMARY CIRCULAR REACTION" (SECOND TO SIXTH MONTH)

At the beginning of this phase the infant is noted to "practice" rhythmic mouth and hand movements, to watch and follow things within his visual field (but not to search for them), to listen to or make sounds, etc., as if he is doing these simply for the sake of doing. Piaget refers to the sensory stimuli involved here as "aliment" for the activity: the child looks at a moving object simply because it has value for the development of vision; he is not yet concerned with the identification of the thing looked at. As each of these relatively independent activities becomes established, coordination between them begins to appear. For example, from the second to the fourth month the baby tries to follow with his eyes what his hands do, but he is not yet able to keep his hands within or to move them into his visual field. As long as his hands are in his visual field, he "practices" hand movements and watches them. Now, when an object appears in the visual field the baby will look at it, and if his hand, too, is in the visual field he will also try to grasp the object. No such effort will be made if the hand is not visible to him. Eventually these three patterns of behavior become coordinated and he becomes able to grasp what he sees whether his hand is in view at the time or not.

In the development of visual schemata it is again noteworthy that the human face is particularly effective in eliciting attention. For auditory schemata it is the human voice which arrests the attention of the baby. These then constitute another set of experiences that tend to be reciprocally assimilated. As the mother talks to the baby he watches her face intently, coordinating the two activities of looking and hearing, as if he is trying "to listen to the face and to look at the voice." All such schemata are at the same time being brought into relationship with earlier established patterns, such as sucking. Thus, by four months the baby not only grasps what he sees and brings it to his mouth to suck, but he also responds with preparatory sucking activities to visual or auditory stimuli connected with feeding, e.g., the sight of the bottle. In these developments, Piaget again invokes the concept of assimilation, now meaning that one schema, e.g., grasping, is assimilated to another, e.g., visual, resulting in a new accommodation: the child becomes able to grasp what he sees. This intersensory coordination is actively practiced and extended, the child being seen to search systematically for correlations. The tendency is to generalize each new activity as widely as possible in relation to all the spheres previously exercised. However, a certain hierarchy of preference seems to persist, earlier activities taking precedence over those acquired later. By the end of this stage reciprocal assimilation is complete. All that is seen is grasped, all that is grasped is brought into position to be seen, and then to be sucked, or vice versa.

The second stage thus transcends the limits imposed by the endogenous behavior patterns. The baby now begins to acquire new patterns and then to coordinate them to form from them further new behavior patterns (*"primary circular reaction"*). One circular reaction is activated by its coordination with another and is no longer simply a response to an outside stimulus. This constitutes an essential progress toward objectification, for when a thing can be simultaneously grasped, looked at and sucked, it becomes externalized in relation to the subject quite differently than if it can only be grasped. But this is still very far from the concept of an object separate from the self. By studying his behavior in response to a disappearing object, Piaget demonstrates that the baby is not yet capable of identifying the thing in space as having an identity. If the baby is first shown a toy and is allowed to watch it being put under the coverlet, he limits himself to looking at the place where it vanished but makes no effort to search for it under the cover. If nothing reappears he soon gives up. For the child the object does not yet have an independent existence in the environment; it exists only as long as it is a sensory experience and when no longer experienced sensorially it ceases to exist for the baby. If the disappearing object is the nipple removed from the mouth, thereby interrupting satisfaction of a need, the child may continue empty nursing or sucking, but in so doing he is merely repeating the earlier reflex pattern without adding anything which acknowledges that the nipple is somewhere in space. He may exhibit reflex groping activity but if this is not successful in reencountering the nipple, he gives up and cries. In brief, the image which disappears immediately sinks into oblivion and no longer acts as a stimulus. If the image is related to a current need, the infant becomes distressed and cries, a nonspecific reaction in relation to the missing image (though an effective reaction in eliciting help from someone in the environment). All the evidence indicates that at this phase of development it is only the infant's sensory and motor activity which he experiences as reality; that which is in the external environment has existence only in terms of the baby's experiencing of his own activity. Further, he is not yet capable of performing intentional acts; he cannot seek something with plan or foresight.

Our knowledge of the capacities of the mental apparatus in the first five to six months makes more understandable the nature of the relationships between infant and adult and the consequences of disturbances on such relationships during this period of life. (a) Since differentiation and identification of objects in the environment have not yet been achieved, the infant is relatively tolerant of different adults as long as they satisfy needs. Obviously some degree of differentiation is possible, but this is based more on variations in how the activity with the adult is experienced than on the baby's recognition of differences in the appearance of the adult. (b) If the infant is permanently separated from a mothering figure and is maintained in a relatively sterile environment, as in the situation described by Spitz (Chapter VII), he suffers not only from a reduction in the sources of instinctual gratification but also from a deficiency of "aliment," the sustaining input of nourishing stimulation from the environment which permits practice, repetition, consolidation, integration and extension of the various behavioral schemata. In extreme cases such as those observed by Spitz, it seems likely that the poverty of such opportunities for tension-free activity with the environment seriously cripples the capacity to conceptualize the world in terms much beyond that characteristic of Piaget's second stage. (c) When the mother-child relationship is unsatisfactory because of repeated failures to satisfy basic needs, there is greater call upon the more primitive endogenous behavior patterns and relatively less opportunity for exercise of the behavior characteristic of the second stage, which requires tension-free periods. The chronically crying, distressed or withdrawn infant has less opportunity to practice, consolidate and coordinate the early schemata than does the happy, contented baby with satisfying relationships. This lack may contribute both to intellectual retardation and to an entrenchment of the more primitive patterns primarily serving the function of securing a relationship or insulating against its absence, as was noted in the case of Monica (Chapter VII). The importance of an unsatisfactory mother-child relationship in predisposing to later psychopathological developments remains to be fully elucidated, but is probably considerable. (d) The "global" pattern which occurs after brief separations reflects both the inability of the infant to retain a mental representation of the environmental objects and his great dependence on stimulation from the environment as "aliment" to maintain the functioning of the mental apparatus. He scans the environment and looks past or through familiar objects in an effort to continue the actions which were associated with earlier relationships. This is a transient behavior pattern which is soon overcome as needs are gratified and the environment again becomes familiar. It is not known whether it has any later consequences in respect to psychological development. (See Chapter VII.)

The notable tendency toward repetition for its own sake, observable in these first two stages, might be regarded as evidence of the operation of the drive activity of the nervous system itself (Chapter III). Each behavioral activity—sucking, grasping, looking, listening, etc.—although originally in the service of a more basic need, in itself engenders a further need to repeat itself even in the absence of the initial need. The baby sucks for the sake of sucking, looks for the sake of looking, grasps for the sake of grasping, and appears to enjoy doing so. Thus, needs which were originally organic, e.g., the need for food, become elaborated into functional needs as well, which extend beyond the primary biological need and give rise to operations which concern the interrelation of things in the environment. When, for example, the need for food is taken care of, the baby utilizes the same schemata to explore and extend his knowledge of the environment. In this fashion psychic development is influenced by the existence and activity of drive systems while at the same time extending far beyond them, eventually becoming relatively autonomous (cf. also Chapter XXII).

THE THIRD STAGE: "THE SECONDARY CIRCULAR REACTIONS" AND "PROCEDURES DESTINED TO MAKE INTERESTING SPECTACLES LAST" (FIFTH TO EIGHTH MONTH)

At this stage the first intentional acts are performed. The child transcends the level of simple bodily activities (sucking, listening and making sounds, looking and grasping, etc.) and begins to act upon things and to utilize their interrelationships as means to an end. This begins around the fifth month, when the baby "discovers" that some activity has produced a result and then repeats the gesture in an apparent effort to reproduce the same result. For example, while reaching to grasp a suspended rattle his poorly coordinated hand movement instead strikes it and causes it to swing. Now the child looks at the swinging rattle with surprise and when it stops, rather than resume the grasping, he repeats the striking movement in order to reproduce the swinging. If successful, he practices the action over and over again, often with evident pleasure, laughing, squealing or smiling. This extension to a new pattern Piaget calls a "secondary circular reaction," for the movements are now centered on a result produced in the external environment and the aim of the action is to maintain the result. Thus, the interest has shifted from the action itself to the result of the action. Further, the child may begin to introduce intermediaries into his proceedings, as when he causes a rattle to swing by shaking the crib bars. As he rediscovers the movements which led to the observed result these schemata are reciprocally assimilated, i.e., he notes that a particular arm movement yields a visual experience, the swinging rattle, and he combines the two as a single act. But it must be emphasized that the original activities which evoked the unexpected response were schemata that had been in use for some time. He had already learned how to grasp for the rattle which he saw. The new development is the interest in the result and then the attempt to duplicate the result. Since the original discovery (the swinging rattle) was accidental and not intentional, this is not yet an act of intelligence. Although the child now seems to have a need to perpetuate the interesting result discovered by chance, the intention still is limited to reproducing the act. Thus, when the rattle stops moving the child experiences some kind of inner tension (or need) which he attempts to relieve (or gratify) by utilizing the movements which he had just performed and which induced the rattle to swing. If he is successful, there is recognition, pleasure and an inclination to repeat again. At this point there is no evidence that the rattle is seen as a discrete object, but only as something to swing. For the child the experience is still a complex of interrelated sensations, visual, tactile, kinesthetic, etc., connected with his own motor and sensory apparatus.

As such secondary circular reactions are extended and consolidated, the baby in the next two or three months begins to use these as gestures to perpetuate a variety of spectacles. Thus, he may use the striking motions to induce another person to make the rattle swing or even to make something else swing, which cannot be made to swing. Here we see an inclination to equate the movement or gesture with the result, a magical procedure. His preoccupation with the activity and its result now leads the child to utilize all varieties of external things as "aliments" for this now established behavior pattern. At the same time this pattern becomes a means for having some kind of contact with heretofore strange things, all of which are for the moment being dealt with as "things to be shaken," "things to be rubbed," "things to make rattle," etc. Procedures evolve "to make the interesting spectacle last," which now may include only fragments of the original movement, or token gestures, so to speak.

During this stage it is clear that for the baby the existence of things in the environment is still experienced primarily in terms of and as extensions of his own actions. If a bright object is rapidly passed in view, he will follow it with his eyes or with his hand but only within the extension of the trajectory of these movements. He behaves as if he expected to find the vanished object in the place where his eyes or hand would go if they continued their movement. In brief, the object has no independence outside the movement of the baby in respect to it. If he fails to find it he now evinces distress and will look for it at the place where he last saw it. Thus, if the adult hides a ball under a coverlet in full view of the baby, he will continue to look in the extension of his own visual movements and when he fails to see it he will look in the hand of the adult where he last saw it before the adult hid it. If it is neither within an extension of the movement started nor in its original position, he makes no further attempt to search for it. Yet it is clear that there has developed some kind of visual permanence of images, otherwise the baby would not have initiated the search in the first place.

Since things do not yet have an objective identity, there can hardly yet be a knowledge of spatial relations. When the thing disappears and is beyond the range of the visual or motor trajectory, it ceases to exist for the baby. This unawareness of spatial relations is revealed in the baby's response when the nursing bottle is reversed so that the nipple is out of his view. He now attempts to suck the bottom of the bottle and although obviously not satisfied, he not only evinces no sign that he realizes that the nipple is at the other end, but also makes no attempt to turn the bottle around, even though other observations reveal that in terms of motor development he is quite capable of so doing. In brief, he behaves as if the two ends of the bottle are unrelated and the nipple has vanished. The object is not yet endowed with substantial permanence.

Piaget likens the baby's view of space beyond prehension ("distant space") to the uninformed adult's view of the heavens, the stars appearing as images without depth in some sort of unrelated pattern and the moon seeming to follow his movements. The baby's experiencing of space begins within the range of his own prehension and motor activity. Through groping and repetitive action the baby moves things back and forth or from side to side in space and thereby begins to assimilate these visual and kinesthetic experiences of depth, but still mainly in terms of his own movements.

The third stage also marks the beginnings of an interest in causal relations, as, for example, when the baby first pays attention to the results of his shaking something. He seems at first merely to establish a link between the experiencing of his own movements and the final result evoked thereby without seeming to pay attention to the necessary temporal, spatial or causal connections between them. It is through such activities that the baby comes to endow his own action with the capability of producing a now-desired result, but this still has the quality of a magic gesture, since he attempts thereby to elicit the same result without the action necessarily having any direct logical relation to the result. In this respect, imitation becomes an important activity in furthering such magical expectations, for the adult characteristically responds to the baby's imitation by repeating it or by expressing approval in some way if he wishes the act continued. When imitating an adult, the baby not only incorporates into himself behavior external to himself but he also exerts an influence on another person, inducing in him some kind of behavior in the form either of a pleasurable reaction or of repetition. This, then, is but one of many ways in which the baby comes to use his actions and gestures as means of inducing a person in the environment to repeat interesting acts. At this stage of development merely the coincidence of the baby's efforts and the consequences in the environment may suffice to link these two in his mind as causally related. Since humans, in contrast to inanimate objects, are more likely to respond to the baby's gestures with behavior, there is a great wealth of possible interactions now experienced by the infant as the magical result of his own activity. This is obviously pleasurable and may acquire the quality of a need in its own right, as evidenced by the smiles or squeals of delight when the baby's gestures evoke the hoped-for response on the part of the adult and by his disappointment when they do not. Here, obviously, are evolving new modes of pleasurable (or frustrating) interaction between the infant and the adults who care for him, extensions, so to speak, from biological to psychological means of relating. In brief, while this characteristic behavior of Stage III is an important step in the development of intelligent behavior, it is also important in extending the range and variety of means whereby the baby establishes and maintains relationships with others.

THE FOURTH STAGE: "THE COORDINATION OF SECONDARY SCHEMATA AND THEIR APPLICATION TO NEW SITUATIONS" (EIGHTH TO TWELFTH MONTH)

The fourth stage marks the first time that the infant reveals a capacity to assign to external objects a consistency independent of the self. Instead of simply repeating and extending the circular patterns characteristic of the third stage, these now become coordinated and interrelated in such a way that behavior evolves which has an aim. By arriving at new combinations the baby learns to put things in relationship to each other. He no longer merely tries to repeat or prolong an effect which he has accidentally discovered, but he pursues an end not immediately attainable and tries to reach it by intermediate means. Thus, when he sees a desired object being hidden, he no longer tries to reach it by by-passing the obstacle or by magic gestures of waving or kicking, but instead removes the obstacle first with one motion and then takes hold of the object with another motion. In this he reveals a capacity to keep in mind the "goal" he wishes to achieve while he is in the process of dealing with the obstacle which stands in the way of his achieving that goal. Hereafter he clearly is seen to search for new means to overcome obstacles to the goal. The dissociation of means and ends indicates the operation of *intention*, which is now differentiated from simple repetitive habits. The means used are borrowed from earlier reaction patterns (schemata), but now the infant has the capacity to remember and to use the appropriate ones at the right time and to adapt them to the current situation. The final result, however, still has a conservative aim, namely, to achieve the same kind of results as before, i.e., to grasp, to hold, to mouth, to shake, etc.

In the course of these developments the baby begins to use instruments or intermediary means to an end. He will push or touch one thing with another or push the adult's hand to make him perform the act. Two aspects can now be related to each other, yet not be confused with each other. Similarly, patterns of behavior are separated one from the other, yet are related to each other, such mobility permitting an increasing range of behavior in the service of attaining the end, whether it be reaching a toy or overcoming an obstacle. This facilitates the discovery of new relations between objects. In the same sense, events and behaviors achieve some degree of independence and relationship so that signs or symbols come to indicate specific events or classes of events. A particular sound—for example, footsteps on the stairs—means that father is home, or putting on the hat means that mother is going away. This recognition implies some mental capacity to grasp what is coming for which the action in progress is merely a sign, but one is not yet justified in assuming that the baby is picturing the objects to himself in their absence, only that the sign sets in motion a certain attitude of expectation and a certain schema of recognition.

It is noteworthy that now the baby begins to deal with a new external object more as an external reality to which he must adapt himself. He subjects it to a sequence of exploratory movements relating to the object rather than to himself. He feels it, explores the surface and the edges, turns it over, moves it, displaces it, etc., all as if he is trying to understand it. This exploration, however, is done by successively trying out in turn each of his repertoire of previously established behavioral schemata, and from these he derives information in terms of its fit to his own body use. This is part of the process whereby the concept of an object having a separate existence is developing. The external object does not yet have permanence in his mind, however, as is demonstrated by the manner of his search for a vanished object. The baby looks for it and conceives of it only in a particular position, namely, the place where he first saw it hidden and then found it. If he watches a ball being hidden under a blanket, he immediately removes the blanket and picks up the ball. But now if he again is permitted to watch it being hidden under the blanket and then removed and placed under a second blanket, he will continue to search for it under the first blanket even though he has seen it disappear under the second. Although the baby behaves as though the ball has existence independent of his own action, it still does not yet have permanence, for its existence in the baby's mind is still linked with the last successful activity which led to its discovery. Eventually he is able to follow displacements successively to second or third places, but if it is not immediately found, he again returns to look for it in the first position. For the baby the ball is not yet a thing which is displaced; it is independent of the displacements; it remains related to certain actions and experiences of the baby.

Further awareness of spatial field is also developing during this stage. The baby is observed to add to his examination of things by slowly moving them toward and away from his face or by observing them while moving his head from side to side or up and down. This would appear to be an attempt to grasp the relations between size and distance and to separate his own movements from the movement of the things being manipulated. By rotating things slowly he acquires the concept of the other side, whereby an invisible part is permanently related to the visible part. He no longer has any difficulty in knowing how to turn the nursing bottle around in order to find the nipple. The third dimension has been recognized, but still only in relation to what the child himself can manipulate. With this beginning mastery of third dimension, his searching activities are no longer limited to the trajectory of his own movements but include the capacity to conceptualize the thing as having shape and dimensions and as undergoing changes in position in relation to himself.

These developments of the fourth stage are noteworthy in a number of respects. In the first place, as was true of the earlier stages as well, it is a consistent finding that the baby repeats and practices each new behavior that he accomplishes. This repetition appears to represent a general principle of mental and nervous system functioning, namely, that behavior or mental activity involved in the successful satisfaction of a need itself becomes a source of pleasure increasingly independent of the original biological need. The consolidation and extension of the new pattern is thereby facilitated through the operation of the pleasure principle, now considerably detached from the immediacy of the more primary biological needs. In the fourth stage we see the first clear evidence of this principle extending to mental activities per se as compared to the pleasure experienced earlier in the consolidation of reflexes and motor activities.

The fourth stage is also marked by the first clear-cut behavior indicating that things in the environment are endowed with some separateness, though not yet permanence, and that they can be recognized and differentiated. This stage coincides with the time (eighth month) when the capacity to distinguish the familiar face from the strange face has developed, when anxiety is first exhibited in response to the stranger, and when grief reactions first occur in response to extended separations (Chapter VII). Now for the first time the baby seems to have some awareness that the mother (or any other adult), who satisfies needs, is separate from himself, and he is aware not only of her comings and goings, but can also anticipate such movements through learned signs. But this mental experience has not yet achieved such permanence that the baby can tolerate separation of any duration, especially if needs are not being fulfilled. If the separation is brief, the baby manifests anxious crying, if it is prolonged, he exhibits a depressive response. Furthermore, an unfamiliar figure who is differentiated from mother either serves to interfere with the mental expectations of gratification associated with the now recognizable figure of mother or acts as a disturbing stimulus in its own right. The baby experiencing anxiety at the sight of a stranger seeks haven in his mother's arms and from this position of security and support is able, with a little time, to assimilate the stranger to the familiar mother figure and thereby establish a relationship. Thereafter the stranger is no longer a stranger and is no longer responded to with anxiety but more likely with pleasurable recognition.

THE FIFTH STAGE: THE "TERTIARY CIRCULAR REACTIONS" AND "THE DISCOVERY OF NEW MEANS THROUGH ACTIVE EXPERIMENTATION" (TWELVE TO SIXTEEN MONTHS)

In this stage the baby truly adapts himself for the first time to unfamiliar situations not only by utilizing schemata acquired earlier but also by seeking and utilizing new means to do so. This process involves the combination of experimentation, the coordination of schemata and the development of apparent categories of thought, so that now the thing in the environment is definitely detached from the activity itself and is placed in coherent spatial, temporal and causal relationships which are independent of the self. When in the previous stage the baby encountered a new object, he subjected it to all sorts of action in order to reproduce some particular result. The present stage is notable in that he is no longer content with reproducing the familiar result; instead, he tries to produce new and unfamiliar responses and finds the novelty pleasing. Thus, when presented with a new toy, he feels it, pushes it, drops it, tilts it, throws it, etc., and his interest is aroused in what is new and different about the results produced thereby. Such procedures are then repeated and modified in order to see what else will happen to the toy. (These combinations of experimental variations on a procedure are called the "tertiary circular reaction.") These behavior patterns constitute a search for novelty and imply that the baby is able to grasp with his mind the object as an entity which can be made to do different things. He behaves as if he knows in advance that there is more to the object than he has so far observed. That his intent now is to make the thing do something is revealed by the general attitudes of expectation, surprise, excitement and pleasure which appear when, for example, he for the first time induces a ball to roll by itself. In contrast to the behavior of the preceding stage, when his interest was mainly on the range of his own activity in relation to the thing being dealt with, now his concern is more with discovering the properties of the thing and its range of behavior. Through such experimentation objects come to be more or less independent centers of forces rather than being largely parts of the baby's own schemata of action, and now his efforts become directed to discovering the properties of these centers. While he is so engaged, other behavior patterns are noted which truly involve the discovery or invention of new means to an end through active experimentation. When confronted with an obstacle, the baby innovates, as when he uses a stick or a string to bring a distant object near. The awareness of spatial or causal relations is being further extended beyond the range of prehension and of his own experience of movement. In the course of the systematic groping and experimentation that eventuate in solutions there is developing in the mind a relationship between patterns of activity and results, the necessary basis for conceptualizing means to an end. The baby now can achieve a familiar goal in circumstances which are strange to him.

The progress in the objectification of things is revealed in how the baby deals with the visual displacements involved in successively hiding an object. It is characteristic of this stage that he now looks for the object where he last saw it disappear, not where he last found it. Thus, if the baby is permitted to watch a ball being hidden under A he immediately finds it there. Now if it is successively hidden under B, C and then D, he will promptly go to D. The baby has clearly become able to take into account all the visible displacements he has observed and has dissociated the ball from his own first activity. However, the ball and its possible displacements do not yet have permanence in the baby's mind, for if he does not actually see all the displacements he will be unable to imagine where it might be and he is unable to solve even the simplest invisible displacement. If the baby sees the ball hidden under A and then under B, but does not see the move to under C, he will look for it under B, but not under C. In brief, the object has identity only in relation to the continued perceptual cues that reach the baby's mind. If these are interrupted he cannot yet imagine what takes place in the interval.

Along with the ability to give objects substance comes the discovery and utilization of complex relations among objects themselves in addition to just between such objects and the subject's body. This ability develops through extensive experimental study of distant as well as near space. The baby now studies the movement of objects from place to place, a feat which is aided by his greater mobility now that he is able to crawl, creep or toddle. Other explorations concern position, equilibrium, rotations, reversals and the contents of containers. Finally, he examines the relations of his movements and positions with respect to other bodies. In the course of such activities the baby succeeds in constructing objective groups which are in spatial relationship to each other and to his own displacements. But this knowledge of relationships does not yet transcend perception. He does not yet have the capacity to utilize such knowledge when its corresponding sensory experience is not also available.

THE SIXTH STAGE: THE INVENTION OF NEW MEANS THROUGH MENTAL COMBINATIONS (BEGINS AT 16 MONTHS)

In the final stage, which ushers in the beginning of true intelligent behavior, the child not only is able to conceive of the object in the environment as an entity with dimensions, qualities and spatial, temporal and causal properties, but is also able to do so even when the object is no longer being perceived. In short, there has finally developed a mental representation which includes the object not only as it is actually perceived but also as it might appear under other circumstances. The external object remains identical to itself and separate from the subject and his actions regardless of how it is displaced or hidden. This development is revealed in the child's ability to persist in the search for and to find hidden objects, all the displacements of which were not visible to him. An ability to imagine displacements in space and to internalize cause and effect relationships must be involved. Mental inventions and representations now complement concrete actions as means of dealing with reality. Before carrying out an act, the child can experiment mentally, he can review past actions, he can contrast various possibilities, and he can consider various consequences in advance. Such processes clearly constitute the beginnings of intelligence.

A further consequence of this capacity to represent objects mentally is that the child's body also can be subjectively experienced as an independent object, differentiated from inanimate objects and from other persons. He now has the capacity for mental representations of the self as differentiated from others and can imagine his own movements and activities independently of those of outside objects.

It is important to emphasize that the permanence of mental representations, whether of objects, schemata, etc., is relative and that they must continue to be reinforced by repeated perceptual experience if they are to be maintained. Further, the child must have ever-continuing active experience in order to sustain and advance the objectification of the environment. But as we shall see in subsequent chapters, the varieties of experience encountered in the course of the child's growing up are not limited to the relatively simple kinds of conflict-free situations described by Piaget. To a large extent they also include a host of complex and conflictful situations, some of which may have to be mastered at a time when the child does not yet have the capability to do so and others of which constitute aspects of the environment perhaps correctly perceived at the moment but not necessarily representative or appropriate for other circumstances. Since the child must use what he has available at the moment, and must adjust to changing internal needs as well as to a complex environment, he can never be fully protected from assimilating whatever complex structures are being presented to him at the time he is attempting to accommodate to the particular environmental situation in which he finds himself. Thus the child may learn much that is partially or wholly incorrect and hence may develop patterns of behavior or signal systems which are inappropriate or later on maladaptive. It is mainly in relatively tranquil times, when pressing needs are in abeyance and when the environment is not excessively frustrating, that the child (or adult, for that matter) is able to make maximum use of the techniques of intelligence that evolve in Stage Six. Under less favorable circumstances there tends to be increasing utilization of the earlier patterns, including even the reflex behavior patterns of stages one and two. But even under the best circumstances, the complexity of the environment for the child is such that he leans much more heavily than Piaget's scheme would lead one to expect on conceptual models derived from biological drives and his own bodily activities to form the basis of his mental representation of the environment. This fact is clearly revealed in the nature of children's fantasies, as will be discussed later. In short, although the requiremenents for intelligent thought and for accurate interpretation of reality have been achieved by the end of the second year, only a small fragment of the child's world is accessible to such handling at this age. Indeed, a purely intellectual and rational attitude to the environment in all its aspects is unattainable, even in the healthiest adult. As Piaget expressed it, "Intellectual organization merely extends biological organization," which means also that it can never be freed from its sources in the biological soil of the individual.

REFERENCES

1. Piaget, J.: The Origins of Intelligence in Children (1936). New York, International Universities Press, 1952.
2. Piaget, J.: The Construction of Reality in the Child (1937). New York, Basic Books, 1954.
3. Wolff, P. H.: The Developmental Psychologies of Jean Piaget and Psychoanalysis. *In:* Psychological Issues, vol. 2. New York, International Universities Press, 1960, p. 1.

CHAPTER IX

PERIOD OF MASTERY
OF THE BODY

By the end of the first year in some children, and by the end of the second year in most children, certain important new lines of development are beginning. These developments make available new means of adjustment, but they also introduce new problems. The push toward new activities is discouraged by the disappointments and dangers of these new experiences, and temporary regressions occur. The initial efforts to stand or to walk may fail or succeed, may result in a painful fall or new horizons, or may be greeted by mother's groan or by her applause. The important developments in the second year are the following:

1. As described in the last chapter, the second year marks the time when the child first succeeds in giving objects in the environment substance and identity separate from himself. He now is capable of representing them in mental terms without the necessity for uninterrupted sensory guidance. He can conceive of himself as an object among and yet separate from other objects. And finally, he shows clear evidence of the beginnings of intelligence, with the capacity to solve problems, exercise intention and pursue goals.

2. The child shows curiosity about the various parts of his body. He explores the moving appendages, the orifices, the protruding structures. He begins to be interested in what goes into and what comes out of his body. Part of this activity is in the service of assimilation of and accommodation to the environment, as discussed in the last chapter, and part involves experiencing body pleasure of a decidedly erotic nature. Finger sucking, rhythmic movements and genital play are pleasurable accomplishments for the child, though potential sources of conflict with the environment.

74

3. The achievement of standing and walking increases greatly the range of activity and perception but at the same time introduces dangers not comprehended by the small child. The pleasure of achievement may be countered by painful accidents or by parents' concern about the dangers to which the toddler may be exposed. There is manifest pleasure in the mastery of the neuromuscular system. He enjoys being active and learning new motor skills. He is persistent and intent in overcoming difficulties and usually is overjoyed with success. His successes generally are also a source of pleasure to the parent. The child's own pleasure in accomplishment and the parent's pleasure both serve to reinforce and facilitate the learning process. But not all accomplishments are necessarily pleasing to the parents or even safe, so that conflict and struggle are inescapable.

4. Sphincter control begins to develop in the second year. Because of the needs and expectations of the mother this becomes an important area of communication between mother and baby. It is one of the increasing number of activities in which the baby must conform to the mother's demands and expectations or suffer a disturbance in his relation to his mother. The mother's own feelings and conflicts, which originated in her relation with her own mother, significantly influence how she deals with her child, although sometimes only at an unconscious level. For example, the mother who as a child was strictly toilet trained may unconsciously communicate to her child her own unconscious childhood wish to defy her mother and soil, a wish to which her child may then conform. Such a tendency on the part of the child to act out the unconscious, repressed wishes of the parent at the parent's unwitting behest is an important source of later aberrant behavior or intrapsychic conflict (see Chapter XXVIII).

5. Speech and language as means of expression and communication generally begin to develop in the second year and provide new means of functioning which are distinctively human. Speech and language become means of communication and discharge that will gradually supersede the more primitive behavioral patterns of earlier life. More and more will the child in subsequent years think about or say what he wants before acting. This is another important progress in the development of ego and the ability to interpose a delay between drive and action (cf. Chapter XXII).

The rates of development of these various activities are uneven in each child and from child to child. For example, one child may walk early and talk late, but the reverse may be true with another. This asynchronous development in itself may make for problems. The child whose interests and motor skills outstrip the development of language and speech may be frustrated in his inability to communicate his wishes. At the same time, the parents may be thwarted in their attempts to satisfy or protect him. In all spheres of development, the parents' conscious and unconscious expectations of and wishes for the child's performance will have an important influence on their relationship. The child who disappoints by not living up to the parents' expectation or who provokes anxiety by behavior not desired by the parents is placed in a situation of potential conflict. In general, however, the developmental (and instinctual) pressure is great. This may be seen both in the extraordinary perseverance of a child in some activity, even when his parents disapprove, as well as in his rage when frustrated by a task. Although there may be selective inhibitions in response to parental attitudes, in general, children persevere in their attempts at mastery, major retardation occurring mainly in settings of privation.

FURTHER DEVELOPMENT OF SEXUALITY: ORAL, SKIN, AND MUSCLE EROTISM

The sexual component of mouth activity as represented by sucking has already been commented upon. Involved in this, and essential to it, is the special pleasure experienced in the mouth through sucking. This has a rhythmic character and even, at times, a climactic quality, which can be best described by the term *erotic*. We can speak of zones of the body which possesss this quality as *erotogenic zones*. The buccal mucus membrane is one of the first of the erotogenic areas to develop. Some of the ways in which the drive for satisfaction of oral pleasures influence total behavior have already been discussed. The erotogenic zones are important nodal points not only in the development and nature of object relations, but also in the development of mental apparatus. As avenues whereby pleasure is achieved and experienced, they provide a certain intensity to experience which colors the subsequent mental representation of the experience. This accounts for the prominence of oral imagery and oral language which originates in the early period of life and persists thereafter. Skin and muscle, as expressed through contact and rhythmic movements, are probably also early erotogenic zones.

ANAL EROTISM

At some time, usually by the second year, the irregular rhythm of the bowel also acquires the qualities of erotogenicity. In many infants there is no evidence of this in the first months; some infants, however, show clear reactions of pleasure on the passage of feces and, indeed, their rhythms of crying and quiescence seem to be more closely linked to bowel evacuation than to feeding. In general, most babies are noted to participate more actively in the evacuation process sometime during the first year. Fullness of the rectum, to a degree, and expulsion of the fecal mass seem to give pleasure, stemming both from relief of physiologic tension and from the act of expulsion itself. The baby's attitude toward its feces is at first quite bland; from unawareness and disinterest, he develops interest and pleasure. The baby handles, examines, plays with, smears, smells and tastes the feces with no evident disgust. His interest in and curiosity about feces develop along with the baby's exploration of his body. In general, fecal play is a secondary interest, easily superseded by interests in persons (objects) and new activities. The child whose object relationships are disturbed, however, may show increasing preoccupation with feces, including coprophagia (eating feces), while being correspondingly withdrawn from his external environment. This is usually an indication of a serious disturbance in psychological development (Spitz[4]).

The adults' attitudes toward urine, urination, feces and bowel movements are quite different from the baby's, and out of this interaction important psychological conflicts develop—basically, the conflict between the baby's wish to gratify a body pleasure and the parents' need that the baby conform to the adult standard as determined by his parents' past. Eventually, the baby must give up his pleasurable play with feces and uninterrupted enjoyment of urination and bowel movement and conform to the standards of cleanliness of the culture. In contrast, in the feeding and sucking experience the mother has more control over the situation, for although the baby may refuse food, eventually hunger lowers his ability to resist the mother. Use of the sphincters, on the other hand, is entirely inaccessible to any direct control by the parent. Until a certain degree of maturation of the neuromuscular mechanism has been achieved and until the child can actively cooperate, the parent cannot hope to have the child urinate or defecate when and where the parent wants. New experiences for the child result from this situation, for mother may have to cajole, plead, beg, threaten or bribe in order to get the baby to perform as she wishes.

Interaction between child and parent over bladder and bowel training is of most importance during the second and third years. A number of possible relationships may be noted:

1. The child may retain urine or feces in order to prolong the pleasurable sensations. If these bodily sensations yield greater pleasure than does satisfying his mother, he may persist even at the risk of incurring his mother's displeasure.

2. The child may retain in order to defy the mother—the beginning of a pattern of stubbornness. This is part of the child's pleasure in

mastery over his body, a feeling of relative independence from his mother, a source of strength in face of separation.

3. The child may retain urine or feces to please his mother. In so doing, the child denies himself the immediate pleasure of urination or defecation, even tolerates some discomfort, in order to enjoy his mother's pleasure that he is able to perform when and where she wants.

4. The child may urinate or move his bowels as a defiant act. Soiling and smearing may be deliberate or unconscious hostile acts by children (or disturbed adults). Urethral, anal and fecal profanity in most languages clearly betray the aggressive implications of such infantile activity now carried over into speech.

5. The child may move his bowels for his own pleasure. Soiling may then be an erotic pleasure in its own right for the child. This is a more self-centered (narcissistic) pattern, in which interest in and awareness of the needs and expectations of the environment are relatively ignored. It may include coprophagia.

6. The child may urinate or move his bowels in order to please the parent. The child's ability to enlist his mastery of his motor system in the service of object relations is an important contribution to the development of psychological control over motility.

7. The feces, something coming from the child's own body and associated with pleasure, may be regarded by the child as a valuable possession, something to hold on to and to treasure—the child's own creation. The mother's attitude toward the feces, as a praiseworthy production or as dirty and disgusting, helps to determine the child's attitude. Actually, the mother's attitude can be contradictory; she may be pleased with the success of the defecation but disgusted with the feces.

8. The act of defecation may be equated in the mind with the concept of getting rid of or destroying something. The child gets rid of (defecates) that which is bad; holds on to what is good. This provides another model for *projection* as a mental mechanism. Also, the "bad" feces can be the model for a later delusion, the internal persecutor, the idea of something bad or rotten inside.

9. Urination, especially by boys, may yield pleasure in terms of the powerful stream which may be directed playfully or aggressively. This may evoke envy in the little girl.

Although emphasis is properly placed on the importance of bowel activity in this period of development, it is also the period during which the child is achieving muscular control. Pleasure in mastery—destroying, breaking and tearing—is prominent at this time. Clearly, the same psychological qualities also apply to the various relationships between the child's developing control over and utilization of his skeletal muscles in the service of his own gratifications and development and the wishes and prohibitions of the parents. Much of the child's activity at this time is in the service of gaining control and mastery of the neuromuscular system and thereby of the environment, but many of the end results are destructive or are seen by the environment as destructive, regardless of whether or not the aim originally was destructive. The conclusion is unavoidable that the child comes to derive great pleasure from activities which accidentally or incidentally prove to be destructive. The prominence of these types of activities at this age has led to the use of the concept *anal-sadistic* to designate these tendencies.

Important at this time also are the relationships which develop between developing motor capacities and pain. Whereas earlier in life pain was experienced more or less by chance, now the child's activity not only exposes him to situations in which he suffers pain, but also he becomes capable of inflicting pain on others. The experience of pain, whether it is suffered accidentally or is deliberately inflicted on the child as punishment, comes to constitute a deterrent to whatever activity resulted in pain. By the same token, the child learns that by inflicting or threatening to inflict pain on others he can force them to conform to his wishes. Through such interrelationships threat and fear of pain become powerful intrapsychic influences in controlling the child's activities as well as in molding the patterns of his relationships with others. The link between pain and punishment also proves to be important in relating pain and guilt, and later we shall see how pain may attenuate feelings of guilt and how guilt may result in pain (cf. Chapter XXXII).

The Evolution of the Anal-Sadistic Impulses

The ego has the task of mediating between the instinctual demands pressing for gratification and the demands of reality. The relatively unrestrained anal and sadistic activities must be given up or fitted into patterns imposed by the parents and their culture. If sphincter control and muscular control are demanded too early and too vigorously, or too late and too feebly, conflicts may be intensified which may be reflected in the subsequent development of the mental apparatus. In general, *how* bowel training is carried out is more important than *when* it is carried out. In the interaction between parent and child over these issues, the conflicts that result may leave lasting impressions in the form of fixations, so that later under stress modes of expression and gratification peculiar to this anal period may be reactivated. Some of the reflections in later life of unresolved problems of this period may include the following:

1. Disorders of bowel function, such as constipation, diarrhea or incontinence, may persist or recur as unconscious modes of expression of aggression or erotic impulses.

2. Morbid stubbornness or obstinacy as character traits may reflect patterns that evolved during the period of bowel training.

3. Overcleanliness or meticulousness may appear as an over-

determined reaction against soiling impulses, or exaggerated sloppiness or disorderliness may reflect the intensity of the early anal pleasures or defiance of the controlling environment. Miserliness, stinginess, penuriousness, hoarding are character traits stemming from the need to hold on. These character traits are sometimes referred to as "anal."

4. There may be persistence and exaggeration of the sadistic impulses and behavior of the earlier period.

While the child is passing through this phase and is more or less successfully mastering the problem of bowel control and anal erotism, various displaced manifestations may be observed. These include smearing and mushing of food, mud or dirt, the collection of objects, first dirty and finally glittering things, and general disorderliness.

REFERENCES

1. Abraham, K.: Contributions to the Theory of Anal Character (1921). *In:* Abraham, K.: Selected Papers on Psychoanalysis. London, The Hogarth Press, 1948, pp. 370–393.
2. Engel, G. L.: Psychogenic Pain and the Pain-Prone Patient. Am. J. Med., *26:*399, 1959.
3. Freud, S.: Character and Anal Erotism (1908). *In:* Standard Edition of the Complete Psychological Works of Sigmund Freud, vol. IX. London, The Hogarth Press, 1959, pp. 167–177.
4. Spitz, R. and Wolf, K.: Autoerotism. Some Empirical Findings and Hypotheses on Three of Its Manifestations in the First Year of Life. *In:* Greenacre, P. et al. (eds.): The Psychoanalytic Study of the Child, vol. III/IV. New York, International Universities Press, 1949, p. 85.

CHAPTER X

STAGE OF
PRIMARY SOCIAL AND
SEXUAL DIFFERENTIATION

By the third year new forces are being added to the already turbulent stream of life. Some of the earlier activities and drives are beginning to be superseded. The child's horizon is broadening, and new, often puzzling, stimuli are impinging upon his perceptual apparatus. With the development of locomotion, motor skills and speech, the child becomes more venturesome in relinquishing his tight hold on his mother and exploring the world with his own sense organs. But the external world still holds many dangers for the small child, and there are many tearful retreats to the security and safety of mother's arms.

The child's individuality now is being more clearly asserted. The mother has had to grow with him through a rapid succession of changes and just as the child has to begin to relinquish some of his earlier infantile pleasures in the course of exploring the world, so, too, mother has to relinquish some of her feelings about having a small, cuddly baby. Here, already, significant differences may be seen in the mother's attitude. Some mothers may begrudge the development of the toddler stage, with its relative independence compared to the earlier period of comparative helplessness, and may be reluctant to permit this development to take place. Such reluctance may take the form of feeling a sense of loss, even depression, that she no longer has a little baby; or it may take the form of unrealistic fears about the dangers to which the toddler may be exposed, or of unrealistic anger at the disorderliness or destructiveness of the toddler. Other mothers may find the stage of helpless dependence a burden and may welcome the appearance of the

81

toddler stage. Such mothers may think of their little babies as unresponsive or as messy little creatures with no feelings and may be overanxious for them to sit, walk and talk. There are many patterns of relationship between the mother and her child, and what must be clearly understood is that the mother's effectiveness and capacity as a mother and her satisfactions in motherhood may not be the same at all points of development. These variations in the mother-child relationship may become a source of conflict and may influence the development of the child's mental apparatus and character structure.

We have already described the role of the mother in the earliest development of the mental apparatus. In earliest infancy the mother's success in providing satisfaction of needs and, therefore, in enabling the child to have relatively prolonged periods of comfort, enhances the capacity of the child to examine and explore the external world. The recognition that the source of gratification comes from the outside-from the mother—and that the mother may come and go, contributes to the development of the sense of a self, namely, the distinction of the "I" from the "not I." With confidence that needs will be fulfilled, the child appears to have more and more energy left over, so to speak, to explore and to relate to objects in the external world. The first exploration is a self-oriented one, i.e., the child refers that which he sees in the external world to himself and to his body. His concepts are animistic. To the chair and to the table are ascribed qualities and feelings similar to his own. He may speak of a table as if it could hurt him or love him or be comforted by him. While he is busy identifying things and persons in the external environment and distinguishing them from himself, only the third person is used. A clear-cut concept of personal identity, as exemplified by the use of the pronouns "I" and "you," develops only gradually.

THE PLEASURE PRINCIPLE AND THE REALITY PRINCIPLE

The major factor in the development of the mental apparatus continues to be the operation of the *pleasure principle*. In general, the child seeks that which provides comfort or pleasure and avoids that which yields pain or unpleasure. We have already described how the internalizing of past successful and unsuccessful experiences permits delay of gratification and contributes to confidence that gratification will take place. The mother, who exists for the baby both as a satisfying and as a frustrating object, lays the basis for the techniques necessary to achieve gratification and to avoid pain and discomfort through the internalization of images of "good" and "bad" mother. These internalized images are not yet clearly differentiated from the child's developing concept of himself. Though he has progressed from the phase in which the mother is experienced only in relationship to the satisfaction of needs to being able to recognize mother as a separate person who satisfies or who frustrates, he has yet to be able to recognize her as an individual who also has needs of her own—needs which may be in conflict with his own needs. The concept of consideration of others is yet to develop. Now the child must begin to "learn" the limitations of conditions under which his own needs can be gratified. In other words, he must begin to recognize the particular requirements of those in the external environment which must be satisfied in order for his needs to be satisfied if he is not to suffer pain or disappointment instead. In this manner the pleasure principle gradually becomes modified by the demands of reality. To continue to operate on the basis of the primitive pleasure principle would fail because when efforts at gratification conflict with the needs or expectations of others upon whom the child is dependent, punishment or rejection rather than gratification may be the result. Gradually and painfully the child must learn to delay or even renounce some of his own wishes in order to retain a satisfactory relationship with his objects. The *pleasure principle* as the regulator of psychic life and behavior is being modified by the demands of reality to become the *reality principle*. Pleasure and satisfaction of needs are better assured by taking into account the external reality, the actual conditions under which satisfaction can be achieved. Important in this development is the capacity to *anticipate* what will yield pleasure and what will result in pain, frustration or disappointment. This becomes a potent new motivating force to learn about and understand the environment and represents an important determinant of intellectual growth.

As motility, perception and language mature, the child's range of experience increases and his means of satisfying needs and avoiding unpleasure also expand. The further development of the mental apparatus permits an increasing measure of independence from mother, but this development does not take place in a haphazard way. It follows and is determined by the biological as well as environmental conditions imposed upon it in the past as well as affecting it currently. Thus we find the child enlarging the circle of persons who become objects through whom satisfaction of needs may be achieved. He has already learned to differentiate between the persons in his environment. Now he increasingly selects and develops psychological and behavioral techniques which assure greatest satisfaction by virtue of repeated successes while trying to avoid those which might lead to frustration. He begins to know what mother likes and dislikes, what father likes and dislikes, what grandparents like and dislike, etc. Similarly, he begins to increase the variety of ways in which he can satisfy himself. These include the use of his own body, as in oral activity, anal activity, running, jumping, rocking, etc., as well as the use of fantasies whereby a certain measure of pleasure can be experienced from the mental products of imagination.

Thus the child is acquiring not only an increasing number of objects in the external environment but also an increasing number and variety of internalized objects. The relatively greater degree of independence from the real external objects comes about mainly because they have become established within ego as internalized psychic representations, and as such they provide not only guides and models for behavior but also material for fantasy. The child can work out in his mind how to behave in relation to real objects and he can also imagine pleasurable activities with them without necessarily translating it into behavior or even communicating it in words. Much of the play of young children involves such fantasy activity. The child's concept of himself is developing in relationship to internalized objects and, to varying degrees, he will come to identify with these objects, as evidenced by the various ways in which he behaves, feels and thinks like them. It is out of the kaleidoscope of experiences with objects that satisfy and objects that frustrate that further ego development takes place. Continuity of relationship with objects is of great importance in this formative period if the child is to "learn" satisfactory ways of relating and is to internalize reliable images. If relationships are interrupted or if the adult behaves inconsistently or unpredictably, then the child's psychological development may suffer by virtue of the instability of the resulting psychic object as a guide for behavior and as a source of gratification. Further, since the development of the child's concept of himself includes the psychic representations of these early objects as sources of satisfaction or frustration, such unsatisfactory early relationships may impair self-confidence, may increase the need to be dependent on external objects, may cripple the capacity to love, or may expose the child to excessive degrees of frustrated rage. These and other consequences of disturbances in early object relations will be discussed further.

THE DEVELOPMENT OF THE SEXUAL DRIVES

If development is normal, the dominance of the oral organization begins to wane by the third year. The mouth is no longer the main testing organ, and sucking comes to occupy more the position of a periodic regressive phenomenon, i.e., during fatigue, sleep or frustration. Similarly, the inclination to use the mouth and the teeth in an aggressive or biting fashion becomes less. This change means that ego development has now reached the point where such impulses are no longer quickly or immediately translated into behavior. Nonetheless, the corresponding fantasies and feeling states persist in the unconscious mind as ideas of oral bliss, of oral aggression and sadism, of eating and being eaten, of biting, etc. These continue to achieve direct expression in the form of conscious fantasy, play, and the responsiveness of children to stories having such themes (e.g., "Hansel and Gretel"). In adult life they can be recovered in the dreams, fantasies, legends and myths of all peoples, and fragments of oral behavior continue to achieve expression in various oral mannerisms and oral pleasures, such as smoking, chewing, kissing, etc., and in our language (the oral terms of endearment such as "sweet," "I could eat you," etc., and the oral terms of aggression such as "biting sarcasm," "a sharp tongue," etc.).

Similarly, the anal components come under the control of the ego so that bowel training is successfully achieved and the standards of the grown-ups of the environment are taken over by the child. But to varying degrees the drive representations of these impulses, as described in the last chapter, will also persist in the mental apparatus, at unconscious and preconscious levels.

In some children as early as the second year, and in most children in the third or fourth year, there is increasing evidence of awareness of and pleasurable sensations from the genitals. Casual fingering of and playing with the genitals and actual masturbatory activity may begin within the first year, but this usually does not take precedence over such forms of auto-erotic activity as thumb-sucking, playing with the lips, playing with the ears, nose, hair, limbs, etc. Spitz[6] reports that genital play is more likely to develop during the first year when there is a sustained object relationship with the mother, whereas, when object relations in the first year are contradictory or change intermittently, rocking and headbanging or fecal play may result. Genital play in the first year is, if anything, an accompaniment of more successful early development. However, it usually is not until the third or fourth year that genital sensations become more insistent, as evidenced by the ubiquity of masturbatory activity in this period. It is interesting that few adults recall such early masturbation, yet observation of children leaves no doubt of the frequency of its occurrence. Evidently, at some time the child discovers the pleasurable sensations evoked by manipulation of the genitals, the penis by the boy, the clitoris by the girl (the vagina remains unknown). Now the penis and the clitoris become the new erotogenic zones. (For this reason, this period of psychosexual development is also referred to as the *phallic* stage.)

A number of psychological and behavioral developments result from this shift of erotism to the genitals:

1. There is a decided increase in the child's curiosity about its own

body and about the bodies of others. This is manifested by explorations of his own body, exhibiting himself and exploring others. In this the child experiences excitement, but he also encounters social barriers and taboos. It is of interest in this regard that while the parent usually helps the child to identify by name the various parts of his body, the genitals usually are omitted or are given some neutral name; or the name that the child invented is the one used by the parents. Often the parents associate the genital region with or identify it as an excretory organ, something dirty, not to be touched. The child's interest in displaying his own body, which previously was thought of as "cute," now, when the genitals in particular are exhibited, is often forbidden, as is the child's exploration of the genitals of other children. This sudden change in the parents' attitude requires an adjustment on the part of the child, involving a compromise between a drive and a social reality, since the discharge of pleasurable sensations in relation to the genitals is now disapproved. As we shall see, this provides the basis for conflict but does not determine that its outcome will necessarily be harmful or pathological. We may recognize in this early childhood conflict about displaying and exhibiting the genitals factors contributing to the adult perversions of exhibitionism and scoptophilia, to the character traits of "showing off" and curiosity, and to certain other psychopathological developments (see Chapter XXXI).

2. The insistent sensations and the involuntary tumescence of the little boy's penis are now a source of pleasure to him, but they may also evoke anxiety. The fact of a visible change in structure of a part of the body which cannot be controlled may be disturbing to some boys, particularly if the parents actively or passively disapprove. The little boy who has consciously or inadvertently stimulated an erection may become panicky because he cannot make it go away at will.

3. The discovery of a difference between the external genitalia of the boy and the girl is a momentous one, and it has wide ramifications for both. The boy is curious and puzzled to discover that the girl has no penis, and he draws, for him, the logical conclusion that the penis can be lost, can be cut off, can disappear. With the primitive tendency to experience the environment in terms of his own body and his own experiences, the boy has no reason not to assume that everyone is constructed essentially as he is. He becomes curious when he notes bodily differences and he wants to know the explanation. When such differences involve matters such as the color of the skin, the amount of hair, the presence of teeth, or even an amputation, the parent usually responds fairly readily. But the difference between the male and female genitals is less easily and less comfortably responded to by most parents. This, plus the fact that the penis is a source of pleasurable sensations and, hence, an object of pleasure for the child, makes the issue a more critical

one. Children readily verbalize or act out their fantasies in this regard, if permitted to do so. The boy clearly reveals his anxiety that his penis may be lost. This anxiety about castration does not depend upon an overt threat by an adult, although obviously when such a threat does occur, the fear may be intensified. Some children interpret the passage of the fecal mass as an example of how the penis may be lost; feces, too, have the quality of a valued object for some children. This anxiety about possible loss of the penis may be expressed in a number of ways, all of which may appear in the content of the fantasies and play of a little boy:

(a) He refuses to abandon the idea that women and girls really do have a penis. He speculates that it may be hidden in the pubic hair, that it is inside and will grow out, that the clitoris, if he sees it or is told about it, will grow into a penis, and so forth.

(b) He tries to convince himself that a lost penis will grow back. Such activities as hiding the penis between his legs and letting it pop out, comparing the feces which he produces to a penis, and playing games or indulging in fantasies in which things are cut off and grow back are all attempts at such reassurance. Many of the seemingly innocent questions of the little boy, such as whether the flowers will grow again, etc., are reflections of his attempts to master this anxiety.

(c) He may repeatedly exhibit his penis, talk about it or hold onto it, to reassure himself that it is intact.

(d) He may displace some of his fear of castration to other parts of his body and develop unusual concern and fear about injuries, cuts or bruises.

(e) He may depreciate girls and women as inferior creatures and dissociate himself from them as a group.

(f) He may threaten others with castration, actually and symbolically.

(g) He may attempt to suppress his impulse to handle and play with his penis, even at the expense of relinquishing pleasure; or, conversely, he may accentuate his masturbatory activity as a means of reassurance against the castration idea.

The little girl, too, must deal with her discovery of being different from the boy and having no penis. To varying degrees, the little girl may experience this as a deprivation. This will be particularly likely if the mother herself depreciates her own role as a woman, shows preference for boys or depreciates the little girl's more feminine inclinations. This development may manifest itself in a number of ways:

(a) She, too, may use denial. She may claim that she really has a penis or that her mother has one, or that her penis is inside and will grow out, etc. She may play various games with sticks, hoses, etc., to simulate a penis. She may attempt to urinate standing up, like her brother or father. She may equate her feces with a penis or she may attempt to substitute the clitoris for a penis. She may even equate her body with a phallus.

(b) She may feel that a "bad" mother deprived her of the penis, just as she once deprived her of the breast or nipple on weaning.

(c) She may so successfully repress the whole idea of penis that later in adolescence she will be surprised to discover its existence. She may then see it as a dangerous, damaging or dirty thing.

(d) She may feel envy of the boy, feeling that he has something that she does not have, and she may ascribe the parents' preference for the boy to this difference.

4. The discovery of the parents' genitals may be a further source of stimulation and of anxiety. The child of this period may be surprised, impressed or frightened by the size of the father's penis; the mother's pubic hair may seem mysterious, as though hiding something; the discrepancy in size of the penis may contribute to the little boy's feeling of inferiority compared to the father. And to both the little boy and the little girl the father's penis may be seen as a threatening weapon.

5. The sexual activity of the parents contributes further to these developments. In the first place, it is something usually carried on in secret, from which the child is excluded, and this in itself evokes curiosity and bewilderment. The child may feel rejected and angry that he is excluded and that his parents have secrets; yet this is one of an increasing number of reality events which the child must accept. At the same time, the witnessing of the sexual act may be exciting, stimulating and frightening for the child. Whether seen or overheard, it may be interpreted by the child as a fight or a struggle in which one party injures the other. Ample material for fantasy is provided by such situations. Even children as young as two years are more aware of and more affected by such experiences than many parents realize. For the very young child, this may achieve the quality of a traumatic event. The witnessing of parental intercourse by the very small child is referred to as the *primal scene*.

6. Curiosity about pregnancy and birth inevitably arises at this period. The child begins to ask questions about where he came from or where his baby siblings came from. The enlarged abdomen of the mother may lead to the idea that the baby is in the stomach and that it got there by ingestion. This is a logical development from the earlier oral dominance and is further reinforced when parents speak of the baby as "being in mother's stomach." The child may also believe that the baby is conceived or born through the mouth or may take the process of defecation as a model for the birth process. He may now retain feces or pass feces as part of his identification with the pregnant mother. The concept of something growing inside the body is difficult for the child to

comprehend and often provokes anxiety. There is concern as to how the baby gets out. Is it the mouth, penis, the umbilicus? Or is the abdomen cut open, or what? Both boys and girls believe themselves capable of having a baby, and it may be a disappointment, for the boy to discover that he cannot have a baby just as it may be a disappointment for the little girl to discover that she does not have a penis. Here again parental preferences and attitudes about girls versus boys play a role. The little girl's gradual realization that she, rather than the boy, can have a baby has important consequences for future development. At the time it may provide an adequate compensation for her earlier discovery that she has no penis.

These developments make this period of life (age 3 to 5) one during which new sources of conflict are evolving. It is during this period that the important differentiation of maleness and femaleness is being made in respect to the self and to the figures in the environment. With the recognition of these differences, not only do the courses of development of the boy and the girl begin to pursue different paths, but also the maleness and the femaleness of the father and the mother begin to assume special importance. Social and cultural factors now play important roles in establishing the concepts of sexuality which are acceptable to the group. (Valuable information on this score is to be found in the literature of anthropology.)

REFERENCES

1. Ferenczi, S.: Stages in the Development of the Sense of Reality. *In:* Ferenczi, S.: Sex and Psychoanalysis: Contributions to Psychoanalysis. New York, Robert Brunner, 1950, pp. 213–240.
2. Freud, S.: On the Sexual Theories of Children (1908). *In:* Standard Edition of the Complete Psychological Works of Sigmund Freud, vol. IX. London, The Hogarth Press, 1959, pp. 205–227.
3. Freud, S.: Sexual Life of Man (chapter 20) and Development of the Libido and Sexual Organization (chapter 21). *In:* Freud, S.: A General Introduction to Psychoanalysis. Garden City, N. Y., Garden City Publishing Co., 1943.
4. Freud, S.: Three Essays on the Theory of Sexuality (1905). *In:* Standard Edition of the Complete Psychological Works of Sigmund Freud, vol. VII. London, The Hogarth Press, 1953, pp. 125–231.
5. Mead, M.: Male and Female. New York, William Morrow & Co., 1939, pp. 51–77.
6. Spitz, R. A. and Wolf, K.: Autoerotism: Some Empirical Findings and Hypotheses on Three of Its Manifestations in the First Year of Life. *In:* Greenacre, P. et al. (eds.): The Psychoanalytic Study of the Child, vol. III/IV. New York, International Universities Press, 1949, p. 85.

CHAPTER XI

STAGE OF PRIMARY SOCIAL AND SEXUAL DIFFERENTIATION: II. THE OEDIPUS COMPLEX

As we continue our discussion of the sexual development of the child, it is essential to appreciate that we deal with material which for the adult is unconscious, no longer accessible to memory or recall and, therefore, not testable by attempts at retrospective reconstruction from the memory of one's own experience. Some of the sources of evidence will be alluded to. The usual test of "Does this make sense in terms of my own experience?" will not prove helpful. Later we will discuss the mental mechanisms involved in this inability to corroborate the concepts from our own memories.

With successful differentiation between male and female, mother and father, sister and brother, the path is cleared for investment of sexual feelings in the parents on a different basis than before. At first the pleasant sensations associated with masturbation may be accompanied by fantasies of the pre-oedipal period—to be loved, cuddled, comforted or nursed by mother. This fantasy may take the form of being a pet which is caressed by mother. Or it may involve anal erotic concepts—to be wiped, to be given an enema, to have the buttocks stroked. Or sado-masochistic concepts may appear—to be whipped and then comforted, to be lost and mourned over, some other child being beaten, etc. Gradually the sexual discoveries and the sexual theories of the child lead to new fantasies and activities in which the masculine-feminine polarity becomes evident. The development of the

90

boy and girl now begins to differ. Increasingly, however, does the culture play a role, both as it circumscribes and determines the parent's attitude and behavior, and as it impinges directly on the child. What constitutes "masculine" or "feminine" behavior in any society is determined by both biological and cultural influences. (For examples, see the anthropolgical studies of Mead,[6] Roheim,[8] Benedict,[3] Kardiner[5] and others.)

THE BOY'S DEVELOPMENT

The boy, becoming aware of anatomical differences, begins more and more to associate himself and to identify with the males of the family, especially father and older brother, and of his peer group. Part of the identification with father involves doing what father does, and this eventually extends to involve father's relation to mother and doing what he thinks father does with mother. But the development of phallic erotogenicity, a biological development, has a crucial influence on the subsequent course of behavior. Just as in the earlier oral and anal phases the relationship to mother was influenced by certain needs experienced in these areas of the body, so in the phallic phase, the physiological activities of the penis influence this relationship, even though the boy may have no conscious awareness or understanding of coitus per se. The boy wishes to exhibit his phallus, to have mother admire it, and he may even attempt to induce her somehow to participate in the pleasure he experiences from it. In fantasy he conceives of it as a boring, penetrating structure. Without actually knowing what men do with women or what father does with mother, what intercourse literally is, the boy of four to six begins to wish or try to use his phallus as an instrument of pleasure with mother. Innocently, this is first only an addition to other more acceptable body pleasures enjoyed with mother, such as being held, cuddled, fondled, etc., but it then may be elaborated to include frankly masturbatory activities, exhibitionistic behavior, and a wide range of fantasy much less accessible to direct observation. In essence, a new biological drive mechanism has been added to those already operating and is pressed into the service of the continuance of existing object relations. The consequent behavior and fantasy may be seen as psychological elaborations of primary biological behavior; they arise, like other basic biological processes such as feeding, excreting, walking, etc., from the activity of a basic organization within the nervous system which follows an intrinsic developmental timetable. Biological maturation determines the time of appearance of such behavior. As has already been pointed out in respect to oral and anal drive behavior, it is the functional characteristics of the penis, both as represented in its anatomy and in its controlling nervous system organization, which are responsible for the fact that the boy in behavior and fantasy conceives of and uses the penis as a penetrating, boring and even threatening instrument. This is part of the general psychological attitude of maleness, just as the function and anatomy of the female genitals underlie the attitude of receptivity, which is more typically feminine. Such biologically determined tendencies toward genital sexual activities apparently appear in man and animals long before sexual maturity in the sense of full reproductive capacity has been achieved, and it may be considered that this allows for a certain kind of trial activity and learning before maturity is finally achieved. As we shall see, this has very different consequences in man than in animals, for it initiates a new series of conflicts which must be resolved if psychological and biological maturity are to be achieved.

As this development evolves, then, the boy may begin to see himself as a little man and to see his father as a rival. The mother, as a woman, responds to this with some degree of pleasure (or anxiety, depending on her relationship with men) and she may unwittingly foster the innocent, immature romance. The boy may become protective of mother, possessive of her, he may imitate his father's behavior with her, he may drive his father away, mock or attack his father, etc. In addition to such overt behavior, he enjoys games in which he assumes the father's role, and he delights in stories and fantasies in which a bigger rival is overcome or befriended. These are the common themes of stories which have great appeal for children. In some stories, such as "Jack and the Bean Stalk," the boy kills the giant. In others, such as "The Little Engine that Won a Medal," the little boy (engine) succeeds in doing what the big one (engine) failed to do, and they become friends.

The hard facts of reality for the little boy are not only that he does not know exactly what father does, but even if he did he would be physically incapable of doing it. Father's size, strength and dominant position make the rivalry one-sided. Father may then be perceived more and more as a threatening figure and this threat may take the form of possible castration. Further, the mother sooner or later must also reject such approaches. The result of such rebuffs is the initiation of a new developmental phase in which the fear of castration plays an important role, a fact that is amply supported by direct observation of children's play and fantasy, by the data of anthropology, by the material of dreams, by the productions of psychotic persons, by the myths and legends of all peoples, and by data obtained during the psychoanalysis of patients. The readiness of the boy to respond to this situation with a fear of castration has a number of possible determinants, as follows: (a) the role of the phallus as the erotogenic zone, making the penis a focus of attention and fantasy; (b) the uncontrollable tumescence, which not only betrays the boy's fantasies, but also renders the offending organ conspicuous; (c) the discovery of the absence of the phallus in the girl, which is taken as evidence that there can be a state of "no penis"; (d) direct or indirect castration threats which may actually be made by the father or mother in response to the boy's sexual play; (e) earlier experiences of losing the breast and losing feces, which are also related to rebuff and frustration.

Whatever may be the determinants of the castration anxiety, it is expressed unmistakably by the little boy in various forms, such as manifest concern about his penis, excessive fears of injury, phobias, nightmares, etc. The role of castration anxiety in subsequent development will be spelled out in later chapters.

THE GIRL'S DEVELOPMENT

Subtle psychological differences between boy and girl are early apparent, but the girl, like the boy, also starts out with her mother as the main object, and therefore her earliest erotic fantasies also may have her mother as the object. As early as the second or third year, however, the little girl may begin to show some differentiating behavior between father and mother in the sense of being more coy and coquettish with father than with mother. Such behavior is usually pleasing to father and often does much to facilitate the relation between father and his little daughter. In such respects the behavior of the little girl and of the little boy with father may begin to differ. With the beginning of the phallic phase, the clitoris becomes an erogenous zone. It may now be used for masturbation in much the same way as the boy utilizes his penis. The vagina, however, remains largely unknown. This constitutes one decisive difference between the sexual development of the girl and that of the boy, for the vagina must eventually replace the clitoris as the primary erotogenic zone. A second decisive difference is that to achieve adult heterosexual status, the little girl must shift her strivings from her first object, mother, to father. The boy's first object is a woman and, hence, suitable for the first stirrings of heterosexual fantasy. The turning of the little girl from mother to father may begin abruptly or may be gradual and it may involve a great deal of antagonism and hostility toward mother, with many complaints about her. This change is likely to have its beginning at the same time that the little girl notices the anatomical difference between herself and the male. The first impulse is to want to repudiate the difference and to attempt a masculine identification. The fantasy of having been deprived of a penis (i.e., castrated) by the mother may occur, and this may engender antagonism toward or fear of the mother, while the wish for a penis may facilitate interest in the men in the family group, especially the father. During such strivings the girl may give up clitoric masturbation or may develop a passive wish to obtain the penis from her father. Such concern with the penis and with her differences from the male may receive considerable reinforcement from the behavior and attitudes of one or both parents, in which case the feminine development of the girl may be jeopardized. Ordinarily, however, biological factors foretelling later reproductive function influence the girl's development in the direction of anticipating motherhood. As with the boy, this eventually also involves a turning toward the parent of the opposite sex, the father, as the object with whom a relationship already exists and with whom fantasies of sexual activity and pregnancy may now be entertained. But these are primitive fantasies, often determined by inappropriate oral or anal concepts or by other inexact concepts of anatomy. And as with the boy, the little girl too now finds herself in a rivalrous relationship with the parent of the same sex, the mother.

The phallic stage is thus marked by the appearance of sexual strivings which bring the child into an erotic relation with the parent of the opposite sex and a rivalrous relation with the parent of the same sex. This is known as the Oedipus complex. There is an important difference between the development of the Oedipus complex in the boy and in the girl. The boy's Oedipus complex develops out of the phase of phallic sexuality, but under the influence of castration anxiety he is forced to abandon it (age five to six). With the girl, there is no castration anxiety in the same sense. She may envy the boy's possession of a penis and the temporary advantage he seems to enjoy with the mother, and soon with father as well, as father's rivalry changes to pride when the boy brings his oedipal strivings under control and begins to emulate father. Under these circumstances she may pass through a period of masculine identification, a tom-boy phase. For the girl, the oedipal phase begins with the discovery of the genital difference but is not resolved until puberty or later. No such decisive influence as the castration threat forces her to abandon father as a love object as the boy must give up his erotic strivings for mother. Instead, the relation with father develops slowly, spanning the whole period during which sexual maturation is evolving.

THE OEDIPUS COMPLEX

The Oedipus complex, the development of which we have just described, is a discovery which has provoked and continues to provoke much controversy and resistance. Freud derived the name from

Sophocles' drama "Oedipus Rex." A similar theme is to be found in many great works of literature. In "Hamlet," for example, Hamlet's problem stems from the task imposed upon him by his father's ghost, to take vengeance upon the man who did away with father and took his place with mother, a reflection of his own repressed childhood wishes.

The complex may be viewed as an outgrowth of the biological and psychological conditions under which the human child develops: the long obligatory dependence on the parents, the need of the child to be loved and to love, the fact that the parents are the first love objects, and the biologically determined sexual developments which occur before physiological and anatomical sexual maturity have been achieved. If some of these factors are interfered with the complex may not develop or may be very weak, in which case psychological development is impaired and maturity cannot be achieved. Some of the consequences of failure to achieve or to resolve the Oedipus complex are discussed in Chapter XII.

It is necessary to emphasize that as important as the forces involved in the Oedipus complex may be in the child's personality development, they color and influence rather than replace what has gone before. In other words, the child continues to need, enjoy and profit from his or her relations with the parent figures as before, and much that transpires between child and parent is little influenced by the issues just presented. This constitutes a developmental phase, the conflictful aspects of which can easily be overstressed in the attempt to present it in capsule form. Except for certain situations which tend to intensify the conflict or in one way or another to interfere with its resolution (as discussed in the next chapter), the problems posed by this new situation serve as spurs rather than as barriers to further maturation. The child, in fantasy, in play, in his activities may from time to time betray a considerable preoccupation with these sexual conflicts, but this does not necessarily reflect a comparable degree of psychological disturbance. Indeed, much of such overt expression is natural and relatively matter-of-fact, but it is still noteworthy that in time it passes into the realm of the taboo. Although from time to time it erupts in some blatantly obvious manner, for the most part the ability of the child to maintain tender, affectionate and physically intimate relations with both parents is not significantly interfered with. The ties are too strong and the need for the relationship too insistent to allow for any easy disruption; indeed, it is the strength of this need for sustaining relationship which, while it brings up the possibility of conflict in the first place, also contributes to the resolution. In time the two aspects of the bond between parent and child, the anaclitic (or nurturing and supporting) and the erotic, become dissociated, and this is what marks the resolution of the complex and the beginning of the ability to relate sexually with new objects without conflict.

So far, no culture has been studied in which the complex is not found to exist in some form. National and racial myths and legends reveal this motive repeatedly. Incest taboos and totem taboos are found in all primitive societies. The necessity for a taboo in itself indicates the presence of an impulse that is forbidden. There is no need to forbid what there is no inclination to do. The nature of the cultural organization influences considerably the importance of the complex. In cultures in which the family unit is relatively small and compact and the relations between child and parent are correspondingly more intense, the need for taboo is strong, and, indeed, the whole complex is subject to a stronger repression. The range of institutional devices to prevent incest and to insure exogamy provides illuminating insight into the social-cultural vicissitudes of the complex.

REFERENCES

1. Freud, S.: Development of the Libido and Sexual Organizations (chapter 21). *In:* Freud, S.: A General Introduction to Psychoanalysis. Garden City, N. Y., Garden City Publishing Co., 1943.
2. Freud, S.: The Psychology of Women (chapter 5). *In:* Freud, S.: New Introductory Lectures on Psychoanalysis. New York, W. W. Norton & Co., 1933.
Other cultural patterns are described in such sources as:
3. Benedict, R.: Patterns of Culture. Boston, Houghton Mifflin Company, 1934; Baltimore, Pelican Books, 1946.
4. Freud, S.: Totem and Taboo (1913). *In:* Standard Edition of the Complete Psychological Works of Sigmund Freud, vol. XIII, London, The Hogarth Press, 1955, pp. 1–162.
5. Kardiner, A.: The Individual and His Society. New York, Columbai University Press, 1939.
6. Mead, M.: From the South Seas: Studies of Adolescence and Sex in Primitive Societies. New York, William Morrow & Co., 1930.
7. Mead, M.: Male and Female. New York, William Morrow & Co., 1949, pp. 104–127.
8. Roheim, G.: Psychoanalysis and Anthropology. New York, International Universities Press, 1950.

CHAPTER XII

DEVELOPMENTAL CONSEQUENCES OF THE OEDIPUS COMPLEX: THE PARENT-CHILD RELATIONSHIP

The period of life from about four to six years of age is for the child one of rapid change. The intensity and the complexity of the forces besetting the child pose pressing problems in adaptation, involving intensified conflict between drive-induced behavior and conditions for continuing relationships imposed by the environment. At this age this is more important for the boy than it is for the girl, since the boy faces a more immediate problem. The mother, who has continued as his object through the oral, anal and now phallic stages of libidinal development, becomes the object of sexual fantasies which he is not only physically incapable of implementing, but which also tend to bring him into rivalry with his father. Both the strong sexual impulses toward mother and the strong aggressive impulses toward father (and siblings) must be attenuated and controlled, and here a decisive factor is the fantasied fear of castration. In essence, the boy has to accept the reality of giving up something which is not his to have. But relinquishing this fantasied relationship with mother must be accomplished in such a way that later on these feelings and impulses can be transferred without difficulty to another girl. It must be made clear that when we speak of "giving up mother as an object," we refer to giving up mother as an object for gratification of phallic sexual wishes, for the mother continues as an object who gratifies a variety of needs, for care, for nuturing, etc., and she has already made a lasting contribution to the formation of the boy's ego, as described in earlier chapters. In the course of dealing with these impossible (phallic) wishes, the boy encounters a critical developmental problem. He might give them up entirely, remaining thereafter attached to his mother in ways characteristic of an earlier (pre-oedipal) period or he might relinquish mother as the object of his phallic aims yet still maintain an object relationship with her that satisfies his other needs. The varieties of devices, successful and unsuccessful, utilized by the boy to accomplish this constitute a large part of character formation and psychopathology, and will be discussed later in this section.

The girl, too, has the need to sustain a relationship with the mother for satisfaction of long-established needs. Yet this relationship must undergo a strain on several grounds. First, with the discovery of sex differences, the girl goes through a period of greater or lesser identification with father and brothers, during which she tends to be antagonistic and depreciating toward mother and often has the notion that father admires and mother loves the boy more than the girl. But then, as the more passive, receptive feminine aims assert themselves, there is a change in the direction of becoming a feminine object for father, from whom she may first have the fantasy of obtaining a penis and then a baby. Mother then becomes her rival for the affection of father, but, like the boy, she too identifies with her rival, thereby acquiring another source for feminine development. Unlike the boy, the castration threat is not a factor in forcing an abrupt solution of the Oedipus conflict and, therefore, normally this situation often persists until well into puberty. The changes of puberty, especially the development of the breasts and the beginnings of menstruation, bring into the foreground the feminine, procreative functions and oblige the girl to abandon the father as a sexual object and to turn to other males. In this she is more likely to succeed if her mother has provided an adequate feminine object for identification.

The issues involved in the evolution and resolution of the Oedipus complex highlight mainly the role of changing biological drives and object relations in psychological and social development. As the sexual drives develop and have impact on the child's mental processes and behavior, changes are initiated which are completed only after puberty. These include progressive modification in the relationships with old objects, parents and siblings, and the development of new object relations free of earlier taboos. This is the period during which sexual differentiation is being accomplished and more distinctively masculine and feminine roles arrived at. Such changes take place slowly and unevenly, and include pressing conflicts which are as often reacted to with regression as with progression. Thus, for a long time the need to be loved and taken care of is the stronger drive, so that when the child meets rebuff or disapproval he is likely to abandon temporarily the phallic strivings and manifest more dependent, babyish behavior. If in the phallic period the child is separated from the parents, he may manifest not only patterns of grief and longing but also disturbed regressive behavior, including loss of sphincter control, finger sucking, rocking, deterioration of speech and motor skills, demanding, whining or infantile behavior, aggressive and destructive outbursts, sleep disturbances, etc. Only when the earlier needs are assured will he again turn toward more frankly phallic aims. Clearly, the earlier developed drives and the modes of object relating through which their satisfaction is achieved take precedence.

As is so throughout development, success in earlier phases provides the child with the confidence that his needs will be satisfied and that his objects can be relied upon and thereby liberates him to engage in the new experiences and cope with conflicts engendered by the biological impetus of the phallic phase. In this respect the Oedipus complex may be seen as an apprenticeship for heterosexuality and the development of male or female identity. This new reality of sexual differences and sexual urges must be mastered before the individual is ready to assume his eventual role as a sexual partner and as a parent. Although biological and social factors determine that the first objects will be found among near family members and therefore impose the necessity for major renunciations, the child in act and fantasy also engages in considerable sexual play and curiosity with less taboo objects, especially with other children. When successful, the child may be said to have learned with and through his parents what it is to love and to be loved while he is at the same time developing sexually. The fact that the parents and siblings must be given up as sexual objects is not in itself deleterious. It poses problems and engenders conflicts which must be resolved, but it also requires and facilitates the development of relationships and activities with objects of both sexes and all ages outside the family unit, thereby extending and enriching the child's experience. In the course of finally resolving successfully the oedipal conflicts, the child in play and fantasy has enjoyed and experienced an apprenticeship as "husband," "wife," "mother," "father," "baby," "wage-earner," "housewife," etc., through which little by little he has learned the responsbilities, limitations and, to some extent, the pleasures of each of these roles. Further, the unconscious use of childhood love objects as models for the choice of a mate creates a continuity with the family one establishes and thereby perpetuates tradition (Erikson[4]). This is a means of continuing into the next generation what was learned in preceding generations. The final renunciation of the infantile love objects, although it inevitably involves some struggle and conflict, is, if successful, experienced as satisfying progress and maturation. Thus, we emphasize, the Oedipus complex is a normal and necessary developmental phase and is not in itself pathogenic. On the other hand, if the Oedipus complex is not experienced or if it is not successfully resolved, serious psychological defects may and often do result. A brief description of some of these will help to illuminate the role of such failures of development or of resolution of the Oedipus complex in psychological development.

1. The child whose early upbringing does not include a sustained relationship with two parents, as may occur in institutions or with multiple, brief foster home placements, not only may suffer the consequences of early deprivation as already described, but also may be denied the opportunity to relate to a father and mother in their sexually differentiated roles. Under such circumstances there may be a serious crippling of sexual development and identity, with a tendency to persist in infantile, dependent modes of relating in adult life. Such persons are notoriously deficient in their capacity to love and to feel loved and to fulfill the roles of spouse or parent. Indeed, all their relationships are likely to be shallow and tenuous. Their control of impulses, aggressive and sexual, is likely to be weak, while at the same time such activities provide little satisfaction. Such cases provide by contrast the most convincing evidence of the salutary consequences of achieving and successfully resolving the Oedipus complex. The most serious crippling of all occurs when circumstances deprive the child of the opportunity to live through and resolve these first trial sexually motivated relationships long before biological sexual maturity has been reached. Of interest in this regard is the demonstration that infant monkeys brought up from birth with a cloth model "mother" and deprived of any contact with adults, male or female, upon reaching physical and sexual maturity prove incapable of mating. The males are impotent, the females frigid, and neither show any interest in or talent for love-making. If successfully impregnated, the females evince remarkably little capacity for mothering behavior. In brief, when the full range of physical contact, including nursing and clinging, with mother and other adults does not take place, further sexual behavior is stunted. This suggests that the development of mature genital and reproductive sexual behavior is dependent upon an orderly sequence of physical relationships during infancy and early childhood (Harlow[5]). The relevance of this finding to the psychobiological significance of infantile sexuality and the Oedipus complex in humans remains to be established.

2. In certain instances, through an intrinsic defect in the child or through the behavior of one or both parents, the child either suffers such extreme frustration or is so overindulged at an infantile level that he never really becomes normally engaged in the oedipal situation. With extreme frustration he is too occupied with efforts to maintain himself; with overindulgence he tends to be maintained in a position of infantile dependence. The difficulties involved in coping with the oedipal situa-

tion are not worth the candle, so to speak. He simply avoids the frustration and clings to more infantile patterns of relating. The consequence is the pathetic, helpless, dependent adult, much of whose behavior and relating activity is predicated on the continuing need to be mothered and cared for like a child, in a nonsexual manner.

3. If the parent of the opposite sex has been removed from the scene before the beginning of the phallic phase and remains absent, establishing object relations with members of the opposite sex may prove difficult. The child may then become overattached or involved with the parent of the same sex, sometimes with the intensification of a homosexual rather than heterosexual object choice at a later time. This is not a decisive factor, however, since many other influences, such as association with siblings, other relatives and friends, the social groupings, etc., may provide sufficient opportunity for other identifications, minimizing the impact of the relationship with the single parent. A great deal depends on the behavior of the single parent, especially whether he or she takes the child as a symbolic substitute for the lost spouse.

4. The parent of the opposite sex may unconsciously behave in an unduly seductive manner, thereby unwittingly encouraging the child to greater expectations of sexual gratification than are justified, leading to the danger of a permanently unresolved Oedipus complex. The little girl may find that the father is more responsive when she behaves in a coquettish manner; or the little boy may find his mother responding to his aggressive, affectionate, sexually provocative behavior. Children may exploit such responses for more dependent rather than erotic needs, since this is actually how they succeed in gaining attention and love from the parent. Such mutual seductive behavior intensifies the sexual conflicts of the oedipal stage and may thereby interfere with its resolution. In both the boy and the girl, intense rage toward the parent of the opposite sex may be mobilized because of the hopelessness of ever gratifying the wish. Both the wish and the rage must be controlled. Later object choice, i.e., the type of marital partner sought, may be largely determined by the wish to duplicate, hopefully more successfully, this situation with the parents.

5. Poor relationships between the parents are also conducive to an unsuccessful resolution of the Oedipus complex. The very fact that the parents quarrel or are incompatible encourages the child to think of himself or herself as a more suitable mate. In addition, one parent may consciously or unconsciously invest more in the child if he or she finds the spouse unsatisfying. The best insurance for successful resolution of the Oedipus complex is to have happy, compatible, mature parents.

6. The death, illness, injury or desertion of the parent of the same sex during the period of the Oedipus complex may mobilize serious conflict because such an event would coincide with the unconscious or

thinly disguised wishes of the child. This may have important pathogenic implications for later development because it is in keeping with the magical thinking characteristic of that period of development. The child's concept is that a wish or a fantasy is equivalent to an act, a concept which stems from the power of his first words, his early feelings of omnipotence, and it may be echoes in stories and fairy tales which he hears. He then is in danger of believing the illness or death of the parent to be the result of his own aggressive wish or fantasy. Such a conviction may mobilize guilt and lead to the development of strong defenses against entertaining hostile or angry thoughts about loved people. The child in this period of development does not yet have the resources necessary to carry through successfully the work of mourning (cf. Chapter XXVI).

7. Excessively harsh or punitive attitudes of the father make more difficult the solution of this complex. To the boy, such a father may seem so threatening that he may give up not only mother but all women and in addition assume a passive, compliant attitude toward the father in particular and men in general. The boy may then aspire to be the passive love object of the father and see the mother as his rival (so-called negative Oedipus complex). Impotence and homosexuality are two possible consequences of such a development. The boy may develop exaggerated character traits of passivity, compliance, ingratiation, timidity, etc., or he may solve the problem by being more harsh and punitive than the father himself, leading to an overly aggressive and often sadistic character structure. In childhood this aggression may be displaced toward younger siblings. The castration complex is of great importance in determining the boy's behavior in such a situation.

The girl dealing with such a father may identify with him and hence remain with strong aggressive masculine traits and never achieve femininity. Or she may assume a masochistic attitude toward the father and carry with her the concept of the sexual experience as a sadistic attack to be passively accepted by the woman. Frigidity is a common outcome. Women with such backgrounds are sometimes found to marry brutal, sadistic men who mistreat them and to whom they submit without complaint. In brief, they tend to repeat the first object choice, for which the father was the model.

8. If the mother is an aggressive or a relatively masculine person and the father passive or feminine in character, other difficulties are introduced. The boy in such a situation has to deal with an aggressive, punitive mother, usually a woman who has failed to overcome her own penis envy and masculine strivings and who has strong aggressive, castrating attitudes toward men. The husband and son now become the targets of such attitudes. Further, such a boy usually has an inadequately masculine father with whom to identify. A boy in such a situa-

tion may follow in the father's footsteps and develop a passive, feminine and masochistic character; he may be forced to retreat to pregential levels of adaptation; he may become timid and fearful of women and be impotent; he may turn to overt homosexuality; he may look for the same kind of wife.

The girl brought up in such a setting also faces difficult problems. Since such a mother generally rejects the feminine as well as the maternal role, the girl is likely to have been relatively deprived in her pre-oedipal period and to have had her own feminine qualities depreciated as well. Such a mother often rebels violently against all homemaking and maternal activities, including pregnancy and child care. The daughter may take over her mother's aggressive, "masculine" character, eschewing the femine qualities and regarding passivity as dangerous. Or she may adopt a passive attitude toward the mother, maintain the mother as her object, depreciate the father and men, and develop a latent or overt homosexual relationship to women. Or the girl may assume a strong, apparently maternal, protective attitude toward the father, establishing strong bonds toward him which she is never able to relinquish.

9. If the parent of the opposite sex has a strong preference for the boy or the girl and has correspondingly rejecting attitudes toward the child of the other sex, the advantage of being like the child of the preferred sex may lead to feminine identification among boys and masculine identification among girls.

10. The presence of an older sibling of the opposite sex often provides a substitute for the parent and oedipal problems may revolve about the sibling. It is also clear that siblings are rivals and that the size of the family will have bearing on the fate of the complex. The single child may have difficulties in later life because of lack of such rivalry, for the situation is more realistic when there are several siblings. When her siblings are much younger, an older girl may enjoy a substitute mother role; but when parental relations are poor or the girl is realistically deprived, this situation may intensify the deprivation and frustration of an older girl and lead to an increased hostility toward her younger siblings.

It is a testimony to the extraordinary adaptive capacity of the human being that none of these situations are necessarily pathogenic. Many individuals successfully cope with such difficult constellations and achieve a successful resolution of the Oedipus complex. Important in these successes under such difficult circumstances may be other figures, teachers, guides, counsellors, scout leaders, religious leaders, etc., who may provide more adequate objects for identification than do the parents.

REFERENCES

1. Bowlby, J., Ainsworth, M., Boston, M. and Rosenbluth, D.: The Effects of Mother-Child Separation: A Follow-up Study. Brit. J. Med. Psychol., *29:*211, 1956.
2. Flugel, J. C.: The Psychoanalytic Study of the Family. London, The Hogarth Press, 1921, chapters 2, 3, 6, 7, 10, 14.
3. Freud, A.: The Bearing of the Psychoanalytic Theory of Instinctual Drives on Certain Aspects of Human Behavior. *In:* Loewenstein, R. (ed.): Drives, Affects, and Behavior. New York, International Universities Press, 1953, pp. 259–277.
4. Erikson, E.: Ego Development and Historical Change. *In:* Freud, A. et al. (eds.): The Psychoanalytic Study of the Child, vol. 2. New York, International Universities Press, 1946, p. 359.
5. Harlow, H.: The Heterosexual Affectional System in Monkeys. Am. Psychologist, Jan. 1962.

CHAPTER XIII

RESOLUTION OF THE OEDIPUS COMPLEX: DEVELOPMENT OF THE SUPEREGO

In the last chapter we discussed some of the forces which interfere with the development of the Oedipus complex or influence its development unfavorably. Now we shall consider the more successful resolution of the Oedipus complex and the alterations in the mental apparatus that characterize this period. The Oedipus complex contributes importantly to the development of the child's sense of identity as male or female and its successful resolution consolidates this process. In the process of relating to the mother and the father, the child is now required not only to differentiate between his parents but also to see himself more as an individual, personally and sexually. In the resolution of the complex, the child must abandon his expectations to replace the opposite parent as a sexual object and must thereby further consolidate his identity as a person in his own right. He has to accept the fact that the parent of the opposite sex cannot become a sexual object and that in this area the parents belong to each other and not to him (her). In the preceding phases of development the assurance of the love of the parent provided the strongest incentive for giving up activities and satisfactions disapproved by the parent. Now the love for and of the parent, having become attached to phallic aims, itself becomes under certain conditions a dangerous and taboo instinctual aim. This is a painful and difficult renunciation, and it is therefore not surprising that such situations as described in the last chapter make the acceptance of such a deprivation a difficult one. The realistic fact which finally turns the tide is the hopelessness of the rivalry with the parent of the same sex.

105

But the child does not give in at once; various defensive maneuvers are utilized which attempt to deny or avoid this reality. Some examples follow (cf. A. Freud[2]):

1. The child often displays much interest and pleasure in stories in which the final result is the opposite of what reality dictates. These stories for children gain their popularity by virtue of how well they fit with the child's psychological situation at the time. Thus, themes of killing the giant or wicked ogre and marrying the princess, gaining the love and admiration of the big, powerful man, killing the wicked witch or stepmother and being found by the handsome prince, the magical fulfillment of wishes, lost parts growing back or reappearing, etc., all are in accord with the prevailing oedipal fantasy and involve an attempt to achieve in fantasy what is impossible in reality. Life experience eventually consolidates the judgment that these are indeed "fairy tales," but for some time they help the child to avoid a reality for which he is not yet prepared.

2. Children also make up stories and act out games which grossly disregard reality, but which satisfy the oedipal wishes in fantasy. Thus, children imagine that they are powerful and invincible, that they are daring cowboys or soldiers, or that they have powerful animal friends. For example, a little boy may make believe he owns a lion who loves him and terrifies everyone else. Another common fantasy of the child is that as he grows bigger, the parent will grow smaller. Through such devices the child, in essence, denies in fantasy what is inescapable in reality, that he is small and weak and the parent is big and strong.

3. During this period nightmares and phobias are not infrequent. The child may experience an intense inappropriate fear of something in the environment. It may be a harmless animal or a dangerous animal which, however, is not really a source of danger (such as a wolf or lion when none exist outside the zoo). This fear is entirely out of proportion to the realistic danger, but the child is quite inaccessible to reasoning. As a result he may greatly restrict his activity on that account. For example, at first the child may simply show fear of the animal; then he may become anxious even if someone simply talks about or shows a picture of the animal; then he may avoid all situations with which the animal might be associated. Eventually he inhibits his activity so as not to run the risk of coming in contact in any way with the feared animal. The feared animal may appear in nightmares or may be associated with darkness. Dynamically, such childhood phobias are thought to develop out of the conflicts engendered by the burgeoning sexual impulses and fantasies and the opposition they encounter from the environment. The particular character of the phobia is determined by the child's own infantile aggressive fantasies and may be oral or anal (to be bitten, eaten, torn, crushed, trampled, smothered, buried, etc.)

or primitively phallic (to be stabbed, penetrated or mutilated). Characteristically, safety is sought by remaining close to the love object. Fear of being alone or of the darkness at this age often includes a more explicit phobic content of this character. One proposed structure of a childhood phobia is as follows: Dynamically, the boy experiences hostility toward the rival parent, here the father, and erotic wishes toward the mother. Because of the dangers such fantasies bring up ("castration" anxiety), they are repressed. Both the hostile wishes and the fear are displaced to an animal and now he feels afraid of an animal (representing the father) which threatens him. The child is thus able to replace his hostility toward the father by hostility and fear of an animal, thereby also permitting him to feel love for and not be afraid of the father, who even becomes his protector. Instead he fears that the animal will do to him what he wished to do to the father or what he was afraid the father would do to him. At the same time, under the guise of avoiding the feared animal, he can be more with the mother, get into bed with her, etc. The symbolism of the phobic animal usually condenses all the forbidden wishes of the oedipal conflict. The nightmares and night terrors of this period have a similar theme, accentuated by the less effective control of ego during sleep and in darkness.

4. In addition to denial in fantasy, which the child either keeps to himself or relates as a story, he may act out or talk out his denial. He plays at being big, being grown-up, being father, mother, pirate, lion, tiger, etc. As long as this exists as a "game" and as long as the child promptly reverts to the reality of going to bed or eating supper at the parent's request, such behavior is condoned and encouraged by the parent. Through this device, the child denies for the time being the less satisfying reality and displaces from the true objects the love and hostility which cannot otherwise be expressed. During this period, the child moves easily and quickly from fantasy to reality and back again; the invincible cowboy hero is quickly converted to the hungry little boy who demands that mother feed and take care of him.

5. Occasionally a child for a period restricts his activities (his ego) in all areas which might bring him into competition. He becomes cautious, timid, and limits the range of his curiosity and exploration. This restriction is usually of brief duration and may be regarded as a defensive maneuver normal for this period.

In general, this period is marked by vigorous activity and play during which verbal and motor skills are rapidly developing and knowledge of the environment is expanding. The child is enlarging his circle of relationships, especially with other children, and society provides him with certain structures, such as play groups, nursery school, kindergarten, etc., in which trial action in the form of games, play and fantasy acting becomes possible in a group setting. At this age the child is full of curiosity and endless questions about the world around him, much of which is of a frankly sexual nature. He inquires about sexual and anatomical differences, where babies come from, and insists that his questions be answered. He himself engages in sexual explorations of and with his playmates. This kind of behavior as well as his first rough, aggressive, destructive acting out is met by controlling or punishing reactions from the environment, though, from the child's point of view, such responses often seem highly inconsistent. Nonetheless, lines are unmistakably being drawn as to what is and what is not acceptable behavior and language in the social environment in which he is growing up. But the drives underlying such activities are by no means eliminated by these external pressures. They continue to seek expression and satisfaction. Though the child may learn to hide or control his behavior and curiosity in his parents' presence, he still pursues them in secrecy, either with his playmates or in solitary play. This is the beginning of a degree of self-control which reveals development of an internal organization whereby the child internalizes some of the warning and punishing functions of the parents and thereby forestalls their disapproval while at the same time enabling him still to enjoy some of the forbidden gratification. This development will now be discussed in terms of *superego*.

FORMATION OF THE SUPEREGO

We have already described how, as a result of the conflicts engendered in this period, there is first an attempt to deal with the realistic situation by denying or avoiding it or by minimizing the unpleasant consequences. But if development is to proceed and if the child is to be acceptable to his family and to the social group in which he and they live, he must more and more conform to and accept reality as defined by the personal and socially determined standards of the parents. In the accomplishment of this acceptance, a new organization of the mental apparatus, the *superego*, evolves from the ego. It has its beginnings in the oral phase when the baby is totally dependent on the mother and when the mother functions for the baby's as yet undeveloped ego. In the course of assimilating the external world, the child not only learns what gives him pleasure or pain, but also what gives the mother pleasure or pain. These experiences form guides to behavior but also provide grounds for internal conflict. Little by little the images of mother and later of father build up within the child as guiding and ɔontrolling influences which direct the activities and impulses of the child in conformity with the parents' demands and needs, even when the parents are not physically present. At first the child may curb his activities only in response to a direct threat or a punishment by the parents, or he may respond to the parents' unconscious expression of discomfort when he does something disapproved by the parents' super-ego; the threat or punishment or the disapproving expression of the parent need not be repeated, but the child responds as if it had been. In brief, what was once an external influence now becomes an internal influence.

The main development of the superego as a separate institution in the mental apparatus takes place at the time of the developing Oedipus complex. As the child must more and more conform to reality, he must also give up dependence on such unrealistic ego devices as denial, by which that which is unacceptable or disagreeable in the environment is dealt with as if it does not exist. One device that the child uses to deal with the undeniable fact that he is smaller, weaker and less competent than the parent is to aspire to become like him. This is accomplished by the process of *identification*, whereby the child consciously and unconsciously emulates and tries to be like the parent whom he both loves and fears. Identification acknowledges, at least to some extent, the reality of this discrepancy in size and ability and hence serves both as an impetus toward development and as a means of defense against the unacceptable hostile feeling toward the rival parent. When identification is successfully accomplished, many of the characteristics of the loved and feared object actually become an integral part of the self. With this, the boy, for example, is able gradually to give up the idea of displacing his father and becomes willing to wait and work to be like him. Now the boy may enter a phase of admiration and even hero worship of his father. Overt hostility toward his father (her mother) may now even be replaced by greater affection. Through such a process of internalization of the characteristics and standards of the parents the child is establishing an internal system concerned with expectations, goals, punishment and reward. This includes a psychological (personal) ideal of what he should be like, first modeled on the parents (*the ego ideal*), in relation to which he compares how he actually feels himself to be and how he feels he should be. When he does not live up to the ideal, he may feel *shame;* when he does, he feels *pride*. This is a superego function and provides a goal to live up to, a spur for achievement and development. In addition, the superego is made up of the internalized representation of all the do's and don'ts of the parents (and later teachers, guides, etc.) and through them representatives of the mores and moral code of the culture. Thus, there also develops an internal agency for reward and punishment. When one does what he conceives of as being wrong, something to be disapproved of, one feels *guilt,* and with it a feeling of worthlessness and a need for punishment and atonement. This leads logically to the concept of social conscience (see Chapter XVIII).

The steps in the development of the superego may be schematized as follows:

1. "I do or wish something, and mother (or father) punishes or disapproves of me."

2. "I don't do something because I *will be* punished or disapproved of."

3. "I don't do something because it *will make me feel bad* if I do it. Indeed, even entertaining the wish to do it makes me feel bad." (The wish and the act are considered equivalent.)

4. "I don't do something because it just isn't a good thing to do."

The first three steps represent behavior when the superego is immature. The last stage is representative of more mature superego function and may become quite automatic. The magical thinking of earlier childhood, wherein distinction between a thought and an act is not made, then disappears. With such successful development of the superego, the child more and more is able to use his own feelings and behavior as guides without requiring the actual physical presence of the parent. Further, he can anticipate and avert punishment or disapproval by the parents through this internalized representation of them. He thus borrows strength from the parents.

As a special internal motivating force of ego, superego (and ego ideal) may function unconsciously as well as consciously. It is an important factor in circumscribing what mental processes become conscious and what behavior becomes manifest. As a self-punishing agency it may operate before as well as after the fact. Thus, at times certain thoughts or fantasies may never be permitted access to consciousness, being prevented simply by the threat of punishment (experienced as feelings of guilt). At other times such wishes, fantasies and even acts may become conscious or manifest and then may be followed by feelings of guilt or shame. Feelings of guilt are relieved by punishment and forgiveness. It is not uncommon to find children at this age soliciting punishment at the hands of the parent in order to relieve feelings of guilt, sometimes provoked by fantasies or acts about which the parents are ignorant. This may be accomplished by misbehaving in some other, usually less serious, way. Thus the child who feels guilty because of a destructive, hostile fantasy toward the parent or a sibling or because he has masturbated may deliberately be naughty until punished. Sometimes he may "accidentally" fall and injure himself or deliberately hurt himself by some act such as banging his head against the door. It is characteristic of the function of superego in childhood for the child to be even more severe with himself than the parent would be.

The formation of superego and ego ideal also marks the beginnings of the development of moral and ethical feelings in the child, a process which extends into early adulthood. The sense of what is right and what is wrong, what is admirable and what is reprehensible, what is honest and what is dishonest, what one should aspire to and what one should avoid—all such concepts are evolving as mental constructs in the course of the child's interaction with his particular social environment. It is both a necessity as well as an advantage for the child to find the conditions under which he can grow and develop as well as be accepted by the social group in which he finds himself. Through such learning and internalizing of the standards and requirements of his group do his own standards evolve. But it must be emphasized not only that the most potent influences are those of the persons most directly concerned in the child's nurturing (the parents), but also that what is explicitly taught by them or by others may not correspond with the parents' actual behavior or the conditions under which the parent-child relationship actually takes place. Double standards on the part of parents in respect to their children are notoriously commonplace. In general, the child is more responsive to that which is closest to the wish or actual behavior of the parent than to that which the parent voices or displays for the child's benefit.

REFERENCES

1. Frank, L. K.: Cultural Control and Physiological Autonomy. Am. J. Orthopsychiat., *8*:62, 1938.
2. Freud, A.: The Ego and the Mechanisms of Defense. New York, International Universities Press, 1946, chapters 6, 7, 8.
3. Piers, G. and Singer, M.: Shame and Guilt. Springfield, Illinois, Charles C Thomas, 1953.
The classic case of childhood phobia is:
4. Freud, S.: Analysis of a Phobia in a Five Year Old Boy (1909). *In:* Standard Edition of the Complete Psychological Works of Sigmund Freud, vol. X. London, The Hogarth Press, 1955, pp. 3–148.

CHAPTER XIV

THE DEVELOPING
MENTAL APPARATUS

Having given attention to the many forces which influence the child's development during the first five years, it is worth while now to examine more systematically how the mental apparatus has evolved during this period. The fact that biological processes having to do with survival and growth determine behavior long before such behavior has any psychological equivalent and before the child has awareness of his own behavior justifies the perspective that the biological has primacy in the development of mental functioning. Thus, as earlier material has illustrated, there already exists at birth the organizations in the central nervous system for such functions as nursing, clinging and other ways of relating to the mother basic for survival, but only over an extended period of time does there evolve psychological awareness of such behavior. This can come about only as the baby becomes capable of differentiating himself from his mother and his own behavior from that of others. The baby nurses, eats, clings to the mother, etc., long before he knows about nursing, eating, clinging, or about mother. Because the child learns about the environment through the actions and functioning of his own body, especially in relationship to gratification or frustration of needs, his early psychological constructs are likely to be much influenced by how he experiences the activities of his own body. This accounts for the oral, anal, phallic and other body-functioning ways of conceptualization and thinking, as evidenced in the fantasies of children, in dreams, etc. The data of Piaget also demonstrate the importance of body action and experience in the development of the mental process (Chapter VIII).

The primacy of the biological in psychic development also accounts for the fact that much of behavior and mental activity takes place without conscious awareness, and some never becomes accessible to consciousness. The child masters certain behavior in the service of survival and growth without ever necessarily having to "know" about it. Other biologically determined behavior evokes conflict and, as we shall see, is not subjected to the transformations necessary for conscious knowledge. To become conscious in a mental sense means to be able to attach words, concepts and symbols to what is experienced and to be aware of their meaning. The capacity for conscious awareness and understanding and the associated ability to exert conscious will over impulses and behavior distinguish the developed mental apparatus of the healthy adult from that of the child. This development involves the progressive acquisition of autonomy of mental functioning in the sense of a relative freedom from the necessity to respond "thoughtlessly" to either internal or external forces. It is experienced in terms of a sense of mastery and control over one's impulses and environment as contrasted to helplessness or passivity in the face of internal or environmental pressures. Such capacities are unevenly acquired in the course of development, being earliest achieved in aspects of functioning that are relatively free of conflict, as already discussed in relation to the development of intelligence (Chapter VIII). In the final analysis, the degree of development of the mental apparatus is measured by the extent to which mental functioning achieves autonomy in relation to the basic biological influences, while at the same time assuring satisfaction of these needs and adequate adjustment within the environment. Adequate adjustment includes the capacity not only to accommodate to the environment but also to modify or resist it and the judgment to know when and how to do so. These much-to-be-desired final characteristics of mature mental functioning must be kept in mind as we consider the development of the child's mental apparatus.

INSTINCTS, DRIVES AND THE "ID"

Psychoanalytical psychology has placed great emphasis on the biological forces which exert their influence on behavior and hence on the development of the mental apparatus. To these forces the term *instinct* has been applied (see Chapters II and III). Instinct is a biological, not a psychological, concept referring to the influence of the needs of the body on mental activity and on behavior. Such influences are, of course, mediated through the central nervous system and are experienced psychologically in the course of the behavior evoked thereby. What is experienced is not "instinct" but rather various aspects of body sensation associated with satisfaction or frustration of the needs and, in time, various perceptions of the environment associated therewith. Little by little, in the course of development psychological representations of these body and other experiences become established in the mental apparatus. As such they then begin to assume some measure of independence from the body itself and may then be referred to as *drives*. *Hunger*, for example, reflecting the needs of body tissues for nutriment, achieves psychological representation as *appetite*, which may influence eating behavior over a much wider range than that determined by body needs alone. *Drives are the psychic representations of instinct*. Drives are inevitably linked to the body experiences of the infant and, consequently, take forms determined by both developmental and experiential factors. Drives have the effect of initiating, implementing or modifying behavior and thought. Their psychic expression exists in the form of *unconscious fantasy*, fragments of which become available to the observer in the form of verbal fantasy, children's play, dreams, myths, legends, the productions of psychotics, neurotic symptomatology, etc. Unconscious fantasies express the gamut of drive activity. They may include all the variety of wishes or impulses described in the preceding chapters, such as oral incorporative, clinging, oral-sadistic, anal, phallic, oedipal, castrative, etc. And, as we have seen, even though instincts are in the service of survival, growth and reproduction in a biological sense, at various times and under various circumstances the drives may lead to conflict, first with the invironment and later intrapsychically.

These processes and activities constitute the *Id*, as defined by Freud.[2] The Id is not a thing or a place within the mind but represents a category of processes and functions, the drive part of mental functioning, with all the elaborations brought about by phylogeny, ontogeny and experience. Those processes encompassed under the heading "Id" are always unconscious. Only the derivatives, after they have been successively modified by ego and superego activity, reach consciousness. As such, they may then reveal the nature of the drive in the psychological form of a wish or an impulse from which have been eliminated those aspects of the drive which are unacceptable. In early childhood such drive expression is relatively less disguised and is more readily translated into behavior which at times blatantly expresses the underlying impulse. But it would be a mistake to assume that this is fully conscious and understood by the child. For one thing, the child's capacity for verbal expression and concept formation is still decidedly limited so that his often picturesque and pungent expressions of a sexual or aggressive character do not necessarily carry the full literal meanings known to the adult. (But they have much more meaning than some adults who believe the child to be utterly innocent are willing to concede.) Further, much of the drive activity of the child is experienced primarily in the form of feelings (affects) which do not yet have meaning on the form of words or concepts but which lead more directly to action that serves to gratify a need or relieve a tension. Some aspects of such behavior are generally acceptable or even desirable to the environment, whereas other aspects must be modified or inhibited altogether. For example, the baby masters eating quickly, but must learn the conditions and manner of feeding himself; he urinates and defecates, but must learn acceptable ways of so doing. Similarly, he manifests sexual and aggressive behavior in response to inner pressures, but much of this is unacceptable and must be suppressed or inhibited. Behavior and feelings subject to such forces are less likely to achieve mental representation in the form of words and concepts and, in this sense, tend to remain unconscious. Intellectual learning and conscious knowledge are achieved much more effectively in the conflict-free sphere. The child can be much more aware and knowledgeable in respect to those aspects of his behavior that involve hunger than those that have a sexual meaning. This is seen most clearly in the fate of the biologically determined sexual impulses which underlie the Oedipus complex. The sexual aspects of the child's behavior may be quite manifest to the observer, but after the child grows up what he is able to recall of his childhood may be largely devoid of sexual content, though the memory may continue to have a strong affective tone. We shall later consider the role of ego and superego in determining what is permitted access to consciousness. It is a function of ego to reconcile the inconsistencies between drive-determined behavior on the one hand and reality as represented by the environment on the other.

In understanding instinct and drive it is important to keep in mind that these forces reflect the fact that for survival, growth and continuation of the species, the organism is dependent upon certain elements in and input from the environment which it cannot secure from its own internal resources. It is literally driven to behave in ways that assure the supply of these necessary environmental elements. Hence, it is meaningless to consider instinct or drive without taking into account the object in the environment toward which the drive is directed. In earliest infancy this takes place reflexly, without the necessity for knowledge, conscious or unconscious, on the part of the infant of what constitutes the suitable object in the environment. Piaget referred to this as the stage of "The Use of Reflexes." The fact that instinct must have an object means that drives, the psychic representations of instinct, must also include psychic representations of the drive objects. To put it in the simplest psychological terms, the child has not just a wish, but a wish *for* something, be it food, body contact, mother, etc. It is an important psychological fact that the development of psychic representation of the drive object is facilitated by some degree of frustration of the need. The child is unlikely to be consciously aware of a need for air unless he experiences some difficulty in breathing, and then he is more aware of a need to breathe than of a need for air. Knowledge of air as the substance breathed comes much later. In contrast, awareness of food and of mother evolve out of repetitive experiences of being hungry and being fed and of separation from and reunion with mother. The developments in the first years of life involve the acquisition of increasingly complex psychic representations of satisfying and frustrating experiences with environmental objects. It is this which contributes the individuality of drive expression for each person. Although the biological organization underlying instinct is probably similar for all humans, the development of drives is much more influenced by the nature of early life experiences, which help to establish what aspects of instinctual activity are both satisying and acceptable and what aspects are frustrating or unacceptable. The material of the preceding chapters indicates some of the varieties of drive expression that evolve out of this interaction between biological developments and environmental conditions. Again, it is a function of ego to resolve conflict by assuring a suitable object for drive gratification. The Oedipus complex is an example of a situation in which drive expression must be delayed until a new object relationship can be established. Unacceptable drives must be inhibited, taboo objects must be avoided, and suitable compromises must be found if the child is to function with reasonable comfort and with basic needs gratified. Drive systems, however, tend to persist in their organization around early objects and so continue to exert an influence on psychic activity and behavior. What becomes conscious in the form of wish or fantasy, whether or not translated into expression or action, represents that aspect of drive activity which either is acceptable to ego and superego or which is strong enough to break through the controls of ego. The period of development that has been considered so far is marked by the evolution of drive systems and the beginnings of their control.

THE EGO

If we can recognize in the infant the existence of instinct (the *Id*, as described above), we can also recognize the presence of an organization to assure satisfaction of needs. This is the *autonomous ego*—those processes, the organization for which is present at birth, which have immediately to do with survival, development and growth. The processes include systems of perception; threshold apparatuses to permit access to certain stimuli and to protect against others (the so-called "stimulus barrier"); systems concerned with learning, memory, retention and recall; systems concerned with communication, internally and with the environment; systems concerned with motility in the service of survival, as in nursing, sucking, feeding, excretion, etc.[3, 4] These autonomous ego functions have their basis in the properties and functions of the central nervous system (see Chapter III). As psychological processes they evolve through utilization of the neural systems in the course of development. These aspects of ego function are called "conflict-free" because they exist before the development of intrapsychic conflict and do not develop out of the necessity to resolve conflict, as do the defensive functions of ego. Rather they constitute the apparatus through which drive action is achieved. They play an important (but not exclusive) role in the development of cognitive functioning, as described by Piaget (see Chapter VIII), and in the functions of reality testing.

The functions subsumed under the term "autonomous ego" operate originally under the behest of instinct, i.e., of the Id. They assure satisfaction of needs and they follow essentially the operation of the pleasure principle. But, as has been already developed, the operation of the pleasure principle alone eventually becomes incompatible with continued survival and growth. The child must learn the conditions under which the environment will provide or permit gratification, and this requires that there be a delay between the stimulus of the need and its perception by the mental apparatus on the one hand, and the action to satisfy the need on the other. The *defensive functions* of the ego are concerned with such processes. They probably originate first from the threshold apparatuses of the autonomous ego, the capacity to block perceptions from the outside environment or from within, as well as the capacity to delay or block affect or the discharge of drive. In the service of maintaining an optimal dynamic steady state ego, functions develop which ultimately have the purpose of mediating between drives and the requirements of external reality and its representatives. The material of the preceding chapters has already served to outline the nature of the conflicts operating during these first years. The ego defenses, as psychic mechanisms, modify mental experience and behavior so that pain and discomfort, physical or mental, will be avoided while at the same time some degree of gratification of needs is achieved and growth and development can continue. Since at this early age gratification of needs is very much dependent on continuing object relations, the nature and availability of such relations prove to be important limiting factors determining which aspect of mental activity or behavior is to be modified or relinquished. The nature of the early object relationship also determines what other aspects of external reality must be ignored or distorted in order that this relationship not be disrupted.

The defensive aspects of ego function include signal or warning functions, which operate to warn of the possibility of painful states before they actually develop. These will be discussed further in terms of affects. The signal or warning functions of the ego develop in relationship to particular past experiences of the child and provide a means of anticipating difficulties as well as a means of warning of the necessity for some type of action. The danger signals of the ego serve to initiate other defense mechanisms. The important early ego defenses have already been mentioned but are summarized again here:

1. The pattern of withdrawal, the raising of the threshold to stimuli from the external world, eventually is elaborated into various forms of *denial*, which may be directed not only toward processes in the external environment but also toward mental processes, including affects, which have become conscious. Thus, the child may ignore aspects of the environment, awareness of which might be disturbing, or may claim he has not thought or felt something which actually did become conscious. The manifestly angry child may say, "I am not angry," and the little boy may insist that the girl has a penis in spite of visual evidence to the contrary. He refuses to acknowledge what would be painful or frightening at this point in his development, but eventually he must accept reality and acknowledge the evidences of his senses.

2. *Repression* refers to the ego process whereby drive representation is blocked from achieving consciousness. Thus, repression may operate to keep drive representation from ever being experienced consciously, or it may operate to return to an unconscious state drive expressions, fantasies, etc., which at one time had been conscious. Repression requires continuous expenditure of energy, for that which is subject to repression, being an expression of drive, continues to seek discharge. In so doing it continues to exert an influence on mental activity and behavior, and from time to time derivatives may attain discharge in some form. The fate of much of the psychic content of the early years, as described in preceding chapters, is that it is subjected to repression. What was so blatantly expressed at ages three, four, five or six is largely forgotten, though indications of its continued existence in unconscious mental terms is clearly evident in later life. The evidence for this will be discussed in subsequent chapters. In essence, the net effect of repression is that the child no longer knows or never learns about that which is repressed. Repression may be directed toward the drive itself or toward the object of the drive, or both. Thus, the child's sexual curiosity about a parent may become curiosity about the parent

but may no longer be concerned with sexual matters; or it may become sexual curiosity about someone else; or just curiosity about someone else. Yet observation of the child's behavior during play may clearly reveal evidence that he is still operating under the influence of sexual feeling toward the parent. Repression takes place without conscious awareness; it is not the same as *suppression*, the deliberate withholding of something because it may be considered not acceptable to the listener.

3. *Displacement* refers to processes whereby the aim or the object of the drive may be changed. For example, an aggressive drive may be displaced from a dangerous object to a harmless object or to a less dangerous symbol. This was illustrated in the mechanism of the phobia (Chapter XIII).

4. *Reversal into the opposite* refers to the process whereby an unacceptable impulse may be turned into its opposite, such as love into hate, or vice versa. Thus the child who is disturbed by too strong aggressive feelings towards a parent may talk and think mainly of the ways in which he likes the parent.

5. *Introjection* has already been discussed in some detail. It is an ego defense mechanism which evolves out of the primary oral organization of the infant and is the chief mechanism used by the immature ego to maintain an object relationship and to avert the painful consequences of object loss. Hence it operates in the service of development as well as of defense. The object psychologically is experienced as being taken in as a whole and is felt to be inside. It is as if the child were to say to himself, "I will prevent mother from going away by keeping her inside me; then I will not feel tension." The model for this is the relief of tension and the satisfaction which occurs with nursing.

6. *Identification* eventually evolves from introjection after a more clear distinction between self and object has developed in the child's mind. It too plays an integral role in growth and development, a process whereby the child unconsciously takes for himself qualities of his objects and thereby adds to his evolving concept of himself. Identification may also operate as an ego defense, as when unpleasant feelings of helplessness or fear are avoided by becoming like the lost or threatening object. This is an intrapsychic process whereby the desired or envied qualities of the object are assumed for the self and thereby the self is enhanced and changed. The sense of weakness or helplessness is reduced by feeling strong like the object, or the feeling of fear is counteracted by feeling as threatening as the aggressive object (identification with the aggressor).

7. *Projection* refers to the mechanism whereby unacceptable impulses, feelings or drives are ascribed to the outside rather than to oneself, or to the object rather than to the self. They are thereby disowned.

These and other defense mechanisms of ego will be discussed further in different contexts (Chapter XVII). They constitute the various mental mechanisms whereby a compromise is achieved between the demands of Id and the requirements of reality, whether it be represented as it actually exists in the external world, or by the internal representatives thereof (including superego and ego ideal). It is characteristic of the operation of the defensive functions of the ego of early childhood that reality is more often disregarded or is more seriously distorted than it is in later life. Although the same ego functions are utilized by the healthy adult, they are not so resistant to the facts of external reality as are those of the child. This is particularly evident in the child's use of denial and projection.

From these considerations we can see that ego function includes many types of active processes and that work is accomplished. Energy is required for such work and it is evident that ego functions may both facilitate and inhibit activity at the same time. In terms of the reality principle, it is the function of ego to permit activity which is appropriate to reality and to block or inhibit activity which is not. Ego functions also serve to save energy for the organism as a whole. By interposing a delay between the drive and action upon it, or between the need and satisfaction of the need, opportunity is afforded to test mentally the various possibilities of action and to select that which will be most successful and most satisfying. In this sense, thinking can be seen as a preparation for action, or, as Freud put it, ". . . a trial action with minimal expenditure of energy."[2] It is the development of ego which brings about the modulation and control of behavior characteristic of the adult as distinguished from the infant or small child, whose behavioral expressions are more immediate and impulsive. It is also the development of ego which permits the tremendous range of creativity and accomplishment that characterize human beings. Integration of past and present and synthesis of new solutions are functions of ego. It is also ego development which provides the quality of autonomy of mental functioning. This will be discussed further in Chapters XVII and XXII.

SUPEREGO

The development of the superego was discussed briefly in Chapter XIII. We can see that the superego represents a particular sampling of the persons and influences of the external world, which is then permanently established within the mental apparatus. The superego provides a third force (in addition to the instinctual drives and the forces of external reality), in relationship to which ego processes must operate. We have recognized the punitive and disapproving aspects of the superego as representing the voices and examples of important figures. Ego processes are involved in maintaining oneself in the good graces of this institution. *Guilt,* as affect, becomes the special signal of ego that disapproval is threatened. Later we shall describe some of the particular mechanisms that operate in response to guilt. The *ego ideal* represents the internalized expression of goals, standards and aspirations, many of which were established through relationship with the important figures in one's early life. The ego functions of self-observation and self-examination keep tabs on discrepancies which may exist between actual performance, behavior or plans and those established within the ego ideal. *Shame* becomes the signal mechanism of the ego which warns of a failure to live up to the ideals. We note that the aggressive aspects of object relationships are involved in the formation of the superego. Thus, many of the harsh, punitive attitudes people hold toward themselves arise not only from attitudes of the parents, who may once have behaved that way, but also from the children's attitudes toward the parents. That is, a child's earlier, but unacceptable hostility toward a parent may become turned upon himself, so that his angry, accusing attitude toward himself actually corresponds to how he himself once felt toward the parent. Similarly, the ego ideal evolves from the child's love for the object and the object's love for the child.

The Id, ego and superego represent the classic tripartite structural concept of the mental apparatus as formulated by Freud.[2]

THE CONCEPT OF OBJECTS AND OF THE SELF

In earlier chapters we have discussed the role of objects and object relations in the development of the mental apparatus. It was pointed out how the ego develops and is modified by the nature of the object relationships of early life. As part of this process we postulated the formation within the mental apparatus of object representations, that is to say, of complex and dynamic memory traces which evolve from the gratifications, frustrations and experiences with the external objects during the course of development. We learned that only gradually does the child develop a concept of himself, a distinction between himself and the not-self, and that this is contributed to considerably by how early experience with objects determines their existence in the child's mlnd as object representations. Many aspects of ego and of superego function express intrapsychic relationships between the developing concept of the self and objects. Successful development requires an increasingly clear delineation of oneself as an individual. Nonetheless, some measure of confusion between self and objects always persists, so that seif-observation and self-evaluation at times actually express one's feelings about objects and at times express the feelings of objects about the self. As will be developed later, there are many individual variations and expressions of such processes. The ability to establish and to maintain object relationships and to maintain an identity will prove to be an important influence in the regulation of health and disease.

Narcissism

This refers essentially to the processes whereby love (libido) is directed to the self. The infant is said to be primarily narcissistic, in that before objects exist for him, all libido is concentrated on the self. In a sense, this is an ambiguous concept because in infancy there is no clear concept of self either. Nonetheless, there is some justification for using the term "narcissism" to refer to such self-directed and oriented feelings and attitudes. The small child is normally much more narcissistic than the adult, in that he is more self-centered and less altruistic. Later we shall recognize in the adult healthy degrees of narcissism, having to do with self-esteem, pride and self-satisfaction.

TOPOLOGY OF THE MENTAL APPARATUS

We recognize that mental activity may exist in three states: *conscious, preconscious* and *unconscious*. Consciousness may be thought of as the "sense organ" of the mind. With effort or attention we bring something to consciousness. It may be a word, a thought, an impulse, a concept, a wish, a sensory image, a feeling, or a bodily sensation. At other times, something may intrude into our sphere of consciousness whether we will it or not. The first remains in our sphere of consciousness only fleetingly and will disappear as soon as we withdraw our attention. The second comes into consciousness against our will and usually displaces other processes from consciousness. In either instance the stimulus may originate from within the body or from the outside. The process of something becoming conscious thus involves the concept of a threshold. The stimulus is either strong enough to overcome the threshold, or work must be done to raise it to an intensity that can overcome the threshold. These processes of keeping something from becoming conscious and of permitting other things to become conscious are ego functions. Similarly, the failure to keep something from becoming conscious may represent a failure of ego function. When work is done to bring something to consciousness, what appears does so in an orderly, organized form. Here again we see the operation of ego, which uses processes of logic, coherence, organization and orderliness to bring the particular content into consciousness. Except for bodily and mental feelings (including affects), that which comes into consciousness must do so by being associated with a symbol or a word. It is this capacity to organize conscious experience in a logical, coherent, reality-oriented fashion which marks the evolution from primitive to more mature mental functioning in the child. The term *"primary process"* has been used to refer to the illogical form of mental activity characteristic of unconscious mental processes and the manifest mental processes of small children. The work of ego converts this to the *secondary process,* the orderly mental activity in the form of words, abstractions and symbols which is organized with due regard for logic, coherence, temporal and spatial relationships, and which avoids contradictions.

Content which can relatively easily be brought into consciousness by the exertion of effort is regarded as being *preconscious.* That which we regard as "on the tip of the tongue" is something preconscious against which some resistance is still being exerted. When something is *unconscious,* it is not directly accessible to consciousness by any device. The largest part of mental functioning takes place at an unconscious or preconscious level. This includes all the processes which we have so far subsumed under the headings of Id, ego and superego. If it were necessary to deal with everything at a conscious level we would be paralyzed; most of our moment-to-moment mental and physical activity goes on automatically, as is obvious in such an activity as guiding a car through traffic while carrying on a conversation. The data of psychoanalysis and particularly the insight obtained through the analysis of dreams, errors, slips of the tongue, parapraxis, wit and humor, as well as the material revealed during hypnosis, organic and metabolic brain disease and psychosis, indicate the nature and operation of unconscious mental processes. As we have already described, most mental processes are unconscious before they become conscious.

AFFECTS

Affects originate in infancy as the communicative and behavioral expressions of drive. As the psychic apparatus evolves they come to acquire the qualities of ego functions as well. Affects have two essential characteristics: they are felt subjectively and are expressed nonverbally, indicating to oneself and to others one's current state of need, desire, satisfaction or pleasure. We have already emphasized the importance of the polarities of pleasure-unpleasure and comfort-discomfort as early regulators and organizers of infant behavior and psychic development. In whatever way they are experienced in infancy, they constitute the basis for the subjective aspects of affect, something felt. This may properly be thought of as an internal communication, indicating the status of the organism in terms of whether or not needs are fulfilled, and as such it is mediated by central nervous system organization which is in operation before (phylogenetically as well as ontogenetically) the psychic process comes into being. In the prepsychic stage this internal communication may be seen as the afferent end of the neural organization mediating behavior necessary to assure satisfaction of needs. It constitutes the input from the body that lets the organism "know" whether needs are being met. Though we have no way of knowing how and when this becomes psychic experience for the infant, obviously during some phase in development the child begins to be able to differentiate in a psychological sense feelings of "pleasure" from those of "unpleasure." At the same time the adult "knows" from the baby's behavior how he is feeling, and this fact identifies the other essential aspect of affect, that it is also a communication to the environment of the infant's status in respect to need or satisfaction, comfort or discomfort. The baby's behavior, facial expression, movements, posture and the sounds he emits indicate unmistakably this status. Further, the adult is geared to respond with behavior that is intended to sustain the baby's comfort and to terminate his discomfort. This has already been discussed in earlier chapters in terms of the mother-infant unit.

In brief, then, affects as psychic experiences evolve from internal communicative processes (information) within the infant and from communicative processes between the infant and others. These are concerned with the regulation of basic life processes which for their success demand the presence or participation of another person. For the helpless infant this includes a great deal. In other words, affects are concerned not only with the internal awareness of drives and the needs they express, but also with the communicative processes whereby the object of the drive is secured. As the mental apparatus develops these processes progressively come under the aegis of ego. The perceptual processes whereby one knows *how* one feels are functions of ego, as are the processes whereby one learns *what* one feels. The latter involves the differentiation of affects into distinct qualities and their eventual identification in terms of language. In the course of time the relatively undifferentiated qualities of "pleasure" and "unpleasure" become differentiated into such feeling states as contentment, joy, confidence, trust, hope, love and affection, on the one hand, and anxiety, depression-withdrawal, fear, shame, guilt, disgust, sadness, helplessness and hopelessness on the other. Feelings of "tension requiring relief" include not only such biologically distinct qualities as hunger, thirst and sexual urges, but also their more complex derivatives already considered under the headings of libidinal and aggressive drives, the affect part being what is felt.

In addition, there are numerous mixed affect and mood qualities. This array of differentiated affects indicates awareness of qualitatively different states of psychic adjustment which are also communicated nonverbally (and with development become capable of being communicated verbally as well) to the environment. These will be discussed in Chapter XVIII, but for present purposes it must be appreciated that affect differentiation is an important aspect of the developing mental apparatus.

In earlier chapters reference was made to contentment and confidence as two early pleasure affects and to anxiety and depression-withdrawal as two early unpleasure affects. Their derivation from more primitive biological states was considered. A fuller discussion of affects will be reserved for Chapter XVIII, but it is worth while at this point to consider how the primary affects of unpleasure, namely, anxiety and depression-withdrawal, evolve as the mental apparatus develops. Keeping in mind the origins of affect, it is useful to examine these affects from the perspective of ego, self-object and drive, indicating thereby that affects constitute multifaceted psychic processes.

Anxiety

Beginning in the nonspecific crying fit, the undifferentiated active reaction to the rising tension of unsatisfied needs, the anxiety reaction comes to occur more specifically in response to actual separation, the absence of the familiar face configuration, darkness, strange places, the stranger, and finally threats to the body, including mutilation and especially the castration threat. All of these come to be experienced as danger situations, seen as originating in or arising from the outside world, and they become stimuli for anxiety, an emergency reaction, the relief of which requires flight from the dangerous situation to the object(s) who affords protection and assures satisfaction of needs. What began as a biological response indicating mounting tension and an unsatisfied need acquires the psychic meanings of a warning of impending danger while at the same time initiating both internal (physiological and psychological) and external (behavioral) responses which prepare the body for protection against damage and the individual to resist or flee the danger. Central to our understanding of how anxiety evolves as a specific affect quality, a true ego state, is that it involves not only the concept of a danger, but also relief through relationship with an object.

THE EGO ASPECT. With repeated experience the child becomes able to anticipate what is "dangerous" for him, whether it be an unacceptable impulse or an external threat, and with varying success learns how to cope with it. In terms of the mental apparatus this means that to a considerable degree the earlier diffuse reaction becomes refined to the quality of a mere signal, a danger signal, so to speak. The warning function has become internalized as an ego process. At its most effective level the signal is responded to rapidly and silently, the danger situation is averted, and no anxiety is felt. This result may be accomplished by means of ego defenses, by behavior intended to alter the environment in order to reduce the threat, or by the resolution of the conflict or problem through mental processes and behavior. This silent operation of signal anxiety provides an efficient means for responding to change and avoiding stress. The concept of learning is appropriate in that when a successful solution has been achieved the signal operates to initiate promptly the same solution on subsequent occasions. (Avoidance-conditioning studies of animals reveal a similar acquisition of an efficient response to a signal with marked reduction in the degree of activation of the nervous system to accomplish this.) However, if past experience provides no immediate solution or if an old solution is no longer appropriate, the signal initiates the more general reaction, which not only is felt as anxiety but also includes the physiological and behavioral changes preparatory for flight and danger, and the communication to others of a need for help. It is through ego processes that the anxiety is felt, with all the ideational content peculiar to the individual, and that attempts at resolution are made. The diffuse anxiety, including as well sensations from the bodily changes that accompany anxiety, now is also experienced as a danger signal in its own right.

THE SELF-OBJECT ASPECT. Basically, anxiety is experienced as danger to the self, which may be seen as arising from within, as when the person feels in danger of being overwhelmed by his own impulses which he cannot control, or from without, as when he feels the danger to arise from some situation in the external environment. In either circumstance the self-image is felt to be relatively weak and ineffective, and this feeling is often experienced as a loss of self-confidence, leading to a need for help from others which may be communicated nonverbally and verbally. This state is responded to psychically and behaviorally with efforts to re-establish a more effective object relationship and thereby strengthen the self. When anxiety is overwhelming this capacity to seek an object actively (in reality or intrapsychically) is lost, and the more passive state of helplessness ensues (see Chapter XVIII).

THE DRIVE ASPECT. This aspect of anxiety appears in the ideational, behavioral and physiological processes, many of which reveal the frantic effort to assure gratification of needs which have been placed in jeopardy in the course of the danger situation. Basically, the attempt to secure gratification involves an external object or an intrapsychic object representation and includes the reactivation of more primitive psychic, behavioral and physiological mechanisms concerned in the preparation for defense and flight. Such processes continue and even are reinforced through the mechanism of negative feedback until help in the form of a suitable object or solution arrives or exhaustion supervenes.

Anxiety plays a central role in psychic regulation, acquiring the quality of a sensitive indicator of both internal and external changes for which some response is necessary if pain or discomfort is to be avoided or minimized. This signal function may be regarded as the psychic (more specifically, ego) aspect of the so-called alerting or activating systems of the brain which render the animal vigilant and ready to respond to danger situations. Its importance in learning is obvious. (See also Chapter XXXIII.)

Depression-Withdrawal

This may be seen as the less differentiated affect warning of loss of supplies *and* as indicating the need for conservation of energy, from which evolve other more complex affects, notably helplessness and hopelessness, as we shall discuss later.

THE EGO ASPECT. This involves a signal warning of loss of supplies. It is evocative of psychic mechanisms and behavior to insure the supply, to retain the object, to enhance self-esteem and to maintain the illusion that the loss is not significant. It may lead to behavior to hold, to cling, to ingratiate, to reward, to force or to seduce an external object to these ends. With the failure of such changes to provide a solution, the defenses shift more to withdrawal and heightening of the stimulus barrier in the course of which we presume the painful affect is felt with increasing intensity.

THE SELF-OBJECT ASPECT. In its more primal aspect, depression involves a regression toward a pre-object stage, and includes extreme withdrawal, even sleep or coma. From the psychobiological perspective, this may finally include withdrawal from all external sources of supply, giving up nursing and clinging, and raising the barrier against stimuli from the outside. It is important to note that the manifest behavior of depression-withdrawal tends to elicit a response to hold, succor and comfort from the person in the environment.

THE DRIVE ASPECT. This is self-preservative but in a primitive, "last ditch" sense. It involves essentially the conserving of energy, and includes a heightening of the stimulus barrier to reduce incoming stimuli and a reduction of activity to save energy.

This perspective of ego, self-object and drive is also useful in highlighting some aspects of the differentiation of affects in the course of the development of the mental apparatus. As affects become more differentiated it becomes clear that some are more prominently characterized by signal or scanning properties while others are characterized more by discharge properties. We have therefore subgrouped the differentiated affects according to these characteristics, namely as the *signal-scanning* affects and the *drive-discharge* affects, admittedly a purely descriptive terminology.

The *signal-scanning affects* have as their distinguishing characteristics a warning or signal function and a "How am I doing?" or scanning function, yielding judgments of good or bad, success or failure, pleasure or unpleasure. They serve as signals and means of reality testing for orientation to both external reality and internal reality, this being an ego function. When some satisfactory defense or behavior is immediately available in response to a change in internal or external environment, the signal evoking it operates instantaneously and silently and no affect is felt. When such a simple, economical signal is ineffective, some quality of affect is felt, this, too, functioning to provoke further ego mechanisms or behavior to end the conflict and distress. Thus, the signal-scanning affects reflect the operation of the reality principle, warning against that which is dangerous and sustaining that which assures adjustment. What is felt, ideationally and in terms of body sensations and physiological changes, does not primarily include discharge in the classic sense of a pleasurable increase in excitation and its release. Instead, the signal-scanning affects provide information which is then used by the self-inspection part of the ego as a guide for subsequent ego activities in the service of the reality principle. Success and failure are indicated in the modalities of comfort and discomfort, pleasure and unpleasure. Accordingly, we subdivide the signal-scanning affects into those indicating unpleasure, such as anxiety, shame, guilt, disgust, sadness, helplessness and hopelessness, and those indicating pleasure, such as contentment, confidence, joy, pride and hope.

The *drive-discharge affects*, relatively speaking, show more discharge quality and less signal quality. The feeling state experienced and the ideational content are more directly the expression of drive seeking discharge. The felt affect achieves a climax and is then dissipated as the goal is achieved, or it is blocked if the underlying drive is incapable of fulfillment. In either case, the drive-discharge affect is then replaced by signal-scanning affects, pleasurable or unpleasurable, depending upon the ego's evaluation of the consequences of the drive seeking discharge. The discharge affects cannot, therefore, be classified as either pleasant or unpleasant, this being an ego judgment which is reflected by the appropriate signal-scanning affects, as when an angry feeling may on one occasion be associated with guilt or anxiety and on another with satisfaction. We classify the discharge affects in relation to the main drive tendencies, anger and rage being the affects of aggression, and love, affection, tenderness and sexual feelings being the affects of the libidinal drive. Hunger and thirst reflect more specific biological affect qualities, which may, however, become contaminated with other discharge affects. In addition, we may note the affects of partial or fused drives, such as envy, greed, impatience, stubbornness, sympathy, pity, etc.

The differentiated affects will be considered in more detail in Chapter XVIII.

REFERENCES

1. Engel, G. L.: Anxiety and Depression-Withdrawal, the Primary Affects of Unpleasure. To be published (Int. J. Psychoanal., *43*:1962).
2. Freud, S.: The Ego and the Id (1923). *In:* Standard Edition of the Complete Psychological Works of Sigmund Freud, vol. XIX. London, The Hogarth Press, 1961, pp. 3–63.
3. Hartmann, H.: Comments on the Psychoanalytic Theory of the Ego. *In:* Eissler, R. S. et al. (eds.): The Psychoanalytic Study of the Child. vol. 5. New York, International Universities Press, 1950, p. 74.
4. Hartmann, H.: Ego Psychology and the Problem of Adaptation (1939). New York, International Universities Press, 1958.
5. Hartmann, H. and Kris, E.: The Genetic Approach in Psychoanalysis. *In:* Freud, A. et al. (eds.): The Psychoanalytic Study of the Child, vol. 1. New York, International Universities Press, 1945.
6. Hartmann, H., Kris, E. and Loewenstein, R.: Comments on the Formation of Psychic Structure. *In:* Freud, A. et al. (eds.): The Psychoanalytic Study of the Child, vol. 2. New York, International Universities Press, 1946, p. 11.
7. Rapaport, D.: The Theory of Ego Autonomy: A Generalization. Bull. Menninger Clin., *22*:13, 1958.
8. Schmale, A. H. Jr.: Relationship of Separation and Depression to Disease. I. A Report on a Hospitalized Medical Population. Psychosom. Med., *20*:259, 1958.

CHAPTER XV

THE LATENCY PERIOD

The next phase of development, the so-called latency period, beginning at about age six, is marked by the growing importance of ego and the development of social relationships outside the family. It is the period when the early sexual conflicts and aggressive impulses are coming under the control of the ego within the framework of the cultural milieu in which the child lives. It is a phase during which intellectual growth and development are taking place and character structure is being established.

The reduction in manifestly sexual interests and activities during this time has led to the concept of a dichronous sexual development in humans, the first phase reaching its peak at around age four to six, and the second phase beginning at puberty; hence, the term "latency" for the intervening period. This apparent reduction of sexual interest probably does not have a biological basis. Although it is true that the sexual ambitions of the child in the oedipal period cannot achieve expression because of the taboos as well as the limitation imposed by anatomical and physiological immaturity, the apparent disappearance of overt sexual activity more likely is culturally determined. In those primitive cultures (specifically, in the Trobriand[8] and Marquesas Islands[5]) in which there is less restriction of sexual activity among children (except the incest taboo), such activity continues uninterruptedly throughout childhood and intercourse is frequently accomplished before puberty. Even in our culture sexual activities among children are not uncommon under certain circumstances, as when the Oedipus complex is not successfully controlled or when the group setting is permissive.

Hence, the latency period is a latent one only in a relative sense. The sexual drives, although latent, continue to press for discharge and to exert an influence on fantasy and behavior. Since the expectations of our culture call for complete subjugation of sexual activity by the child, however, overt sexual activity generally is considered to represent a deviation from the cultural norm. For the most part such activity during the six to twelve-year period is carried out in secret and often involves considerable internal struggle, with accompanying anxiety, guilt or shame. It includes solitary masturbation, with a wide range of sexual fantasies, most of which are forgotten; homosexual activity, usually mutual masturbation, less often oral or anal activity; sexual games, such as the "doctor" games where the body is examined; varieties of sexual curiosity, including peeping; and so forth. Children vary greatly in regard to how inhibited or how preoccupied they are with such activities, which for the most part remain at a pregenital level. In the culture which demands control of overt sexual activity, excessive preoccupation and activity at this age reflects poor ego function. In those primitive societies in which children are permitted to indulge in heterosexual activity (with due regard for the restrictions of exogamy), pregenital aims are less prominent and genital intercourse is said to be accomplished earlier.

The successful control of sexual and aggressive activities reflects the growing effectiveness of ego function in its role as moderator between, on the one hand, drives, and, on the other, reality as represented in the external environment and its internal representatives in the form of superego and ego ideal. Most important among the defenses is *repression*, which, when successful, operates to keep the unacceptable impulses from consciousness and from spilling over as overt behavior. For the most part the child is increasingly successful in controlling his impulses and conforming to expectations. Yet derivatives of unconscious activities do from time to time become conscious, especially in the form of daydreams, which, however, are usually sufficiently modified and changed as to be both acceptable and gratifying. Indeed, daydreaming is an important mental development of the latency period. It represents one way in which the child can deal with the problems of having to wait until he is bigger before he can have certain experiences and gratifications. Instead he enjoys fantasies in which he secretly indulges in the forbidden activities or acts out his ambitions in an exaggerated manner. Although in real life the child may deny any interest in the opposite sex (boys more so than girls) and would be ashamed to be discovered to have any such interest, in his secret fantasy this plays a significant role. The boy's fantasy of great feats of bravery and daring often includes in the background an admiring girl (mother ?), and the girl daydreams of her prince charming (father ?). These are often continuations of earlier fantasies which did manifestly include the parents and which also accompanied masturbation. The "family romance," a common daydream of this period, is one in which the child imagines that he is really not the child of his own parents, but of other parents, usually of a different social status. Another fantasy involves being an orphan who is free to gratify himself. Such fantasies provide ample means to experience in a disguised fashion both aggressive and sexual feelings toward the real parents.

The daydream represents an important stabilizing and maturational activity of ego during this period of development. In the daydream the child is able to enjoy gratifications and triumphs that in reality are denied him, either because they are forbidden or because he is not yet sufficiently developed to be able to achieve them. The taboo-determined fantasies are especially likely to undergo considerable modification under the influence of the superego so that the forbidden activity is no longer easily recognizable. In this we see the censoring operations of the ego, especially displacement and projection, making it possible for the child to enjoy his primary impulses by disguising them so well that he himself does not recognize them. In the fantasied sexual and/or aggressive act the subject or object or both are replaced by other figures or the acts themselves are modified so as to be no longer obviously sexual or aggressive. Such fantasies are usually enjoyed when the child is alone and they may be accompanied by masturbation. Occasionally such fantasies exceed even the bounds imposed by the child himself and he may then experience anxiety, guilt or shame. This may lead him to intensify his efforts at self control, especially when masturbation is also involved. At such times he experiences his own impulses as too strong, threatening to place him in a dangerous position. The wish seems as real as the act and he fears that his wishes will be known or discovered by others. In spite of this apparent disturbing feature, the daydreams involving taboo areas represent an important type of mental working through of what cannot be acted out in reality, and unless they so preoccupy the child as to preclude other activities they may be regarded as contributing to development. The very fact that the daydreams are progressively modified in order to be enjoyed in itself constitutes a gradual acceptance of the restrictions demanded by society. Gradually and over a period of time not only does the child become more and more able to differentiate between what is possible only in fantasy and what is permissible in reality but also the fantasies themselves more and more approximate reality. This process is especially evident in the less conflictful fantasies that occur in compensation for the limitations imposed by physical immaturity. In these the child imagines himself to be bigger, stronger, more skillful, etc., and takes as his models older children or adults. Eventually, what was possible only in fantasy does indeed become possible in reality. Here, again, the fantasy provides occasion for a kind of working through and practice which prepares the child for the eventual mastery. As successes are achieved self-confidence is enhanced, development is spurred, and the range of gratification within reality is greatly extended. The daydreaming of childhood thus may be seen as serving both defensive and constructive functions and helps to prepare the child for future reality. He can have some gratification, yet at the same time can test the fantasy against reality without committing himself to overt action.

CHARACTER FORMATION

As the child assumes more and more responsibility for his own behavior and learns what is expected of him, the various patterns of ego defense concerned with impulse control tend to become crystallized in characteristic ways for each child. He now begins to show habitual patterns of reacting to external as well as to internal demands. These patterns in the aggregate make up what is generally known as character. As one examines character structure one recognizes that the various types of psychic adaptation and ego defenses so far described all may contribute in various proportions, but now in more consistently sustained forms. The partial stabilization of the intrapsychic equilibrium that occurs in the latency period, with the ego activity suppressing many of the earlier pleasure-seeking impulses under the pressure of external reality and superego, gives rise to more or less characteristic patterns of behavior of the child. What appears as the overt behavior and manner of the child is an expression of this equilibrium and the characteristic ego mechanisms used. Usually a combination of ego mechanisms is used, though one or another may be more prominent in a particular child. Several new ego defenses achieve importance in the latency period and also contribute to character formation. These are *reaction formation, undoing* and *isolation,* all of which are related to the growing influence of superego.

Reaction Formation
This is the solidification of a rigid attitude or behavior which is the opposite of that which exists unconsciously. Now instead of repeated repression to deal with a dangerous impulse, the ego takes a "once and for all" definitive stand against the impulse or danger and thereafter presents the opposite facade. Reaction formation thus makes an important contribution to character formation, for it is responsible for certain consistent patterns of behavior and response. Occasionally, if the need to resist the pressure of drives is very great, whether because of the strength of the drives or because of external and superego influences, exaggerated character traits may result. For example, excessive cleanliness or orderliness may be a defense against the impulse to soil;

excessive kindness or compassion may be a defense against an impulse to cruelty; excessive generosity may be a defense against a wish to take; excessive aggressiveness may be a defense against the fear of passivity or dependence. These, then, become relatively inflexible patterns which tend at times to be inappropriate and unrealistic and constitute the basis for pathological consequences. Under normal circumstances reaction formation operates in a relative sense and is encouraged not only by the need for defense against impulse but also by the gratifications experienced when impulses are mastered and the child becomes able to fit satisfactorily in a social group.

Undoing

Since animistic thinking and concepts of magic rather than of logical causality are characteristic in children of this period, various types of magical gestures are often used by children to ward off forbidden impulses. Undoing is the corresponding ego defense whereby something positive is done which actually or magically is the opposite of the forbidden impulse and in that sense negates it. Certain oaths, vows, rituals and superstititions of children (as well as of adults) incorporate this principle. Examples are found in such activities as touching picket fences, stepping on cracks, etc., the idea in the child's mind being, "If I do so-and-so, something bad will happen to someone (a hostile impulse); if I do not, they will be safe," or vice versa. The ambivalence of such behavior is obvious. Underlying undoing are not only the more primitive concepts of black magic and white magic, but also more sophisticated concepts of atonement and recompense. Magic forestalls the evil consequences to oneself or to others of the tabooed drive; atonement punishes the self or indemnifies the other. In either case an attempt is made to undo or take back to avoid injury.

Isolation

This ego mechanism operates to keep apart thought and feeling. In its most flagrant form it permits a person to have, for example, a thought with an obviously hostile intent unaccompanied by the corresponding feeling of anger or hate, the cold, unemotional "I hate him." Isolation also takes the form of ritualistic behavior and thinking, which serve the same purpose. These may include rigorously ordered thinking or rituals which symbolically achieve this end, such as counting rituals, arrangements, etc. Isolation plays an important role in logical thinking. Since the meaning of words and symbols used in thought is often psychically overdetermined—a cigar, for example, potentially being a cigar, a smoke, rolled-up tobacco, a phallic symbol, etc.—a requirement for logical thinking is that one be able to concentrate on the relevant meaning of the word or thing and not be distracted by the affect that would accompany a sexually or aggressively charged symbolic meaning. Similarly, the rituals characteristic of isolation serve the purpose of interposing time or distance between things which must be kept apart lest their association evoke an unpleasant affect.

Identification

The ego mechanism has been discussed in earlier chapters, but it is of increasing importance in character formation during the latency period. To a considerable degree early character formation is already molded by the nature of the early object relations and the identifications with parental and other family figures. But as the child begins to emancipate himself from the family and to establish extrafamilial social relationships, other persons become important as objects for identification. This was mentioned earlier in reference to daydreaming, but it takes place also in the course of day to day experience. Teachers, counsellors, guides, older children, peers, neighborhood idols, more distant relatives and even public figures of the past and present come to constitute meaningful objects and thereby contribute to the multiple identifications which are so important in eventual character development.

THE SUPEREGO AND EGO IDEAL IN LATENCY

The latency period is characteristically a phase during which superego development and function assume great importance. As the child becomes more capable of fending for himself and consequently less dependent in a literal, physical sense on the parents, he at the same time becomes more dependent on their internalized influence in the form of the superego and ego ideal. No longer do the parents operate to so great a degree in a surrogate ego manner for the child, performing ego functions of which the child is not yet capable, as was true in infancy and early childhood. Now as the child ranges at a considerable distance from the parents, he carries their influence with him. But it is typical of these developments that the latency superego often tends to be more exacting and strict than the parents. In part this reflects the relative lack of confidence of the child in his ability to deal with his own impulses and in part it is a projection onto the parents of the child's own aggression, which now is turned against himself. Such exacting, often rigid, superego requirements play an important role in the consolidation of character structure which occurs during latency, particularly in the new ego defenses of reaction formation, isolation and undoing, all of which may, when extreme, be marked by stringent opposition to impulses and by techniques of self-punishment and atonement. One may truly say that moral character is being formed in the latency period. Yet the very rigidity of superego function at this age renders it less effective and less adaptable, with the result that the child repeatedly breaches or threatens to breach its barriers. He does not actually conform consistently to his own superego standards and hence periodically has to intensify his efforts again to be "good." Variations and inconsistencies in the demands and expectations of the parent may at times be important in such lapses. Indeed, the parent not infrequently unwittingly induces the child to act out his own (the parent's) forbidden wish and then punishes him for so doing.[4] A mother, for example, with strong impulses to soil and mess in retaliation against her own mother, reacted against such impulses in herself with an excessive need and demand for cleanliness. But she unconsciously manifested pride in her son's defiant messiness while at the same time punishing him severely. When exaggerated, this mechanism plays a role in some forms of delinquency. (See Chapter XXVIII.)

INTELLECTUAL DEVELOPMENT

Age six as the year to begin school was empirically arrived at, yet it coincides with the beginning of the latency period. With resolution of the conflicts of the early stages, not only is more energy available for learning, but also learning in itself has its gratifications. Some of this energy arises from a shift of attention away from the sexual object to nonsexual objects. In terms of ego mechanisms we see the gradual consolidation of defenses and a greater development of those ego functions concerned with learning, reason, judgment, integration and synthesis. These developments also assist the child further to postpone gratification and to block the tendency toward inappropriate activity or behavior. He literally now becomes more able to "think out" and to make judgments as to the meaning of his behavior. In other words, his understanding of reality is developing rapidly during these years. This process is aided by identification with the parents and with others in their nonsexual interests. Children who have not accomplished this may do poorly in school because of their persistent preoccupation with infantile sexual goals. Healthy children, meeting intellectual or other frustration, may revert to earlier activities (masturbation, finger or pencil biting, etc.). With favorable development gratifications revolve to a very large extent about achievement, learning, building, collecting, etc.

SOCIAL ADJUSTMENT

It is during the latency period that social adjustments beyond the confines of the intimate family circle are initiated and established. These include adjustment in school, neighborhood play groups, various social organizations such as scouting, camps, etc., and a general introduction into the varieties of social groupings and roles of children as well as of adults extant in the setting in which the child lives. In the course of such activities the child learns the "rules of the game" as prescribed by the group and by society. Further, although he comes to enjoy relationships that should be relatively free of the taboos and conflicts of the intrafamilial relationships, it is inevitable that he tends to project and transpose the same conflicts onto the new relationships. It is in the course of working through these new relationships that he also has new experiences that help him to learn that the world is not exactly as it appeared in the more restricted confines of the family. The characteristics and requirements of the particular social groups are helpful both in setting new boundaries and in opening new vistas. In these new settings he has the experience of living a variety of roles—the school child, the scout, the camper, the ball player, the follower, the leader, etc., in addition to the new roles that evolve at home. Through such role playing, which is contributed to by identification and interaction with others, new images of the self begin to emerge and new patterns of success and failure help to consolidate skills and provide tangible goals. With increasing self-confidence and with trust in others, the child is able to achieve greater independence from his parents and a greater opportunity for the development and application of his own talents and assets. But in spite of all the evident attempts to break away from the parents, the dependent needs still remain strong. The youngster still requires and yearns for the parents' encouragement, advice and approval, and suffers when it is withheld. When he meets frustration, a return to more infantile behavior is readily provoked. Enforced separation from a parent, as through death, illness or divorce, imposes a hardship with which the child is not yet ready to cope. Enforced dependency of the child, as might result from prolonged illness or from the parent's deliberate intent, also places serious barriers in the way of successful maturation. Such children are often excluded from their contemporaries' groups and have much difficulty in establishing identity and in cultivating social relations. In the years of latency, the child is likely to be peculiarly intolerant of another who displays the weaknesses and fears that he himself is trying to hide and overcome, and he therefore tends both to exclude and to attack such children. Scapegoatism is a common phenomenon at this age.

GANG FORMATION

Studies of boys' gangs have provided helpful insight into how the group structure reflects the distinctive psychology of latency and provides a setting in which individual psychological needs are handled.[7] Gangs organized by the boys themselves are the most revealing. They have the following characteristics:

1. The gang is essentially homosexual in composition. If girls are included, they have to be tomboys who can compete with the boys at their own level. The gang is often the scene of secret sexual play.

2. Contempt and hostility for the opposite sex is the accepted code of the gang. This is a means of repression of earlier sexual feelings for mother, since the manifest goal is to demean the object of the opposite sex.

3. There is a leader who does things first and who provides a counterbalance to the superegos of gang members. Being admired by the leader and by the group may outweigh the superego restrictions which come from the parents. What makes for leadership is a subject in itself.

4. There are various initiation rites which have as their purpose the overcoming of the castration threat and the reinforcement of the defenses against castration. He who can't "take it" is "a sissy," i.e., like a girl. To have successfully passed the initiation provides confidence in one's masculinity and permits a shift from passivity to activity, from the one being initiated (symbolically castrated) to the one who initiates.

5. An identification with adult gangs and groups is often a function of the gang formation, but the adult groups selected are frequently ones that are in opposition to the parental group. This is also a means of dealing with the threatening parents and of overcoming the castration threat. It provides a further illusion of strength and invulnerability.

6. There is an intense group loyalty within the gang with rigid adherence to the laws and mores of the gang, even when these customs are in opposition to the laws of the adult culture. This gives a feeling of strength to the boy who otherwise feels weak in his opposition to his parents. The strength he gains by merging his identity with the gang more than compensates for his feeling of relative weakness when alone.

7. The importance of being one of the gang is clear. To be excluded means to be weak, to be castrated. To belong gives strength and status.

8. The cruelty and sadism of the gang are regressive phenomena and represent a return to the earlier anal-sadistic level of organization, part of the result of having to give up phallic aims. Rituals and compulsions are prevalent at this period. The boys act out in sadistic play what they are unable to act out at a more adult sexual level. Their

pleasure in this cruel activity is striking. It is always directed at the weak, the eccentric, the deformed, the aged, etc.

The social milieu and the family situation of the boys have much to do in determining the character and the activities of their gang. It seems likely that there is a greater tendency to turn toward an independent gang when the family unit and its interrelationships are unstable, marked by intrafamily aggression, insecurity or sexual threat. Under such circumstances a boy finds greater protection and security within the gang, where aggressive impulses may remain at frankly sadistic levels and may be released in gang fights, sadistic attacks, etc. In gangs formed among boys with greater self-confidence and family security, aggression is more likely to be deflected into socially acceptable channels, such as feats of endurance and skill, athletic contests and other types of intergroup competition. Skillful use of the gang psychology by adult leaders provides a valuable avenue for further growth, development and maturation of children in the latency period.

Girls in the latency period do not show such a strong interest in gang formation except for those who persist in their masculine identification. Such girls may join the boys' gang or even form a rival gang that functions like a boys' gang. More often the girl at this age tends to be more docile, more dependent, and, if she is successfully identifying with a feminine mother, is enjoying more feminine activities, such as playing with dolls, homemaking, etc. Yet at other times much tomboyish behavior is evident. Girls' groups are much less cohesive and are not characterized by the strong group identifications so prominent among boys. Instead, close, intimate friendships with a few girls are likely to develop.

The latency period is thus only a period of relative latency, in contrast to the more tumultuous phallic phase and adolescence. There is tremendous push in the direction of intellectual and physical growth and development, but there is also an active struggle to deal with and master the unresolved problems of the earlier periods. The most striking change that occurs with the beginning of adolescence is a revival, in a new form, of many of these old problems.

REFERENCES

1. Bornstein, B.: On Latency. *In:* Eissler, R. S. et al. (eds.): The Psychoanalytic Study of the Child, vol. 6. New York, International Universities Press, 1951, p. 279.
2. Fenichel, O.: The Means of Education. *In:* Freud, A. et al. (eds.): The Psychoanalytic Study of the Child, vol. 1. New York, International Universities Press, 1945, p. 281.

3. Friedlander, R.: The Psychoanalytic Approach to Juvenile Delinquency. New York, International Universities Press, 1947, chapter 9.
4. Johnson, A. M. and Szurek, S. A.: Etiology of Antisocial Behavior in Delinquents and Psychopaths. J.A.M.A., *154*:814, 1954.
5. Mead, M.: From the South Seas: Studies of Adolescence and Sex in Primitive Societies. New York, William Morrow & Co., 1939.
6. Peller, L.: Reading and Daydreams in Latency: Boy-Girl Differences. J. Am. Psychoanalyt. A., *6*:57, 1958.
7. Redl, F.: The Psychology of Gang Formation and the Treatment of Juvenile Delinquents. *In:* Freud, A. et al. (eds.): The Psychoanalytic Study of the Child, vol. 1. New York, International Universities Press, 1945, p. 367.
8. Roheim, G.: Psychoanalysis and Anthropology. New York, International Universities Press, 1950.

CHAPTER XVI

ADOLESCENCE

Adolescence may be defined as the phase of psychological development during which full genital and reproductive maturity is reached. This period of psychological adjustment does not correspond precisely in time to the underlying biological phases, puberty and nubility. There are, for example, girls who menstruate before they reveal the beginning psychological changes of adolescence and girls who enter adolescence who have not yet begun to menstruate. *Puberty*, the first phase, extends from the first appearance of secondary sexual characteristics to the inception of reproductive capacity. *Nubility* is the period during which full reproductive potentiality is finally established. Among boys the secondary sexual characteristics, hair growth, genital growth, voice change, muscular development, etc., usually become evident between ages 12 to 14, while spermatogenesis with fertile sperm, the beginning of nubility, does not take place until ages 15 to 16. Among girls the onset of puberty is marked by the development of breasts and nipples, pubic hair, growth of internal and external genitalia and menarche. These changes occur between the ages of 11 to 14 years. The first menstrual periods appear at an average age of 13½ (range, 9 to 17 years) and ordinarily are anovulatory. On the average there is a lapse of two to four years after menarche before ovulation finally takes place and conception becomes possible. Accordingly, both the adolescent boy and girl are usually incapable of conception until after age 15 to 16, even though the girl may already have been menstruating for some time. Full reproductive capacity in the girl is not achieved for another two to four years after ovulation has been initiated.

These bodily changes presumably are secondary to developments in the central nervous system and mark also the maturation of the reproductive drive system within the nervous system. Neural or neurohumoral stimuli from the hypothalamus cause the secretion of gonadotrophic hormones by the anterior pituitary, resulting in gonadal development, increased secretion of sex hormones and their secondary effects on genital and bodily development. In the girl, puberty, including the menarche, is marked by a rise in follicle stimulating hormone (FSH) from the pituitary, and nubility appears with the secretion by the pituitary of interstitial cell stimulating hormone (ICSH), which, with FSH, permits the ovum to be shed and to pass into the uterus, the remaining follicular cells then forming the corpus luteum. Luteotrophin from the anterior pituitary induces the secretion of progesterone from the corpus luteum, and it is this hormone which prepares the endometrium for nidation. A discussion of the influence on behavior of the hormonal changes of the menstrual cycle will be reserved for a later chapter (XXI).

These biological changes have a profound influence on psychic development, making adolescence a period of considerable upheaval. Although, as we have already discussed, certain preparatory sexual developments had been taking place during the preceding years, the adolescent now has at his disposal the necessary apparatus for the completion of the sexual act. This in itself contributes a new drive quality to psychic activity, namely, a genital sexual drive, which must come under the control of the ego. Genital responses must not be permitted to occur without the individual's consent, so to speak. With the appearance of these changes, the balance established during the latency period is again threatened. The conflicts of the phallic period are now revived with renewed intensity and must be resolved. Earlier, however, the ego was helped in its struggle by outside forces, particularly the controlling influence of the parents, which was dictated by the continuing dependent needs of the child, for whom the parents remained appropriate objects for the satisfaction of many dependent needs. In adolescence, relative emancipation from the parents and a greater measure of autonomy and independent function must be achieved; therefore, the youngster has to rely to a much greater degree on his own controls. Those internalized controls which had developed in relationship with and on the model of the parents are jeopardized for the very reason and to the extent that they are derived from the parents' influence. A different kind of relationship with the parents is called for, one in which the old sexual components are once and for all eliminated. With the revival of the strong sexual drives and the development of genital potential, the parents can no longer occupy the same role as objects; hence, new objects must be found, both for the satisfaction of dependent needs, and, of course, for the satisfaction of sexual needs. The adolescent, therefore, has to give up his former dependency on the parents, because it now is threatening to him.

THE ADOLESCENT BOY

The boys' puberty and corresponding physical development lag behind those of the girl. When puberty begins he is still mainly oriented toward the peer group, the boys' gang. The first stirrings of puberty are not manifested in genital terms and are not yet directed toward girls, who at the same age are more fully developed and often taller. Instead, there is first an intensification of pregenital strivings, expressed in increased motility in the form of physical restlessness and fidgeting, in oral greediness, in anal and sadistic activities, dirty language, disregard of cleanliness, etc. Rebelliousness and lack of submission to the parents, shame and embarrassment in response to displays of parental affection, and increased rivalries with peers are prominent. Within the peer group the boy is often boastful and exhibitionistic and may even begin to brag about his sexual knowledge or precocity. This sexual talk, however, is still largely pregenital. It is a manifestation of the need for self-glorification, a pregenital aim of phallic origin. In brief, during this early phase of puberty the genital impulses are strongly resisted, while pregenital drives are intensified. Gradually, however, more manifestly erotic heterosexual inclinations appear, and the character of the peer group begins to undergo a subtle change. In the largely homosexual façade that characterized the latency period, a crack develops as one boy acknowledges or demonstrates a genuine interest in girls. At first this is regarded as a breach of loyalty and this boy is subjected to kidding and taunts while at the same time he is being envied. The nature of the kidding itself betrays the latent wishes of the other boys, who have not yet mastered the anxiety of breaching this group taboo. This type of kidding is a trademark of adolescence and is a means of dealing with anxiety. The blush betrays the latent yet unacceptable wish. Both boys and girls, however, cling to the advantages of group identification. The boys "hunt in packs" and the girls band together for flirtatious forays. They boast to their own group of their own exploits (often imaginary) with the opposite sex, and they set themselves apart from the parent groups by dress, manners, speech, customs, etc. Curiosity and exhibitionistic behavior are rampant, but the underlying anxiety about the first sexual experience is clearly revealed by the nature of the group activity, which, in the beginning, at least, often effectively pre vents any such experience. Similarly, the need to get away from the parents and from the parents' scrutiny is evident, yet the controlling influence of the parents may be essential to avert too impulsive action.

The preliminary struggle of the adolescent boy before he is able to deal with his genital strivings in a heterosexual manner also reflects the revival of the earlier castration anxiety which marked the phallic period of earlier years. For a while the boy is acutely aware of his masculine inadequacy in comparison to older men, a situation reminiscent of the earlier rivalry with father. But he also sees women (mother) as dangerous, even potentially castrating figures. It is of interest in this regard that many societies, especially primitive societies, have highly structured initiation rites for the pubescent boy, marking the transition from boyhood to manhood. For the most part these rites involve a disruption of the dependent relationship with the mother, a symbolic castration and an assumption of some symbol of identity with the father and the adult male group. Following successful initiation, which is always an ordeal, the boy is formally regarded as having been inducted into the role of mature male with all the privileges and responsibilities thereof. In Western culture such rites are not formalized, yet there is a sequence of experiences which serve essentially the same purpose, such as the Bar Mitzvah, initiation into clubs and fraternities, examinations and graduation, induction into military service, etc. All of these are transitional experiences whereby the boy bit by bit comes to assume his role as an adult male, identifying with and eventually succeeding his parental counterpart. Some of the anxiety commonly associated with such experiences, especially when inappropriate, has its origin in the separation and castration anxiety episodes of earlier childhood.

The development of genital maturity takes place over an extended period of time and is marked by increasing heterosexual play, alternating with masturbation with heterosexual fantasy. For some time this sexual play falls short of intercourse, and for the most part it is quite self-centered, an exploratory or "practice" sexual activity in which the boy tests his capacity for arousal and control and his ability to attract and arouse the girl. But he does not yet have genuine interest in the girl as a person or as a reproductive partner. Although such boy-girl relationships may be very intense, they tend to be transient and superficial. The girl sought after often is either one who will enhance the boy's prestige in the group because of her beauty and popularity or one who gives promise of fulfilling a wish for sexual experience. Marriages contracted during this period, for whatever reason, often are doomed to failure because of the inadequate basis of the object choice for the long haul of a life-long relationship. Eventually, however, as the boy successively and successfully works through these transitional stages, he achieves the capacity for full genital maturity and object relationship.

THE ADOLESCENT GIRL

The beginnings of puberty in the girl are not marked by as spectacular developments as occur in the boy because the girl has already turned away from the mother in respect to the pregenital strivings and is aspiring toward a more independent role. In latency this had been achieved by assuming the role of the tomboy or of the independent little girl, in both instances the love object being a close girl friend. With the onset of puberty, the girl defends herself against a regressive pull toward the pre-oedipal mother by more manifest and active heterosexual interests. Such behavior, however, is not yet truly feminine in its aim. In general, it is either directed toward the less developed boys, who are not yet a real threat and toward whom the girl can safely behave aggressively, or it remains at a fantasy level with inaccessible men, often figures of the day. This aggressive heterosexual play-acting generally goes on under the protecting shadow of a warm and confiding relationship with another adolescent girl with whom secrets are shared. It serves the dual purpose of resisting a regression to dependence on the mother and of helping to turn her budding sexual interest away from the father. For the girl in early puberty, too great attachment to the mother is an obstacle to a desire to grow up and is a greater danger to future development than is attachment to the father (Deutsch[1]).

The girl generally welcomes the physical changes of puberty and she begins to devote more attention to grooming and appearance, a source of self-satisfaction not yet used too freely as a means of sexual attractiveness. She is beginning to assume a physical identity as a woman, setting her apart both from the little girl and from the boy. Breast development in particular is for some girls at last an outward physical attribute of femaleness, comparable to the penis as the boy's anatomical badge of masculinity.

As puberty develops the girl loosens her ties with her girl friends and turns more to boys. This reflects an important struggle for the girl, whether her ultimate object choice will be homosexual or heterosexual. Because of the strong, unconscious ties to the mother, the woman maintains a stronger bisexual tendency than does the man. This is evident in the fact that girls in early adolescence are more willing to stress their masculinity than boys are to acknowledge femininity, to them a source of shame. Normally the early homosexual ties of girls dissolve slowly; girls often go through a phase of crushes on older, inaccessible women as they become detached from their peer-age girl friends.

Girls do not easily relate their genital organs to their yearning for love and more than boys keep apart their psychological and somatic tensions. They more often carry out masturbation or experience somatic sensations without appreciating their sexual nature; quite different is the boy's experience of erection and ejaculation as obviously sexual.

As heterosexual feelings intensify, negative attitudes develop toward both mother and father. The father in particular loses his charm and attractiveness and is no longer regarded with admiration. Indeed, quite intensely antithetical feelings may develop. The girl now is inclined to avoid her father's bodily atmosphere, which may even seem disgusting. She progressively detaches herself from both father and mother and preoccupies herself with fantasies of her future as a woman. Or she may turn her activity to reality by engaging in many experiences with boys, which also serve the purpose of trying out her sexual capacities and responsiveness. Eventually, she comes to a resolution of her conflicts and emerges into the full blossom of mature womanhood.

THE EGO OF THE ADOLESCENT

The decisive issues psychologically in adolescence relate to the biological maturation of the genital and reproductive drive systems on the one hand and to the necessity for object change on the other. These processes place a great demand on ego function if the transition from childhood to adulthood is to be accomplished successfully. It must be recalled that ego development, to begin with, was greatly influenced by the nature and effectiveness of early object relations. Further, in the course of childhood it was necessary to control certain pregenital drives directed toward the parental objects in order to maintain the relationship and assure basic needs. These pregenital drives were not eliminated; they were repressed, inhibited or toned down during the latency period. They continued to exist in the form of unconscious fantasies and their disguised conscious derivatives. They were not abandoned but were simply postponed under the exigencies of the moment. That they contributed importantly to learning how to love and be loved in the full sense is revealed by the barrenness and poverty of the relationships and the defective capacity to love commonly found among persons whose early childhood was marked by interrupted or inadequate affectionate relationships with consistent parental figures. This may also be true among higher animals, for infant monkeys brought up exclusively with a cloth model of a mother as a substitute for a live mother prove incapable of mating upon reaching adulthood (Harlow[6]).

With the development of biological maturity, the heretofore controlled sexual impulses receive a powerful impetus and the adolescent is threatened with the danger of both revived pregenital and new genital impulses being directed toward the old objects. This is experienced psychically not so much in terms of a real, conscious danger, but more in terms of a danger of being overwhelemed by intense inner feelings, often accompanied by confusion about the self: "Who am I?", "What am I here for?", etc. Such confusion reflects the need to establish an identity freed from its earlier origins in the parental objects. This disruption of the earlier established and relatively stable ego defenses calls for the development of new ego activities to cope with these changes and to reachieve a new status. Old issues are reopened and must be settled. This takes time, actually a matter of years, and accounts for the fact that adolescence normally is marked by turmoil and upset, sometimes of such magnitude that it is difficult to distinguish normal from pathological adolescence. These upheavals are the external indications that internal adjustments are in progress, that the temporary preliminary balance of latency is being abandoned so that adult sexuality can be integrated into the individual's personality. Tranquility during adolescence may mean that the youngster has built up excessive defenses so that he remains wrapped up with his family, considerate and submissive. Such an individual may achieve tranquility at the cost of not "growing up."

Anna Freud has categorized eight ego patterns typically utilized in adolescence as means of defense against infantile object ties and against pregenital and genital impulses:[3,4]

1. The adolescent attempts to detach himself from his infantile objects and to displace his feelings to other persons and interests. This involves an object loss and to some degree requires the work of mourning (see Chapter XXVI), a process, however, which is facilitated by the discomfort of the conflict involved in retaining old objects. Normally this takes place gradually, though not smoothly. Sometimes it takes place abruptly, essentially a flight, leaving the youngster for the moment with a passionate longing for other relationships. Under such circumstances there is strong likelihood that the identical (but unrealistic, since they are still pregenital) wishes will be transferred to parent substitutes (provided these persons seem to the adolescent to be diametrically opposite in manner, culture, etc., to the original parents) or to ideal leaders or contemporaries. The new allegiance is strikingly overemphasized, as is the detachment from the parents, and it is this exaggeration which marks it as a defensive action rather than a healthy progression to new relationships. So detached from the parents, the youngster then feels free to act out both aggressive and sexual impulses outside the family, acting out which may range from harmless to idealistic, dissocial or even antisocial behavior. The success or failure of this technique of defense in terms of maturation is determined by the degree to which the aims change from what existed originally in relation to the early objects. When they are carried over essentially in their infantile pregenital form to the new objects, the same conflicts will persist and the consequence may well be unsuccessful adjustment or illness later in life.

2. When the adolescent does not succeed in displacing his libidinal attachment from the parents, the ego response may be to reverse the feelings, to turn love into hate, dependence into revolt, respect and

admiration into contempt and derision. This may occur normally from time to time in any adolescent, but some adolescents utilize such devices in a sweeping manner. Such adolescents imagine themselves to be free, but actually they remain as securely tied as ever to their parents and to their great distress and suffering continue the same struggle within the family circle. They do not actually move away from the parents, but instead linger as hostile, belligerent, irritating youngsters, rationalizing their behavior and projecting their hostility by claiming that they feel and act as they do because of the controlling and hostile behavior of the parents. Even when the latter is true, it is still likely to be exaggerated. In some cases this aggression may instead be turned on the self, resulting in depressive, self-destructive and even suicidal consequences.

3. Another ego device for dealing with the frustration which arises when feelings are detached from the parents but not successfully invested in substitute objects is to direct the feelings to the self (narcissism). Earlier disposition toward withdrawal and narcissistic attitudes predisposes to such a development. Again, this may occur from time to time in the normal adolescent but it constitutes a pathological process when it becomes a pervading feature of the adolescent's mental life. Such a process may be manifested by inflated ideas of strength, beauty or power, by fantasies of unlimited achievement or popularity, or of great suffering and sacrifice (the latter when the superego is strong), or by excessive preoccupation with the body in terms of appearance, blemishes, odors, awkwardness or unpleasant body sensations (hypochondriasis).

4. Regression, from time to time and to a minor degree in normal adolescence and in a prolonged and sweeping manner in pathological adolescence, is another important ego defense. Such periodic retreats to the infantile objects ordinarily serve a function in temporarily reestablishing ties and are also useful in cushioning the separation experience for the adolescent as well as for the parents. Some adolescents, however, under the pressure of anxiety, retreat to early childhood techniques of relating, especially primary identification with the object. As a consequence they often suffer some degree of confusion in their ability to distinguish the self from objects, and they tend to project their thoughts and feelings onto the object. Further, they use identification excessively as a means of relating, altering their own personality to conform to someone else's, rather than developing their own identity. Some adolescents carry this regression to identification so far as the main means of relating that they achieve little identity of their own, utilizing instead the borrowed (and unstable) identities of others. They forever seem to demand information from the outside to "know" who they are, and they function "as if" they are first one person and then another. Their goals are fluid and shift as they assume one pseudo-

identity after another. In the more severe examples of regression serious disturbances in reality testing may result. These may be manifest in a state of confusion or an inability to distinguish between the internal and external world. Primary identification as a method of dealing with early object ties is temporarily effective because it substitutes "being like" for "liking." Instead of relating to objects and experiencing all the associated feelings, these adolescents try to be like the object, but as a result they live a very impoverished and unsatisfying life, since they do not actually experience real affection for or from the object of identification. By controlling their feelings so extensively they come to experience any intense feeling as threatening their self-image, as was true in early childhood when the distinction between self and objects was not easily maintained under stress. But in contrast to the small child, they can no longer readily turn to the parent for support and hence are in danger of social isolation.

Defenses may also be directed against the impulses themselves rather than or as well as against the early object ties, as illustrated in the following types.

5. The inhibited, shy adolescent attempts to postpone development by repressing and denying pregenital and genital strivings and by maintaining a dependent relationship with the parents. This reaction may actually be encouraged by a parent who is reluctant to relinquish ties with the offspring. In such instances the youngster attempts to retain the ties by giving up the impulses.

6. Among some adolescents there is an antagonism toward impulses which far surpasses in intensity anything in the way of repression ordinarily seen. It resembles the asceticism of religious fanatics. These youngsters mistrust enjoyment in general, and counter more urgent desires with more stringent prohibitions. This may begin with the instinctual wish proper and then extend even to the most ordinary physical needs. Such individuals may renounce any impulse which even remotely savours of sexuality. They may avoid their peers and all their activities and interests, such as music, dancing, teen-age clothing, etc. This asceticism may even extend to involve repudiation of protection against the weather, limitation of food, drink and sleep, and postponement of urination and defecation as long as possible. When of such magnitude it approaches psychotic behavior. Usually, however, such periods of asceticism are countered by sudden swings in the opposite direction, to excesses in an attempt at restitution. Such extreme ascetic behavior expresses a blind fear of all instinctual activities, an abandonment of all pleasure except masochistic pleasure. Fortunately it is usually a transient phenomenon.

7. Certain adolescents develop an insatiable interest in abstract subjects. They gather together for erudite discussions of all varieties of philosophical problems. But a gross disparity exists between the

idealistic views expressed by the adolescents and their actual behavior. What they engage in is a thinking-over of the instinctual conflict, not so much as preparation for action as a means of avoiding (deferring) action. The nature of the arguments and of the subjects discussed reflects the conflict within the youngsters' mental apparatus. It becomes a means of surmounting the danger until the individual is ready to engage himself more actively in life. This over-intellectualization may, in some cases, persist and effectively paralyze activity thereafter. Again, this may merge into a psychotic state.

8. Adolescents commonly deal with both impulses and early object ties by taking uncompromising positions on both practical and idealistic grounds. They stand up for their ideas. They take pride in their moral, aesthetic and ethical principles, and they refuse to make concessions to their elders, whom they see as lacking in standards and principles. In such respects these adolescents may be more controlled in their behavior and more exacting of themselves in maintaining self-imposed standards than are their elders or peers. This may be particularly glaring when the parents actually do have lax standards, and it represents a resistance by the adolescents against identification with the parents, often because of a fear of the intensity of their own impulses were they to be like the parents.

Emphasis properly has been placed on the defense aspects of ego functioning in adolescence, but these must still be recognized as stabilizing influences which, if effective, make possible further development and maturation. As is true throughout development, periods of relative tranquility are necessary for the individual to be free to interact with the environment, to learn, to synthesize his experiences, to experiment, to test, to create, etc. The ego defenses assure such periods of relative peace, and although from time to time the results may be distressing and upsetting to others or even pathological, from the point of view of the adolescent they should be seen as potentially useful ways of regaining and maintaining mental stability. When successful, they become integrated with other defenses and enable the adolescent to deal in his own good time with the two basic tasks, detachment from early objects and reproductive maturation. The typical inconsistency of the adolescent reflects the alternation between fighting against and trying out his impulses, being dependent on and revolting against his parents. In each phase he is consolidating constructive experience which allows him to progress toward the adult structure of personality.

THE CONSCIENCE (SUPEREGO) OF THE ADOLESCENT

Derived from the standards, expectations, prohibitions and restrictions of the parents and designed to guide the behavior of a child, not an adolescent or adult, the childhood superego must undergo major modification in the course of adolescence. Many standards so internalized prove to have lasting value and meaning, but much of what acquired for the child the value judgments of good and bad, permissible and forbidden, was so categorized in terms of the realities of childhood. With the advent of adolescence standards must change. Some activities forbidden to the child now begin to be acceptable while others permissible for a child become inadmissible. The adolescent struggles with these changing standards and periodically suffers guilt when he questions whether it is all right to do what he had earlier been forbidden to do and shame when he does what earlier had been acceptable but now no longer is age-compatible or fails to do what is age-appropriate. The development of new standards, more independent of the standards derived from the parents, is not easily accomplished since this is taking place at a time when the youngster has to depend more on his own internal resources. In his attempts to break away from the parents and at the same time to remain intact, the adolescent actually may become for the moment more rigid and exacting than even the parents expect. As he assays his new roles, tests out his new sexual urgings, he may find a very narrow margin between feeling guilty for indulging in previously forbidden activities and ashamed for not trying or succeeding. Group sanctions become a force of major importance in overcoming these obstacles and in aiding the progress toward greater independence of conscience. Through peer group discussions and activities the adolescent is able to achieve a modification of his internalized standards. But this is still a transitional phase to the formation of the mature superego, and in order to accomplish this, the adolescent again temporarily depends on outside influences as sanctions change. Eventually, these too become internalized and constitute part of the evolving identity of the adolescent.

THE DEVELOPMENT OF IDENTITY IN THE ADOLESCENT[2]

One of the important features of adolescence is the development of an identity. Many of the characteristics of adolescent behavior are understandable in terms of the attempt to establish an identity that is not so dependent on the preceding identifications of childhood. As already described, the early object relations contribute through identification to the development of ego and superego and to the concept of the self. With the necessity to break away from the parental and other family figures and to adjust in a broader social context, the adolescent suffers a disruption of his earlier image of himself. This is characterized by varying degrees of introspective ruminations about his role, destiny and identity, about life and death: "Why are we here?", etc. It may also be manifested in rapidly shifting, superficial identifications, borrowed identities, so to speak, in which the adolescent behaves "as if" he is first like one person and then another. These are usually persons for whom he rapidly develops tremendous admiration and he wants nothing more than to be like them, only soon thereafter to acquire an entirely different idol and assume a different role. Eventually, as the adolescent has successes of his own in school, in work, in social relations, etc., his own identity begins to emerge. It includes the successful identifications of earlier life, but these must undergo modification and resynthesis. Erikson emphasizes that the adolescent process is conclusively complete only when the childhood identifications are subordinated to a new kind of identification developing in the course of social relationships and competitive apprenticeship with and among age-mates. He contrasts the playfulness of childhood and the experimental zest of youth underlying the earlier identifications with the "dire urgencies" of the new identifications, which force the adolescent into serious choices and decisions, leading to more final self-definitions, roles and life commitments. Higher education, job apprenticeship and other kinds of training experiences are some of the ways in which society sanctions intermediary periods between childhood and adulthood, during which such crucial decisions can be worked over before finally being settled ("psychosocial moratoria," according to Erikson). It is during such periods that the adolescent more or less settles a place for the future, blocks out a pattern of inner identity to be completed and a schedule for its accomplishment. It no longer is possible to speculate about or play with the wonder of what it will be like "when I grow up." It is no longer a game or fantasy which can be abandoned at will. This process goes on unconsciously and consciously and it still receives strong impetus from forces and influences originating in earlier childhood. It does not represent nearly the break or discontinuity with earlier life that it sometimes seems to. On the contrary, it involves a "sense of inner continuity and social sameness which will bridge what he *was* as a child and what he is *about to become*, and will reconcile his *conception of himself* and his *community's recognition* of him" (Erikson[2]). The community's responses to the adolescent's need to be recognized by those around him are of great importance, for it is through these responses that the adolescent is able to develop his capacity for work and occupation, to extend his roles into wider sections of society, at the same time maintaining ego defenses against the intense impulses invested in a mature genital apparatus and powerful muscular system. This turning toward and receiving from society, as compared to the earlier transaction with family objects, marks the end of the usefulness of identification as an ego mechanism in the service of growth and development (though it remains useful as a defense). Now it is recognition and acceptance by society, as variously represented by subsocieties and key individuals, which becomes the crucial influence in determining how the individual sees himself and wants to see himself. The community has various institutionalized devices for giving such recognition and at the same time for being recognized by the individual, but it may reject him if he does not seem to care to be recognized. The family moves to the sidelines. They may share their offspring's satisfaction in being recognized by the community but they no longer are the major source of such recognition. Mere recognition by the parent no longer suffices. The youngster who continues to look primarily to and be regulated by the parents' standards, wishes and expectations in his search for identity will not easily achieve it, if he achieves it at all. The earlier identifications upon which such goals were based must be modified and changed and even given up if he is to find his own unique place in a changing society. When fully developed, identity implies a clear picture of oneself as an individual operating within and belonging to a group. This is a mutual and social relationship in which one not only is able to sustain a sense of constancy, consistency and sameness while operating within the group, but also is able to do this while sharing and giving of oneself to the group. This capacity to share with and to merge into the group without threat to or loss of the sense of personal identity, to feel a part of the group, to have a well-defined role, to have function and status, to be responded to and given recognition, marks the attainment of mature adulthood as compared to adolescence. Many adults do not achieve this, as we shall see later.

THE PARENTS OF THE ADOLESCENT

It is well known that the experience of adolescence may be as disrupting for the parents as for the adolescent himself. Some parents have difficulty in tolerating the efforts of the adolescent to detach himself and feel the loss intensely. Especially do they suffer when the process of detachment is marked by the kinds of aggressive, hostile behavior described earlier. Other parents are sexually stimulated by their adolescent son or daughter, a feeling which may come to consciousness with shock and dismay. In this respect the parent must go through some of the same struggles against impulse and suffer the same need to detach himself as does the adolescent, though this usually takes place on a lesser scale. The growing adolescent may also serve as a disturbing warning of the parent's impending decline in sexual attractiveness, vigor and strength, leading mothers to compete unrealistically with their daughters and fathers with their sons. Other parents may with varying success try to utilize the adolescence of their children for their own vicarious gratifications.

Most parents successfully weather their children's adolescence, but these examples suffice to illustrate some of the sources of difficulty that may render the experience of adolescence stormy for some parents.

REFERENCES

The papers by Anna Freud and by Erikson are especially valuable sources of material on adolescence, including the pathology of adolescence, which is not dealt with in this chapter.

1. Deutsch, H.: The Psychology of Women. New York, Grune & Stratton, 1944, vol. 1, pp. 1–149.
2. Erikson, E. H.: The Problem of Ego Identity. J. Am. Psychoanalyt. A., 4:56, 1956.
3. Freud, A.: Ego and Mechanisms of Defense. New York, International Universities Press, 1946, chapter 12.
4. Freud, A.: Adolescence. In: The Psychoanalytic Study of the Child, vol. 13. New York, International Universities Press, 1958, p. 255.
5. Friedlander, K.: The Psychoanalytical Approach to Juvenile Delinquency. New York, International Universities Press, 1947, chapter 10.
6. Harlow, H.: The Heterosexual Affectional System in Monkeys. Am. Psychologist, Jan. 1962.
7. Josselyn, I. M.: The Adolescent and His World. New York, Family Service Association of America, 1952.
8. Lorand, S. and Schneer, H. I. (eds.): Adolescents. Psychoanalytic Approach to Problems and Therapy. New York, Paul B. Hoeber, Inc., 1961.
9. Montagu, M. F. A.: The Reproductive Development of the Female. New York, Julian Press, Inc., 1957.

CHAPTER XVII

ADULTHOOD:
THE MENTAL APPARATUS

Adulthood, in the physical sense, roughly corresponds to the attainment of full growth and development. The absence of further change in stature, however, obviously does not mean that change does not continue to take place; change continues, but at a different rate and of a different character. The biological processes of aging from the beginning of adult life into senescence remain an almost unexplored area. Psychologically, the successful transition from adolescence to adulthood represents only the beginning of a new developmental phase. It cannot be regarded as an end stage, although obviously the rates of change are considerably slower than what we observed earlier. Indeed, in Chapters XIX and XX we shall consider a number of what might be called normative developmental crises in the course of adult life, such as courtship, marriage, child-bearing, parenthood, job achievement, role changes, menopause, etc. The life of the adult is thus influenced by past development, by the biological changes occurring in the course of adulthood, and by the vicissitudes of current life experience.

The concept of maturity has always been a confusing one. By convention we have come to regard the adult as physically mature as compared to the child. In one sense this is correct, but it seems more in keeping with the facts of growth and development to establish a range of maturity for each age period, as well as to specify what systems we are referring to. Thus, one may be more or less mature at birth, at one year, five years, ten years, twenty years or at fifty years, or one may be mature in the sense of some physical attribute at twenty years but immature in the sense of some psychological attributes at the same age. In subsequent chapters we shall consider the developmental phases of the adult man and woman and indicate some of the ranges of behavior appropriate at each level (Chapters XIX and XX). Before that, however, we shall consider in general terms how the function and organization of the mental apparatus of the adult differ from those of the child and adolescent.

THE EGO

The distinguishing characteristic of the mental apparatus of the adult is the relative dominance and autonomy of the ego. The mental developments described in the preceding chapters involve in essence the acquistion of a relatively effective internal regulatory system to handle and integrate the input from both the internal environment (drives) and the external environment (reality). This development is evident in the following respects:

1. The adult shows a good capacity to delay action. He can, better than the child, use thought, self-examination and self-judgment in dealing with the pressures of drives and the influences of the environment. He can call upon the resources of past experience from which he can synthesize new ideas and make a judgment as to the proper course, timing and character of his action. This means that he now has the potential capacity to carry out the right action at the right time with maximum effectiveness and to learn from his errors. The degree to which an individual is capable of this capacity is one measure of ego strength.

2. Because of a better developed sense of personal identity, he not only has a clearer conception of himself and his own needs but also has the capacity to understand and respond to the needs of others. A clear self-identity permits an appreciation of the identity of others. As will be discussed further, the intactness of the psychic self, experienced in terms of self-identity, self-confidence and a capacity to tolerate deprivation of the sources of supply for the self is an important determinant of psychic as well as physical health (cf. Chapters XXV and XXVII).

3. The development of a sense of reality means that the person no longer functions as if a wish in itself could bring about a satisfaction or as if a need for a satisfaction guaranteed the satisfaction. He relinquishes the childhood concept that symbolic actions by themselves necessarily can bring about satisfaction and that persons in the environment can be influenced in the same manner that one can influence or utilize one's own body. Symbols and words are used in thought and feeling and are not equated with objects. In other words, there is a

diminished tendency to use techniques of magic and omnipotence. The ability to identify, characterize, categorize and utilize what exists in the environment and to differentiate such objects and phenomena from each other and from the mental experiencing of them is now well developed. The beginnings of this capacity were identified in the second year of life by Piaget (Chapter VIII).

4. The adult has a considerable capacity to tolerate tension and discomfort. Past success in problem-solving and the fact that many other painful or difficult situations in the past have been overcome or pass by themselves, provide a quality of confidence and hope which permits such tolerance.

5. The confidence and the capacity to maintain contact with reality and to maintain control over the drives underlie the capacity for love, full sexual enjoyment, work and play. In addition, they permit the periodic abandonment of reality in the form of fantasies, play, joking, humor, etc., all of which can be tolerated as well as enjoyed because of the certain knowledge of one's capacity to terminate such activities at will.

6. The utilization of defense mechanisms is adaptive and reality-oriented. Although all the mechanisms previously described continue to be used, they can be more readily challenged by the requirements of reality, and thought and behavior can be modified accordingly. The principle of economy tends to facilitate the re-utilization of previously used ego mechanisms preferentially, but the adult ego is more able to recognize discrepancies and failures and to develop new techniques to deal with stress or to solve problems. Actually, for the most part the old mechanisms are perfectly useful and their manifestation in a fairly characteristic way for each individual serves in good measure to identify his character structure. How each of these defense mechanisms operates in the adult will now be described briefly:

REPRESSION.   It is inevitable that a large part of psychic activity remains subject to permanent repression, even in the healthy adult. The chaotic, pleasure-seeking impulses of the Id cannot be permitted access to consciousness indiscriminately, not only because they are incompatible with the requirements of reality, but also because they would interfere with and disorganize the smooth functioning of the mental processes required in daily life. The largest part of what is repressed early in life remains under repression, and under most circumstances there is no need for this status to be changed. It is mainly when the repressions of early life are of such a character and of such a magnitude as to interfere with later reality testing and reality adjustment that symptoms may develop later in life. The successful accomplishment of the developmental work of adolescence permits the lifting of repressions as they concern many activities and objects which previously came under the sweeping taboos related to the Oedipus complex. This will be elaborated later on when we discuss the object relations and the instinct expression of the adult.

DENIAL. Since it is directed against the external world, denial plays a much smaller role than repression in the mature person. Nonetheless, all adult persons use denial. They tend to avoid painful external reality until it has to be coped with. The necessity to carry on "life as usual" when confronted by all sorts of difficult, painful or tragic events in the world around us, especially when such events cannot be controlled or influenced by us, requires that they be excluded from our sphere of consciousness much of the time. In the same manner we are able to block out or minimize a wide variety of disturbing or disrupting stimuli that impinge upon us from the outside in order that we can proceed without distraction with whatever we are doing. Such stimuli may include potentially uncomfortable or unpleasant body sensations arising from environmental conditions or internal changes. They may also include affects and symptoms of illness. Ordinarily such denial does not take place at the expense of reality testing, so that if reality adjustment requires it, that which is being denied can fairly readily be brought to the attention of the individual.

INTROJECTION. This primitive, orally-derived defense whereby an object is dealt with by being symbolically ingested plays a relatively small role in the adult. The chief circumstance under which it may be observed transiently is in response to object loss, when a temporary regression may take place, reactivating the tendency to replace the lost object in a manner more characteristic of infancy and early childhood (see also Chapter XXVI).

IDENTIFICATION. This intrapsychic process whereby one takes on the qualities or characteristics of objects already represented intrapsychically also is less prominent in the adult than in the child. In the child it operates more in the service of development than of defense. In the adult it is more likely to be a defense, usually utilized during periods of real, threatened or fantasied losses, or in reaction to a threatening object, in relation to which the individual feels relatively depleted or weak.

IDENTITY FORMATION. This is a process whereby one progressively adds to one's concept of oneself during successes and failures in many different roles by virtue of mutual interactions and transactions with other persons and groups. Usually contributing to continuing psychological growth and development, it may also operate as a defense mechanism, since the sense of identity adds considerably to the capacity to deal with pressures, whether they arise from within or from without (see Chapter XVI).

PROJECTION. To some degree, the adult continues to project to the outside that which is felt as unacceptable or undesirable. This is revealed by the fact that a person often sees another's faults more clearly than his own, or more readily notes another's hostility than his own. But again, the adult is more able to subject this to reality testing when it is important to do so.

DISPLACEMENT. The objectionable impulse or wish which is repressed may be displaced to another object or location. Displacement represents a compromise in that a second choice is accepted because the one really desired is repudiated internally or frustrated externally. This will be recognized both as a common conscious as well as an unconscious activity of many people. However, the adult ego, when confronted with a reality demand, is more able than was true at an earlier developmental level to recognize, acknowledge, modify or give up such displacements.

RATIONALIZATION. Since all thought and behavior are determined by multiple impulses, some more acceptable than others, the tendency is to select for conscious use the explanation which is least objectionable to the self and to society. Thus, the usual explanations of our behavior that we offer are generally the more palatable ones. Much of the time rationalization is influenced as much by a consideration for the other person as it is by a concern for ourselves. Again, the adult is more capable of recognizing the other motives of his behavior if reality so requires.

UNDOING. This ego defense, which was relatively so prominent during latency, continues to operate in the form of a host of minor mental and social rituals, some of which have become part of ordinary social custom. They represent essentially symbolic devices that indicate to the self and to others, at an unconscious level, that undesirable impulses are under control. Many formalized social customs such as handshaking, for example, serve to communicate to the other person and to reinforce for the self that a dangerous impulse, in this case aggression, is not present or is under control. This kind of communication is necessary because such impulses persist at an unconscious level, a fact which is quickly revealed to us when someone does not conform to the accepted rituals. Not shaking hands is recognized as an unfriendly if not frankly hostile gesture. However, in contrast to earlier ego states, undoing as utilized by the adult has much less of an omnipotent, magical quality and is more readily subjected to reality testing.

ISOLATION. This is an ego defense essential for logical thinking, because it serves in the interest of economy. A charged feeling is detached from the thought or from an object when that feeling is not relevant or necessary. A great number of symbols which are used in logical thinking and reality testing not only have real meaning in terms of the external environment, but also may refer to body or sexual concepts of early life. This is most clearly revealed in dreams, where ordinary things in the environment may also be used to symbolize parts of the body. The adult ego for the most part successfully isolates and keeps out of consciousness this symbolic connection when realistically no such connection actually exists. This is very important in logical thinking since the other symbolic meanings are often associated with conflictful feelings or painful affects. Later we shall discuss types of psychopathology in which the individual has a tendency to respond unconsciously to the symbolic rather than to the real meaning, or in which the individual has to overdo the isolation, or in which the individual deals with the symbolic meaning exclusively.

There are many other patterns of ego defense, such as those which evolved in adolescence, as well as others not discussed, some of which represent quite distinctive, idiosyncratic characteristics of individuals and are not readily defined. A common one is *conversion*, but since this almost always results in symptom formation, discussion of it will be reserved for a later chapter (Chapter XXXIII). Regardless of the details of such ego patterns, the adult quality is seen in the individual's capacity to achieve a reality-oriented adjustment. In general, it is not the ego defense which is to be regarded in terms of normality or abnormality, but how the defense is used and what the consequences are. We shall return to this later.

THE SUPEREGO

Ideally, superego function in the adult, as compared to that in the child or adolescent, more closely approximates ego function. In contrast to the situation in childhood, when the superego existed as a more or less separate institution personifying the standards and the do's and don'ts of the parental figures, oscillating between extremes of harshly punitive attitudes on the one hand and unrealistically approving ones on the other, these functions now become a more integral part of the self and of one's own identity. In other words, the healthy adult is able to feel a much greater and more assured sense of responsibility for his own behavior. This, too, is a function of his sense of identity, which now includes a reliable feeling of what is right and what is wrong, The superego no longer exists as a foreign body, so to speak, and no longer includes, willy-nilly, all the standards and demands of the parental figures, regardless of how appropriate or inappropriate they may have been. Reality testing functions of the ego have permitted the adult to make judgments concerning these past standards and to evolve a new edition which is more in keeping with current reality. The signal function, however, continues much the same. Guilt and shame continue to be the warning signals that one has done wrong or has failed to live up to expectations (see Chapter XVIII). In further contrast to the situation of childhood, the reality testing capacity of the adult ego is able to make a distinction between impulse, thought or fantasy on the one hand and the actual act or behavior on the other. The adult superego does not respond as if the two were equivalent. Similarly, the responses are more realistic. Thus the adult is more able to evolve appropriate behavior in response to superego warnings, and should he unwittingly transgress, he is more able to make proper amends. In other words, the superego provides an impetus to appropriate action and is not simply a punitive agency. In this sense, superego (and ego ideal) constitute newly developed motivating forces. It motivates ethical, moral and socially considerate behavior, and even when transgressions take place, the adult is more likely to experience regret or remorse and to respond with appropriately constructive behavior rather than with paralyzing shame or guilt.

DRIVE EXPRESSION OF THE ADULT

The preceding discussion of ego and superego already characterizes to a considerable measure drive expression in the adult. Nonetheless, there are certain developmental changes which deserve comment.

Sexuality

Two basic changes must occur in libido development before the adult level may be said to have been reached. First, there must be a shift in erotogenic primacy from the pregenital (oral, anal, phallic) to genital primacy. Second, there must be a change in object from self to parent to extrafamily heterosexual object. That such development has been accomplished may be revealed by the following criteria:

The mature adult has the capacity to achieve a successful heterosexual love relationship. In our society this eventually culminates in marriage and having children. It requires a capacity to love and be loved. It also includes the capacity to achieve orgasm at the genital level. A successful orgasm involves a period of mounting excitation during foreplay and a climax which can be more or less synchronized with that of the partner; it is followed by satisfaction, relaxation and feelings of love for and gratitude toward the partner. A wide variety of essentially pregenital activities or fantasies may take place in the period of foreplay, but no one of these constitutes an obligatory requirement for orgasm. When some such specific activity is necessary before orgasm can be experienced, it is usually an indication of some failure of sexual maturation, a perversion (for example, the man who can experience orgasm only if he is beaten first or the woman who can experience orgasm only if her husband tells her of his sexual experiences with other women)

(Chapter XXXI). With the attainment of genital primacy, the conscious and/or unconscious confusion that existed in the pregenital period between the sexual and the other nonsexual physiological functions of the erotogenic zone disappears. Thus the sexual functions of the genitals cease to be confused with the excretory functions, the urethra and the rectum are not used or conceived of as sexual organs, and the nutritive and the sexual functions of the mouth are separated. The developmental aspects of adult sexuality, including child-bearing and parenthood, will be discussed in Chapters XIX and XX.

Aggression

The adult is able to gratify the basic needs to overcome and master the environment in ways which are essentially in conformity with the realistic situation. Pleasure is derived from doing the job well, from mastering difficulties in work, from the feeling of conquering nature, building, organizing and successfully supporting one's family (the man) or mastering the problems of child-bearing and child-rearing (the woman). Other adult means of expression of aggression are to be found in play, games, identification with athletes or teams, membership in competitive groups, etc. The adult finds satisfaction of aggressive needs in any of these ways, and his sense of reality prevents him from overdoing (as, for example, the man who is not satisfied until he has ruined all his business rivals) or from withdrawing (the man who can't accept a promotion or who can't defeat his father in a card game). In addition, the adult is able to handle aggression successfully in the situation of being attacked. Now he uses his aggressive abilities in self-defense and the object of the aggression is a real enemy. Under such circumstances the amount and character of the aggression discharged is appropriate to the provocation and to the realistic dangers and gains. Further, such appropriate aggressive activity is not accompanied by feelings of guilt. Hence, such aggression is expressed in such ways as to immobilize or harm the enemy and not hurt oneself. The mature adult is able to plan his expression of aggression, to make realistic judgments, and, if necessary, to withold the attack altogether if reality so dictates. When aggression needs to be expressed, it can be expressed directly, appropriately and with a clear goal in mind.

SELF-CONCEPT AND IDENTITY

The development of a sense of identity, as described in the last chapter, constitutes a most essential feature of the mental development of the adult. This sense of being, this capacity to feel and experience oneself as an individual among individuals, as a sentient, thinking human being with wishes, ambitions, goals and roles in life, is a function of ego, but it is being considered under a separate heading to emphasize its importance. As already discussed, the self-image of the child has evolved through a series of interactions with objects, experienced as good and bad, which provide the basis for representations of both psychic objects and psychic self. The development of the concept of self comes about by virtue of the degree and kind of support which has been provided by objects, yielding for the child periods of satisfaction and frustration and perceptions of himself as good or bad. Later, through identification with objects and through the judgments by objects of the child's "goodness" and "badness," further contributions are made to the child's image of the self. And finally the child's own experience of himself, through the successes and failures of his own efforts in various situations and roles and his relations with other objects, completes the basic processes whereby a self-concept develops and identity finally evolves. Obviously, these processes are subject to a wide range of variation from individual to individual, depending on original endowment, the vicissitudes of experience and the nature of early objects. To a large degree, the final self-concepts are precipitates and derivatives of the earlier object relations. But each person reaches chronological adulthood with a capacity for self-experience and identity based largely on what has gone before. This proves to have major importance in determining the kind of object relations currently sought after and the capacity of the individual to establish and maintain new object relations or to tolerate the loss of old objects. Continuing and sustained object relationships are also necessary in order to maintain the intactness of the self-concept and identity. It is for this reason, as will be discussed later, that object loss, real, threatened or fantasied, constitutes such a ubiquitous psychic stress (Chapters XXVI and XXVII). When, for whatever reason, there is a loss of or a decrement in the experience of the self as competent, secure, confident, strong and capable of dealing with changes in the internal or external environment, then psychic changes are set in motion in order to re-establish the previous status when the self was intact, changes which may or may not be successful or adaptive. Later we shall discuss the importance of this in relation to health and disease (Chapter XXV).

OBJECT RELATIONS OF THE ADULT

The attainment of a sense of identity which marks the transition from adolescence to adulthood involves a significant alteration in the nature of object relationships. It means that the real dependence on the earlier family objects no longer is as binding or as obligatory and that the capacity to establish and maintain relationships with new objects is correspondingly enhanced. This does not mean that the relations with the old objects can now be dropped. Rather, it involves the resolution of many areas of conflict with the early, usually familial, objects and the evoltuion of a new relationship relatively free of such conflicts. Thus the adolescent who goes through a period of rebellion and alienation from the parents should, in adulthood, succeed in re-establishing with his family a new and gratifying relationship. Most important in this process is the detachment of the childhood sexual aims from the familial figures and their displacement to other figures. This constitutes, in essence, the final successful resolution of the Oedipus complex and carries with it then the corresponding reduction in the necessity to maintain active the kinds of defenses and mechanisms which previously were necessary in order to function successfully in the family circle. It makes possible a much more realistic appraisal of the family objects, who are now neither excessively idealized nor feared. When this process is not successfully accomplished, not only are many of the old conflicts with the family objects continued, but also they are to varying degrees displaced onto the new objects. This must be understood as a relative matter, and it can be regarded as almost axiomatic that to some degree the qualities and characteristics of the earlier relationships will be carried over into the new relationships. During periods of stress or deprivation the apparently well-resolved conflicts of an earlier period may be revived with quite unexpected intensity. Ideally, however, in spite of the persistence unconsciously of such feelings and attitudes, the new objects are endowed with a relatively discrete identity of their own. Thus, the wife is not confused with the mother nor the husband with the father and it is possible for the healthy adult to have both sensual and tender feelings toward the spouse. The mature couple can be tolerant of each other's and of their own periodic dependent needs, they can allow themselves to be mothered by the spouse without jeopardizing the more adult and the sexual part of the relationship. The adult is not afraid to have warm and affectionate feelings toward friends of the same sex, and he is also able to feel affectionate toward his parents without either being too dependent or stirring up the old conflicts. He does not carry into his relationships with peers his unresolved conflicts with his siblings, and he does not displace onto his boss or other superior his unresolved feelings toward his parents.

In brief, the sense of personal identity also carries with it the capacity to ascribe identity and invidivuality to others and to relate to them more realistically in terms of their assets and deficits with appropriate consideration for their needs and aspirations as individuals.

This ability to experience the full measure of personal gratification in a relationship without at the same time sacrificing consideration and respect for the other is the hallmark of the mature adult object relationship. It makes possible the ability to relate gratifyingly to a wide variety of people even under trying circumstances. Such a mature individual is not so readily threatened by the other person's difficulties, problems or defects, which he can understand or accept and even be helpful about, without serious danger to his own sense of personal identity and confidence. Such persons are generally seen by their fellows as strong characters.

SOCIAL ROLES AND WORK

The mature adult is also a socially adjusted human being. This means that he has an awareness of the social structure in which he plays a role and of his responsibilities and obligations to society and his place within society. As already discussed in respect to identity formation (see Chapter XVI), his sense of himself, his identity, involves his roles and status within society, in terms both of his own activity and of the feedback of approval, recognition or disapproval from the social group. The mature adult is responsive to the goals, needs and destiny of the social group, of which he feels an integral part. He is able to make judgments or decisions relating to the welfare of the larger group and to face and deal with the conflicts of interest and value attendant thereon. At times he may have to subordinate his own interests or the interests of smaller groups to which he belongs, such as family.

Work is the main means whereby one's function in society is fulfilled. It is through a work role that one establishes a position as an effective member of the society, which in turn provides recognition and reward in the form of money, rank, responsibilities, awards, publicity, etc. The mature adult experiences satisfaction in his own work effectiveness and achievement, regardless of social recognition, but his gratification is enhanced if his work is in some way also regarded or recognized as socially valuable or useful. His sense of personal identity evolves in the course of the development of his work role. Thus, whether and how one is successful or unsuccessful as a housewife, a carpenter, a physician, a bookkeeper, an artist, provides an important nutriment for the maintenance and development of identity throughout adulthood. When social or environmental influences restrict or prevent fulfillment of work roles, there may be decidedly harmful effects on continued personality growth during adulthood. (See Chapters XXI and XXVIII.)

CHAPTER XVIII

ADULTHOOD: THE MENTAL APPARATUS: II. THE DIFFERENTIATED AFFECTS

The origin and early development of affects are discussed in Chapter XIV. The continuing development of the mental apparatus results in an increasing richness and variety of affect experience while at the same time an enhanced capacity to control affective expression is achieved. The adult's repertoire of feelings evolves from the earlier so-called primal undifferentiated affects in the course of ego and superego development and the acquisition of psychic representations of self and objects. Throughout life affects continue to constitute the basis upon which object relations are established and controlled (to "know" someone is affectively, not intellectually, determined). Further, affects continue to provide the main medium of interpersonal communication, since it is the affect quality which often determines the meaning of the interpersonal verbal exchange. Intrapsychically, affects provide information concerning the status of the self per se and of the self in relation to objects, and they indicate the level of drive tensions. In the adult such intrapsychic activities are ego functions having motivational and warning properties. As signals, affects anticipate on the basis of past experience intrapsychic changes, thereby permitting the ego to initiate psychic processes or behavior to maintain psychic balance. Such controlled ego response is in contrast to the relatively uncontrolled affect expression characteristic of the infant or child. Now intrapsychic resources are such that affects can inaugurate psychic defenses and behavior without the necessity for full-blown affect expression to assure satisfaction of needs. Through ego control the adult also is more capable of modulating affect expression or delaying its full expression until time and circumstances are most suitable. By the same token, decrease or loss of this ability for appropriate affect expression, whether it appears in the form of uncontrollable display of affect or an inability to feel or express the appropriate affect, indicates failure of normal ego development or a loss of ego control.

In Chapter XIV the differentiated affects were subdivided into two major categories, the *signal-scanning affects* and the *drive-discharge affects*. In addition, affects of fused drives are identified. The reader is referred to that chapter for the basis for such a differentiation.

THE SIGNAL-SCANNING AFFECTS

The signal-scanning affects may conveniently be subdivided into those indicating unpleasure and those indicating pleasure, referring to the conscious subjective quality at the time experienced.

The Signal-Scanning Affects Indicating Unpleasure

Anxiety

Primal anxiety has already been discussed (Chapter XIV), and its subsequent differentiation involves the successive phases of ego and libido development. Thus, the child successively manifests anxiety in response to separation, strangers, body integrity, castration and, finally, to loss of control over self, with many variations of coloring in between depending on the nature and strength of drive activity and the conflicts evoked thereby. In different individuals during childhood there may be various more or less specific anxieties concerning biting, eating or swallowing, or being bitten, eaten or swallowed; soiling or being soiled; penetrating or being penetrated; bursting, castration, mutilation, pregnancy, etc., as were discussed in earlier chapters. Such content of unconscious fantasy, the conflict engendered thereby, and the various ego defensive processes developed to cope with the conflict, although not significantly modifying the basic experience of anxiety in respect to the characteristics already described, nonetheless add distinctive feeling qualities and ideation to what is felt as anxiety, even though these determinants remain unconscious. This is reflected not only in where and how one may feel what he calls anxiety (in the back or abdomen or chest, etc.; in the dark, in crowds, in examinations, etc.), but also in some of the physiological and behavioral concomitants (e.g., grinding the teeth, aerophagia, nausea, cremasteric response, muscle cramps, etc.). (See also Chapter XXXIII.) Further, the ideation accompanying the anxiety may also betray the nature of the underlying impulse and the defense against it. This is seen most classically in the phobias, in which the internal source of danger, an unconscious fantasy, is projected to the outside, while the threatening object is displaced. In general, the details of the anxiety and its accompanying ideation reflect the psychogenetic and dynamic factors that contributed to its development. Clinically, this is true of all anxiety experiences, whether the external danger is real or is an unrealistic projection, as in a phobia. Examinations, surgery, danger of bodily harm, etc., not only may provoke differing intensities of anxiety, from none to panic, in different individuals, but the details of what is felt as anxiety will show variations from individual to individual even though the basic pattern, including the ego, object-self and drive aspects, is much the same in all.

Anxiety, as here characterized, is a fairly consistent accompaniment of any psychological decompensation regardless of how brief it may be. Since ontogenetically anxiety always precedes and experientially frequently precedes the other unpleasure affects, some of the qualities of anxiety are to be found during almost every unpleasure state. In terms of what is felt, this may range from vague feelings of uneasiness, restlessness and foreboding ("free-floating anxiety") to more specifically identified fears, which may be realistic to varying degrees or may be totally unrealistic (phobias or delusions). When the person identifies a reason for his anxiety, whether it be realistic or not, the reaction tends to be more organized and more related to the circumstance alleged to be or actually responsible. Free-floating anxiety is more diffuse and involves more disorganization of behavior. It is an intensely unpleasant state which is not likely to persist for very long without some other psychological and behavioral processes developing intended to terminate the discomfort and somehow resolve the situation. For this reason, we may expect to observe free-floating anxiety, if only briefly, as the most frequent first manifestation of psychic stress, and therefore a common accompaniment of any illness. But we must not overlook the role of anxiety as the primary system alerting to danger and mobilizing all the systems, biological, psychological and social, concerned in the maintenance of life. Anxiety must be recognized as the psychological part of the activity of the critical defense organization concerned with maintaining and protecting life.

The ego, self-object, and drive aspects of anxiety are discussed in Chapter XIV, the physiological aspects in Chapter XXXIII.

Shame[1, 8]

Shame is experienced chiefly in terms of feelings of inadequacy, inferiority, failure and worthlessness. It comes into being as the child becomes capable of internalizing the admired standards and expectations of his important objects, first the parents and then others throughout childhood, who become models for such positive identifications. Like guilt, it probably begins after the child reaches the toddler stage and is responding to approval and disapproval transmitted over a distance as something heard or seen. Two important elements are involved in the process whereby such internal standards (the ego ideal) are set up. The first is the internalization, through identification, of the standards and ideals of the loved and admired object upon whom the child feels dependent and whom he wishes to be like. These include the positive identifications with the loving, reassuring parent, the parent who gives permission to be like him, and the parent who imposes his own ideals (sometimes unachieved) on him. But this internal image is not an exact replica of the external object. Through projection the child also imparts to the admired object qualities that he wishes him to possess (beauty, wisdom, strength, etc.) as well as qualities that the child may himself possess, such as, for example, strong aggressive impulses.

Shame, then, is the affect felt when ego makes the self-judgment of a failure to live up to the performance required by the self-imposed standards. It is finally expressed as "I am ashamed of myself," rather than "They are ashamed of me." The earliest content of shame is likely to be related to body image or function, the child feeling ashamed of his weakness, smallness, nakedness, lack of control of his body, etc., as compared to the parent. To feel ashamed of deformity and disfigurement is a derivative of this. One may also feel ashamed of another, as when a parent feels shame if the child fails to live up to the parental expectation. In adult life shame involves more abstract concepts as well. *Embarrassment* describes a special quality of shame, that occurring when one's failure or error is suddenly discovered or exposed.

THE EGO ASPECT. The ego aspect of shame includes signal and scanning functions. It is part of the self-evaluating function of ego to provide a warning that some impulse, thought, fantasy or act will fail or has failed to satisfy the standards of the internalized ideal (ego ideal). When the signal is effective, the unpleasant felt affect is averted by psychic processes and/or behavior which insure that standards are maintained. This may include not only ego defenses to ward off impulses the expression of which would cause shame, but also ego processes in the service of maturation and accomplishment, a spur to activity, achievement and creativity. With failure, the unpleasant affect is felt with increasing intensity and various secondary psychic and behavioral processes appear, such as to hide, to cover up, to blame oneself, to depreciate oneself, etc. The typical behavior of the person experiencing shame is to hang the head, cover the face, blush, slouch, stand immobile or even sink down.

THE OBJECT-SELF ASPECT. This involves, first of all, the discrepancy between the idealized self (the ego ideal) and the self as actually perceived. The failure to achieve such standards invokes a *fear of abandonment* by the internalized love object, expressed in the terms "I am unworthy." From the developmental perspective, the susceptibility to shame is greatly increased when internal standards are too high, when too great perfectionism is demanded of oneself. This may come about especially when early childhood feelings of omnipotence are projected onto parental figures who also imposed unreasonable demands for performance as a condition for love. The shame then involves the feeling that one is unlovable, as a result of which attentive or loving behavior from persons in the environment becomes unacceptable. In addition, projection may lead to the interpretation that "No one loves me because I am unlovable" or "Because no one loves me I must be unlovable." With the loss of an object the person may feel responsible for the loss, the object having left "because I am unworthy of love." This feeling may occur even when no such responsibility exists, as when the other person dies. This feeling of utter worthlessness and of being held in contempt or finally abandoned expresses the most extreme of the unfavorable judgments of self in comparison to the ideal. Lesser degrees of shame involve correspondingly less harsh and final judgments and allow for greater potentialities of making good, of reachieving a favorable opinion of the self, of again feeling pride.

THE DRIVE ASPECT. This aspect of shame is two-layered. At one level we see restitutive or compensatory features in the direction of accomplishment and achievement, attempts to attain the goals and to re-establish the object relation as represented intrapsychically. We would relate this to some of the processes underlying primal anxiety, the tendency to correct a disturbed dynamic steady state and to re-establish the conditions for growth. The other drive quality relates to the conservative, self-containing properties of the depression-withdrawal response, specifically in relation to the idea of prospective abandonment. With the judgment that one is unloved and unlovable, the trend is toward withdrawal and insulation. The relative strength of these tendencies, which is determined by early developmental factors, will decide whether shame will be a spur to accomplishment or whether it will deteriorate into hopelessness. (See also Chapter XXXIII.)

Guilt (Guilt Feelings)[1,8]

Guilt is the affect which comes into being with the development of the superego, the internalization of the punishing and prohibiting standard of the early objects and their culture (see Chapter XIII). These internalized standards stem both from the actual demands and standards of early objects and from the projections of the child's magical and destructive impulses onto the object. Thus, the parent who provides the model for the superego standards may actually have been harsh and punishing or the child may ascribe to him his own sadistic impulses which are then reintrojected to form a powerful, forbidding, punishing intrapsychic influence which keeps him from transgressing. Whatever the factors resulting in a particular superego structure, guilt feelings are experienced when through fantasy or act the requirements imposed by the superego are transgressed. The feeling is of having committed a wrongdoing or a crime, and the fear is of annihilation or mutilation, the avoidance of which may be accomplished by atonement or self-inflicted punishment. The punishment, expected or self-imposed, tends to follow the primitive law of talion, to inflict the same on the self as one wished to inflict on the other.

THE EGO ASPECT. This aspect of guilt involves the perception of the disparity between the impulse or deed and the internalized prohibiting standards as represented in the superego. In this instance, it is the superego which takes over the warning function, alerting to the danger that a transgression has occurred or might occur. Now the superego acquires a drive quality in that it exerts a force, counteracting the drives, and requiring adaptive ego responses. The latter may include any of the ego mechanisms serving to keep out of consciousness and/or to deflect or inhibit the disapproved impulses. Or it may include processes which result in atonement or punishment instead of the acting out of the impulse, as when one hurts oneself rather than another. Thus, signal guilt, like signal anxiety, operates silently without a felt affect as long as ego mechanisms are successful either in dealing with what would be guilt-provoking before it occurs or in effecting punishment afterward. The operation of signal guilt often can be correctly inferred when manifest psychic processes or behavior involve self-punishment. atonement and aggression turned inward in any of its manifold expressions, When the response to the signal is inadequate, the affect of guilt is felt with rising intensity and with various efforts at restitution and atonement. This includes intense feeling of anguish and badness during which the sufferer either tends to exhibit his badness and to expose himself to punishment, injury or retribution, or withdraws, depriving himself of opportunities and of satisfying human contacts.

THE OBJECT-SELF ASPECT. This includes, first of all, the harsh, disapproving, destructive attitude toward the self originating from the disapproval of the child by the angry parent. It is experienced, however, as a self-judgment, meaning that all the harshness, all the fury, all the destructiveness are concentrated in the superego, resulting in the subjective experience of a harsh judgment of oneself. The person sees himself as bad, black, the "worst person on earth," despicable, dirty and deserving of punishment. In this process we see some loss of boundaries between self and object since the person feeling guilt may only dimly be aware of the origin of the disapproval ("Father would be angry") or may not be aware of its origin at all, sometimes indeed ascribing to the real external object only beneficent qualities: "He is so good to me, but I don't deserve it." In this way, aggression toward an external object, in fact or fantasy, is effectively blocked and concentrated on the self instead. This blurring of distinctions between self and object is also revealed in the tendency for the person feeling guilt to see and describe himself in the terms in which he really sees the object toward whom he is ambivalent. With extreme degrees of guilt, the judgment is of the self as being so bad that only death (annihilation) can satisfy the need for punishment. The transition to hopelessness will be brought out later.

THE DRIVE ASPECT.   The drive aspect of guilt most prominently includes the aggressive drives turned on the self. The original drive activity to destroy the object which frustrates is now to be found in the harsh attitude toward and cruel, merciless judgment of the self. The aggressive drive activity designed to force the unsatisfying object to supply needs may remain unconscious although it often continues to be expressed behaviorally in disguised form, as when the guilt-ridden person insists that the object listen to his confessions of badness. The restitutive drive components are found in the expectation that sufficient atonement and self-punishment will eventually re-establish serenity and permit a satisfying object relationship. (See also Chapter XXXIII.)

Disgust

This is an affect quality developing as a reaction against oral and anal drive activity involving tasting, swallowing and smelling. Its anlage is the primitive reflex physiological organization to expel from the mouth that which tastes bad, and includes nausea and vomiting. With subsequent developments the neutrality toward or even pleasure with certain tastes and smells (notably feces) has to be countered and disgust becomes the specific affect response to a variety of stimuli or fantasies symbolically associated with such oral or olfactory intaking tendencies, the content of which has become classified as dirty (fecal). Disgust thus contributes to the development of the standards which go into the make-up of ego ideal and superego and, in a sense, is a special kind of shame and guilt, as indicated by the expression "I am disgusted with myself." It is important in the development of ambivalence, another instance in which what was once enjoyed (e.g., fecal play) becomes bad or dangerous.

THE EGO ASPECT.   The ego aspect of disgust involves first the unconscious signal warning against the eruption of such primitive oral and anal (olfactory) wishes as well as against exposure to bad smelling or tasting stimuli realistically originating in the environment. Further, it mobilizes the specific defenses against the anal, coprophilic or coprophagic impulses, notably reaction formation and various patterns of cleanliness, fastidiousness and neatness. When the drive is too strong, the more primitive reaction pattern is evoked and disgust is felt along with the behavioral and physiological patterns associated with spitting, gagging, retching and vomiting. It is important to appreciate all the possible symbolic equivalences of the soiling tendencies, which may involve psychic activity not originally anal as, for example, when genital sexual activities or thoughts thereof are judged to be dirty and hence disgusting.

THE OBJECT-SELF ASPECT. This is closely related to the comparable aspects of shame and guilt. To be disgusted with oneself involves particularly the idea of being dirty, an anal judgment which may include processes not actually anal as, for example, sexual impulses. "I am disgusted" also carries with it the connotation of expelling or getting rid of an ambivalently held object. Disgust, then, involves a self-judgment of being dirty and malodorous, and therefore untouchable, to be pushed away, segregated, isolated. Again, such a self-judgment may actually be the opinion that the person holds of the object (now ascribed to the self) or it may represent an aggressive soiling (anal sadistic) wish intended for an object but turned instead on the self. To feel disgusted with someone else is to regard him as dirty, unacceptable, unpleasant, and includes a wish to be rid of him.

THE DRIVE ASPECT. The drive aspect of disgust has two sides. The first is the wish to taste, smell or indulge in that which has fallen under a taboo as dirty. The second is the reaction to rid oneself of something felt to be bad by spitting it out. The first expresses persistence of certain early body pleasure wishes; the second is more in the service of survival and reality, to expel what is bad, using the primitive physiological defenses of spitting and vomiting. (See also Chapter XXXIII.)

Sadness

This is a differentiated affect more specifically indicative of object loss, real, threatened or fantasied. It is that part of the response reflecting the absence of the source of gratification but not yet a giving up. This is a transitional affect since it includes some elements of pleasurable recollection of the lost gratifications. The pleasure quality is to be found in the expression "sweet sadness" and the associated feelings of nostalgia, homesickness, longing, all of which include the capacity still to enjoy the missing object in fantasy and memory or the hope and expectation of an eventual reunion. When these are not possible, other more unequivocally painful affects are felt, finally helplessness or hopelessness, the affects indicative of giving up.

THE EGO ASPECT.   This includes the warning of the possibility of loss of the source of gratification and the mobilization of psychic mechanisms to avert such loss before it occurs or to deny or to compensate for it after it occurs. When these attempts are unsuccessful, sadness is felt and it now includes the ego processes concerned with memories of past gratifications and expectations of reunion. The feelings are those of loss, emptiness, longing and unhappiness, associated at the same time with some qualities of pleasant recollection.

THE OBJECT-SELF ASPECT.   This aspect of sadness involves primarily the discrepancy between the wish and longing for the missing object and the actuality of its real or impending unavailabliity. Commonly, it includes an exaggeration in fantasy of the gratifications obtainable from the missing object, whose psychic image is thus aggrandized as a supplier of needs. Correspondingly, the image of the self is felt as impoverished, deprived, empty, weakened or in some way missing an essential part. As compared to helplessness or hopelessness, however, the relative identity and intactness of self and object are fairly well retained, and the person still feels worthy and deserving of love and attention.

THE DRIVE ASPECT.   Combined in the drive aspect of sadness are both the more active tendency to re-establish the lost or threatened object relationship, especially through the use of fantasy when the object is unavailable, and the more conservative tendency to withdraw and conserve energy until the object again becomes available. The forms of expression of the object-directed drives will be determined by earlier patterns of object-relating activity. The characteristic behavior of sadness includes a slowing up, a lowering of muscle tone which produces a slumping posture and sad facies, and a readiness to cry. This behavior may be replaced by increased activity and forced cheerfulness which are part of the attempt to deny or minimize the loss or the painful feelings of sadness. (See also Chapter XXXIII.)

Helplessness and Hopelessness[10,11]

These affects indicate the greatest degree of disorganization in response to stress and reflect giving up, the feeling that it is or will not be possible to carry on, to cope with the stress, that it is too much, the end. For their elucidation we are indebted to the work of Schmale.[10, 11] Helplessness and hopelessness differ in respect to the developmental factors determining the predominant patterns of early object relationships. With persistence of the more anaclitic (leaning) type of object choice, in which sources of supply are felt to come from external objects, the giving-up affect is *helplessness*. The feelings are of being left out, let down and deserted, but the individual considers himself neither responsible nor capable of doing anything about it, instead feeling that help must be provided from an outside source. With a more narcissistic object choice (taking the self as the model for objects) and with greater development of the internalized institutions of superego and ego ideal, the giving-up affect is *hopelessness*. Now the feeling of giving up includes more despair, futility, "nothing left"; the self-judgment that one is completely responsible for the situation leads to the feeling that there is nothing he or anyone else can do to overcome the feelings or change the situation. Further, one is not worthy of help so that even if help is offered it cannot be accepted.

Hence, helplessness tends to develop in the person who is more manifestly dependent on external sources for gratification, especially when objects are seen as sources of supply having no needs of their own, as was characteristic of early childhood.

Hopelessness, on the other hand, is more likely to occur in the person whose institutions of internal judgment (superego and ego ideal) impose rigid requirements as to the conditions under which gratifications can be achieved. Such persons are likely to have fewer satisfying relationships and even these are highly ambivalent. They have a pseudo-independence or a pseudo-self-reliance which hides their difficulty in object relating. Guilt and shame commonly precede hopelessness in the response to stress.

Helplessness has its anlage in the undifferentiated anxiety of infancy in which the baby is truly helpless and must be supplied by the parent or surrogate. Helplessness, as experienced later as an affect, involves the memory of this situation as it existed when the capacities of the infant for survival and satisfaction without an external object were exceedingly limited. It involves the unconscious memory of the self as the crying or sobbing baby, unattended and without expectation of relief unless help comes. Symbolically as well as behaviorally, the person feeling helplessness may feel like crying or calling for help, yet feels unable to initiate activity to help himself.

The anlage of hopelessness, on the other hand, is to be found in the primal depression-withdrawal indicative of the fact that no help is possible and that exhaustion threatens. To the person feeling hopeless it seems that neither external objects nor internal resources will suffice to restore him. The ancient biological mechanism of withdrawal and insulation from the environment is called upon.

Helplessness and hopelessness are the affects resulting when object loss, real or fantasied, includes to a major degree a self-judgment that one can no longer function without the object. This is in contrast to sadness, in which fantasy about the object still provides support for the self and therefore some confidence. Sadness evolves into helplessness or hopelessness when it includes the inner awareness of the absence of the object and a corresponding deterioration of the self as an intact, effective, integrated, confident entity.

THE EGO ASPECTS.   These are related mainly to signals warning of dangers of object loss and leading to the many psychological and behavioral devices which serve to retain the object and the source of supply and thereby the intactness of self. If these devices are successful, the feelings of helplessness and/or hopelessness will be avoided, although any or all of the other affects and responses to affects, including anxiety, anger, guilt and shame, may be mobilized before this is achieved. If they are unsuccessful, helplessness or hopelessness is felt as a painful mental state which may then be responded to by denial or projection or by withdrawal and inactivity. The ego responses to the signal represent attempts to ward off an object loss or to re-establish a lost object relationship, whereas the responses to the felt affects are more indicative of the ego's attempt to deal with the painful state itself (through denial or projection) or to avoid further drain (through withdrawal and inactivity.)

THE OBJECT-SELF ASPECT.   Helplessness and hopelessness are the affects most expressive of loss of object and damage to the self image. Helplessness refers to the inability of the self to function or to survive in the absence of supplies ordinarily afforded by the lost (in fact or fantasy) object and the inability to initiate activity that would regain the lost object and supplies. However, the capacity to respond to the activity of an object is retained. Hopelessness, on the other hand, includes the same qualities but with the difference that help seems to the hopeless person to be neither possible nor acceptable. The self is seen as more damaged and inadequate during hopelessness than during helplessness.

THE DRIVE ASPECTS.   In helplessness the drive activities include features seen in both the primal anxiety and the depression-withdrawal patterns. There is a readiness to respond to external objects or sources of supply in an anaclitic fashion, but such sources are enlisted mainly by signals of despair or "cries for help" rather than by activity. In the absence of available or potential objects, the self-preservative drive is expressed in the energy conservative withdrawal response.

In hopelessness the drive processes involve predominantly withdrawal and insulation, a last ditch conservative effort which, however, is not compatible with life for very long. Paradoxically, the decision for life or death may be based on whether aggression can be aroused, even if largely self-directed. A hated self to be punished and reviled is still a self, and the intensity of hopelessness may be attenuated as long as punishment can be directed to the self. In this sense, guilt attenuates hopelessness.

Both helpless and hopeless persons behave similarly in that they exhibit reduced activity, interest and initiative with respect to external objects. In hopelessness, however, the degree of such behavior is greater,

occasionally to the extent of being mute, motionless and largely unresponsive. In helplessness one sees more manifestation of the wish for
help in the sense of a capacity to respond to the helping figure. (See also
Chapter XXXIII.)

The Signal-Scanning Affects Indicating Pleasure

These affects are indicative of self-judgments of intactness, success and gratification. For the most part they are less urgent and less
intense than the affects indicating unpleasure, except when the achievement or success is of unusual degree or follows great effort. In contrast
to the unpleasure affects, the ego processes involved act to facilitate the
continuation or repetition of the conditions responsible for the feelings
of pleasure.

Contentment
Contentment is a general feeling that needs are being or have been
fulfilled and goals achieved. Unpleasant tension is absent. It is quiet
and restful and includes satisfying bodily as well as psychic experience.
One is at ease with oneself and with one's objects.

Confidence
Confidence here refers to faith in one's own strength, capacity and
potential to achieve goals, satisfy needs, avert or overcome dangers
(courage) (i.e., "self-confidence") as well as reliance on one's objects as
sources of gratification ("trust"). It includes also sureness of one's
capacity to establish new and maintain old relationships, to love and
to be loved. Confidence looks to the future on the basis of past satisfactions and successes.

Joy
Joy is expressive of a more climactic fulfillment of needs and
achievement of goals. At its peak there is a sense of fusion of self and
object which is felt as greatly enhancing the strength, capacity and
invulnerability of the self without at the same time damaging or destroying the object. In it are likely to be revived previous developmental
experiences indicative of such fulfillment, which then contribute to the
tone and quality of the individual experience of joy. With joy, aggression is neutralized and is felt neither toward or from the object nor
toward the self. But, perversely, there may be joy in destruction (orgies).

Pride
Pride is the affect specifically indicating success in living up to
the standards of the ego ideal. It pronounces satisfaction with the self,
which feels correspondingly strengthened, loved, admired and in-

vulnerable. The person feeling pride is eager to display himself and to be seen, in contrast to the behavior in shame, the opposite affect. Pride, therefore, is particularly related to all varieties of achievement, the various ways in which mastery is achieved in relation to the environment and to objects. The earliest expressions of pride are particularly related to development and mastery of the body.

Hope

Hope, as an affect, is a derivative of confidence with an ambiguous quality. Actually, hope may replace confidence when uncertainty develops concerning one's capacities. This implies a decrement in the concept of self as competent and a shift to objects and the environment as the expected source of support and/or gratification. It means that control is no longer felt to be in one's own hands, to so speak, but somewhere else. Past experience may justify the confidence and trust in the object so that one can feel hope. Or there may be a return to more magical thinking to justify the hope. Thus, confidence is based more on past reality and on the judgment of the self as able; when one feels sure one does not need to feel hope. Hope, on the other hand, is less reality-based. Hope, therefore, is a mixed affect, reflecting a degree of unpleasure, an uncertainty, the pleasure side of which reflects continuing confidence in external objects and on chance. Accordingly, it is possible to feel helpless and yet to feel hope. When one is *hopeless*, reliance on the objects has been lost.

From the clinical point of view, the ego affects indicating pleasure reflect the intrapsychic state, that is, the ego's perception (self-judgment) of success in the solution of conflict and the gratification of needs as experienced intrapsychically. When this is in concordance with reality it is indicative of health. But such self-judgment of success may be at the expense of reality or in spite of reality and, hence, may be indicative of disease or may obscure disease. As examples may be cited the elation and feelings of well-being in mania (in which loss and depression are being denied) or when a serious threat (e.g., an unsatisfactory life situation or cancer) is successfully denied.

THE DRIVE-DISCHARGE AFFECTS

The group of affects already discussed, the signal-scanning affects, have as their distinguishing characteristics a warning or signal (ego) function and a "How am I doing?" or scanning function, yielding judgments of good or bad, success or failure, pleasure or unpleasure. They do not have specific discharge activity. When the pure ego signal fails,

the felt affect functions to provoke further ego mechanisms and behavior to end the conflict and distress. Thus, these affects reflect the
operation of ego in the sense of structured warning systems against
that which is dangerous and structured sustaining systems for that
which assures adjustment. What is felt, ideationally and in terms of
bodily sensations and physiological changes, does not prominently include either goal or prospect of relief, climactic or otherwise, the necessary qualities of discharge. Instead, the signal-scanning affects provide
information which is then used by the self-inspection part of the ego as
a guide for subsequent ego processes in the service of maintaining a
satisfactory dynamic steady state. The *drive-discharge affects* show
much less signal quality and much more discharge quality. The feeling
state experienced and the ideational content are more directly the expression of the drive seeking discharge; the feeling dissipates as this
goal is achieved and is replaced by a signal-scanning affect, pleasurable
or unpleasurable, depending on the many dynamic and developmental
factors that determine conflict. Nor can the drive-discharge affects be
categorized as pleasant or unpleasant per se, this being a function of
whether the goal is or can be successfully achieved or whether there is
expectation of success or failure. We know, for example, that anger can
be experienced as either pleasant or unpleasant. This judgment of
pleasure or unpleasure is a function of the ego affects. Later we shall
discuss further how these two classes of affects are interrelated.

The drive-discharge affects derive from the two main drive qualities, anger and rage being the affects of aggression, and love, affection,
tenderness and sexual feelings being the affects of the libidinal drive.

Anger or Rage

This is the affective expression of the aggressive drive directed
toward an external object, rage representing a greater degree of anger.
When the direction of the drive is turned inward or altered by virtue
of an unfavorable judgment of superego, anger is no longer felt but
rather a signal-scanning affect, e.g, guilt, shame, anxiety, etc. From this
alone it should be clear that anger or rage is not the same as the aggressive drive but only that aspect of drive which can penetrate into consciousness as something felt. Developmentally these affects originate
in the primitive, undifferentiated crying fit which includes not only the
expressions of unpleasure (later to become anxiety) but also the primitive drive activity to be rid of whatever is associated with unpleasure
and to secure what is necessary to reachieve comfort and to satisfy
needs. The latter includes the object, the existence of which as an
entity is unknown to the infant. As eventually differentiated, manifest
anger or rage may be felt with or without awareness of an object ("I
am furious at so-and-so," or "I am furious, but I don't know why or at

whom" ["blind rage"]); or it may be felt in terms of its physiological and bodily concomitants, which any observer can recognize as those of rage, but whose meaning or content is denied ("I am *not* angry," said with clenched fists and an angry voice). In the last example the affect reaches consciousness but its recognition is promptly rejected through the mechanism of negation; the concept "angry" is conscious but then is refuted by the negation "not" placed before the word "angry." What is felt and manifested *is* anger, even if not so recognized by the angry person.

THE EGO ASPECT.   Anger does not have or does not achieve a warning quality in the same sense of anticipation that characterizes the signal-scanning affects. Indeed, the warning function of the signal-scanning affects is part of the ego system which determines whether or not anger evolves, is felt and/or is discharged. The ego aspects of anger are to be found mainly in the various ways in which anger is experienced and discharged in the course of "taming" the aggressive drives. Specific modes of psychic expression of anger, including sarcasm, wit, argumentative capacities, aggressive fantasy, etc., are examples of anger coming partly under the aegis of ego and no longer requiring the pure discharge of explosive motor activity characteristic of the less mature organism. Some modes of handling aggression and therefore of expression of anger may become so stereotyped as to constitute character traits of the individual. *Hate* represents a more structured, deliberate, sustained, consciously object-directed form of anger-rage in which both the feeling and the drive expression remain under ego control.

THE SELF-OBJECT ASPECT.   The affect of anger is always object-directed, consciously or unconsciously. It has two meanings: one is to destroy the object who threatens, damages, frustrates, etc., and the other is to force the object through pain or punishment or threat thereof to provide gratification, to satisfy needs (Schmale[10]). The first is more primitive and develops out of the infantile situation in which the external object existed for the infant only as a supplier, without needs of its own. It is further entrenched by the oral experience of the early infant-mother relation whereby the satisfying object appears to be taken in and disappear (as the baby falls asleep). When this developmental level of expression of anger and rage persists into adulthood, such lack of regard for the object may result in the object being seriously injured, even murdered, without the aggressor feeling guilt or remorse. It is in this sense that anger and rage are primarily destructive.

The second level of organization of anger becomes possible when objects as sources of gratification are recognized not only as being outside, but also as having needs and vulnerabilities of their own and hence as being subject to force or threat. Indeed, part of the developmental process whereby self and object are distinguished from each other is through mutual expressions and experiences of aggression, whereby the "other" is hurt or forced. The expression of anger then is used to force the object to "behave," meaning not to disturb but to provide gratification. The child learns that the parents' expression of anger usually has such an aim and he soon follows suit in his own developing relationships. At this level of development the destruction of the object as a goal now exists more in the form of deep unconscious fantasies, which, however, continue to exert an influence on psychic processes.

Although anger is always object-directed, this fact is not necessarily conscious to the angry person. Even when the angry person suddenly directs the blow onto his own person, he is taking his body as an external object in place of the real object. As mentioned above, aggression directed toward the psychic self remains internalized (an intrapsychic process) and is experienced with a different affective tone (guilt, shame or disgust). When the person feeling guilt or shame injures himself it is usually not felt as anger or rage, but rather as a deserved punishment.

THE DRIVE ASPECT. This is, of course, the most prominent aspect of anger. As discussed in Chapter III, what is called the "aggressive drive" is primarily in the service of survival, growth and development. The understanding of aggression is sometimes confused by equating it with the observer's judgment of destructiveness and postulating a primary destructive drive. Initially the element of destruction not only is purely incidental but also has no reality for the infant or small child, only for the observer. In actuality, aggression is concerned with the overcoming of obstacles in the environment for the assurance of need gratification. This includes vigorous efforts to cope with frustrations and the mastery of the body and of the environment, which is a normal part of growth and maturation. The voluntary neuromuscular system is the main body system through which aggression is discharged. Anger, the affect of aggression, includes both the bodily changes concerned with discharge of aggression and unconscious and conscious fantasies reflecting the urgent need to gain control, to master or to overcome opposition. The drive then provides the impetus to violent fantasy and vigorous activity toward this end, and the feeling is relieved (or discharged) when something external, in fact or in fantasy, is dealt with, destroyed or in some way brought under control. If for any reason this goal cannot be achieved and the drive affect cannot be discharged, ego affects such as anxiety, guilt, shame, etc., may be felt. The ideational content and the body activity during anger may include any or all of earlier modes of expression of aggression, such as biting, swallowing, tearing, crushing, breaking, squeezing, soiling, mutilating, castrating, blinding, hurting, etc. While much or all of such ideation may remain unconscious, the bodily processes corresponding to such fantasies may still be activated as if such acts actually were being carried out (e.g., clenching the fists and grinding the teeth). (See also Chapter XXXIII.)

Love, Tenderness, Affection, Sexual Excitement

These terms are various ways of designating the affects associated with libidinal drives. These are terms commonly used but they are neither sharply defined nor well delineated from each other. Like their aggressive counterparts, as affects they are directed toward external objects (which may include one's own body or parts thereof). The affects refer to what is felt, even when the feeling may not be identified by the subject and when the ideational content (including the identity of the object) may be in some way and to some degree kept from consciousness. Again, some variety of discharge is characteristic of these affects and this is achieved through various degrees and types of transaction, action and union with an external object. Sexual excitement, of course, involves special types of bodily tension and discharge. These affects are neither mutually inclusive nor exclusive, i.e., it is possible to feel sexual excitement with or without tenderness or to feel love with or without sexual excitement, even though all may spring from common instinctual sources. Again, these affects cannot be defined in terms of pleasure or unpleasure, these qualities being determined by the success or failure of the drive wish as well as by the consequences thereof. Developmentally, they originate from primal experiences of satisfaction and pleasure, but with the development of "good" and "bad" object and self concepts and of conflicts between drive and reality (external and psychic), the libindinal drive affects no longer guarantee pleasure.

THE EGO ASPECTS. These include the various ego activities in the service of satisfaction of the drive wish. They are individually and experientially determined and include not only the ego processes of the moment but also character traits, the more or less characteristic ways of executing the drive. Such ego processes contribute particular color and tone to the affect experiences, rendering them more distinctive and individual in each case. The ego aspect also includes various alerting and preparatory signals indicating rising or falling drive activity, internally derived or externally provoked, and facilitating in an anticipatory manner the fulfillment of the drive need.

THE SELF-OBJECT ASPECTS. These are central since they are the affects experienced in relation to the drives directed toward some level or type of communion, transaction, contact, union or consummation with objects. Through processes already discussed, object-directed strivings are also the origin of and nutriment for the concepts of self. Hence, although the affect as felt consciously is object-directed, unconsciously the libidinal drive may be directed to the self as well as to the object.

For example, by identification with the object loved, one may also feel loved, even though in reality the object does not reciprocate.

Accordingly, the tremendous variations possible and inherent in development determine that the mode of experiencing and the capacity to experience these affects will evolve out of the variety and nature of all previous, and especially early, object relations.

THE DRIVE ASPECTS.   The drive aspects appear in the form of the various bodily as well as psychic activities in the service of contact and union with the object, many of which are experienced in the form of body sensations or varieties of ideational expression thereof. For the most part they are experienced in the form of longing for and/or discharge through the modalities of mutually shared sensations: hearing, seeing, touching, tasting, smelling, etc., and all the nuances thereof, ranging from the sensual to the spiritual. Again, the individuality of affect expression and experience is determined by the past of the individual and includes expression and feeling tone derived from all levels of libido development, oral, anal, phallic and genital. For example, such affects may be accompanied by marked changes in appetite, which may increase or disappear. (See also Chapter XXXIII.)

THE AFFECTS OF PARTIAL DRIVES AND FUSED DRIVES

The vicissitudes of drive development determine multitudinous affect tones which reflect not only specific modes of drive expression or discharge (e.g., oral, anal, etc.) characteristic of different developmental phases, but also gradations of fusion of the two main instinct streams, libido and aggression. Such affects are more structured and and more specific and become more involved in total character structure. Thus, when we refer to a person as "angry" or "affectionate" we may refer to the capacity for or tendency toward such expressions (character traits) as well as to the current presence of such affects. On the other hand, such designations as "greedy," "envious," "miserly" more typically refer to character traits, even though the person so described may only periodically feel greed, envy or miserliness. From the developmental point of view, such affects reflect the responses to more or less specific psychodynamic situations of childhood through which each individual normally passes. Later circumstances may reactivate memory of such situations and with it may be re-experienced the corresponding affect. Or developmental problems may interfere with the normal resolution of these early states and lead to their perpetuation. This takes the form of a readiness to feel such an affect and the development of character traits in keeping with the drive underlying the affect.

Because such affects reflect unresolved drive tendencies dating from childhood, they are not easily discharged (i.e., the drive is not readily satisfied). This in itself contributes to their chronicity and accounts for the development of character traits corresponding to the affect quality and the unsatisfied drive. Further, because of the conflict surrounding the drive, we may find these affects readily contaminated by signal-scanning affect responses (e.g., anxiety, guilt, shame, etc.) or even by ego mechanisms converted to the opposite behavior (e.g., greed to generosity). Thus, although we are including these among the drive-discharge affects, their lesser capacity for discharge brings them into closer relationship dynamically with the signal-scanning affects. These affects will be described only briefly.

Greed

Greed is an orally derived affect reflecting the need to receive, to be given and its frustration, namely, the feeling that one has not received enough, that one is unfilfilled. It has an aggressive tone in that it includes the wish to take, to get, to fill oneself, if necessary. It has an anxious quality as well, relating to the discomfort of not getting enough. In object-relating terms it involves holding onto or forcing the object to supply and a readiness for anger at the object who does not.

Envy

Envy also involves an intensification of the wish to receive but includes hostility toward the person who has what one wants. In this feeling state we can see the perpetuation of the infant's uncertainty that hunger will be followed by satiation or that the bodily felt need to be held and cuddled will be satisfied. This is compounded by hostility toward a rival whose needs are being, or are believed to be, fulfilled. In object-relation terms it includes the aggressive wish to force the object to give as well as the wish to take from the rival. The self is felt as deprived, but deserving. *Jealousy* is very similar except that it usually refers more specifically to sexual wishes, affection and love. The person who feels jealousy wishes to exact exclusive devotion and is intolerant and suspiecious of rivals.

Impatience

Impatience is another orally derived affect, originating in the infant's anxious waiting to be fed, and includes a strong component of impulsive devouring or seizing. "I can't wait" is the characteristic expression of impatience. It, too, fuses libidinal and aggressive tendencies toward getting what is wanted without regard for the object's needs or wishes. Impatience reflects the operation of the pleasure principle in infancy, "I want what I want when I want it."

Stubbornness or Obstinacy

Stubbornness or obstinacy (here referring to the subjective feeling, not to another's judgment of behavior) reflects the wish to hold on, to retain, to maintain control, which derives from childhood anal retentive or bodily mastery drive activity. In object-relating terms it indicates a lack of confidence in the object's capacity or inclination to satisfy needs and a necessity to retain strict control over objects through control over oneself and one's body. The anxious wish to retain is the affect content of miserliness.

Sympathy[6]

Sympathy is a feeling involving identification with a person who is suffering in some way from pain, a loss, a defeat, etc. The suffering person is taken as a love object, but in a special sense, namely, through a psychic sharing of the suffering and a wish to help. But by virtue of identification with the suffering person, the psychic self also gains love. The capacity to feel sympathy requires maturation to the phase of psychic delineation of self and object, but at the same time involves some loss of this capacity to maintain separateness in the sense that the person feeling sympathy may also suffer like the object. A low threshold for sympathy is often a means of dealing with guilt, whereas the seeking of sympathy is often the means whereby an unconsciously guilty person solicits and establishes relationships. *Empathy*, on the other hand, involves the capacity to know how and what an object feels and yet to maintain identity and separateness.

Pity

Pity is a more ambivalent feeling toward an object in which there is an element of hostility and contempt toward the suffering person. The receiver is humiliated and the donor is placed in a superior position. The aggression toward the object remains unconscious, hidden behind the facade of pity. The identification with the suffering person is less intense so that the person feeling pity experiences only a modicum of suffering.

The foregoing descriptions do not exhaust the variety of complex affect tones which characterize psychic life, but it suffices to indicate how genetic and dynamic processes lead to the differentiation of the primary drive tendencies into complex and at times highly individual affect qualities. Other affect nouns and adjectives of our language only partly reveal this heterogeneity, since much that is affective is simply not translatable into words. Such terms as cruelty, meanness, kindness, generosity, disdain, contempt, admiration, inquisitiveness, courage, timidity, and a host of others describe particular affect qualities that not only have motivational aspects but also serve to identify more fixed character traits of the individual. From the clinical point of view, they are revealing of the past psychological development and of the current state of the individual and hence are helpful in understanding something of the individual's adjustment and problems.

THE AFFECTS OF SUDDEN DRIVE RELEASE

When forces blocking the expression or satisfaction of a drive are suddenly released, the resulting affect experienced has certain distinctive qualities which deserve mention in passing. Often there is a feeling of relief, which may be associated with laughter or crying or both. The laughter in response to wit and humor has been ascribed by Freud to the sudden release of tension associated with the unexpected experiencing of something previously tabooed.[4] Surprise, astonishment, awe and horror are other affect qualities in response to the unexpected— that which is too big, too small, too strong, too stimulating, too soon, too quick, or in some way exceeds the immediate capacity to grasp and comprehend. These usually brief affects include the feeling of an abrupt loss of orientation of the self in respect to the provoking stimulus.

THE INTERACTION OF AFFECTS

This presentation has classified affects into two distinct categories, the signal-scanning affects and the drive-discharge affects, but we must appreciate that what is subjectively felt, whether or not it is identified and/or reported by the subject, represents only one facet, albeit a complex one, of rapidly changing, dynamic pyschic processes. Affects do not have substantive quality. Rather, they provide information to oneself, as well as to objects and observers, of the changing status of the organism as experienced psychically, particularly in respect to the vicissitudes of drive activity and self-object status. The central position of affects in the psychic economy means that the information of the affect always has a motivational quality. It defines the immediate necessity to continue or to change in terms of the pleasure principle and the reality principle. But each change may introduce new conditions and, therefore, the necessity for other change. Hence, it is common to see one affect quickly provoking another affect or even a series of affects. For example, an unconscious hostile wish toward a love object may reach consciousness as *anger*, but with no conscious object or direction; this may mobilize *anxiety* which may lead to projection of the hostile wish in the form of *fear* of attack, perhaps from some relatively innocuous animal; such manifest fear may then be grounds for *shame*, that one is weak and afraid, and this is now controlled by discharging *anger*, this time to a less dangerous or more accessible object; if successful, the first new feeling may be *pride*, but the fact that the original hostile impulse meant for the love object was discharged, even though to a displaced object, this may lead to superego disapproval and *guilt*. Or, rejection by a love object may lead first to a feeling of *sadness*, then *anger* toward the rejecting love object, which is countered by *guilt* and *shame* and then finally *helplessness* or *hopelessness*, the affects of "giving up." Thus, one affect may mobilize a whole cluster or series of affects, the sequence of which gives information as to the successive psychic processes being used in the attempt to restore and maintain a successful dynamic steady state.

For these reasons, affects provide a major source of information concerning states of health and illness. It is not by chance that our first inquiry of a patient is, "How are you feeling?"

THE CONCEPT OF CONSCIOUS AND UNCONSCIOUS AS APPLIED TO AFFECTS

Since affects are not entities but a complex of dynamic processes, the designation "conscious" or "unconscious" has relevance only to the particular aspect of affect under consideration. Obviously, the *subjective* aspect, by definition, refers to what is conscious or easily accessible to consciousness. But what is felt is not necessarily translatable into words or concepts by the person experiencing the feeling and hence cannot be easily communicated in such terms. On the other hand, we know that affects are communicated nonverbally, actually the more primitive means of communication. Hence, there is possible a greater measure of "knowing" what we feel and even what others feel than can be put into words. On the other hand, the drive components, the ego (signal) components, and the self-object components follow all the rules that regulate the disposition of mental activity as unconscious, preconscious and conscious. All three may be represented in ideational terms, as fantasies, and as such may undergo all the vicissitudes of change of which the mental apparatus is capable. Thus, the feeling may be stripped of all ideational content, in which case it may still be strongly felt, but may be unidentifiable. A man may commit murder without being aware that the intense feeling he experienced was rage. The drive components may be completely or only partially kept from consciousness, as may the signal (ego) component which may operate silently; they may be preconscious and easily available (e.g., the calm that's "dangerous"); or they may be conscious and intensely felt, or may be felt and denied ("I'm not afraid"). The object may be disguised, displaced, omitted or replaced by the self; or only the defensive response to the affect may become conscious; or there may be awareness only of the physiological changes, which are felt as symptoms of illness. In brief, the concepts "conscious" and "unconscious" cannot be applied to affects as if they constitute entities, but only to specifically designated aspects of affects.

REFERENCES

1. Alexander, F.: Remarks about the Relation of Inferiority Feelings to Guilt Feelings. Internat. J. Psychoanal., *19*:41, 1938.
2. Benedek, T.: Toward the Biology of the Depressive Constellation. J. Am. Psychoanalyt. A., *4*:389, 1956.
3. Darwin, C.: The Expression of the Emotions in Man and Animals (1872). New York, Philosophical Library, 1955.
4. Freud, S.: Jokes and Their Relation to the Unconscious (1905). *In:* Standard Edition of the Complete Psychological Works of Sigmund Freud, vol. VIII. London, The Hogarth Press, 1960.
5. Freud, S.: Inhibitions, Symptoms and Anxiety (1925). *In:* Standard Edition of the Complete Psychological Works of Sigmund Freud, vol. XX. London, The Hogarth Press, 1959, pp. 77–175.
6. Hollender, M.: The Seeking of Sympathy or Pity. J. Nerv. & Ment. Dis., *126*:579, 1958.
7. Novey, S.: A Clinical View of the Affect Theory in Psychoanalysis. Internat. J. Psychoanal., *40*:94, 1959.
8. Piers, G. and Singer, M.: Shame and Guilt. Springfield, Illinois, Charles C Thomas, 1953.
9. Rapaport, D.: On the Psychoanalytic Theory of Affects. Internat. J. Psychoanal., *34*:177, 1953.
10. Schmale, A. H.: Needs, Gratifications, and the Vicissitudes of the Self-Representation: A Developmental Concept of Psychic Object Relationships Psychoanalytic Study of Society, *2*, 1962.
11. Schmale, A. H. Jr.: Relationship of Separation and Depression to Disease. I. A Report on a Hospitalized Medical Population. Psychosom. Med., *20*:259, 1958.

CHAPTER XIX

THE NORMATIVE
DEVELOPMENT OF THE MAN

Adulthood involves a series of developmental processes. Since there are important differences in the development of men and of women these will be discussed separately. In discussing these processes, we can speak only in generalities since the past individuality, both biological and psychological, makes for the widest variety of possible developments. Further, we discuss developmental processes within the broad framework of the present era and culture without any attempt to specify the differences relating to the multitudinous subcultural, class, social and other patterns. We shall attempt to focus on the more universal developmental experiences. With further clinical experience, the student will gradually familiarize himself with the more individual or unique patterns. The discussion is primarily clinically organized, in that we have selected for discussion the nodal points in life which clinical experience has revealed to be important in the maintenance of health and in the development of disease. (See Chapters XXIII, XXIV, XXV, XXVII.)

For convenience, we arbitrarily divide adulthood into three periods: early, middle and late. The divisions between these periods do not correspond to any fixed biological or social phenomena.

EARLY ADULTHOOD (AGES 21 TO 35 YEARS)

For the man this is a period of relative vigor and activity, during which he is establishing himself in a variety of different roles and different relationships. If formal schooling has not ended by this time,

189

the man is generally engaged in some type of professional or career training. In the present era, most men have either completed or are completing obligatory military training. During these years the man is establishing and developing his role as a working member of society. This is important in achieving identity and status. The man in any society is expected to do something and be somebody in the world of work, and his success is one regulator of his self-esteem. It involves not only certain levels of achievement, but also the working through of new kinds of relationships with peers and superiors. One aspect of the sense of identity is to be able to see himself not only as a farmer, mechanic, salesman, lawyer or doctor, but also as an accomplished farmer, mechanic, salesman, lawyer or doctor and to be recognized as such by the community. Clinically we see problems developing when the man's earlier life experiences have been such that he is unable to establish and maintain the kinds of relationships necessary to develop or pursue a career. Thus, he may be unable to compete without feeling anxiety or other painful affects, or his self-esteem or self-reliance may be too low to enable him to get started, to mention only two possibilities. And certainly trouble may develop when the external environment thwarts these endeavors; unemployment, discrimination, job displacements or other social and cultural pressures may prevent the achievement of job status. The nature of a man's adjustment in the work situation is an important indicator of his mental health.

This is the period of falling in love, courtship and marriage. The transitional love affairs of the adolescent period are now replaced by more serious affairs, in which the goal becomes the establishment of a permanent relationship and a family rather than sexual experience only. The man may have several successes and disappointments before he finally achieves this goal. For the young adult, falling in love is a tremendously fulfilling experience. Probably at no other time in his life will he invest as much of himself in another person. Since the successful love relationship is a mutual one, it involves a considerable enhancement of self-esteem. Here again, a major contribution to identity formation takes place, now involving the man who loves and can be loved When this new object relationship is relatively free of the conflicts associated with the childhood love objects, the experience represents a major developmental achievement. The intensity of the genuine love relationship which culminates in marriage has the effect of recasting and consolidating the new image of the self as a man and contributes to the resolution of the earlier ambivalent relationship with the parental figures. On the other hand, disappointment in or thwarting of such intense love relationships can also be among the most intense and painful experiences of human life. Clinically, such experiences of love loss often constitute precipitating events for illness, both psychological and somatic. Under any circumstance of serious object loss the work of grief and mourning is required for resolution. (See Chapters XXVI and XXVII.)

The formal step of marriage constitutes another developmental turning point with many implications beyond those which have just been described for the "falling in love" experience. It represents the formalization of the relationship, the rituals, ceremonies and legal processes involved testifying to the seriousness with which society regards marriage. It formally acknowledges the change in relationships with the childhood objects and the assumption of new and unique responsibilities. The man now establishes a new identity, that of the husband, the breadwinner. He now no longer works for himself, he works for his family. Further, he achieves a different status in the eyes of society and is required to fulfill certain obligations and conform to certain patterns of behavior to which he was previously not bound. He not only has new and different gratifications and aspirations, but also is bound by new and different controls and restrictions to which he must adjust. This, then, is another developmental crisis which, when successfully met, facilitates further growth and development for the individual and, when unsuccessfully met, may bring with it varieties of decompensation and illness.

The role of husband also involves interpersonal relationships with another family, that of the wife. Such relationships are more likely to be marred by conflict because they are imposed rather than selected. They tend to bring up problems of rivalry and divided loyalty, as well as to revive earlier problems with the man's own family which may easily be displaced to the in-laws.

Marriage also requires that the young man establish his role as the sexual partner in a setting of permanence and intimacy not previously required of him. With the subsidence of the mutual overvaluations characteristic of the "in love" period, day to day adjustment to the marital partner requires some effort, the success of which plays a part in the establishment of this new object relationship.

Marriage inevitably brings into consideration the potential role of father. To have children is the natural outcome and goal of marriage and failure to achieve this goal may represent a significant blow to the self-esteem of the man. The preparation for fatherhood takes place throughout the man's life, culminating in a strong generative or reproductive urge. It began with his relationship with his own mother, identification with whom provided the earliest source for the wish to take care of, to nurture, to support, to provide for his own children.[2] The man whose very early relationships with his mother were deficient in this respect may have difficulty fulfilling the role of father with his children. The second source of fatherlinesss comes from the man's relationship with his own father, which provides further material for the development of the concept of what it is like to be a father. This may be modified and changed with further development and under the impact of the times and of new cultural patterns, but nonetheless, the earlier father-son relationship is an important determinant of the later father role.

The birth of each child brings about further adjustment and development. It should be clear that there are different developments and adjustments and different roles and identities in being the father of one child as compared to being the father of two, three, four, five or six children; in being the father of a girl or of girls, as compared to being the father of a boy or of boys; in being the father of an infant, toddler, a latency period child or a teenager. A variety of experiences with the children tends to recapitulate and often to reawaken for the father comparable experiences of his own childhood, which may include long-buried feelings about parents, sibling rivalry, goals, ambitions, etc. A man projects onto his children, and especially onto the boys, the hopes and expectations that he has not been or may not be able to fulfill for himself. A variety of experiences of the children may prove to have special significance to any particular man in terms of imposing a requirement for some new type of adjustment, failure of which may result in a symptom of illness. (See Chapter XXVII.)

The young man in this period may also have other kinds of social or group experience in which he plays roles different from those already described. These include his social relationships with other men, his memberships in various clubs, lodges and groups, athletic activities, his involvement in play, recreation, etc.

By the end of the period of early adulthood the man has a fairly well established image of himself and of those around him. He has usually by now moved some distance away, psychologically speaking, from his parents, who also may have begun to develop a relationship somewhat more dependent on him, rather than the reverse. By this point his siblings are usually grown up and occasions for the more intense rivalries are generally considerably attenuated. Nevertheless, one still expects to find a persistence of earlier fantasies concerning the relationship to the parents and the relative status with the siblings.

MIDDLE ADULTHOOD (AGES 35 TO 60 YEARS)

This is usually a period of relative stabilization in terms of work and career. During this time the man generally establishes his level of effectiveness and achievement; it varies tremendously from person to person. The man who does not achieve such a phase of stability in this age period may begin to feel himself increasingly in jeopardy. As the years go by, the prospects of gaining such a status become more remote. Hence, failures during this period, whether they are determined by the relative incompetence of the man himself or whether they are imposed by outside circumstances beyond his control, are increasingly likely to be felt as threats to security and to his image of himself and self-esteem. This is particularly important in the United States, where as a youth one hears and sees such emphasis put on success. Loss of job, loss of position, loss of status in respect to work all are potential sources of symptoms or illness, both somatic and psychological, depending on vulnerability and the individual capacity for adjustment under such circumstances.

During this middle period, parents, parental figures and older friends may be lost through illness and death. One can now anticipate a rising incidence of significant losses for the man. Many factors, both early and current, will determine how successful he will be in adjusting to these losses.

In addition, the children are growing up and the father may experience varying degrees of separation from them, as when they go off to college, into military service, and, finally, leave home for work or marriage. One cannot predict from the event alone how such separations will be experienced by the man. The father has already had to work through the adolescent period of his children, which in itself required a considerable measure of adjustment. The man whose self-esteem is high, whose capacity for object relationship and for achievement is good, who feels generally fulfilled, experiences these developmental changes in his children with pride and pleasure, more than compensating for the sense of loss. The reaction of the man who is not so gratified and successful in life may be very different. He may feel jealousy, envy, anger, disappointment or sadness; he may unrealistically identify with his children, he may resist their attempts to achieve independence, or he may feel rejected, deserted and defeated, a failure. Such experiences are also important determinants of illness. (See Chapters XXVII and XXVIII.)

Toward the end of this period, some men begin to show an appreciable decline in vigor and strength. This may be revealed in a reduced capacity to sustain activity in work or play, or in declining sexual interest and potency. Some men will react to such changes by increased physical and/or sexual activity.

LATE ADULTHOOD (AGE 60+)

This is a period of biological aging. There is tremendous variation from individual to individual as to their rate and the character, but in general, the physical changes with aging include the following:

1. There is a progressive decrease in energy and strength available for work and play.

2. Tolerance of stresses of all sorts diminishes. Physiological adaptations become less adequate so that adaptive failures with consequent tissue damage are more easily brought about.

3. There is involution of different organs and systems. This includes decreased strength and substance of muscle; alterations in skeletal structure, bones, tendons and joints, which lead to impairment of locomotor ability and to a greater tendency towards fractures; structural changes in the heart and blood vessels, which impair the circulation of various organs, especially the brain; changes in skin, and a consequent impaired capacity to deal with temperature changes, physical trauma, etc.; loss of teeth, and a consequent interference with nutrition; reduction in various modalities of sensation, including vision and hearing, thereby reducing the efficiency of the perceptual system as a whole; decreased elasticity of the lungs, and consequent reduced ventilatory function; decline in gonadal function; and loss of brain substance, with consequent reduction of its efficiency as an integrating organ. These changes occur at varying rates and to different degrees in different individuals.

For the man, this is the period of retirement. He may welcome this, especially if he has other sources of gratification and supply or if his work has been particularly burdensome. Or he may see it as a blow, a loss, if he had been particularly dependent on his work as a source of gratification. He may also see it as a loss of status, a loss of strength, being discarded, thrown on the scrap heap, etc. Some men may experience the growing up of their children as a relief of the responsibility of taking care of them, whereas others may experience it as a loss of the special status of being the father who is stronger and who provides. Grandchildren appear, and they especially may be a source of pleasure and gratification. The role of grandfather is a much less ambivalent one than the role of father.* The man's sense of perpetuating himself may be greatly enhanced by having many grandchildren.

On the other hand, other important objects are being lost. The wife, siblings, old friends and sometimes the older children may fall ill and die, and some men are left relatively bereft and alone. The loss of a wife and companion of 30 or 40 years may be particularly devastating, and it is not uncommon to hear of the husband falling ill and dying very soon after the wife dies. (See Chapter XXXIII.)

In our culture, the problem of the aging man is complicated by the generally depreciating attitude towards the aged and by the nature of our social structure, in which economic factors and housing often make

---

* To the Talmud is ascribed the statement that grandparents and grandchildren get along so well together because "they love the enemy's enemy."

it difficult to find a suitable place for the aging man to live and to be taken care of. The situation is especially difficult if his relationship with his children has not evolved in a healthy fashion. The position of the older man is thus one of increasing dependent needs, yet often limited sources of supply. Because our society places so much emphasis on the vigor of youth, the older man frequently finds himself unable to face and acknowledge these changes. Many of the characteristic behavioral patterns of the aged can be understood in this framework. They include the following:

1. Age is marked by a conservatism of outlook and action. This is a reflection of the older person's decreasing tolerance for change and his diminished energy and capacity for new adaptations. Anything new and untried more readily provokes anxiety and is shunned because it may be too difficult. It is easier and more comfortable to remain within the framework of familiar experience and not to have to face and acknowledge declining ability or to experience failure.

2. There is a reduction of recent memory and an apparent sharpening of the memory of things past. In part this is due to organic changes in the brain and in part to a denial of the painfulness of the present, which is lacking in both the dependent security of childhood and the independent powers for maintaining the security that characterized the mature years. The aging person saves self-esteem by turning back to earlier periods of greater security and success as reassurance against the threats of the present. This process may be aided by confabulation and distortion, which heighten past successes or create nonexistent triumphs and minimize or discount past failures.

3. Some older persons compensate for their feelings of inferiority and inadequacy by becoming more self-assertive, aggressive, dogmatic and contemptuous of the younger generation.

4. Mild depressiveness is a common characteristic of older persons, a reaction to the relative isolation and loneliness, the feeling of being left behind by life and the repeated losses to which they are subjected.

5. Older persons become more self-centered (narcissistic). They may be more sensitive, stand on ceremony, become querulous and at times suspicious and defensive.

6. With increasing incidence of illness and death among contemporaries, the sense of invulnerability is undermined. Anxiety and depression are mobilized and are often countered by increased concern with bodily function and minor bodily symptoms. Actual organic changes become psychologically elaborated and, therefore, become more severe and incapacitating. Some old people may react to the same threat by denial, by paying no attention to the obvious physical changes and by attempting to function as though they do not exist.

7. Some degree of regression is an inevitable accompaniment of the

aging process. Previously well-maintained control of personal habits, sexual behavior, expression of aggression, self-indulgence, etc., may weaken, sometimes with disastrous results. Some older men lose their former fastidiousness, others their moral scruples. Earlier, including relatively infantile, modes of expression may reappear.

REFERENCES

1. Benedek, T.: Insight and Personality Adjustment. New York, The Ronald Press, 1946, chapters 1, 2, 3, 9, 15, 16.
2. Benedek, T.: Parenthood as a Developmental Phase. J. Am. Psychoanalyt. A., *1*:389, 1959.
3. Gitelson, M.: The Emotional Problems of Elderly People. Geriatrics, *3*:135, 1948.
4. Meerloo, J.: Psychotherapy with Elderly People. Geriatrics, *10*:583, 1955.

CHAPTER XX

THE NORMATIVE DEVELOPMENT OF THE WOMAN

Many aspects of the development of the woman are not essentially different from those of the man. However, the distinctive functions of childbearing and child rearing introduce certain major differences which have biological, social and cultural implications, even when these functions are not fulfilled.

EARLY ADULTHOOD (AGES 18 TO 35 YEARS)

We place the arbitrary age for the beginning of adulthood in the woman lower than that in the man because there is considerable evidence that the girl matures earlier than the boy, biologically and socially. Although in our culture there are many different socio-economic patterns, in general the woman does not require as long or as complex preparation to assume the role of wife and mother as the man does to establish himself as a breadwinner and father. Although most young women these days hold jobs of various sorts, for the majority the eventual goal is to become a wife and a mother. Even the majority of women who train for and plan careers do so with the hope and expectation that they can also fulfill these functions of womanhood; many succeed in both. This orientation is in contrast to that of the man, who, even though he aspires to be a father and the head of the family, is likely to place greater conscious emphasis on establishing himself in work and career.

The Sexual Cycle

A distinctive biological aspect of womanhood is the menstrual cycle. Here we see the regular and rhythmic operation of a primary drive organization, a biological system, which differentiates a part of the natural development of the female and which is primarily concerned with her eventual childbearing function. The monthly bleeding is only the outward manifestation of this process. In its broadest terms, the menstrual cycle represents the regularly recurring biological sequence whereby the woman's body is periodically prepared for mating and impregnation. This is expressed on the one hand in the changes which take place in the reproductive organs and in the body as a whole, and on the other hand in behavioral and psychic processes which are in the service of assuring fulfillment of the corresponding sexual and reproductive functions. These processes are under the control of a primary organization in the central nervous system which exerts its influence via the hypothalamus and pituitary on the gonads and reproductive tract and also on higher nervous centers and mental processes. Further, this central organization itself is also influenced at the same time both by the gonadal hormones and by the higher mid-brain systems.

The endocrine and physiological changes during the stages of the menstrual cycle may be summarized as follows:

1. At the time that menstrual bleeding begins, blood estrogen and progesterone are both very low. The anterior pituitary responds to this situation by the secretion of a high level of follicle stimulating hormone (FSH). This stimulates the formation of a large number of follicles, which, in turn, secrete estrogen and raise the blood estrogen level. The rising estrogen level contributes to the changes in the endometrium which lead to cessation of bleeding. (Days 1 to 4.)

2. Of the stimulated follicles, one begins to mature and the others degenerate. For several days, then, the blood estrogen level falls slightly and epithelial and capillary regeneration in the endometrium is now completed. (Days 4 to 8.)

3. The single maturing follicle enlarges rapidly, producing more estrogen, under the influence of which the stromal capillaries of the endometrium dilate and rapid endometrial growth occurs. This is a period of rising blood estrogen level. (Days 8 to 12.)

4. Toward the middle of the cycle the high level of estrogen stimulates the hypophysis to liberate enough luteotrophic hormone (LTH) to activate luteal tissue formed in previous cycles to produce a small amount of progesterone. (Days 12 to 14.)

5. The combined action of this small amount of progesterone and the estrogen through the hypothalamus causes the hypophysis to secrete enough luteinizing hormone (LH) to bring about ovulation. The freshly

ruptured follicle now produces less estrogen and more progesterone. (Circa day 14.)

6. During approximately the next ten days the organized corpus luteum is stimulated by LTH and continues to secrete estrogen and a large amount of progesterone. Now the endometrial glands enlarge and the total amount of endometrium increases. Toward the end of this phase the two ovarian hormones, estrogen and progesterone, act to inhibit the hypophysis so that the corpus luteum is no longer stimulated (unless fertilization has taken place and a chorion formed). (Days 14–24.) During the last four or five days the corpus luteum degenerates and the levels of progesterone and estrogen again fall rapidly. The stroma and glands of the endometrium shrink, stasis occurs, then necrosis, and the menstrual flow begins. With the fall in ovarian hormone level the hypophysis is freed from its inhibition, produces more FSH, a new burst of follicular activity begins, and the cycle resumes.

This cyclically recurring biological process exerts its influence in subtle ways on the mental activity and behavior of the woman. This is to be anticipated since it constitutes a basic biological characteristic of the female, the fulfillment of which demands certain appropriate preparatory and consummatory activities. Correlative psychoanalytic and endocrine studies have thrown considerable light on the interrelations between these cyclic biological processes and psychological processes.[1] By examining the correlations between psychological data and the various phases of the menstrual cycle and hormone levels as established by vaginal smears, Benedek has been able to demonstrate consistent psychodynamic trends corresponding to these different phases. Unconsciously, and at the most basic level, corresponding to the ripening of the follicles and the rising levels of estrogen, is an active object-directed psychodynamic tendency which brings forth wishes, fantasies and desires of varying intensity and of different levels of maturity. The aim of the unconscious motivating tendency is to bring about contact with the sexual object and achieve gratification through coitus. How this drive will be experienced and acted on by the woman, whether it achieves any conscious recognition, will be determined not only by the actual situation as it exists at the moment, but also by previous developmental experiences that have influenced psychosexual development. When progesterone production comes into play, beginning in the pre-ovulation state, the active outwardly-directed tendency fuses with a more passive receptive tendency. Parallel with the peak of the cycle at the time of ovulation, the sexual drive reaches its highest level of integration. Although the psychic manifestations of this state may vary, depending upon the individual's chronological and emotional maturity as well as on her external situation, the point of highest hormone production leads to the dominance of the passive-receptive tendency, which motivates reproductive behavior. The content of the psychological material at this time can best be described as emotional preparation for motherhood. This evolves parallel to the effect of the hormone of the corpus luteum (progesterone) upon the uterus, preparing for nidation of the impregnated ovum.

When conception does not occur and the progesterone and then estrogen levels decline, a regression of this genital and reproductive integration takes place, and more primitive, i.e., pregenital, manifestations emerge. The nature of such pregenital trends varies greatly from individual to individual, but in any event they are likely to be associated with residual intrapsychic conflicts originating in childhood. This accounts for the prominence of symptoms, especially tension and depression, in the premenstrual period. Oral or anal patterns, including such manifestations as overeating, a drive toward cleanliness, etc., are fairly frequent in the premenstrual period. When menstrual flow is established, this mood generally relaxes, and after a few days, as the new follicle begins to ripen, the psychosexual cycle begins anew. It should be emphasized that this description concerns the basic innate drive pattern, whereas the various levels of learning and development which modify the individual's response to the drive and influence her actual experience are much more highly individual matters.

Benedek's more detailed examination of the phenomena associated with ovulation[1] provides further information on how mental processes and behavior are integrated toward the goal of reproduction. At the time of ovulation there is characteristically a sense of relaxation and well-being and a shift of the woman's interest to her own body and its welfare. Physiologically, ovulation is accompanied by an increase in metabolism, including an elevation of temperature. Psychologically, ovulation is accompanied by an intensification of receptive and retentive tendencies. The activation of the reproductive drive, a biological process, tends to reactivate the various psychological processes associated with childbearing and sexual development, including the earliest relationships with the parents. At the same time, some of the developmental factors concerned with the formation of both ego and superego are also reactivated. Thus, not only the drive but also factors which inhibit the drive, postpone its gratification, negate its meaning and significance, organize for its avoidance, etc., may come into being psychically. This is a repetitive process, beginning with the menarche, which serves the function of bringing about the repetition of the developmental conflicts and of achieving their working over toward reproductive maturity. Under ideal circumstances, then, the regularly recurring sexual cycle of the young girl provides repeated opportunities for her to "learn" to work through her sexual development and to achieve reproductive maturity in both a biological and psychological sense. The fact that many of the early cycles are anovulatory helps to insure that this can occur before pregnancy is possible.

Although not part of normal development, the influence of psychic apparatus on the sexual cycle might also be mentioned here. There is good evidence that both the menarche and the development of secondary sexual characteristics may be delayed and inhibited in the presence of certain types of psychic conflicts. It is also well known that menses may be delayed or the periodicity of the cycle disturbed in the course of certain psychic conflicts as well as during depression and physical deprivation. Similarly, irregular and/or prolonged bleeding during and between regular menstrual periods may occur. There may be anovulatory cycles on the one hand, and false pregnancies on the other.

Such biological factors provide, of course, only an undercurrent and do not determine the final form or character of the girl's mental processes and behavior. They do contribute, however, the signature which is distinctly feminine and which psychobiologically differentiates the woman from the man. It is a soft and silent voice that exerts its influence subtly and gently and for the most part unconsciously. It constitutes a background influence on psychic activity and behavior, operating while the young girl is much preoccupied with establishing her role and status. Like the young man, she too finds herself working through a separation from her parents and other family members and achieving a certain level of independence both in relationship to work and with other girls and boys. She is further consolidating her identity as a particular young woman and she experiences the elations and disappointments of love, culminating eventually in courtship and marriage. There are many social pressures and influences which color and circumscribe the behavior and activity of the young girl. For the most part there are differences as to what society expects of the young girl as compared to the young man. Particularly in respect to decorum and sexual behavior, standards of behavior are generally more strict and circumscribed for the girl. Failure or inability to live up to such standards may be a source of conflict or may intensify old conflicts and may precipitate symptoms of illness. (See Chapters XXVII and XXVIII.)

Marriage

The woman is likely to marry at a younger age than the man. Always present and operating at an unconscious level is the biological drive toward conception and motherhood, the manifest expression of which may range all the way from the most overt, frank and conscious wish to have babies to the complete denial of such a wish. Such an unconscious influence plays a much stronger role in the woman than in the man in determining the choice of marital partner and the decision when to marry. In many different ways the woman tends to be more oriented toward fulfilling her eventual role of mother and homemaker. In this regard the woman more often operates under the influence of a longer term perspective than the man. The woman is inclined also to be more accepting of a relatively dependent role both in relationship to her husband and in relationship to society in general. She maintains closer links with her own family, especially with her own mother. Her sexual activity is also more influenced by these longer term factors, biologically under the control of the hormones and psychosocially under the influence of many other factors. Although the young wife may continue to work, either voluntarily or because of necessity, this is generally experienced as a goal secondary in importance to that of raising a family. The largest part of her psychobiological development has been to prepare her for this goal. Failures or difficulties in this preparation, resulting from the vicissitudes of early development, play a large role in determining the nature and variety of conflicts and problems that may develop for the woman. The more successful her own development has been, particularly in relationship to a healthy and mature mother who, in turn, had enjoyed a good relationship with a healthy husband, the better are the girl's prospects for success and for the maintenance of health. Because the girl's life is likely to have much more in common with that of her own mother than is true of the man in relationship to either of his parents, there is a stronger tendency for reawakening of and repetition of old conflicts which existed with the mother during infancy and early life. The awakening of such conflicts should not be taken to mean that they will not be successfully resolved.

For the young girl, as with the man, the early phase of marriage involves a period of mutual adjustment. The girl must succeed in effecting a further degree of separation from her own parents, especially the mother, upon whom she becomes less dependent, both psychologically and realistically. Part of this separation is accomplished by and during the state of "being in love," during which the husband is endowed with many qualities, some of which may be exaggerated at best. This enables the girl to span the process of separation from her own family and to consolidate a relationship with her husband. During the early years of marriage the relationship gradually becomes established on a more realistic basis. Some girls, however, may experience varying degrees of disappointment in their husbands and some adjustment is necessary. Eventually, the young wife succeeds in establishing her own identity as a wife. This includes both the stabilization of her relationship with her husband on a more realistic basis, as well as with friends, neighbors, other members of the family, and so forth.

Pregnancy

Conception may take place at any time during the childbearing period of marriage. (We shall not discuss here pregnancy in the unmarried woman, pregnancy which may force a marriage, or pregnancy resulting from an extramarital relationship. Needless to say, there are important psychological processes underlying such occurrences which in turn introduce a host of psychological and social problems which are of great importance.) Whether or not pregnancy is planned, its possibility is always present. Young women differ greatly in how prepared psychologically they are to become pregnant. There are many potential sources of conflict in relation to pregnancy:

1. The girl may be ready, but a variety of realistic external factors may make pregnancy inadvisable or impossible.

2. The girl may be ready, but the husband may not be prepared emotionally to assume the role of father.

3. The girl may be ready and eager, but either she or her husband may have some organic defect which renders one of them infertile.

4. The girl may not yet be ready, but her husband or family or social group expects her to be.

5. The girl may not really be ready, but may unconsciously use pregnancy for other ends, such as satisfying an unresolved childhood fantasy, as a means of replacing a lost object, as an adjustment to disappointment in the marriage, etc.

When religious or other scruples do not intervene, there is the possibility, through contraceptive devices, for the couple to regulate the timing of the pregnancy. A failure of contraception may catch the woman unprepared and impose a sudden demand for an adjustment which she may or may not succeed in accomplishing. Also, when there are religious or other interdictions on the part of either partner, the use of contraception can, of course, be another important source of conflict.

The various factors concerned in the preparation of the woman for pregnancy have already been discussed in preceding chapters and may be summarized as follows:

1. There is the biological component as represented in the original endowment and development of the reproductive organization, including the central neural organization and the reproductive organs.

2. There are the particular cultural attitudes in the environment in which the girl grows up.

3. There is the relationship with the mother. The degree to which the mother is experienced as a good, nurturing, supporting, succoring figure in early life helps to determine through the early introjections and later identifications the woman's own capacity to feel herself as a potential "good" mother. In addition, the mother's attitudes toward the woman's role, pregnancy, labor, child-raising, etc., all are important

in influencing the girl's attitudes toward acceptance of her own femininity and procreative functions.

4. There is the father's relationship to the mother and to the girl. This includes his acceptance of her as a girl and, of course, the successful transformation and resolution of the Oedipus complex. Related to this are also the development and fate of the girl's birth and pregnancy fantasies during childhood, as well as some of her actual experiences with such matters, as they may concern the mother, older sisters or younger siblings.

5. There is the development during puberty and the repeated "working over" associated with the sexual cycle, as already described.

Conception and pregnancy are, first of all, biological processes, but they also have their influence on the psychic apparatus. A primary drive organization subserves the aims of pregnancy. Its first influence appears in the postovulatory period as the level of progesterone is rising. When conception takes place and a chorion is formed, progesterone secretion continues, and this then sets in motion all the psychobiological processes concerned with the subsequent pregnancy. The psychic trends associated with high progesterone, as described earlier, are continued and intensified. Both the bodily and the psychic economy are now concentrated on the task of nurturing the developing fetus. Psychodynamically this is expressed in greater interest in the body and the self, in an intensification of the intaking (oral) trends, in a reduction in heterosexual interests. There are many and rapid physiological changes taking place in the body, some of which are experienced as symptoms. The explanation of the nausea of early pregnancy, which occurs in a high proportion of women, is as yet unknown, but there is good reason to believe that it is at least in part contributed to by some of the psychological processes associated with the intensified oral drive. There is much better evidence that such factors operate among the women who continue to vomit throughout pregnancy; such women are generally found to have considerable unconscious conflict about the pregnancy. The increased appetite and food intake are also expressions of an intensified oral drive and they simultaneously serve both the need for increased nutriment for the growth and development of the fetus and the psychological need of the woman to receive.

In spite of the symptoms that may be experienced in the course of these rapid physiological changes, the healthy woman experiences her pregnancy with exquisite joy and fulfillment. She feels serene, contented, expectant and fulfilled in a way which is entirely unique. There is a normal increase in narcissism in the sense that she derives the largest part of her satisfaction from experiencing what is going on within her body and from the attention and affection which is directed toward her by the various persons in her environment. By the same token, certain women may become disturbed and have symptoms, as, for example, the woman whose previous development had predisposed her to experience bodily sensations or changes in the body image as uncomfortable or dangerous; the woman whose earliest life experience had not included sufficient care, love and attention to render her confident of such feelings within herself; and the woman whose external environment realistically is deficient, depriving or inadequate. Obviously, the woman who is not prepared emotionally for pregnancy for any of a host of reasons will have difficulty in enjoying this experience.

As the pregnancy develops the woman waits eagerly for the first sign of life, the movement of the fetus, and now, for the first time, her fantasies about the baby assume a more realistic quality. As her abdomen enlarges and as fetal movements continue, she not only is much preoccupied with the reality of her baby but also becomes occupied with preparatory "nesting" activities. She makes many preparations in fact and in fantasy to welcome the new baby. During the last weeks of pregnancy, the woman begins to feel impatient and uncomfortable. The pleasures of the state of pregnancy grow less and the prospect of terminating the discomforts that develop make her also more able to accept some of the pain and difficulties of the delivery.

Delivery

The delivery itself is another complex psychobiological process for which women are variably prepared. Again it is justified to say that the whole life experience of the girl up to this point has contributed to this preparation. Most crucial is the early psychosexual development during childhood and the degree to which the woman has achieved the maturity of adulthood. Of next importance is her actual life situation at the time, meaning, in essence, that her ability successfully to experience the delivery without undue disturbance will be optimal if she is not concerned with unrelated conflicts, frustrations or losses at the same time. In this regard the relationship with the physician is of great importance, since she comes to rely upon him and on his skill and knowledge to protect her and her baby from pain and harm.

As labor begins, most women enter into the experience with reasonable confidence of success, but not without some stirrings of anxiety concerning injury, pain, and, at times, the possibility of death either for themselves or for the baby. Under normal circumstances, these concerns are fairly readily taken care of by the woman herself with the aid of her physician and her family. Ideally, her physician will have prepared her for what to expect during the course of the labor and delivery and will have clarified for her what will be expected of her and what she may expect of him.

Confinement

The most important first experience of the mother is the discovery of and the reunion with the baby. The first cry and the first physical contact with the newborn infant is generally experienced by the woman as a joyous moment. Intense motherly feelings well up and there is a sense of serenity and completeness in holding the baby. In mammals there is a regular, orderly sequence of events whereby the mother animal establishes a relationship with her newborn, the interruption of which may interfere with the subsequent relationship. There is good reason to believe that such a biological factor also operates as a drive in the human female. This is of some practical importance because it is noted that some women who have had anesthesia and who are unconscious during the birth experience or for some time afterwards may have a sense of estrangement and distance from the infant which is not otherwise experienced to this degree.

Motherhood and Motherliness

Many aspects have already been discussed in the chapters on infancy and early childhood, to which the reader is referred. The quality of motherliness develops and evolves throughout the life of the girl and is intimately related to her development and her relationship with her own mother. "Motherliness" is not dependent upon the fact of being a mother. It exists before the woman ever becomes pregnant and may be manifested in many different ways. Further, the childless woman does not necessarily lack the qualities of motherliness; indeed, some women who for one reason or another are incapable of bearing children succeed in displacing and sublimating these qualities in many other activities, often having to do directly or indirectly with the care of children. In some women the quality of motherliness is exaggerated and is expressed in a need to have or to take care of innumerable children, occasionally a sign of psychopathology. As already described, the expressions of motherliness are different at different ages of the child and also are different with the successive children.

Like the father's, the woman's role and identity will be different depending on the ages, number and sex distribution of her children. And, of course, she learns from experience with each successive child. Her attitudes and feelings also change and develop as each child assumes a different identity and behaves in different ways. As the children appear, the woman becomes increasingly involved with the problems of child care and home care—much more intimately than does the father, since hers is commonly a full-time job. The close reciprocal nature of the relationship between mother and small child is such that she is likely to be more sensitive to and more responsive to the successes, failures, illnesses and developmental thrusts of her children. She is more closely tied to the children and suffers more from having them grow up and go away from her. Hence a mother may unwittingly oppose the efforts of the child to achieve some measure of independence and to separate from her, since she may feel these as some degree of loss. Going to school for the first time may be experienced not only by the child as a separation from the mother but also by the mother as a separation from the child. The woman who works, whether by design or by necessity, must make provisions for the care of her children, and under either circumstance she may have conscious or unconscious conflicts that she herself does not fill the mother's role.

Wife-Mother

The young wife who has become a mother assumes a different identity and a different relationship with her husband than existed before. She also sees her husband in a different role than previously. Both are now parents and the woman may have difficulty if the husband-father does not adequately assume his new role. Many of the day-to-day problems and adjustments of the young woman are concerned with the interrelationships between herself, her husband and her children. These will be discussed in somewhat greater detail in the next chapter. The woman also achieves a new status in relationship to other women and in relationship to other members of the family by virtue of being a mother. She must now fulfill certain expectations set both by herself and by those around her. Failure to live up to those expectations may be one source of psychic stress. (See Chapter XXVII.)

MIDDLE ADULTHOOD (AGES 35 TO 60 YEARS)

By the beginning of this period, most women have had either all or most of their children. Although the reproductive potential continues, usually into the mid-forties or later, it is unusual for the woman to have more than one child after 35, and many women have none. For those women whose childbearing begins relatively late, more of their middle adult life is spent in the care of young children than is usually the case. Those women who continue to have children until the end of their reproductive period usually have the help of their older children to participate in and share some aspects of care of the younger ones. As long as the sexual cycle continues, the woman is under its phasic influence and hence the various psychic aspects of reproductive experience are kept alive. In this age period, conflicts about becoming pregnant may be different since even women who earlier very much wanted children now may no longer do so. Or there may be disappointments about not having had a child or not having had more children earlier.

The children now are at different ages and in different phases of development and they are going through varying stages of separation from the mother. The period of middle adult life is marked by the possibility of very important losses for the woman. They include not only the loss through illness or death of her own parents and older family members, but also the loss through school, work, military service and marriage of her older children. It may be especially difficult for the mother to adjust to the loss of the oldest child, particularly the oldest son. It may be even more distressing when the youngest child finally leaves home, leaving the mother for the first time with no children to take care of. There may be an intervening period during which one or more grown children are home but they no longer have the role of children and the mother does not feel as needed as she did earlier. As these changes take place, the woman who has devoted the largest part of her energy and efforts to child rearing and homemaking gradually, sometimes suddenly, finds herself relatively less occupied and less needed. Thus, in addition to the actual separation from her grown children, the woman may also to varying degrees experience a loss of status. This constitutes a change in the image of herself and may require a developmental adjustment. Some women are unable to make such an adjustment and have difficulty as a consequence. The more healthy woman is able to achieve new interests or to reinstate old interests which she had had to drop, and she develops for herself a new phase of her life. She may not be able to turn to her husband for help in this respect since this is generally the period in his life in which he is either deeply involved with his own work and career, or, if not, he is having troubles of his own. (See also Chapter XXVII.)

The Menopause
This is a biological event marking the end of the reproductive period of the woman's life. It generally occurs in the forties unless artificially induced at an earlier age by surgery or disease. It usually takes place gradually over a number of months and is associated with the gradual decline of gonadal function. Contrary to common notion, there are no regular predictable symptoms of the menopause. Not only do many women have no symptoms, but even among those who do have symptoms careful investigation usually reveals that these symptoms had existed long before the menopause and were accentuated during the menopause rather than developing for the first time. In general, the psychodynamic trends already described during the premenstrual period tend to be reactivated during the menopausal period. The woman whose premenstrual symptoms had been severe and persistent throughout her reproductive cycle is likely to have correspondingly severe menopausal symptoms. She experiences the menopause as a loss, a depletion and a decline in her sexual attractiveness,

her usefulness and her function as a woman. Oral and narcissistic needs are intensified, but because the change is experienced as involving her own body, there may be a feeling that such needs can no longer be fulfilled. For this reason, as we shall see later on, menopause is particularly likely to be associated with depressive symptomatology. The more fortunate woman whose life adjustment has been good and whose life achievements have been significant tolerates these changes much better. She may even feel herself relieved of certain pressures or unconscious obligations related to still being potentially reproductive. The decline of gonadal function does not necessarily influence the woman's interest and capacity to respond heterosexually. Indeed, some women are more able to respond sexually when the possibility of pregnancy no longer exists. Some women make a vigorous effort to cover up or overcompensate during the period of menopause.

Toward the end of this period, most women begin to show definite physical changes associated with aging and some show decline in strength and vigor.

LATE ADULT LIFE (AGE 60+)

Most of the considerations discussed in relationship to the man apply also to the woman during this period of life and need not be repeated. Perhaps of most distinctive significance for the woman is her role as grandmother. Through being a grandmother, the woman is able to continue vicariously her reproductive role and to enjoy many privileges which she could not have with her own children. Sometimes the relationship with a grandchild may be extremely important, compensating for the loss through growing up of her own children.

REFERENCES

1. Benedek, T.: Psychosexual Functions in Women. New York, The Ronald Press, 1952: The Sexual Cycle in Women (chapters 1–11); Climacterium, A Developmental Phase (chapter 13, also Psychoanalyt. Quart., *19*:1, 1950); The Functions of the Sexual Apparatus and Their Disturbances (chapter 14); Some Psychophysiological Problems of Motherhood (chapter 15).
2. Benedek, T.: The Organization of the Reproductive Drive. Internat. J. Psychoanal., *41*:1, 1960.
3. Deutsch, H.: The Psychology of Women. Vol. 2, Motherhood. New York, Grune & Stratton, 1945.

4. Donovan, J. C.: The Menopausal Syndrome: A Study of Case Histories.
   Am. J. Obst. & Gynec., *62*:1281, 1951.
5. Donovan, J. C.: Psychologic Aspects of Menopause. Obst. & Gynec.,
   6:379, 1955.
6. Markee, J. E.: The Relation of Blood Flow to Endometrial Growth and
   the Inception of Menstruation. *In:* Engel, E. T. (ed.): Menstruation
   and Its Disorders. Springfield, Illinois, Charles C Thomas, 1950.
7. Mead, M.: Male and Female. New York, William Morrow & Co. 1949.

CHAPTER XXI

THE FAMILY

Any discussion of growth and development is incomplete without some consideration of the family as a dynamic social grouping within which the individual grows, develops and relates to others and through which he relates to the society and culture.

All cross-cultural surveys have shown that some form of family is found in every society. Although there are many variations as to how families are organized, the basic structure involves an institutionalization of sexual and parental roles in a formal pattern of small nuclear groups integrated with other groups and structurally related to all other units of the social system. We shall not be concerned with all these cross-cultural variations, but rather with the types of family structure encountered in America. It is important to appreciate that the family structure familiar to most students through their own life experiences is not necessarily typical as far as peoples the world over are concerned. Further, there are many exceptions to it even within this culture. For example, many ethnic and national groups in this country have attempted to maintain family structures typical of their homeland. An important tension for the individuals in such family groups stems from attempts of the second and sometimes third generations to break away from the old family patterns and to conform to what is considered the more typical American pattern.

Elucidation of the structure and the function of the family is not a problem which can be handled with the techniques and concepts of individual psychology. The family may be regarded as having a well-defined, organized structure of its own. For any one family member, the family consists of the nuclear group (husband, wife and children), the lateral extensions (the range of collateral relatives such as aunts, uncles and cousins), and the vertical extensions (the range of generations,

211

including grandparents, great-grandparents, and grandchildren). It also includes persons with whom the individual may not necessarily have any personal relationship but who have a lasting influence on the family and its members in terms of traditions, standards, accomplishments, faults or failures. Further, the structure of the family is very much related to the structure of the society of which it is a part. Thus, in the urban middle class there tend to be small family groups with a continuous demand for maximum mobility, both geographical and social. Upper class families are more likely to place emphasis on the importance of the continuity of the generations, with their traditions and hierarchical systems. In certain rural areas and with certain ethnic groups the collateral relatives may be more important. But even such limited generalizations have a way of changing with the times, as indicated by the larger number of children that characterizes the middle class family now as compared to a decade or two ago.

Some functions of the family are universal. These include the socialization of children, the satisfaction of sexual needs and the psychological, biological and material maintenance of the members of the family. Of course, the family is the source of the first objects, which are so important in the psychic development of the child. These functions are carried out in many different ways, depending on, among other things, the social milieu in which the family exists. A father of one occupational or one social grouping may be expected by the social group in which he relates to have different responsibilities and attitudes and to carry them out differently than might be true of the father in another grouping.

Kluckhohn and Spiegel[3] have suggested five frames of reference within which to consider the family. In the *first* place, they note that the family is a collection of individuals. So far, this has been the main frame of reference in which the "family" has been considered in this book, namely, in relationship to the needs and conflicts of the individual. We have examined how the developing individual relates to each family member—mother, father, siblings, spouse, offspring, etc.—and what the role of each is in his development. But the family is not simply a collection of individuals, it is a dynamic group. Therefore, a *second* point of reference is that of the small primary group with its characteristic action processes in group dynamics. Here the factors involved in how the group functions in relation to other groups and in how the members of the group interact with each other in relation to the existence and behavior of the group as a whole cannot be dealt with simply in terms of the psychology of the individual. Factors which maintain or disrupt the cohesiveness and integrity of the family as a group or which bring it into conflict with other groups may override, or at least considerably complicate, the psychological requirements of the individual. The family, of course, is only one of several groups of which the individual is a member. Intragroup and intergroup dynamics thus constitute the second important frame of reference for consideration of the family. *Third,* the family is also a major unit of the total social system. Characteristics of its structure and function ramify through the whole social system, with all sorts of subsystems with which it articulates. Thus, the family must be seen in terms of the social system of which it is a part. This leads to the *fourth* point of reference, the system of values characteristic of the social system. The family is a main medium for transmission of these values. The family is the main carrier of the cultural values of a given historical period. So strong is its influence in this regard that political movements which wish radically to change these values generally find it expedient to disrupt the family structure by removing, or at least alienating, the children from their parents. *Fifth,* the family has a geographical as well as occupational status and both are important variables in the structure and function of different families. There may be considerable contrast between families in urban as compared to rural settings.

Kluckhohn and Spiegel view these five reference points as a system of interrelated and more or less integrated component parts. They illustrate it with the following example: "A married woman may or may not be a mother. Whether she is or not probably will depend on her biologic and psychologic state. But if she is a mother, her parental attitude will vary according to her geographic location and status in the social system. She will have different techniques for taking care of her child if she lives on a farm with her husband usually within hailing distance, from those she will develop if she lives in a city as the wife of a traveling salesman who is gone for long periods. Not only geographic location and occupational status, but the size of the primary group will produce variations in the parental attitudes and the child care arrangements. The farm wife who has ten older children will delegate much more responsibility than the traveling salesman's wife who has two children under five." Even from such a limited example it should be clear that if we are to understand the forces impinging upon any individual, it is necessary also to know something of these other points of reference as they apply to the family as well.

THE RELATION OF THE FAMILY TO THE SOCIAL SYSTEM

The structure and the function of the family are closely related to the form of the social system. At the same time the more or less universal functions of the family provide a certain stability and resistance to change in the social system. At times, changes in the social system bring about significant and sometimes rapid changes, even from generation to generation. For example, we are quite familiar with how industrialization, changes in housing, suburban living, transportation, mobility, conveniences of living, availability of labor, etc., have changed many of the aspects of family life in the current generation as compared to the past generation. This is in contrast to some relatively stable cultures where patterns of family living have remained essentially unchanged for many, many generations.

When we examine the roles of the various family members and what is expected of them, we find that they differ considerably depending on what social system one is concerned with. In this country the position held by the father in the occupational world is particularly important. It may depend upon his family status, his class position and his educational attainments. When a man of the upper middle class does not have the intellectual capacity to obtain or hold a position commensurate with the family expectations, whether he holds a more menial job or whether he is protected in a job in which he really does not have commensurate ability, the situation can be a strain on other members of the family. A similar circumstance involving a man from a lower social stratum would not present a problem of the same magnitude either to the individual or to the members of the family. In considering the psychological stress for an individual, one must be aware of the implications not only for the man who fails to live up to the expectations of other family members and to the family standards, but also for other members of the family who may experience this failure as a blow to their pride and self-esteem. On the other hand, the unsuccessful or deviant member of the family may serve as a scapegoat and as such may be a compensating influence for lesser failures.

There are also certain rules of residence which characterize a society and which determine certain conditions of living. In general, members of the nuclear family group (husband, wife and children) live together in the same residence. From the point of view of the individual, it is this which determines what he calls home, with all its implications in terms of his sense of personal identity and feelings about local, regional and other matters. In our society, especially in urban groups, it is expected that the residence will include the nuclear family but not other relatives. Thus, the husband or wife who is obliged to make room for another member of the family may feel imposed upon, and all involved may suffer to some degree. This is in marked contrast to certain other societies in which the sharing of household facilities by a large number of relatives is the usual state of affairs.

SOCIALIZATION OF CHILDREN

A basic and universal function of the family is to be a medium for the socialization of children. We have already discussed in detail the significance of the biological-psychological dependence of the child upon the parents and the implications of this for the development of the child. The family also serves, however, as a system whereby a society makes possible the systematic and orderly introduction of children into their roles and places in society. Some of these functions, of course, are also performed by the educational and other systems. To a large degree, however, the child learns through and within the family the conditions for living within this small group, and through this experience he learns the expectations of the larger groups and of society. He does not actually grow up in a random way but has to learn his status and the range of possible future roles available to him within the society. In addition to the largely intrapsychic and interpersonal aspects of development earlier described, the learning of social role behavior and of techniques of adjustment to the various kinds of situations he will meet with as an adult is best accomplished in the framework of the family. Needless to say, the roles so acquired will tend to reflect or mirror those appropriate not only for the social system as a whole, but also for the particular systems characterizing that family. The sense of belonging which evolves thus concerns not only object relationships in terms of individuals but also an identity within a group, an identity which involves a number of different roles. The child who is brought up in an institutional setting or whose family is unstable or breaks up tends to have much more difficulty in achieving such a sense of belonging. Similarly, the deviant family, whether because of individual psychopathology or because of different social origin, makes a less adequate if not seriously defective contribution to the child's socialization.

THE SIGNIFICANCE OF ROLE

The concept of roles has been useful in describing the characteristics of a system of relations within a group over a period of time. In respect to the family as a system, one may describe the behavior of any one member in terms of his role in transaction with a role partner or partners. Spiegel[5] has defined a role as "a goal-directed pattern or sequence of acts tailored by the cultural process for the transactions a person may carry out in a social group or situation. No role exists in isolation but is always patterned to gear in with the complementary or reciprocal role of a role partner (alter). Thus, all roles have to be learned by the persons who wish to occupy them in accordance with the cultural (or subcultural) values of the society in which they exist." The role concept is a way of describing dynamic processes occurring among the members of a group who are related to each other in part at least through the medium of the group. It should be appreciated that in the context of group dynamics we are now considering processes which in the context of intrapsychic dynamics were referred to as object relations and identity formation. The emphasis now is on the forces involved in the structure and function of the group, here specifically the family. For any one individual the other persons constitute objects, and we have conceptualized his ways of relating in terms of "object relations." This concept viewed the situation from the perspective of the individual. When the situation is viewed from the perspective of the group (the family) and the processes concerned in the structure and function of the group, other ways of conceptualization are necessary. It goes without saying that the maintenance of successful and satisfying object relations by the individual is also importantly influenced by the factors operating within the group which maintain its integrity as an effective system for interpersonal and social relations. The consideration of roles thus provides us with a different set of data elucidating the influences impinging on the individual as he functions in various groups, of which the family is one of the most important, but not the only one.

By and large, as individuals we are relatively unaware of our roles and of the various devices that we use in maintaining our roles and in behaving appropriately. In general, we know unconsciously what to do and how to do it under a wide variety of circumstances. This is important in terms of psychic economy because it enables the individual to know what to do and how to behave in many situations without having to think it out. When operating in familiar situations one is able to be spontaneous and need not be self-conscious or self-guarded. On the other hand, when one moves suddenly to a strange situation, a foreign culture, or even a new neighborhood, for example, one immediately becomes aware of all the subtleties involved in knowing what one's role is, as well as in knowing what the role of other persons is. Each individual plays many different roles and each role is culturally patterned, meaning that it fits into the needs of the particular social system in question. By the same token, there are standards or norms for each role. In the course of growth and development one learns the various cues and signals that indicate role expectations. This, then, becomes a form of communication among all those who share the same culture. It is a system of sharing meanings and values having both cognitive and evaluative aspects. Each person unconsciously at least, and consciously to some extent, will know the meaning and intent of the signals and cues and behavior that he manifests, and at the same time he has correspondingly definite expectations of the response of other participants. There are patterns of gratification and of frustration in this situation; success in eliciting the expected or hoped for response tends to be gratifying and the failure to elicit it tends to be frustrating. The capacity to function within the framework of the customary roles of the society within which one lives is an important factor in how one maintains one's identity and one's self-esteem. The person who is restricted in this respect will likely be correspondingly restricted in his range of activity and social contacts. Similarly, one can anticipate that being placed in a new situation will always involve to some extent having to learn the systems of communication and the role expectations idiosyncratic to the new situation. The child first experiences this when visiting a new family or when going to school. When a person comes into a hospital as a patient for the first time he has to learn the rules and cues of this new social environment, a new role. If he has difficulty in learning them, he may become disturbed and his progress may be impeded. Indeed, the possibility of such a failure accounts for the reluctance of some patients to enter a hospital even when desperately in need of medical care.

Roles and the conditions involved in roles underlie a feeling of belonging by right of membership in groups. The formal structuring of the various functions of the family, including the cultural and other types of rituals, provides an initial framework. When the family is deviant in one way or another, the child growing up in such a situation not only may feel deprived and be disturbed in relationship to the members of his own family, but also may lose a sense of belonging by virtue of having learned cues and signals for his roles in his own family which differ from those learned by his peers in other families. Such a sense of differing is another factor underlying the distress experienced by a child who has lost a parent. He not only suffers from the loss itself, but he also feels and is seen by others as different from the child who has both parents. Some children will hide the fact that a parent is missing, not only because it is uncomfortable for them to be different but also because it helps them to overcome feelings of having been abandoned.

DISTURBANCES IN ROLE SYSTEMS WITHIN THE FAMILY

Spiegel[5] has pointed out how harmony is maintained in a family (or any group) by complementarity of roles. With the changes in individuals which occur in the course of the vicissitudes of life, however, complementarity may fail. The role partners may disappoint each other's expectations, producing some type of tension which, if persistent, may end in disruption of the group. Spiegel has described five causes for failure of complementarity in role systems in the family.

1. COGNITIVE DISCREPANCY. This occurs when the persons involved in the role system do not know or do not have sufficient familiarity with the roles expected of them. Some of the difficulties between children and parents are of this origin. It may develop in respect to a sudden new situation, in which one or both members are unfamiliar with what is now expected.

2. DISCREPANCY OF GOALS.   The goal of any one person at any time does not necessarily correspond to the goal of the others in the group. For example, for various conscious or unconscious intrapsychic reasons a mother's goal at one point may be to stop what she is doing and rest while her husband or children may insist on their expectation that dinner be prepared. Or a father with phobic symptoms may avoid seeking a certain job because riding in elevators makes him too anxious, whereas his family's expectation is that he be a provider. The persistence or repetition of such goal discrepancies becomes increasingly disruptive to the family group and to the individuals making up the group.

3. ALLOCATIVE DISCREPANCY.   In any particular social situation there is a question of the person's rights to the role he wishes to occupy. Thus, some roles are universally expected, such as age and sex roles. Some roles have to be achieved, involving effort and the satisfaction of certain requirements. One must follow certain formalities to earn the role, and disapproval may occur if the role is usurped without fulfilling the requirements. Some roles may be adopted, consciously or unconsciously. Thus, a person may adopt the role of the generous one, the victim, the defender, the fighter, the strong one, etc. Automatically, the adoption of such roles involves the assignment of the complementary roles to the other persons. Unwillingness of the other person to accept the assigned role becomes a source of conflict. Sometimes a role is consciously assumed in fun or play. This is a means of reducing tension. "I was only kidding," is an example, but it may misfire if the other person does not accept the assumed role.

4. INSTRUMENTAL DISCREPANCY.   This depends on the fact that certain instruments, props, costumes, possessions, etc. (including money), are necessary to fulfill certain roles. When there is a disparity between the role allocated by the self or by others and the instrumentation necessary for the role, frustration and disappointment result. A common situation is one in which the person attempts to assume a role beyond his educational, intellectual or financial means.

5. DISCREPANCY IN CULTURAL VALUE ORIENTATIONS.   This, of course, is most apt to occur when there are differences in the cultural, religious or ethnic backgrounds of the family members.

Restoration of Complementarity
When the family as a group is threatened with disruption by any

of these types of failures, there are a number of processes which come into operation to restore the complementarity. Spiegel delineates the following techniques of resolving conflicts and restoring the balance of the group.

1. COERCING.   One person forces the other to accept the complementary role by threat of present or future punishment. This may be neutralized by *defying*.

2. COAXING.   This involves the manipulation of present or future rewards by asking, promising, pleading, begging, tempting, etc. This may be neutralized by *refusing* or *withholding*.

3. EVALUATING.   A value context is used by praising, blaming, shaming, approving or disapproving.

4. MASKING.   Correct information is withheld or incorrect information is substituted pertinent to the settlement of the conflict. These devices include pretending, evading, censoring, distorting, etc.

5. POSTPONING.   The passage of time sometimes permits changes to take place which will resolve the role conflict. This technique rests on the expectation, often fulfilled, that intrapsychic processes tending toward reduction in tension will bring about a change in attitude and hence resolve the conflict.

6. ROLE REVERSAL.   One person puts himself in the position of the other and, by so doing, is able to bring about changes within himself that permit resolution of the conflict.

There are, in addition, techniques of role modification, such as joking, referral to a third party, exploring, compromising and consolidating, in which there is an active attempt to bring about change in the roles of all the persons involved.

These various processes whereby the dynamic equilibrium of a family may be disrupted or restored are of importance in understanding the experiences of any one individual. They help us to see how the individual helps maintain the structure and stability of the family and, conversely, how disturbances involving one member of the family may affect other members, not only through changes in interpersonal relationships, but also by changes in the dynamics of the family. Of special importance to physicians is to appreciate that when a family member falls ill, especially if it is a chronic illness or an illness which changes his occupational or other status, significant changes may be required in the structure of the family and in the roles and status of its members. Various members of the family may now have to do different things, assume new roles or go without on this account. For some individuals this may involve a gain, such as now having a role and importance they did not have before, and they may actually relinquish it reluctantly. For others it may represent a loss or an additional burden stemming not only from specific areas of conflict between themselves and the sick member of the family but also from the change in their status within the family unit, as well as with other individual family members. Studies of morbidity within families reveal a tendency toward almost chain reaction-like responses to illness in a family member, other members of the family soon themselves becoming sick or disturbed in some way. The ultimate catastrophe under these circumstances may be that the whole family breaks up, the children being disseminated to foster homes or to institutions. For any understanding of the factors involved in the maintenance of health and the genesis of disease, a knowledge of the stability and the resources of the family is of the utmost importance.

The family as a dynamic social group also contributes certain intangible qualities to the individual. To varying degrees the individual family member is identified by others with his family and may be credited with their assets and stigmatized with their failures. One may observe significant reactions of pride, confidence and self-assurance on the one hand, or shame, guilt and disgrace on the other hand, in relationship to what happens within the "family." The tendency toward individualism often leads persons to deny the significance of such factors, but clinical observation usually confirms their importance. Of considerable importance in this respect are some of the problems which arise among the offspring of immigrant parents. These parents, by and large, for their own security and comfort may tend to retain their old value systems and traditions and to maintain a close social and community relationship with families of similar background. Their children's early family life may then be structured around one set of values and one type of role expectation, while their relationships in school with their peers and later on in work impose another set of standards and expectations. The conflicts between children and parents which can be normally expected in the course of growing up are increased and compounded by these additional factors.

REFERENCES

1. Anshen, R. N.: The Family: Its Function and Destiny. New York, Harper & Brothers, 1949.
2. Hill, R.: Families under Stress. New York, Harper & Brothers, 1949.
3. Kluckhohn, C. and Spiegel, J. P.: Integration and Conflict in Family Behavior. Report No. 27, Group for the Advancement of Psychiatry, August 1954.
4. Parsons, T. and Bales, R. F.: Family, Socialization and Interaction Process. Chicago, The Free Press of Glencoe, 1955.
5. Spiegel, J. P.: The Resolution of Role Conflict within the Family. Psychiatry, 20: Feb. 1957.
6. Waller, W. and Hill, R.: The Family: A Dynamic Interpretation. New York, The Dryden Press, 1951.

CHAPTER XXII

THE PSYCHO-
ANALYTIC THEORY
OF BEHAVIOR: A SUMMARY

To a large extent the basic theory of behavior underlying this work derives from psychoanalysis. However, it is by no means obvious from the material so far presented just what this theory encompasses and what constitutes extensions or departures from formal theory as currently held. Accordingly the present chapter is offered as a summary of the basic elements of the theory. No attempt is made to trace the historical developments of the theory or the many changes it has undergone in the seventy years since the first formulations of Freud. Rather, the elements of the theory will be summarized in terms of its current status as recently systematized by Rapaport (1959,[11] 1960[10]).*

Psychoanalysis aspires to the status of a general theory of behavior, embracing both the "normal" and the pathological. As it currently stands, it is by no means a complete theory. Much of the theory resists validation, a task which has posed formidable obstacles. The acquisition of primary empirical or experimental data whereby the basic tenets may be examined has been slow and difficult. To an inordinate degree much of the theory still rests on the accumulated random experiences of individual analysts, which do not lend themselves

---

* Although I have attempted to follow Rapaport's presentation as faithfully and as accurately as possible, this is nonetheless a paraphrase, for the wording of which I assume full responsibility, as I do for the examples, which perhaps are different from what Rapaport might have selected had he included illustrative material. The examples have been chosen to maintain continuity with the rest of this book and as being most appropriate for the audience for which this book is intended. When I have suggested modifications of Rapaport's formulations, these are clearly noted. For a more thorough survey the reader is referred to the original sources.[10, 11]

221

to systematic communication, documentation and study. Nonetheless, in spite of these limitations the theory still provides a framework within which a large number of diverse psychological and behavioral phenomena can be explained. Whether an even more general theory will evolve from the basic corpus of psychoanalytic theory, whether other theories will be incorporated into psychoanalytic theory or whether it will eventually be largely or totally replaced by some other conceptual framework is an issue for the future to settle. At this time a clear conception of the basic elements of psychoanalytic theory is indispensable to the student of human behavior.

THE MODELS OF PSYCHOANALYTIC THEORY

The body of psychoanalytic theory includes a number of models intended to account for conation (action), cognition (ideation) and affect (feeling) as these evolve in the course of development from infancy to adulthood.

The Primary Models

THE PRIMARY MODEL OF CONATION (ACTION). This was illustrated in Chapters IV and V in the infant behavior sequence of restlessness leading to nursing followed by subsidence of restlessness. It may be formulated as the following sequence: (1) *drive reaching threshold*, (2) *drive action on object*, (3) *drive gratification*. This is called a primary action model because it refers only to actions motivated by basic drives and does not include mental activity in the formal sense. (See also Piaget's Stage I, Chapter VIII.) It deals with behavior solely in terms of tension-reduction processes. In this model the restlessness, crying, etc., are the behavioral evidences of tension accumulation; the nursing (or any other activity with the mother-figure which terminates restlessness) describes the tension reducing action on (or with) an object; the subsidence of the restlessness identifies the state of reduced tension. The model does not imply that the object yet has psychological meaning or existence for the infant, but only identifies the agent in the external environment, the availability and action of which is necessary for drive reduction. Since the model specifies that immediate action on the drive object is necessary for tension reduction, it also defines the *pleasure principle*. (See Chapters IV and V.)

THE PRIMARY MODEL OF COGNITION (IDEATION). According to this model previous successful gratifications via a drive object result in the development of the mental capacity to "imagine" (or "hallucinate") the previous gratifications. Then when the drive object is not available and tension cannot be reduced by action on the drive object, the satisfaction can be imagined ("hallucinated") in the form of a wish fulfilled. This is formulated as follows: (1) *drive reaching threshold intensity*, but (2) *drive satisfaction impossible because of absence of drive object*, (3) *hallucinatory idea of previous gratification*. (See Chapters V and VI.) This model implies that when gratification is not possible, the drive energy (cathexis) activates the memory of the past gratification, which is thereby brought into existence in the ideational form of a wish fulfillment. The hungry infant can tolerate delay by mentally recapturing in the form of some imagery what it was like to have been successfully fed on some previous occasion. Here we bypass for the moment what, if any, aspect of this ideation is conscious and what is unconscious and in what form it actually exists in the infant. The theory merely presumes that through some kind of mental imagery of the satisfied state as it had been experienced in the past, the need for drive discharge and action on an object can be delayed or postponed, at least until drive threshold is again approached. It is to be noted that such a mental process not only takes the place of any action but also does not in itself prepare for action. It temporarily reduces tension by substituting the mental imagery for the real thing. In this respect it has limited value in terms of adapting to external reality. But as the primary mode of cognition it paves the way for the later developments. The model provides a basis for conceptualizing primitive cognition as having intention and direction and permits the inclusion in a theory of motivated behavior of apparently illogical phenomena, such as dreams, hallucinations, illusions, delusions, daydreams, reveries, and so forth, and relates them with the more ordered processes of logical thinking. (See Secondary Model of Cognition, p. 228.)

From the genetic (developmental) point of view this model implies that sequences of satisfaction and frustration are necessary for cognitive development and that the patterns of such satisfying and frustrating experiences determine the character of the resulting ideation. Theoretically, cognitive development would be impaired if the infant were to be raised in either a totally gratifying or a totally frustrating situation. Further, it implies that the primary function of such ideation is to enable the infant to postpone drive gratification. The data of Piaget indicate that this is not the only factor in early cognitive development (see Chapter VIII). Clearly this model is most applicable to situations of need, in which the cognitive products do indeed have the character of wishes or wish fulfillment. As we shall discuss later in the book, frustration of needs (drive frustration), in a broad sense, plays a central role in the genesis of pathological states, the clinical material from which psychoanalytic theory has largely been derived. Hence, it is not surprising that the primary model of cognition emphasizes mainly this aspect.

THE PRIMARY MODEL OF AFFECT. When for the infant the drive

object is not available and the hallucinatory ideation of a previous gratification is not possible or is unsatisfactory, some kind of diffuse reaction takes place which is designated as (primary) affect. (See Chapters VII and XIV.) This model may be formulated as (1) *drive reaching threshold intensity* but (2) *drive satisfaction impossible in the absence of drive object*, (3) *affect reaction*. Freud considered the primary affect in terms of an "emergency discharge" (" 'sally gates' for drive tension" or "discharges into the interior of the organism in contrast to alterations of external reality by action"), and psychoanalytic theory in general retains the concept of a discharge function of affects. (See Rapaport,[10] p. 26.) However, as discussed earlier, it makes more sense to stress the intra-organism and object-directed communication aspects of the affect and to place the discharge quality more in relation to drive reduction, if and when it takes place. (See Chapter XIV.) In this view, when a drive object is not available, the reaction which evolves serves either to elicit a supporting response from the object while preparing the organism to resist stress through internal changes (primary anxiety) or to raise the threshold to external stimuli and conserve energy if no response from the environment is forthcoming (depression-withdrawal). (See Chapter XIV.) The intrapsychic aspect of this will be elaborated later. (See Secondary Model of Affect, p. 229.)

These three primary models are related to each other by virtue of the presence of the drive object in the primary model of action and its absence in the primary models of cognition and affect. Further, the "restlessness" which marks drive approaching threshold in the primary model of conation might also be regarded as the beginning of the affect reaction. The primary models of cognition and affect can therefore be combined, as follows: (1) *drive at threshold intensity in the absence of drive object* leads to (2) *hallucinatory idea* and/or (3) *affect reaction*. In this view, whether or not affect reaction develops depends on how effective the hallucinatory ideation is in reducing the tension of the drive. The hallucinatory reconstruction of how it was to have been fed will neither completely nor indefinitely satisfy hunger. This model was derived by Freud from the clinical observation that the activity of a repressed drive can be inferred from either its ideational or its affect representations. Thus, under certain conditions the ideational content of the drive is observed devoid of affect, whereas under other conditions an affect may be experienced unrelated to any ideation. The first may be illustrated by such an obsessive thought as "Father will die" intruding relentlessly into consciousness but unaccompanied by any angry feeling. The second is found in the common experience of an intense unpleasant affect for which no explanation (ideation) becomes conscious to the sufferer. From such clinical experiences the more generalized model was developed to account for all ranges of cognitive and affective responses to drives reaching threshold and seeking discharge in the absence of appropriate drive objects. Affect and idea are thus seen as complementary and/or alternative drive representations.

The Secondary Models

The primary models define processes characteristic of the early developmental phases. The secondary models are intended to account for behavior after further development has been achieved. In part, these developmental changes involve the elaboration in a hierarchical fashion of derivative drives from the basic drives. The latter were based on primary organizations in the central nervous system in the service of survival and growth, whereas the derivatives evolve in the course of learning and experience. This difference may be illustrated in the developmental transition from *hunger*, as a general expression of a body need for nutrition, to *appetite*, as a series of highly individual derivative needs and drives developed through experience and interaction with the environment in the course of appeasing hunger. (See Chapters III and XIV.) The character of the drive derivatives of each individual is determined by how the various biological, psychological, interpersonal and social experiences of the individual have affected basic drive satisfactions or frustrations in the course of growing up. Thus, drives differentiate not only according to ontogenetic laws (e.g., psychosexual development) but also in relation to the conditions provided by the environment, such as periodic inavailability of the drive object, the nature of the object relationship, the appearance of substitute objects, the environment's reaction to and demands for new ontogenetic developments, the social modes provided by the environment, etc. (See Erikson.[3])

The developmental data recorded in Chapters IV to XVI serve to illustrate the range and variety of expression of drive derivatives in the course of biological and psychosocial maturation.

A second important developmental change incorporated in the secondary models concerns the processes involved in the delay between drive reaching threshold intensity and its satisfaction, a delay which reflects operation of the *reality principle*, the necessity to reconcile the requirements of external reality with the conditions under which drive satisfaction can be achieved. This involves the development of structures, more stable psychic systems concerned with means of dealing with the data of external and psychological reality, past and present, to achieve such an adaptive end.

THE SECONDARY MODEL OF CONATION (ACTION).   This model may be outlined as follows: (1) *When drive reaching threshold intensity activates a derivative drive or when a derivative drive reaches threshold intensity, there is* (2) *a structuralized delay (even in the presence of the drive object)* which may include (a) *detour-activity searching for* and (b) *means activity reaching for the drive object* through which (3) *some action yielding satisfaction is eventually achieved.*

According to this model, action may be initiated in several ways. The basic drive may reach threshold intensity, in which case the derivative drives may be bypassed or may be triggered. If hungry enough, one may eat anything edible, disregarding previous preferences, manners, consideration for others and even aversions. But if the basic hunger is less urgent it may merely activate specific appetites to eat certain foods under certain conditions with certain people. Or the derivative drive may itself reach threshold intensity. Here the wish to eat may not be related to hunger or tissue needs for food. Instead the wish to eat may be linked with or replace a wish to be taken care of, to have a social contact, to express aggression, or it may simply constitute a wish for a particular kind of eating experience (a yen for oysters is not indicative of a physiological need for oysters). Or an external stimulation may bring a basic drive or any derivative drive to threshold intensity. The wish to eat may be stimulated by the sight or odor of food. But in any case there then is a detour or delay through mental activity of one sort or another before an action yielding satisfaction is forthcoming. Even in the extreme case of the first example, the action of eating is still preceded by certain thoughts, fantasies, etc. If not, we may speak of regression to the primary mode of conation. The delay has evolved out of the necessity to test the present in terms of the past and to reconcile conflicting motivations and the demands of the environment, whereby a satisfying action, often a compromise, results.

This mode of conation develops in the course of facing the realistic necessity of giving up certain aims. The resulting absence or unavailability of a drive object has the consequence of raising the drive-discharge threshold. In other words, if drive-discharge on an object is not to occur, some intrapsychic process must take place whereby drive is prevented from being discharged. (The term countercathexis is sometimes used to refer to the expenditure of energy to inhibit drive action.) The raising of threshold is accomplished through (a) *defenses* and *controls*, whereby the motivations (drives) against which they are directed are effectively prevented, delayed, modulated or channeled, and (b) *the development of new motivations (drive derivatives)* to achieve a more satisfactory adaptation. Thus, when a basic drive or a derivative drive has to be blocked or channeled by defense or control in order to avoid discomfort, new motivating forces develop which serve the requirements of reality (*the reality principle*). It is through such developmental processes that successive hierarchies of drive derivatives evolve, each one more in keeping with the requirements of reality, including eventually moral and ethical motivations as well—the motivation to do what is right, for example. To return again to the examples, using hunger, appetite and eating, we note that the necessity to give up sucking on the breast or bottle may result in substitute and more acceptable sucking activities, ranging from the finger to the pipe or cigar. Or the necessity to conform to certain manners and modes of eating in order to maintain and enjoy object and social relations leads the child to change from one who feels forced to behave in a certain way while eating to one who wants to behave in this way. Or the necessity to give up certain dependent wishes and behaviors which happen to be associated with the infantile feeding experience may result in a derivative drive which is satisfied by eating, a substitute for the inadmissable dependent behavior.

Delay of discharge in spite of the real presence of the drive object (see (2) above) involves in essence a process whereby from the viewpoint of *psychological reality* the object (drive action on which must be prevented) is absent (unnoticed or unusable) even though actually present in external reality. For example, when one is face to face with the original incestuous object of the Oedipus complex, the structuralized delaying process involves divesting the psychic object representation of those qualities which once made it a suitable object for the satisfaction of the sexual drive. The transformed psychic reality is that no suitable drive object is present and hence no action is taken in relation to the object, who actually is physically present but is simply no longer perceived as the object of *that* drive wish. Hence, in this secondary model we can compare this psychological absence of the object with its real absence in the primary model. This psychological achievement can become possible only when mental development has reached the point where clear differentiation has been established between the psychic representations of objects and those of self. (See Chapters VII and VIII.)

Defenses and controls are conceptualized as structures in the sense that they are more stable and fixed and show less rapid rates of change as compared to the rates of change of drive-accumulation and drive-discharge processes. The development of such structures makes for the contrast between *pleasure principle*, with its tendency for direct discharge, and *reality principle*, with its adherence to the principle of least action. The presence and operation of such structuralized delaying mechanisms of defense and control also allow behaviors other than hallucinatory wish fulfillment or affect reaction when the drive object is absent (whether in external or in psychological reality). It also makes possible detours from the direct route of gratification and search for the drive object characteristic of the primary models. Action on a substitute object is an example. The thumb or something else can be sucked on in place of the unavailable nipple. But more than that, the presence of these structures for defense, control, delay and detour means that it is no longer necessary to have full discharge of drive. Satisfaction may be achieved not only through action on varieties of substitute objects but also through the experience of successfully achieving and maintaining control over drives and external stimuli ("self-satisfaction"), in itself a form of "action" in the sense that deliberately refraining from some action is an active, not passive, process. These are the indications of the developing autonomy of ego which has been achieved in the course of the laying down of structure.

THE SECONDARY MODEL OF COGNITION.   The first two steps in this model are the same as in the secondary model of conation. The third step, following the structuralized delay is (3) *experiment in thought to anticipate and plan, locate and act upon the drive object.* In contrast to the primary model of cognition, ordered thinking now replaces the earlier short cut via hallucinatory gratification. This is a developmental consequence of the fact that the short cut of imagining the wish to be fulfilled when the drive object is unavailable or action is impossible serves only to provide a temporary respite against frustration while contributing little to overcoming the frustration and securing the object. This primary model of cognition ignores current external reality. As mentioned earlier, the hungry man who simply hallucinates food and eating not only does not appease his hunger but also fails to interact with the external environment in which food might be found. In contrast, the secondary model, which becomes possible when structure has been achieved, utilizes this structure and the data of past experience with external reality to think out and plan appropriate action to achieve satisfaction within the framework of current psychological and external reality. Logical thought now precedes action. (See also Chapter VIII.)

The differences between the primary and secondary models of cognition also emphasize two different types of memory organization. In the primary model memories are concerned with the ideational representations of drives, that is, memories of needs and their satisfaction or frustration, pleasure or unpleasure. Such memories operate in terms of primary process mechanisms, in which all memories related to any one drive are equivalent to each other and are capable of being condensed, displaced, substituted and symbolized one for the other, the regulating factor being only whether the ideation means pleasure or unpleasure. Thus, any imagery associated with the satisfaction of hunger is the equivalent of any other imagery of satisfaction. The ideation associated with the act of eating or swallowing may be equated with, condensed with, replaced by or symbolized by the ideation associated with being held (or loved) by mother, for example. In the secondary model the memories relate according to empirical coordinations and logical implications (secondary process). They have to "make sense" in terms of past experience and current reality. This latter conceptual organization of memory and thought is hierarchically higher than that associated with the drive organization and tends to have control over it. These two forms of thought may also be contrasted in everyday thinking in terms of thoughts which are preemptory (as wishes, urges, obsessions, delusions, dreams, etc.) and those which can be taken or left (as practical thought, rational thought, logical thought, etc.). We use the latter to deal with and control the former, but at times also give the former free rein, as in daydreams and reveries. Thus we note that there may be two aspects to any thought, one of which includes intention, anticipation and a sense of pressure which derives from the directedness of the primary model, the other of which maintains relevance to reality, which derives from the structuralized delay. The latter militates against the immediate discharge and gratification characteristics of the primary model and makes possible the development of processes whereby logical relationships are established and maintained. To return to the much used example, we contrast "I'm terribly hungry, let's eat right now" with "Let's arrange to get together after class and have lunch." (See also Chapter II.)

THE SECONDARY MODEL OF AFFECT.   (1) *Drive or derivative drive at threshold intensity*, (2) *a structuralized delay*, (3) *affect signal released by the ego from structurally segregated affect charges*. In contrast to the primary model of affect the affect reaction no longer serves exclusively as a means of soliciting response from the environment (or as "discharge") but now serves more as an intrapsychic signal to mobilize defense and control mechanisms of ego in the service of the reality principle. Affect reaction is no longer immediately manifest, but instead the affect charges are segregated and controlled and a variety of affect qualities differentiate in terms of their roles in psychic functioning. (See Chapters XIV and XVIII.) Now when drive tensions rise, the ego utilizes the segregated, differentiated affect charge to give an anticipatory or warning signal which mobilizes ego processes for defense and for control. Through such low intensity charges situations of danger are warned against and averted and/or preparation for appropriate drive action is initiated. As long as this can be accomplished intrapsychically without the necessity for participation of an external object, affect is not displayed (or discharged). Since, in the secondary model, affects as signals provoke behavioral responses, they may also be regarded as acquiring the character of motivational forces. (See Chapter XVIII.)

THE STRUCTURE OF PSYCHOANALYTIC THEORY

A number of basic points of view underlie psychoanalytic theory. These are summarized under the following headings, each of which is familiar from the material already presented in preceding chapters.

The Genetic Point of View

This view implies that the understanding of current behavior requires taking into account its antecedents, a development dependent on both the biological laws of the organism and the cumulative experience of the individual. This means that the conditions determining and under which particular drive demands were first achieved or apparatuses put to use and all subsequent circumstances under which the resulting behavior takes place constitute historical determiners of the final product. However, as Rapaport points out, in time certain behaviors are less and less shaped further by their recurrence and some cease to be so shaped altogether, becoming automatized and relatively independent of their genetic origins (Rapaport,[10] p. 45). Once this occurs they may be brought into action by particular circumstances or contexts without the original drive or motivation any longer being involved. This stabilization of certain patterns is especially important in the development of character structure and in learning, including the persistence of certain pathological (maladaptive) patterns. To continue the same example, the urgent survival motivation underlying the infant's original urge to nurse is replaced by a great variety of motivations for eating and by patterns of eating which are independent of and usually not stimulated by hunger. Hence, although a particular behavioral response may have originated under drive pressure (e.g., in infancy), its subsequent generalizing adaptive value may be sufficiently great to lead to its establishment as a means of adjustment and development relatively independent of the original motivation.

The genetic point of view assumes the existence of certain innate capacities which mature according to a biological timetable, provided the necessary environmental conditions pertain at the proper time. This assumption underlies the propositions concerning the developmental sequences implicit in the libido development, psychosocial stages and autonomous ego development as outlined in the preceding chapters. Further, it implies that even when superseded by later forms, the earlier forms of a psychological phenomenon remain *potentially* active. This assumption underlies the propositions concerning regression, the repetition compulsion (see Chapter XXVIII) and unconscious fantasies, and plays an important role in the interpretation of pathological states. The persistence unconsciously of an unresolved childhood wish in the form of an unconscious fantasy which has motivating influence on current behavior is an example. In the genetic view it is assumed that all such previously active earlier forms codetermine subsequent psychological phenomena. This also implies that the types of solution and achievement utilized in the past to establish a behavioral pattern are importantly shaped by past solutions and achievements. (See also Chapter VIII for Piaget's formulation in terms of assimilation, accommodation and the circular reactions.)

The Dynamic Point of View

This view holds that there are forces within the organism which determine behavior. Ontogenetically the first of these forces is the drives, but the effectiveness of drives is dependent upon an environmental condition, namely, the presence of the drive object through which the drive is discharged (the need satisfied). (See Chapter IV.) Thus, the drive concept is in keeping with two empirical observations, namely, that much behavior appears to be "spontaneous," as though initiated from within rather than simply triggered by an external stimulus, and that at the same time behavior appears to have purpose.

The influence of drive ranges from an imperative demand to that of only a remote motivational framework. This span defines the development from basic drives, which are the most closely related to the primary biological needs of the organism, to derivative drives, which evolve therefrom as more structured or highly channelized systems, relatively remote from the original biological needs. The derivative drives are elaboration- from, not replacements for, the more basic drives, which continue to exist. Psychoanalytic theory is not yet clear as to how many and what kind of basic drives need be postulated. (See Rapaport,[10] p. 47.)

The drive concept constitutes an important biological referent of psychoanalytic theory. The fact that drive and drive object in environment is an essential transactional system for survival and growth defines the biological and social requirements for the developing relation between the organism and the environment. Hence the drive may be regarded as the psychological referent of the original and developing biological adaptedness of the organism in its environment. (See Chapters I, II and III.)

Drives are not the only psychological forces which motivate and influence behavior. With further development of the mental apparatus other internal influences acquire such capacities. These include affects (see p. 229 and Chapters XIV and XVIII), defense and control systems, including the internalized standards represented in ego ideal and super ego, and the automatized systems that have become relatively divorced from their original genetic sources. (See also Chapters IV, V and VIII regarding influences operating in the infant when basic drives are at a relatively low level.)

Psychoanalytic theory holds that these various motivating forces have a hierarchical relationship, in that many factors from moment to moment determine the relative value to the individual of the various forces operating at the same time; only one gains ascendency, though the total behavior may nonetheless be influenced and modified by the action of other simultaneous motivations. This assumption underlies the concept of intrapsychic conflict as a basic condition of psychic activity. (See Chapter XXVII.)

The Economic Point of View

This perspective postulates the existence of psychological energy in the regulation of behavior. Psychological energy is not equated with any known biochemical energy, though it is ultimately derived from and dependent upon the biochemical energy of the central nervous system. The concept of psychological energy is a quantitative construct restricted to the forces involved in *psychological* processes and their relationships. It does not define the relationships between biochemical or physiological processes and psychological processes or the transformation from biochemical energy to psychological energy. Although quantitative in the sense of more or less, psychological energy is not accessible to measurement, and hence the laws expressing the quantitative relationships between qualities of energy and between energy and output are not yet developed. Information theory and the concept of exchanges of psychological energy in terms of the work of an information network are important avenues of development of the psychoanalytic theory of psychological energy (see Rapaport,[10] Colby[2]). This perspective emphasizes the role of small quantities of energy controlling or setting off networks that carry and dispose of greater quantities of energy.

To speak more explicitly in psychoanalytic terms, this theory contrasts, on the one hand, the more or less free-flowing energy that characterizes primary process, the immediate tendency toward drive reduction by direct discharge (pleasure principle), and, on the other hand, "bound" energy, whereby energy is channeled into the structures that evolve to raise threshold, delay and detour discharge, and deal with reality (reality principle). Through such processes of binding energy into structures, it is postulated that small quantities of energy become available for thought (as experimental action), for the signal function of affects, for defenses, etc. These differences in quality of psychological energy correspond to the observed differences between obsessive thoughts (free energy) and logical thoughts (bound energy) or compulsive and impulsive acts versus planned, thought-out acts.

The Topographic Point of View

This view states that the crucial determinants of behavior are unconscious. It goes further than simply acknowledging that certain mental activities go on without conscious awareness on the part of the subject. Besides categorizing mental processes which are unconscious and incapable of becoming conscious (belonging to system Unconscious) and processes which are unconscious but may become conscious (system Preconscious), it asserts that the rules covering unconscious processes differ from those covering conscious processes, the former following primary process, the latter secondary process characteristics. Further, it is claimed that that which is unconscious exerts an effect on that which is conscious or observable and that therefore the nature of unconscious processes can be inferred from what is conscious and/or observable, especially when the latter deviates from what is expected according to the rules of logic that characterize secondary process.

The Structural Point of View

The concept of structure implies that psychological processes have organization or configuration and can be categorized and examined in such terms. Further, such organization or configuration can be inferred from behavioral data and is conceptualized in psychological terms without reference to the underlying organic substrate and structure, the relationship to which is still unknown. In relationship to concepts of psychological forces and of psychological energy, structure is responsible for the delay, detour, substitution, defense, thresholds, channels, means and tools involved in the final translation of such forces into behavior. Structures, in contrast to drive process, are characterized by relative stability or slow rate of change.

The original conception of Id, ego and superego as categories of psychological processes is a structural approach, for it defines each of these in terms of an underlying organization which determines the nature of the psychic activity characteristic of each. Ontogenetically the earliest structures are inborn apparatuses through which drive actions are executed (e.g., the primitive psychic processes involved in signalling need and establishing nursing). These are called *ego apparatuses of primary autonomy* (also, the *conflict-free sphere of ego*) (Hartmann[9]). They may be viewed as pre-existing organizations which may be triggered by drive, but it is the organization, not the drive, which determines the nature of the resulting behavior. The distinctive details of the nursing behavior of the human infant are determined not by hunger but by the structures through which such behavior is mediated and is different from the feeding behavior of other animals. Other pre-existing structures (apparatuses) include those underlying motility, perception, memory, cognitive styles, language, thresholds, discharge channels, and so forth. These all define the primary state of adaptedness of the organism to the environment. In addition, new structures develop in the course of growth and adaptation within the environment, as discussed earlier. These are acquired structures, some of which are conflict determined (e.g., defenses) and some of which are products of growth, development and interaction with the environment (e.g., processes of identification, identity formation, character structure). The constitutionally given and the acquired structures are not wholly independent one from the other, the former being utilized in conflict situations as well and are modified thereby. Although no statement can be made about the organic substrate, it seems likely that organic factors are of importance in determining differences among individuals both in the disposition of the primary apparatuses of autonomy and the nature of acquired apparatuses possible.

The existence and development of structure account for the more abiding patterns characteristic of behavior in general, and it is against and around this more stable background that the more rapid fluctuations take place in any individual. Character traits, defenses, habits, cognitive styles, concepts, moods, typical gestures, expressions and mannerisms, the persistent effect of the past on the present—all constitute the outward evidence of relative fixed formations, the structure. Further, the concept of structure implies that some psychic systems are and some become relatively independent of the drives or the original motivations. The concept of structure was introduced to account for the fact that motivations do not determine behavior in a one-to-one relation. In the course of the development of structure, motivations are transformed and new motivations evolve. (See also p. 230.)

The Adaptive Point of View

This perspective is concerned with the role of the relationship with external reality in determining psychological phenomena. Reality here refers to the external sources of stimuli, including those from the body via sensory pathways (but not drives as herein defined). This aspect of psychoanalytic theory has undergone the greatest changes of any, for a concise summary of which the reader is referred to Rapaport[10] (pp. 57–61). What follows summarizes the current status of the theory, for which Hartmann and Erikson are largely responsible.

Modern psychoanalytic theory holds that man is born already adapted or potentially adapted to reality in the sense that the primary ego apparatuses of autonomy constitute the means and assurance of "preparedness for an average, expectable environment" (Hartmann[9]). (See Chapters IV and V.) This preadaptation, however, is more potential than actual. It evolves progressively in the course of the continuing ongoing transaction not with one single average environment but with a whole evolving series of environments. These are social environments which provide forms, patterns, institutions and means which mesh with developing modes of behavior (e.g., oral incorporative, anal retentive, etc.) of the child (Erikson[3]). In this view the environment is not set apart from or primarily in conflict with the individual, but rather constitutes a dynamic matrix, which both facilitates and requires adaptation.

According to this view psychological development involves a continuous process of internalizing the reality of the external environment through the process of building models of the external environment. This begins under the impetus of drives, which in part determine the conditions of relating to the external environment but which also change in the course of such transactions with the environment. The whole process of internalizing the environment over time involves the acquisition of information about the environment and the storage and programming of such information in the service of channeling drives into certain directions and not into others. (See Chapters IV to XVI.) This is essential for the evolution of logical thought processes (secondary process), whereby data from the past and current stimuli from within (drives and other motivating forces) and external stimuli can all be processed and programmed internally in order to achieve solutions consonant with the environmental circumstances. The relative autonomy from both drive and environment of secondary process thinking is crucial to the maintenance and improvement of existing states of adaptedness. It provides time not only for an accurate grasp of reality but also for the achievement of a workable relationship (adaptation).

The Psychosocial Point of View
This perspective begins with the "fit" between mother and infant and the prolonged helplessness and dependence of the infant and child on the one hand and the institutions of society which meet, foster, and mold the individual's developing capacities on the other. Erikson's epigenetic psychosocial conception provides the main theoretical framework.[3] It includes the concepts (1) that ego development involves a sequence of developmental phases, each with characteristic features which are universal but which are met with differently from society to society; (2) that the activities of caretaking individuals (parents, teachers, etc.) set the standards and provide the precepts representing the particular society's traditional way of dealing with each phase-specific crisis; (3) that the phase-specific behavior of the growing individual in turn elicits needs in and responses from the caretaking persons, depending on their particular phase of life cycle; (4) that the resulting behavior has an accepted place in society and serves to guarantee the individual's place and survival in the society. According to this view, society and the individual form a unity within which mutual regulation takes place.

SOME ILLUSTRATIONS FROM EVERYDAY LIFE

Certain phenomena of everyday life provide sources of readily accessible material with which to examine the usefulness of psychoanalytic theory to explain behavior. These include dreams, parapraxes, mannerisms of speech and gestures, daydreams, wit and humor. The interested student will find it of value to read the classic psychoanalytic expositions of these phenomena in the light of the modern theory as herein summarized. (See Freud, Feldman,[4] and Brenner.[1])

REFERENCES

1. Brenner, C.: An Elementary Textbook of Psychoanalysis. New York, Anchor Books (Doubleday), 1957: Parapraxes and Wit (chapter 6); Dreams (chapter 7).
2. Colby, K. M.: Research in Psychoanalytic Information Theory. Am. Scientist, *49:*358, 1961.
3. Erikson, E. H.: Childhood and Society. New York, W. W. Norton & Co., 1950.
4. Feldman, S. S.: Mannerisms of Speech and Gestures in Everyday Life. New York, International Universities Press, 1959.
5. Freud, S.: A General Introduction to Psychoanalysis. New York, Garden City Books (Doubleday), 1938.
6. Freud, S.: The Interpretation of Dreams (1900). *In:* Standard Edition of the Complete Psychological Works of Sigmund Freud, vols. IV, V. London, The Hogarth Press, 1953.
7. Freud, S.: The Psychopathology of Everyday Life (1907). *In:* Standard Edition of the Complete Psychological Works of Sigmund Freud, vol. VI. London, The Hogarth Press, 1960.
8. Freud, S.: Jokes and Their Relation to the Unconscious (1905). *In:* Standard Edition of the Complete Psycholological Works of Sigmund Freud, vol. VIII. London, The Hogarth Press, 1960.
9. Hartmann, H.: Ego Psychology and the Problem of Adaptation. New York, International Universities Press, 1958.
10. Rapaport, D.: The Structure of Psychoanalytic Theory. *In:* Psychological Issues, vol. 2. New York, International Universities Press, 1960.
11. Rapaport, D. and Gill, M. M.: The Points of View and Assumptions of Metapsychology. Int. J. Psychoanal., *40:*153, 1959.

Part Two

HEALTH AND DISEASE

CHAPTER XXIII

A UNIFIED CONCEPT
OF HEALTH AND DISEASE

The first part of this book has been concerned with human development, and particular attention has been devoted to the development of the mental apparatus as the intervening and integrating organ relating the internal biological environment and the external physical, interpersonal and social environments. We have been especially concerned with how the mental apparatus and its organ, the central nervous system, come to internalize the experienced external environment of the individual's present and past, thereby establishing a third environment, so to speak, relating the internal and the external environments in terms of past and present, and providing the conditions whereby a future can be anticipated on the basis of what has transpired in the past. And especially have we emphasized the biological factors, including the properties of the nervous system itself, which determine and circumscribe what aspects of the external environment are likely to be or are capable of being so internalized. We have conceptualized the human being in terms of a biologically determined developmental destiny, adapted to and adjusting in a physical, interpersonal and social environment. We shall now examine some of the ways in which development, adaptation and adjustment may be disturbed or interfered with and some of the expressions thereof. Our preoccupation will be with the psychological and social aspects, but it is first necessary that we consider such disturbances or derangements in terms of the total organization of the human being as a biological, psychological and social organism. These encompass the deviations referred to as disease, the proper subject of medicine.

UNITARY CONCEPT OF DISEASE VERSUS UNIT-CAUSES

Medicine is concerned in the broadest sense with the problems of health and disease and, more specifically, with the mechanisms and the processes whereby health is maintained or disease develops. Health and disease are relative concepts which do not easily lend themselves to simple definition. Life itself involves a series of adjustments within the environment, and therefore, health and disease may be seen as phases of life.[1, 2, 3, 5] We may speak of the organism as a whole (or of organs or systems within the organism) as being in a state of health (healthy) when functioning effectively, fulfilling needs, successfully responding to the requirements or demands of the environment, whether internal or external, and pursuing its biological destiny, including growth and reproduction. Disease, on the other hand, corresponds to failures or disturbances in the growth, development, functions and adjustments of the organism as a whole or of any of its systems. Clearly, such a definition is too broad to be of much practical value. Still, it is useful as a starting point, since it does not restrict us to any one parameter. It is to be contrasted, for example, to the cellular concept of disease which, by focussing primarily on changes within the cell as the basic component of disease, is reductionistic and tends to restrict attention to only one aspect of disease, and one which is not necessarily always present. This broader formulation tries to get away from the substantive assumption that disease is a thing in itself, unrelated to the patient, the patient's personality, bodily constitution or mode of life, a concept of antiquity which repeatedly reasserts itself even in our language, as when we say that a patient *has* a disease or that we treat a disease.[6] The broad definition of disease does not confine our attention to any single system or organization of the body. It permits us to conceptualize disturbances or failures at all levels of organization—biochemical, cellular, organic, psychological, interpersonal or social—and to consider their inter-relationships. Further, it does not restrict us to any single etiological concept but permits the application of a multifactor concept.

An important aspect of many concepts of disease in the past has been the tendency to think of disease primarily in terms of a "bad" influence, usually conceived of as something external which gets into the body and thereby causes the disease. This theme characterizes most primitive and prescientific views of disease, and has reappeared repeatedly in various guises in the scientific era. To be able to think of disease as an entity, separate from oneself and caused by an identifiable agent seems to have great appeal to the human mind. Perhaps this reflects the operation of the mechanism of projection, whereby what is felt or experienced as uncomfortable, painful or dangerous is ascribed to the outside. In prescientific medicine such psychological processes achieved expression in the form of demonological concepts, according to which disease resulted from the malevolent influence of demons, ancestor or animal spirits, spirits of the dead, revengeful ghosts, mystical object intrusion, loss of soul, taboo violation, sorcery, or witchcraft.[6] A man became ill because he had an enemy who cast a spell or because he was being punished for a transgression or for breaking a taboo. Essentially similar psychological concepts have continued to influence many interpretations of scientific medicine. Patients certainly, regardless of their level of education and sophistication, prefer to blame their illness on something they "caught," or ate or that happened to them, and consequently to think of disease as something apart from themselves. Many in one way or another formulate it in terms of punishment. Physicians also find attractive such ways of thinking, particularly if they can see the "cause" of disease as something which they can attack and destroy. Indeed, that which can be so attacked is often considered by physician and patient alike as the "cause" rather than as one element or aspect of the disease process. Thus, the tubercle bacillus is the cause of (rather than a necessary condition for) tuberculosis; insufficient insulin is the cause of (rather than a mechanism involved in) diabetes, etc. The thoughtful physician, of course, immediately sees the inadequacy of such formulations. But because such ideas have strong psychological appeal, new scientific contributions repeatedly tend to be translated into such terms, essentially the terms of demonology and of the universal introjection-projection schema of early childhood. A germ theory of disease which identifies a particular micro-organism as *the* cause of a disease is reformulated in terms of demonology to the extent that it postulates an invisible, omnipresent agent which, if it gains access to the body, invariably produces disease. Actually, when it was first proposed, the very physicians who were most vigorous in attempting to introduce scientific methods and concepts into medicine saw the germ theory as a revival of ancient demonology and opposed it on that ground. But when it was demonstrated that certain micro-organisms did indeed bear an etiological relationship to certain disease processes, there quickly developed the expectation that a different germ would be found to account for each and every disease, including mental disease. So attractive psychologically was this idea of the "bad" germ that the emphasis of early workers on factors within the host was often ignored or minimized. In general, lay people and many physicians readily embraced the concept of a single external cause of disease. Certain patients even developed their own idiosyncratic germ theories, suffering from obsessional fears or paranoid delusions about germs, contagion or dirt.

Another tendency is to equate an anatomical lesion with the disease. With the development of pathology and the increasing refinement of techniques whereby deviations from the normal structure can be identified, the temptation has been to consider these findings as the explanation for the disease rather than as manifestations of the disease state. Under such circumstances the disease then tends to be considered in substantive terms, and it is believed that the patient can be cured if the diseased ("bad") part is removed. The fact that such measures often do prove therapeutic, as attested to by the success of surgery, is actually not evidence for the general validity of such a point of view.

The failure of morbid anatomy to explain more than some mechanisms of disease now is leading to the concept of the biochemical defect as underlying disease. Again, the search is for the single defect, an abnormal enzyme or biochemical system, as the explanation for the disease. There are some who even go so far as to anticipate a single biochemical defect for each disease, an idea reminiscent of those advanced in the early days of the germ theory. Regardless of whether disease is equated with an anatomical, a physiological or a biochemical lesion, such concepts again involve the idea of a discrete "thing" inside the body, an entity having an existence of its own, apart from the patient, who is the victim.

Still another variation on this theme is the mechanistic concept, which sees the body as a machine and disease as a condition due to a defective part. In modern medicine this takes the form of the mechanism (the "how") being used as the explanation of the disease state. For example, one is told that peptic ulcer is "due" to overactivity of the vagal outflow. Why the vagus is "overactive" is ignored. In this approach a misbehaving organ or system again fulfills the psycho-economic requirement of the disease as a thing apart. Even the patient who says, "It's my nerves," often is thinking in terms of something wrong with "the telephone wires." Some of the "stress" theories currently popular have also tended to emphasize "stress" as some kind of "bad" force to which the person falls helpless victim. Others formulate "stress" in terms of evil psychological or social influences which cause the person to break down. A variation of this sees the bad influence as inside—for example, the "bad" emotions, such as rage, fear, envy, greed or disgust, which "cause" the patient to fall ill. Physicians thinking in such terms are likely to exhort their patients not to get angry or excited, as if the bad affect or behavior itself would cause illness. Some physicians and laymen have distorted the concepts of psychoanalysis so that instincts or drives are spoken of as evil and dangerous forces which exert a destructive influence on the body or mind. Characteristic of all these concepts of disease, as well as many others not mentioned, is the tendency to concentrate on a single factor which qualifies for condemnation as "bad," and which is then to be attacked (or exorcised).

Whatever qualities permit it to be so designated result in its being given a degree of exclusive importance which rarely is justified.

NOSOLOGY AS A CIRCUMSCRIBING FACTOR

Another difficulty in formulating a general concept of disease has been the inhibiting influence of nosology. Valuable as it is to be able to classify and categorize the phenomena of disease, the application of a name also may have the effect of overemphasizing one aspect of the process at the expense of others or of implying a degree of certainty of our knowledge not actually justified. Names for diseases often have originated from the more obvious, rather than the more important, characteristics of the condition or from some etiological factor. Thus, pernicious anemia is not specifically a disease of the blood and it is no longer pernicious; lupus erythematosus disseminatus is not a skin disease and it is not disseminated. Hypertension refers to the physiological parameter which can be most easily measured. The names used generally reflect the state of knowledge of the conditions at the time they were identified; although names are rarely changed, our understanding of the processes involved is constantly changing. But the name often continues to exert a weighty influence on the physician's concepts, at times completely blocking any approach contrary to what is implied by the name. A classic example is hysteria, so named because the Greeks attributed its manifestations to disorder of the uterus. Obviously, therefore, it could not occur in men and in the last century Freud was ridiculed when he demonstrated some cases of male hysteria before the medical society of Vienna.

What do our diagnostic names tell us? Diagnostic labels are ways of indicating categories of information about our patient. A diagnostic label rarely, if ever, fully defines the illness. Rather it has statistical and predictive value. Thus, if we are told that a man has tuberculosis, we assume that he harbors the tubercle bacillus and we can predict the probability of his having certain signs and symptoms. On the other hand, we cannot assume that he has any or all of these signs and symptoms nor can we assume that he does not have other signs and symptoms which are not statistically related to the diagnostic term "tuberculosis." Nor can we even assume, if the patient does have the predicted signs and symptoms, that all or any of them are necessarily related to tuberculosis. In practice, of course, we begin with signs and symptoms and attempt to reach a diagnosis. We listen to the patient's story and we subject him to various types of examinations and then we attempt to categorize the areas of the patient's illness in which we feel we have understanding and we represent these by the appropriate diagnostic terms. In the course of study of a patient, a great deal of other information is revealed, some of which may and some of which may not bear on the decision about diagnostic categories, but much of which does not lend itself to any such categorization. Yet this unclassifiable information is also essential for the physician's understanding of how, and perhaps also of why, the patient is sick. Thus, with respect to any patient, although the physician's obligation is to establish the clinical diagnosis(es), this is not an end in itself but is the physician's way of indicating those aspects of the patient's illness which he knows and is able to identify, as established by experience and convention. Such diagnostic terms, however, do not include other important aspects or other important knowledge about the patient, nor do they exclude other diagnostic categories or even other phenomena which have not yet been categorized in diagnostic terms.

TUBERCULOSIS AS AN EXAMPLE

Having considered some of the factors that subtly influence how physicians view disease, we are now ready to examine the application of the broad concept of disease. As a hypothetical example, we might postulate the various possible relationships between man and the tubercle bacillus. The tubercle bacillus has the potentiality of producing disease in man in a number of ways:

1. It is a parasite that competes with certain tissues of the body for nutriment and elaborates certain materials which are damaging to cellular systems. It may thereby produce tissue changes which the pathologist identifies as "tuberculosis."

2. The concept of tuberculosis as a known contagious disease may have certain symbolic meaning to a person and may mobilize, or be utilized for, certain phobic or delusional processes.

3. The presence of tuberculosis in one person may alter his relationships with another person in such a way that the latter is frustrated or that certain needs remain unfulfilled. Failure to adjust successfully to this new situation may be expressed as illness in the second person.

Whether or not disease will develop in any of these situations depends upon a number of circumstances. Clearly, only in the first situation is the tubercle bacillus directly involved and is the diagnostic category "tuberculosis" justified. But everything that develops in this first situation will not be understandable exclusively in terms of the relationship between the tubercle bacillus and the cells and organs of the host. Under any of these circumstances, whether or not disease develops will depend upon a variety of factors. Various theoretical possibilities may be summarized:

1. The virulence or number of the organisms may be low. Although inhaled or ingested, they do not have the capacity to penetrate the cellular barrier and gain access to the interior of the body. They are dealt with as inert foreign bodies. No disturbance of existing defenses occurs; no mobilization of new defenses of sufficient magnitude to alter the bodily state is necessary. There is no disease.

2. The organisms are virulent but the resistance of the host is adequate to circumscribe and destroy the organisms locally. This may involve a local tissue change, including the formation of a Ghon tubercle, but no change in the total body economy is subjectively experienced by the person in whom this process is taking place. From his point of view, no illness is experienced. However, an x-ray examination or a tuberculin test may reveal to the physician that this process of adaptation has taken place. This may constitute one of many successful adaptations experienced by this one individual, but it does not constitute a disease. As a result of this adaptation, the person now has a different and usually an enhanced capacity to deal with further exposures to the same organism.

3. In contrast to the previous example, the primary lesion of tuberculosis may be apparent to the person, as when it develops in the skin as a result of a penetrating injury by a contaminated instrument. The development of a painless, indolent skin nodule or ulcer may pass unnoticed by some people or may arouse only slight curiosity. Others may experience considerable concern and may feel it necessary to consult a doctor. A medical student or a pathologist, knowing that he has incurred this injury in the course of autopsying a cadaver with tuberculosis, will most likely experience considerable concern and may have a variety of symptoms, including some that simulate tuberculosis. But such clinical manifestations are largely psychological and have no direct relationship to the activity of the tubercle bacillus per se. Even though this local infection heals spontaneously with minimal tissue change, the patient's total illness experience will be quite different from that occurring when the primary infection is in the lung and runs its course silently, without ever becoming known to the person.

4. Virulent organisms may gain access to the lung and overcome local defenses. This may occur on first exposure or, as is more often the case, when a change takes place in the resistance to organisms already present. In either case we must assume that the capacity of the host to resist the virulent organisms either was inadequate to begin with or that it changed. A series of events is set in motion, some of which are experi-

enced by the patient as symptoms, some of which are manifest to the physician-observer as signs, and some of which are detectable only by special laboratory or other techniques of examination. In the aggregate, these represent the various ways in which the patient responds to the virulent organism as well as to the situation of reacting to it. These processes are taking place simultaneously at many different levels of organization:

(a) There is a local tissue process which results from the destructive effects of the tubercle bacilli on the lung tissue and from the various attempts of the body to overcome and confine the invaders locally, to protect tissues from further damage, and restore damaged tissue. These include the variety of biochemical and cellular responses of inflammation, alterations in local blood and lymph flow, mobilization of phagocytes and other local immune processes, disposal of dead tissue by lysis, phagocytosis, coughing, etc., alteration in the local activity of the lung, and so on.

(b) General biochemical and physiological processes are set in motion as part of the "behind the line" activity to support these local processes. These include shift of circulation to the advantage of the local area, modifications of the ventilatory activity of the lung to protect the damaged part, the formation in and supply from distant organs of chemical and cellular material involved in defense against the microorganism, etc. Some of these are reflected in such manifestations as increased metabolism, fever, sweating, loss of weight, altered respiration, changes in circulating white cells, plasma proteins, etc.

(c) As various systems of the body are brought into action to cope with the local process, the total behavior of the person must eventually be influenced. Central neuro-humoral systems will already have been activated and must eventually have an impact on systems of internal perception of the mental apparatus, indicating changes in the bodily status. This changing status may first be experienced as a general sense of malaise, fatigue, restlessness, uneasiness, vague anxiety, decreased interest in activity, etc., and only a little later may more specific symptoms, such as cough, sputum, etc., be noted by the patient. The former manifestations are nonspecific. They represent the activation of the signal functions of ego, essentially affects indicating a change from the existing dynamic steady state. Such manifestations vary from individual to individual as determined by past psychological experience. They indicate only that the patient is sick. The more specific symptoms—cough, fever, sputum, etc.—are more indicative of the local pathological changes and provide the clues for the diagnosis of the specific infection. Yet since one is dependent upon the patient's report of how he experiences these changes, his psychological development may be crucial in determining what manifestations he presents to the physician and how he does so. From the point of view of the psychic reality of the patient, the general as well as the specific manifestations of his illness will be related to his own personal experience, which may or may not include the concept of tuberculosis. The affective responses to the perception of the pathological changes going on in his body are linked with other past experiences associated with similar affects and not necessarily with past experiences associated with similar pathological processes. (Primary process vs. secondary process; see Chapter XXII.) The defenses that are mobilized to deal with these unpleasant feelings will also be an expression of the person's usual way of dealing with such feelings and they will be highly individual. Thus, one person may focus quickly on a specific manifestation, such as cough, pain or sputum, whereas another may minimize such specific manifestations and present mainly the more general phenomena. Another may need to deny weakness or disability because of his psychological background and hence may acknowledge no symptoms until the tissue changes are far advanced; in such a case it may be a family member who is the first to call attention to the cough or the weight loss. Still another person may respond to the specific symptoms with overwhelming anxiety or depression.

(d) Social and cultural factors will also influence how the disorder is experienced by the patient, by the environment and by the physician. Such factors may determine what symptom the patient selects to present to his family or to his physician and what symptom he may elect to minimize or conceal. Different cultures have different standards as to what is acceptable and what is grounds for shame and concealment. Such factors may also determine when, how and where the patient goes for help. In some social settings and cultural groups, the expected behavior is to seek medical help early; in others, one goes only as a last resort. The various techniques that the person uses to help himself or to get help from others constitute another level of the total behavioral expression of being ill for each individual.

5. Once a person has had active tuberculosis, the degree of recovery may not be uniform in all systems involved. In some patients there may be complete healing of the local process; they may be left with no demonstrable deficiency in respect to pulmonary or other functions, and they may be able to return successfully to their previous level of adjustment, occupation, etc., and to function effectively thereafter. Yet in many respects they are different by virtue of having experienced this illness. In other patients, the tubercle bacillus may be eliminated as an active pathogenic agent, but varying degrees of irreversible damage to the lung or other structures may remain, resulting in some decrement in functional ability. This may require a psychological and social adjustment which he may or may not succeed in achieving. Still other patients may have complete healing of the local tubercular process and no

residual anatomical defect and yet may continue to have a variety of symptoms, sometimes the same as those experienced with tuberculosis, sometimes different. Or patients may be improving or even symptom-free until the time of discharge from the hospital, only then to develop new symptoms. In the last two examples the pathological process at the cellular and organ level has been successfully resolved, but a disturbance in psychological adjustment remains. This is no less an illness than the tuberculosis and may, indeed, prove to be even more disabling or incapacitating.

6. The occurrence of active tuberculosis in one member of the family may contribute to the development of illness in other members of the family. The disruption in a family unit, the loss of an object (husband, wife, mother, father, child, as the case may be), the increased burdens or the deprivations imposed upon the other members of the family, the mobilization of ambivalent feelings toward the sick person— all of these may constitute significant psychological decompensating factors which may in the susceptible individual eventuate in illness. The nature of the illness so precipitated cannot be predicted. One person may decompensate in a largely psychological fashion and manifest neurotic, psychotic, or behavioral disturbances. Another, decompensating with feelings of helplessness or hopelessness in relation to what he is experiencing, may prove susceptible to a pre-existing or an intercurrent process which is eventually manifested somatically, such as diabetes, an infection, cardiac decompensation, etc. A great number of factors will determine whether a person falls ill and if so, when and in what way. In this example, the tubercle bacillus and tuberculosis are only indirectly involved. The stress is primarily psychological and the immediate response is psychological. Whether there will also be decompensation involving somatic symptoms is determined by other factors, some somatic and some psychological. (See Chapters XXV, XXVII, XXXI and XXXIII.)

7. The concept of the tubercle bacillus as a dangerous agent or of tuberculosis as an internally destructive process may become the content of a phobic or delusional system. (In current clinical practice, cancer is the disease which is most commonly used for such phobic or delusional ideas. In times past, tuberculosis and syphilis were more commonly used. However, to preserve the uniformity of our examples, we shall apply this concept to tuberculosis.) In this type of situation the tubercle bacillus and/or tuberculosis is a symbolic expression of some fearful feeling or idea of the patient. As such, it is generally a substitute for some unacceptable aggressive or sexual impulses or may represent his way of dealing with an ambivalent object whom he experiences as actually inside him and destroying him. The fear of contamination, perhaps taking the form of contamination by the tubercle bacillus,

again may represent the projection to the outside of the patient's own feared or unacceptable impulses. (See Chapter XXXI.)

These examples are intended to illustrate in broad terms the many levels of behavior and response characteristic of any disease process. Whether or not the tubercle bacillus is actively involved, the response of the host takes place simultaneously at many different levels. Not all of these responses are adaptive; particularly are they not necessarily adaptive in respect to the interaction with the tubercle bacillus. Thus, both the psychological and the social responses may in some instances help and in other instances hinder successful coping with the pathogenic micro-organism. Not all the varieties of responses are to the tubercle bacillus as a parasite; some may also, or instead, be to the concept of the tubercle bacillus or of tuberculosis. These examples also tell us something of the relativity of the manifestations of disease. At certain times and under certain circumstances, the success or failure of adaptive processes may be of quite a different order in one system as compared to another.

REFERENCES

1. Dubos, R.: The Mirage of Health. New York, Harper & Brothers, 1950.
2. Engel, G. L.: Homeostasis, Behavioral Adjustment, and the Concept of Health and Disease. *In:* Grinker, R. (ed.): Mid-Century Psychiatry. Springfield, Illinois, Charles C Thomas, 1953.
3. Engel, G. L.: A Unified Concept of Health and Disease. Perspect. Biol. & Med., *3:*459, 1960.
4. Mayr, E.: Cause and Effect in Biology. Science, *134:*1501, 1961.
5. Romano, J.: Basic Orientation and Education of the Medical Student. J.A.M.A., *143:*409, 1950.
6. Veith, I.: Psychiatric Nosology: From Hippocrates to Kraepelin. Am. J. Psychiat., *114:*385, 1957.

CHAPTER XXIV

A UNIFIED CONCEPT
OF HEALTH AND DISEASE

II. Disease as a
Natural Phenomenon:
Etiological Considerations

Health and disease have been defined in relative terms. When the organism is successfully adjusting in its environment and is able to maintain this state free of undue excitation, capable of growth, development and activity in an integrated and effective sense, a state of health may be said to exist. This is an active, dynamic process taking place in the face of an ever changing environment. There is continued need for adjustment and adaptation to maintain this state in the face of tasks imposed from the outside and from within the organism itself. When adaptation or adjustment fail and the pre-existing dynamic steady state is disrupted, then a state of disease may be said to exist until a new balance is restored which may again permit the effective interaction with the environment. Obviously there is no sharp dividing line between health and disease, nor are all parameters of the adaptive process necessarily equivalently involved. A person may satisfy all the criteria of health at any point in time simply because the adaptive capacity of a defective system, be it biochemical, physiological, or psychological, has not been exceeded. This may be a matter of fortunate circumstances or of the infrequency or limited intensity of the factors which would put the system under strain. It may also be a matter of time; eventually the system will break down under the impact of accumulated and repeated

250

small stresses. This principle is best illustrated in relation to some genically determined defects which may eventuate in manifest disease only after a lapse of time or under particular circumstances—or perhaps never at all, as will be described later. Another possibility is that, after a disease experience, a limitation in adaptive capacity may result, but the person may be healthy in all other respects unless or until he strains the capacity of the system beyond its limits of adjustment. A mitral valve damaged in the course of rheumatic fever may impose a limitation on the range of possible circulatory adjustment, but this may be in-apparent for many years, during which the person "enjoys good health." The physician's knowledge of the presence of such a potential limitation and the likelihood of eventual breakdown does not alter the fact of relatively good health over a certain span of time, especially when we realize how many persons carry potential limitations completely un-known to themselves or to physicians. But even when there is gross and manifest disability, we must recognize the relative integrity of other systems or modes of function, permitting us to refer quite accurately to the "more healthy" parts of the body or the person.

Such considerations naturally raise the practical question of how we know that someone is sick. We need not concern ourselves with the deviations in structure, performance or behavior that are so gross as to be obvious even to an untrained person. Rather, we need to examine some generalizations that will enable us to identify the state of disease regardless of its severity, etiology or the particular systems involved. We must also be able to identify the potential for breakdown in the apparently healthy person. As a starting point, we can say that the presence of a complaint must be regarded as *presumptive* evidence of disease. It indicates that there is a disturbance in the dynamic steady state, and that this disturbance is now being consciously experienced as unpleasant. The complaint itself does not necessarily give any infor-mation as to the severity or nature of the process. The complaint may be to a physician or a member of an allied profession, a member of the family, or a friend, or it may be kept to oneself. This is a *symptom*—something subjectively and privately experienced which may or may not be communicated to someone else in the form of a complaint. It may also involve something apparent to an outside observer, such as a swelling, a mass or peculiar behavior, in which case it is also a *sign*. Whether or not it is communicated depends on a great number of fac-tors, some personal, some social and some cultural. For example, it may depend on what the person considers to be the proper domain of the physician, a perspective which changes as views of medicine change.

On the other hand, the absence of a complaint (a symptom) cannot be equated with the absence of disease. As will be detailed later, signifi-cant disturbances involving physical as well as psychological processes may be kept out of consciousness so successfully that patients may show the grossest defects or changes in parts of the body, in their physical functioning, in their behavior, or in their thinking processes and yet may deny the fact that any change has taken place. An observer, lay or professional, may immediately recognize that the person is ill. This circumstance, however, differs from the situation already alluded to in which some technique of examination, physical, psychological or laboratory, reveals to the physician a defect which is at the moment compensated for or is simply not involved in the person's current function. The latter conditions fall in the borderland between health and disease, involving as they do relative or potential disability but adequate function under most circumstances. (These may be regarded as belonging more in the domain of preventive medicine than to therapeutic medicine.) Asymptomatic or latent syphilis revealed by a positive serological test would be an example. These considerations should make it clear that health and disease are relative processes in a variety of respects.

The perspective presented here is, of course, much broader than the conventional. It is customary in medicine at the present time, when attempting to establish whether or not a person is ill, to place the greatest emphasis on that which can be determined objectively, i.e., by the physician rather than the patient, often preferably by some impersonal instrument, such as by a laboratory procedure. Regardless of the nature and the severity of a patient's complaint, the failure to discover an abnormality on physical or laboratory examination means to many physicians that there is "nothing wrong." (How this influences what patients feel they must tell physicians in order to be accepted as patients and receive help will not be discussed here.) The common slang is that the patient has "no pathology," and it carries the double implication that he is not sick and often also that he is not worthy of help or that he is "fooling" the physician. If the patient responds favorably to the simple reassurance of "There is nothing wrong" (as some patients do), this may be regarded simply as a demonstration that there really was nothing wrong rather than that the patient had been experiencing some kind of disturbance which was alleviated by this type of reassurance. Another aspect of this is that when some type of objective pathological change is demonstrated, the correction of the abnormality may be equated with cure regardless of the patient's subjective experience. The extreme of this is the not-so-humorous statement, "The operation was a success but the patient died."

Some may argue that this concept of disease is so broad as to be essentially valueless. Experience refutes this argument. The traditional attitude toward disease tends in practice to restrict what is categorized as disease to what can be understood or recognized by the physician and/or what he notes can be helped by his intervention. This attitude has plagued medicine throughout its history and still stands in the way of physicians fully appreciating disease as a natural phenomenon. Disease cannot be defined simply on the basis of the function of physicians, who are changing variables in a social and institutional context. The scientific attitude requires that a clear distinction be made between the study and understanding of disease as a natural phenomenon and the categorization of disease in terms of the function and role of the physician in a society. Only the first is relevant to a scientific concept of disease. The latter changes with time and circumstance. Actually, the patient himself is not always able to make such a distinction and he brings a wide variety of symptoms and problems to his physician, hoping and looking for help. The fact that a physician arbitrarily excludes certain categories of complaints or signs as not appropriate is a reflection of his concept of his role as a physician and does not necessarily bear any relationship to the scientific question of what is disease. Nor does the fact that some patients may use other personal, social or institutional devices to achieve the same end bear on the definition of disease.

Viewing disease from such a naturalistic rather than institutional perspective means that many kinds of processes or experiences may be thought of in terms of disease or related to disease even though they are not currently so regarded. For example, the experience of grief, which ordinarily follows the loss of a loved person, a valued possession or an ideal, fulfills all the requirements of a disease process as we have defined it.[1] The usual arguments to dispute such a point of view are as follows: First, even though everyone recognizes the magnitude of suffering and disability accompanying grief, this is regarded as "natural" and expected, meaning that anyone who suffers a loss would be expected to experience grief. But it is also "natural" for an orderly sequence of events to take place in the tissues following a blow, a thermal injury or the ingestion of virulent typhoid bacilli. And as is also true of exposure to a blow, heat or the ingestion of typhoid bacilli, not everyone experiences grief following a loss and, among those who do experience grief, not all experience it in exactly the same way. A pugilist will have a lesser reaction to a blow than a fragile old man, a dark-skinned person will tolerate the infra red rays of the sun better than a blonde, and a person immunized by a previous exposure to typhoid bacilli will resist the effect of ingested organisms more effectively than a person not so immunized. A second argument is that grief is a self-limited process from which one can expect to recover without help. Even when this is so (and it is not always) the same may be said of many situations which are commonly categorized as disease. Wounds also may heal and infections run their course without any intervention by a physician, but this does not make such processes any the less disease experiences. A third argument (which is not usually verbalized, but which nonetheless influences opinions) is that a person suffering a loss is not usually expected to consult a physician for the diagnosis and treatment of the ensuing grief. If the physician is to consider him as a patient, convention dictates that the patient present with a "legitimate" complaint (e.g., a physical symptom), not with grief. Indeed, this is what usually happens. The grieving patient brings a physical complaint and the physician may never even learn of the bereavement. If he does learn of it, he regards it as "natural" and irrelevant, or "noncontributory," as current medical slang puts it, ignoring the fact that the basis for this judgment was never examined, much less established. Many other types of examples could be given. What I wish to emphasize is that many phenomena of everyday life which are considered natural are not customarily regarded in terms of disease, but nevertheless they involve processes which basically do not differ from those which are involved in disease. The term "pathological" is a relative one and is set by medical, scientific and even social convention. Conventions change, so that what may be considered as illness or disease at one time or by one person may not be so considered at another time or by another person. Epilepsy, drug addiction and psychosis are examples of disease processes which have been variously regarded at different times and by different people. That such conventions have value and use does not bear on the validity of this point of view. The heuristic value of differentiating between normal and pathological should not blind us to the fact that this is a relative matter based on ever-changing criteria.

The main advantage of this point of view is that it helps to focus on natural processes which may then be evaluated in terms of their success or failure in assuring adjustment. Our concepts of etiology need not be dependent on whether or not the end result is designated as "pathological." We are thus free to study any natural phenomenon in its own right and to evaluate its meaning in relationship to success or failure of adjustment, regardless of whether or not convention has established this to be concerned with disease. An anxiety experience is a natural phenomenon justifying our attention whether it involves a student before an examination, a pilot before a bombing mission, a businessman before a law suit, a housewife before an operation, a woman in a crowded elevator, a son opposing his father—regardless of whether or not the person actually comes to us for help and whether or not we can help him. Yet the need for help, whether it is perceived by the person himself or by an outside observer, and whether it is solicited from a physician or from someone else, will provide one of the important criteria of success or failure of adjustment and, hence, of health and disease.

ETIOLOGICAL CONSIDERATIONS: THE NECESSARY AND SUFFICIENT CONDITIONS

We now turn our attention to the factors concerned in the genesis of disease, the etiological factors. *We define etiological factors as factors which either place a burden on or limit the capacity of systems concerned with growth, development or adaptation, or as factors which, by virtue of their physical or chemical properties have the capacity to destroy cells or parts of the body.* They may operate through the impact of something added to or impinging on the system as well as through a deficiency, as when something necessary is taken away, is insufficient or is unavailable. They may originate within the organism as well as in the environment. No etiological factor can be considered in the abstract, but only in relationship to the system or systems upon which it is operating. Further, factors which have etiological significance in respect to a disease process at one time or under one circumstance may at another time or under other circumstances not have such implication. One never deals with a single etiological factor in the genesis of a disease state, although one factor may be more important than others or there may be practical advantages in paying more attention to one factor than to others. To quote Shimkin,[5] "There are few, if any, simple or single causes in biology; there are instead complex situations and environments in which the probability of certain events is increased." The scientific approach to disease assumes multiple factors, some more proximate, some more distant in time; some more specific, some more general in their effects; some necessary, but not in themselves sufficient to bring about the condition of disease. We may qualify the role of any factor by such adjectives as "precipitating", "conditioning", "predisposing", "permissive", "specific", or by indicating its mode of action, viz., genic, biochemical, physiological, psychological, social, etc. Postdictively we seek to identify the conditions necessary and sufficient to bring about a particular constellation of signs and symptoms. As physicians we intervene where we can to aid in the restoration of a state of health. As medical scientists we study these factors in terms of their qualifications as necessary and/or sufficient conditions, and attempt to predict the probability of occurrence of a particular constellation of manifestations characterizing a disease state. Again, as physicians we attempt to prevent the occurrence of the disease state by interfering with the operation of one or more factors before the necessary *and* sufficient conditions have been achieved. The scientific attitude can permit no restriction as to the category of natural phenomena investigated; the scientist's first obligation is to his data, wherever or however they present.

In any consideration of etiology it is necessary to take into account both the *"how"* and the *"why"* (Mayr[2]). The mechanistic tradition of medicine has led to an emphasis on the *"how."* The *"how"* refers to the manner in which things operate. It is essentially a description in dynamic terms of what is happening or what has happened in whatever system one might be examining, cellular, organ, total organism, psychic apparatus, social system, etc. In pneumococcal pneumonia, for example, the "how" will focus attention on the sequence of changes that take place in the lung after the pneumococcus has gained access to it. The question "why" has two possible meanings: *"How come?"* and *"What for?"* The former concerns the conditions which permitted the pneumococcus to gain access to the body in the first place—in other words, *"How come* the person got sick when he got sick?" and *"How come* it was pneumonia?"* "What for?" focusses attention on the purpose or functions of the changes which take place after the micro-organism has gained entry. What function, if any, in the person's adjustment or attempt at adjustment to the "invasion" by the pneumococcus is served by leukocytosis, fever, phagocytosis, cough, etc.? All three perspectives must be kept in mind in considering the etiology of any disease process.

Let us now examine more closely some categories of etiological factors. The strictures of speech prevent us from discussing more than one at a time but this does not obviate the fact that in nature many processes will be operating simultaneously.

Factors Which Determine the Capacity of the Organism to Grow, Survive and Adapt

GENIC FACTORS.[2, 6]   These are factors which are to be understood exclusively in biochemical terms, referring to the chemical composition of the body as determined by genic inheritance. They include factors underlying the individual chemical characteristics of the cells of each person and as such contribute to the basic chemical structure underlying the capacity for growth and development of every cell and system. We may presume that a normal distribution curve will describe the ranges and the capacities of each biochemical system in the population and, hence, the limit of functional or structural potential of the system for each individual. This refers to what we may speak of as the "biochemical universals," those systems which occur in all humans and which are generally regarded as "normal." This perspective emphasizes the genically determined variance within the normal biochemical systems of the body. This variance will describe one of the categories of factors concerned both with the potential for growth and development and with the capacity to adjust to changes imposed from without or from within. It will be a remote factor, one in a chain of events which may prove critical in a breakdown at some later date. Its influence may range all the way from the activity of enzyme systems to what people look like (e.g., pigmentation or body configuration). The influence of skin pigmentation on susceptibility to sunburn or on adjustment in a social group provides a whole range of examples of the remote operation of a genic factor as a determinant of health and disease and will be elaborated on later (p. 268). It is reasonable to assume that such molecular factors also may circumscribe the limits of operation of the brain and of the mind in any individual (e.g., the presence and activity of certain biochemical systems in the brain may be a limiting factor in determining what kinds or ranges of mental or psychic processes are possible in any individual). (See Chapters XXVIII and XXX.)

In addition, genic factors play a role in the transmission of abnormal or defective biochemical systems responsible for the variety of so-called inborn errors. These may include factors which are incompatible with fetal survival, factors which produce or are responsible for major developmental defects, and factors which may become manifest only under particular circumstances and at particular times in development. Among some of the better studied examples are such conditions as sickle cell trait, glycogen storage disease, hereditary phenylpyruvate oligophrenia, congenital galactosemia, gout, porphyria, etc. These relatively rare conditions lend themselves to study because the defect represents such a striking deviation from the normal. Yet it seems likely that many other more common conditions, such as diabetes, pernicious anemia or celiac disease, for example, will prove to involve similar factors. Whether or not genically-transmitted inborn errors become manifest in the form of a recognizable disease state depends on nonspecific as well as highly specific factors having to do with the particular defect as well as with developmental processes. Phenylpyruvate oligophrenia, a form of mental deficiency of infancy, for example, depends on the presence of phenylalanine in the diet for the cerebral metabolic defect to be expressed. Galactosemia, a disorder of infants, becomes manifest only with galactose ingestion. The intestinal malabsorption of the celiac syndrome apparently requires the presence of wheat protein in the diet. These are examples of conditions in which substances normal to the diet are harmful to those individuals who carry the enzyme defect, with a consequent biochemical disturbance involving important body systems. Other types of defects, such as those underlying gout, pernicious anemia and porphyria, may become manifest only after many years, presumably because other factors may be involved and/or because of the length of time necessary for the process to evolve.

The genic determination of the chemical composition of the body is, then, a basic factor in the specific strengths and vulnerabilities of the individual. It plays a role not only in the vulnerability to breakdown but also in the nature and type of development of various systems including the psychic system. It is very probable that some of the factors which determine the strength or character of instinctual drives are, in part at least, genically determined. The sense of taste, for example, which is known to be determined by genic factors, could be a significant influence in the early oral experience of the infant and its relation to the mother. Genic factors are probably important also in the specific development and organization of the brain and hence in certain capacities for mental functioning. There is the challenging possibility that the biochemical characteristics of individuals can some day be established and from this may be anticipated certain potential lines of development, including eventual pathological changes. Beginnings in this direction are to be found in Mirsky's[4] success in predicting peptic ulcer and pernicious anemia on the basis of high and low pepsinogen concentrations in blood. (See Chapter XXXIII.) However, such new knowledge of biochemical determinants does not justify a regression to concepts of "molecular diseases," a reversion toward a single cause-effect relation reminiscent of the oversimplified germ theory.

DEVELOPMENTAL FACTORS OTHER THAN GENIC.   These include all the factors, from conception on, which influence developmental and adaptational capacities favorably or unfavorably. This developmental perspective takes into account all the ways in which the organism and its component parts in the course of development "learn" to secure needs and to adjust to strains, including those provoked by deprivation or insufficiencies. We postulate that within the framework provided by the genically determined structure, the nature and variety of experiences during life will determine the specific ways of development, the particular variety of techniques utilized to relate effectively to the external environment, and the particular varieties of defense, ranging from cellular to psychosocial. The concept of biological and psychological assimilation and accommodation is important here. A wide variety of external things or processes must be taken in physically or psychically and become part of the organism, ranging from molecules to percepts of persons, ideals, etc., and then are utilized in the service of further adjustment and development. All individuals share the need for certain essential elements, but each individual will, in addition, evolve a particular variety necessary for his survival, growth and development, depending on the nature of his individual experience. Thus, at the level of cellular function we note the capacity of the cell to "recognize" and select what it needs for its own development and to reject or actually defend itself against damaging molecules. After a particular micro-organism or foreign protein has gained access to the body, the body may thereafter be permanently changed so that the cells thereafter "recognize" this foreign substance and react differently to it. Some such changes may be permanent (e.g., immunity) while others may develop slowly and last only as long as the substance is present (e.g., tolerance and addiction).

At the level of the organism as a whole we note the variety of influences, notably persons and situations, which the individual comes to experience as providing something necessary for continued effective functioning, and the absence of which may be experienced as a loss requiring some type of adjustment. This has been discussed in the sections on development in terms of object relations and psychic object representations. We emphasize here the highly individual nature of such object relationship capacities and how they help to determine what constitutes the strengths and weaknesses of the individual, what he comes to need from his environment in order to remain comfortable, to grow and to function effectively. These phenomena of assimilation and accommodation are basically biological, their psychological expression being found in terms of objects, object relations, object representation and in learning. (See Chapter VIII.)

In considering the gamut of developmental factors it is important to emphasize the concept of critical periods, both somatic and psychological. For example, only during a very specific interval in fetal life may virus infections in the mother (e.g., rubella) damage the fetus. Similarly, the susceptibility to certain types and modalities of psychic stress is very different at different ages. The consequences of separation from the mother are vastly different at three months, three years and 30 years. A host of processes occurring at a biochemical, cellular or psychological level early in life may be critical in determining the capacity of a person to develop certain pathological changes later in life, but the age at which these occur may be the factor determining whether or not there will be an effect and if so, what it will be. Thus, at any later point in time, what constitutes a stress to any individual will be determined to a large degree by the nature of his past experience (as well as by the character of his genic endowment). This will apply to the nature of the response to micro-organisms as well as to the loss of a love object. By virtue of what has gone before, the person may be more or less able to cope with ingested typhoid bacilli and more or less able to tolerate the death of his mother. (See Chapters XXVII and XXVIII.)

Factors Which Strain Current Capacities

Having emphasized the influence of past experiences on determining both the capacities for adjustment and the specific vulnerabilities and tolerances, we can now consider the varieties of processes which can put such capacities under strain. Because such factors are usually more obvious and certainly more proximate, they are often erroneously designated as "the cause" of the disease process. Not only is this incorrect and misleading, but also at times it tends to exclude other more important considerations.

For convenience we divide such factors into a number of categories:

FACTORS WHICH INJURE BY VIRTUE OF THEIR PHYSICAL AND/OR CHEMICAL PROPERTIES. These include all the varieties of physical and chemical noxae which may impinge upon man from the external environment, (e.g., mechanical forces, poisons, heat, cold, radiation, electricity, etc.) as well as substances which are formed or forces which may develop within the body which injure by virtue of inappropriate quantity or location (e.g., excess insulin, action of gastric juice on the esophagus, increased intracranial pressure). Such internal factors are almost always secondary to other factors, but nonetheless may bring consequences (signs and symptoms) which are specific and not necessarily related to the predisposing factors.

The external noxae come the closest to constituting absolute causes in the sense that beyond a certain degree they will be damaging or lethal to everyone. Even here, however, there are important predisposing considerations. Persons differ in respect to the magnitude of a blow or the dose of a poison that they can tolerate. Further, many other factors of psychological and/or social importance may be critical in determining the circumstance of the exposure in the first place, including suicidal intent, accident proneness, impulsivity, industrial exposure, ignorance, mental confusion, pure coincidence, and so on. Some of these agents, as, for example, carcinogenic substances or radiation, do not necessarily produce their effects immediately or in all who are exposed. In general, the longer the time lapse between exposure and the development of pathological tissue changes, the more complex and multiple are the other conditions necessary for such developments. Some molecular substances achieve a noxious quality by virtue of the host's capacity or tendency at certain times and under certain conditions to develop a specific sensitivity response, the allergic reaction. Such reactions may also take place in response to substances which are part of the person's own cell composition (autoimmune reactions).

PHYSICAL FACTORS WHICH LEAD TO INJURY OR IMPAIRMENT OF FUNCTION WHEN INSUFFICIENT OR UNAVAILABLE. In this group we restrict ourselves to the essential chemical elements (oxygen, water, electrolytes, nutriments, vitamins, etc.) which the organism must obtain from the environment (deficiency states) and the essential substances formed in the body, such as hormones (insufficiency states). Again, we must keep in mind the predisposing conditions which determine "how come" the deficiency or insufficiency occurred in the first place as well as the magnitude and character of the resulting reaction. Here again the less immediately or less consistently developing reactions either involve less critical substances or require the operation of multiple predisposing or intervening processes before the conditions necessary and sufficient for manifest disorder have been achieved. We can contrast the relatively narrow range of resistance to oxygen lack and the more variable response to lack of a single nutritional element, or the pronounced response to insulin or adrenal steroid insufficiency compared to the minor effects, if any, of gastric hydrochloric acid insufficiency. The availability of alternative mechanisms or the capacity for compensatory internal rearrangements are important in determining whether or not deficiency or insufficiency actually will become manifest.

MICRO-ORGANISMS AND PARASITES. These deserve a special category in the etiology of disease because they involve the interrelations between two or more living systems (more than two if intermediary vectors are included). In the case of each agent there are highly specific as well as nonspecific factors which determine (1) whether it gains entry to the body; (2) whether it exists there in a harmless parasitic or a helpful or neutral symbiotic relationship, or whether it damages or destroys its host; (3) in what particular locus, i.e., cell, tissue, organ or body fluid, it can live. The fields of microbiology, parasitology and immunology are devoted to the elucidation of such factors. Suffice it to say that multiple factors in the natural history of the micro-organism and in the host are involved. There are some micro-organisms to which humans are almost universally susceptible on first exposure (e.g., the viruses of measles and smallpox) so that the most significant factor determining susceptibility to infection (though not capacity for survival) may be a previous exposure and the development of immunity. Other micro-organisms may be capable of infecting only a small proportion of people, and others may at some point in the life of the host or of the micro-organism change from a harmless guest to a destructive agent. Here may be involved multiple factors in the host, ranging from fixed (genic or constitutional) biochemical structure to general or local changes associated with other stresses or responses to stresses. As examples of the latter may be cited the clinical observation of an apparent increased tendency to certain infections in diabetes or during certain kinds of psychological decompensation. Some consequences of infection with micro-organisms may be indirect and dependent on the characteristics and condition of the host, so that only certain individuals at certain times may so react (e.g., the relation between hemolytic streptococcus infection and later rheumatic fever or hemorrhagic nephritis).

FACTORS WHICH OPERATE THROUGH THEIR EFFECT ON THE CENTRAL REGULATING SYSTEM (BRAIN AND MENTAL APPARATUS). All the factors so far listed are of such a nature that they *may* exert their influence directly at the level of cells, tissues or organs, involving the central regulating systems only secondarily, if at all. However, if the central nervous system and the mental apparatus are indeed the systems whereby the organism maintains adjustment of its internal environment in relation to the external environment (physical, interpersonal and social) and thereby maintains growth, development and organism integrity, we must anticipate that some factors which determine health or disease are mediated in one way or another through this system. We shall devote the next chapter to a more detailed consideration of this category of etiological factors.

REFERENCES

1. Engel, G. L.: Is Grief a Disease? A Challenge for Medical Research. Psychosom. Med., *22*:18, 1961.
2. Kalckar, H. M.: Some Considerations Regarding Biochemical Genetics in Man. Perspect. Biol. & Med., *1*:3, 1957.
3. Mayr, E.: Cause and Effect in Biology. Science, *134*:1501, 1961.
4. Mirsky, I. A.: Physiologic, Psychologic and Social Determinants in the Etiology of Duodenal Ulcer. Am. J. Digest. Dis., *3*:285, 1958.
5. Shimkin, M. B.: Hormones and Neoplasia. *In:* Raven, R. W. (ed.): Cancer, vol. 1. London, Butterworth & Co., 1952.
6. Snyder, L. H.: Fifty Years of Medical Genetics. Science, *129*:1, 1959.

CHAPTER XXV

A UNIFIED CONCEPT OF HEALTH AND DISEASE

III. The Role of the Mental Apparatus and Central Nervous System; The Phenomenology of Disease

The brain and mental apparatus are the systems concerned with maintaining the adjustment of the organism in its environment and with assuring its potential for growth and development. Therefore, it is necessary to examine the extent and manner to which the predisposition for or precipitation of disease is dependent upon processes mediated through the mental apparatus and the central nervous system and to explore the patterns of disturbance which may be evoked thereby. In terms of etiological factors, the first defines the varieties of primary psychological stress, and the second indicates the direct and indirect etiological consequences of psychological stress. In this presentation we shall not discuss how psychic stress as an etiological factor contributes to disease, but we shall merely emphasize the obvious, that all its effects on the body must be mediated through the central nervous system. More detailed consideration of these processes will be found in the subsequent chapters (XXVI to XXXIII).

PSYCHOLOGICAL STRESS

Psychological stress refers to all processes, whether originating in the external environment or within the person, which impose a demand or requirement upon the organism, the resolution or handling of which requires work or activity of the mental apparatus before any other system is involved or activated. This contrasts, for example, with the factors already referred to, such as micro-organisms, physical trauma, poisons, deficiencies, etc., which affect first the operation or function of biochemical or physiological systems, including sometimes those of the brain, and only secondarily the mental apparatus. Conceptually, for a situation or process to constitute a psychological (rather than physical) stress not only must it pass through the systems of perception of the mental apparatus, but also it must be capable of some type of psychic representation or expression, conscious or unconscious. In other words, it must be capable of being perceived, experienced and represented in the mind of the subject, although not necessarily in toto or consciously, and it must be manifest to the subject and/or observer in psychological terms. The action of a micro-organism or a chemical substance does not satisfy these criteria, but the *idea* of an infection or a poison does. After a micro-organism or a poison has exerted its influence, however, the resulting bodily changes include processes which do have the capacity to penetrate the perceptual thresholds, and hence a somatic disorder can also come to be a psychological stress. Obviously some situations represent both at the same time. A physical injury, for example, may simultaneously be experienced psychologically and physically, or processes which affect the brain directly may also immediately bring about psychological changes by virtue of affecting the physico-chemical substrata of the mental apparatus.

Highly individual factors determine whether a particular situation or process constitutes a psychological stress for a particular individual. The judgment as to whether or not it constitutes a stress for an individual cannot be made from the nature of the external event alone, but requires knowledge of the response as well. A separation may constitute a welcome release as well as a loss, just as the typhoid bacillus may serve to enhance already present immunity as well as lead to typhoid fever. Nonetheless, experience permits us to recognize certain categories of phenomena as being the main means whereby psychological stress may come about. This is a probability statement, meaning that these kinds of events are likely to, but do not necessarily, constitute psychological stresses. A fuller discussion of each category is found in Chapter XXVII.

Loss or Threat of Loss of Objects

Persons, ideals, valued possessions, job, body function and image, social roles, goals, home, country, etc.—there is a tremendous variety of processes originally external to the mental apparatus and psychic experience which in the course of development come to constitute in aggregate the basis of one's concept of oneself and thereby to varying degrees become necessary for effective ego function and for the continued and sustained sense of intactness, fulfillment, success and hope. It is this dependence on psychic objects which renders the individual vulnerable to their loss or threat of loss and imposes the requirement for some kind of adjustment in compensation, of which mourning represents the most familiar response. (See Chapter XXVI.) What constitute the meaningful psychic objects for any individual is determined by many details of his life experience and may be ascertained only through the investigation of his life history. In earlier chapters we have already indicated some of the consequences of separation and object loss at different ages in reference to both patterns of response and of adjustment.

Injury or Threat of Injury

The infliction of pain, mutilation, etc., actual or threatened, is a prominent source of psychological stress. In general, the human being seeks to protect himself from such dangers (except for the special case of the self-destructive individual, to be discussed later), and he responds to psychic experiences that imply such dangers as if they constitute an imminent threat, requiring defense or adjustment. This is so whether the danger is a real external one or whether it is primarily derived from intrapsychic elaboration, unconscious fantasy, persistent infantile conflict, etc. Again, what symbolically as well as actually constitutes such a danger is dependent on the individual's past experience and his past successes or failures in coping therewith. Obviously, all the physical etiological factors already considered become potential psychological stresses to the extent that they can be conceptualized or their effects can be experienced psychologically. Again, we call attention to the neuroendocrine system, which prepares the body for defensive action and for protection against and repair of injury and which to varying degrees goes into action in response as much to the psychological threat of injury as to actual injury. (See Chapter XXXIII.)

Frustration of Drives

This category of psychological stress recognizes the built-in biological drive organizations which press for discharge either in response to developmental processes (e.g., adolescence, the menstrual cycle) or upon stimulation by imagery or the environment. A major aspect of the development of each individual has been the successive mastery by the mental apparatus of the drive apparatuses, so that satisfaction of needs can take place with due regard for the requirements of reality. We have seen how this developmental process carries with it the inevitability of intrapsychic conflict and how internally as well as externally imposed controls at certain times serve to inhibit, deflect or pervert the drive impulses. When intrapsychic conflict develops, the drive can come to constitute a psychological stress for the individual, requiring some sort of resolution in the sense not only that satisfaction of the drive may be conceived as somehow dangerous or undesirable, but also that the drive is not discharged and the need remains unfulfilled. Again the highly individual qualities of this situation must be underscored.

All three of these categories are obviously closely interrelated. Their differentiation is determined mainly by the character of the initiating circumstances, that is, loss or threat of loss, injury or threat of injury, or drive frustration with or without increment, but each may in turn implicate the others. Thus, a sexual or destructive impulse may have to be inhibited because it will threaten an object loss or physical injury; a threat of injury or loss may stir up an intolerable degree of destructive anger or an unacceptable sexual impulse; a threat of injury may be psychologically experienced in terms of an object loss, the loss of a valued body part or function, rather than in terms of pain and suffering. Regardless of the nature of such interrelations, all these psychological stresses not only are mutually perceived or experienced through mental apparatus but also have the capacity to disrupt the dynamic steady state of the mental apparatus. We shall now consider how this may be reflected in the subsequent function of the mental apparatus and in the rest of the body—in other words, the direct and indirect consequences of psychological stress.

PATTERNS OF RESPONSES TO PSYCHOLOGICAL STRESS AS FACTORS DETERMINING THE MANIFESTATIONS OF ILLNESS

In outlining here the patterns of response to psychological stress, we shall in capsule form classify all the patterns and varieties of illness reaction, each of which will be discussed in more detail in subsequent chapters (Chapters XXVIII to XXXIII). Since by definition we specify that psychological stress involves first the mental apparatus, we can also say that the first response to a psychological stress, whether it be primary or secondary, will be psychological and/or behavioral. But there may also by simultaneous and concomitant physiological or biochemical changes in the body which in turn may permit, facilitate or precipitate other types of somatic processes which do not directly involve the mental apparatus. Listed in this order, the range and variety of responses to psychological stress are as follows:

1. An unpleasant affect, or sequence of affects, such as anxiety, disgust, shame, guilt, helplessness and hopelessness, is the first indicator of a disruption of the dynamic steady state. If the stress is brief or if ego processes succeed quickly in achieving a solution, the unpleasant affect diminishes, changes in quality or ceases. If a comparable situation has been experienced in the past and some type of relatively effective ego mechanism has already evolved (or if a solution is available), only the signal (ego) aspect of the affect may be evoked, the mental apparatus quickly responding with psychic mechanisms of defense and solution. When such mechanisms are not immediately available or are unsuccessful, the affects will include various more or less distinctive concomitant subjective physiological, biochemical and behavioral changes. If the affect persists but its ideational representation is distorted, changed or denied so that it remains unrecognizable by the subject, the concomitant bodily changes may still persist. (See Chapters XVIII and XXXIII.)

2. The unpleasant affects, once so induced, may persist for an inappropriately long time or to an inappropriately intense degree. Occasionally they may be replaced by inappropriate pleasant affects, as in euphoria or mania, a defense against the opposite. These may now be considered pathological affective states and are usually associated with manifest bodily changes, generally reversible. (See Chapters XXX, XXXI and XXXIII.)

3. The attempts to overcome the stress, resolve the conflict, and dissipate the unpleasant affect(s) may include inappropriate, unrealistic or repetitively unsuccessful ego mechanisms which in various combinations and constellations make up the variety of psychopathological states known as the neuroses, psychoses, perversions and character disorders (Chapter XXXI).

4. The manifest behavior evolving under (3) may directly or indirectly expose or predispose the person to other varieties of environmental stress, such as injury, poisons, drugs, dietary deficiency, etc., with all the possible consequences referred to in Chapter XXIV. In other words, the inadequacies or inappropriateness of the person's attempt to deal with this now intrapsychic distress may include behavior which does not properly evaluate or avoid the stresess of the external environment or renders the person incapable of so doing (Chapter XXXII).

5. The biochemical and physiological concomitants of sustained or intense affects may in the susceptible individual directly or indirectly put under strain an already defective system (e.g., the effect of anxiety or rage on an already damaged heart) or accelerate, precipitate, enhance

or uncover pre-existing, sometimes latent pathological processes at a biochemical, cellular, organ, or system level (e.g., an infection, neoplasia, diabetes, peptic ulceration, etc.). Clinical observation provides many examples of such a sequence of events (Chapters XXXII and XXXIII).

6. The secondary consequences noted under (4) and (5) in turn have an impact on the mental apparatus which in some cases and in some respects may compound the stress and in other cases or respects may have reparative effects. Some secondary somatic consequences may also directly affect the function or metabolism of the brain, thereby again affecting the mental apparatus. The latter is illustrated by the effects on the brain and on psychic activity of drugs or alcohol consumed in an attempt to alleviate psychological distress or of metabolic deficiencies secondary to psychologically determined abnormal eating or excretory patterns (e.g., nutritional deficiencies or excessive use of laxatives leading to hypokalemia) (Chapters XXXI and XXXII).

These various categories of response to psychological stress are thus mutually inclusive and interrelated. All or any combination may occur in the same individual either at the same time or in sequence or cycles. Also, psychological stress as an etiological factor may operate as the direct or indirect pathway whereby other etiological factors may be brought into activity, as they in turn may achieve the quality of psychological stresses. From the developmental perspective, what was a somatic factor earlier in life may form the basis for psychological stress later by influencing the limit or variety of adjustment possible (e.g., the effect on development of a childhood illness or defect, such as celiac disease, rheumatic fever, cerebral palsy or hare-lip and cleft palate) (Chapter XXVIII).

No linear concept of etiology is appropriate, but rather the pathogenesis of disease involves a series of negative and positive feedbacks with multiple simultaneous and sequential changes potentially affecting any system of the body. The central nervous system is so organized functionally that a reciprocal interrelationship between the mental apparatus and the rest of the body in the pathogenesis of disease states is not only possible but inevitable. Current work on the central nervous system is elucidating the systems concerned in this reciprocal control of internal homeostasis and adjustment within the environment.

The multifactorial concept of the etiology of disease may be illustrated with a familiar example, sunburn.* A *necessary*, but not sufficient, condition for sunburn is, of course, exposure to the actinic rays of the sun. This is the potential physical stress. A genically determined factor, the amount of and capacity to form melanin in the skin determines the

---

* An example first proposed by F. Engel.

capacity to resist the burning effect of the sun, the heavily pigmented person being virtually immune. This is a biochemical factor, which in the rare albino represents a true gene-determined defect. Sufficient exposure to the sun to produce a burn is a function of behavior. This may occur accidentally, through ignorance or during preoccupation, healthy or morbid, which distracts the person from awareness of the risk he is taking. It may even occur deliberately, as when for conscious or unconscious reasons a sunburn (as illness) would serve some psychologically useful purpose. These three factors, the actinic rays of the sun, insufficient melanin to protect the skin, and behavior leading to sufficient exposure, constitute the necessary and sufficient conditions for burning of the skin. Many other secondary factors, some highly individual, will then determine the final picture and course of the disease, sunburn, and its various complications. The imaginative student will have no difficulty in extending this illustration along the lines already considered. But the example does serve to demonstrate the fallacy of considering the actinic rays of the sun as *the* cause, rather than as a necessary condition, for the skin burn. Indeed, radiation from other sources can also produce a burn indistinguishable from sunburn in the susceptible individual. Further, it reveals the weakness of the currently popular concept of "molecular diseases." Were the external factor, namely, the physical effects of sunlight, not so obvious, the insufficiency of pigment in the skin, a genically determined biochemical factor, might be regarded as "the cause," just as the enzyme defect interfering with the metabolism of phenylalanine in the brain is regarded as "the cause" of phenylpyruvic oligophrenia. It is a necessary condition, one of several, but not in itself sufficient. Thus, it may be proper to speak of molecular factors in disease, but not of "molecular diseases."

THE PHENOMENOLOGY OF DISEASE

These etiological considerations serve to draw attention to the complexity of the processes that contribute to the manifestations of disease. In any ill person at any point in the illness the symptoms and signs may consist of a combination of the following:

The Instinct or Drive Aspect

In the course of any threat to the existence and integrity of an organism, activity of the drive systems will tend to be stimulated. These usually are the earlier, more primitive drives, both aggressive and sexual, but they have more to do with personal survival than with species survival. As such they are not necessarily reality-oriented and therefore may not only fail to serve the ends of survival and development but may actually be damaging. As examples may be cited the cardiac patient who races to an open window in response to dyspnea, the patient who overeats in response to feelings of depression, the patient who has erotic feelings in response to a skin or rectal disorder. When increment or change in drive is of primary importance as an etiological factor, the drive phenomena will play a more prominent role in the manifestations of the disease process.

Affects

As already pointed out, affects, usually but not invariably unpleasant, will be manifest at various times and in various forms in every illness experience. Included may be their signal (ego) aspects, their discharge (drive) aspects and their communication (object) aspects, with or without the concomitant bodily changes. As with the drive phenomena, affects in themselves are not adaptive but rather stimuli for adaptive responses, and the consequences of the affects may or may not be helpful in the person's adjustment.

The Adaptive Processes

Many of the signs or symptoms of disease are the manifestations of the adaptive efforts of the organism. These include all the processes concerned with maintaining or re-establishing a dynamic steady state and are to be found at all levels of organization and function, biochemical, physiological, psychological, interpersonal and social. Illustrations were given in Chapter XXIII.

Direct Damage

The direct effects on bodily systems of noxious agents and damaging forces from the external or internal environments will be manifest in biochemical, physiological or anatomical form and not in psychological form, unless it is the brain itself which is damaged.

This classification of the phenomenology of disease has limited practical value since one cannot necessarily deduce from the manifestation itself its place in this scheme, but it is presented primarily to emphasize again that what a sick person presents and what we can observe are complex fragments of many different interrelated processes.

REFERENCES

1. Dubos, R.: The Mirage of Health. New York, Harper & Brothers, 1959.
2. Engel, G. L.: Homeostasis, Behavioral Adjustment, and the Concept of

Health and Disease. *In:* Grinker, R. (ed.): Mid-Century Psychiatry. Springfield, Illinois, Charles C Thomas, 1953.

3. Engel, G. L.: Is Grief a Disease? A Challenge for Medical Research. Psychosom. Med., *23*:18, 1961.

4. Kalckar, H. M.: Some Considerations Regarding Biochemical Genetics in Man. Perspect. Biol. & Med., *1*:3, 1957.

5. Mayr, E.: Cause and Effect in Biology. Science, *134*:1501, 1961.

6. Mirsky, I. A.: Physiologic, Psychologic and Social Determinants in the Etiology of Duodenal Ulcer. Am. J. Digest. Dis., *3*:285, 1958.

7. Reese, W.: The Conception of Disease, Its History, Its Versions, and Its Nature. New York, Philosophical Library, 1953.

8. Shimkin, M. B.: Hormones and Neoplasia. *In:* Raven, R. W. (ed.)· Cancer, vol. 1. London, Butterworth & Co., 1952, p. 161.

9. Snyder, L. H.: Fifty Years of Medical Genetics. Science, *129*:1. 1959.

CHAPTER XXVI

PSYCHOLOGICAL RESPONSES TO MAJOR ENVIRONMENTAL STRESS

Grief and Mourning; Danger, Disaster and Deprivation

We have already made sufficient reference to *stress* to indicate that it refers to influences on the living organism which either are directly damaging or which bring about changes of such a character that, if they are not reversed or compensated for, impairment and damage will result. *At the same time, it must also be emphasized that stress successfully coped with can just as often have a beneficial and stimulating effect on development as stress unsuccessfully coped with may have a harmful or damaging effect.* Stress must not be simply equated with that which is bad or harmful. The concept of stress must of necessity be a relative one, even though some processes allow for no ambiguity as to their stressful nature. Further, whether or not a particular force or situation is experienced as stressful by a particular organism depends on whether or not that organism has in the past developed adequate means of adaptation or defense or has the endowment to do so. As examples one might cite the first encounter with physical agents such as bacteria when specific immunological defenses are not yet available; the child's first behavioral expression of an instinctual need, such as masturbation, which conflicts with the expectations of the environment as represented by the family; or the first requirement to assume adult responsibilities by a person who was greatly overprotected in childhood. These examples differ in that two describe situations in which more complex psychological stresses may occur, and one refers to a physical stress, but in all three the lack of preparation for something not previously coped with is what makes the situation potentially stressful.

Further, a subsequent experience may prove stressful because the earlier attempts at adaptation were relatively unsuccessful or incomplete or are no longer appropriate, or because the first experience produced an unfavorable change. For example, one may respond to a second exposure to a micro-organism with a second infection, to a second dose of drug or serum with a hypersensitivity reaction, or to a surgical experience with revival of infantile complexes associated with past unresolved conflicts about injury or separation.

Stress must also be considered in a quantitative sense: how much, how abruptly and over what span of time. For every living system there is a range defining the capacity of the system to respond successfully to change.

Finally, stress cannot be defined simply in terms of its origin. Although it is easier to categorize stresses in terms of environmental factors or situations, not only do some stressful influences originate within the organism rather than in the environment, but also for any individual the conditions defining stress are to be found simultaneously in the individual and in the external environment. Further, as already emphasized, one rarely deals with a single stress, but rather with a series of reactions of the organism in process with its environment. A complex hierarchy and mosaic of stresses are the result. Nonetheless, experience allows us to identify certain environmental factors or events as likely to prove stressful for a majority of, but not for all, people. These have already been classified in Chapter XXV. The ubiquity of such environmental stress situations makes it possible to study patterns of response among large populations. We select two such common sources of psychological stress as vehicles for further elucidation of patterns of psychological response and adaptation. They are loss of real objects and situations of danger and deprivation.

GRIEF AND MOURNING AS RESPONSES TO REAL OBJECT LOSS

Under this heading are included all the general responses to loss of objects as represented by persons, job, valued possessions, home, membership in a group, country, ideals, etc. (In general, grief refers more to what is felt or experienced, and mourning to the processes involved.) Human life is such that no one is immune to such events, and everyone may be expected to have a number of major grief experiences during his life. Grief responses are not confined to humans, having been observed in animals as well. The most clear-cut loss evocative of grief is the death of a loved person, and we shall take as the model for the grief reaction the response to an unexpected death. The basic principles apply to other varieties of object loss as well, but obviously there are important variations in patterns of grief dependent upon the circumstances of the loss and the significance of the object lost. Grief and mourning present fairly consistent patterns which can be best understood in terms of the sequence of psychological processes concerned in the apprehending of a loss, the attempts to deal with it and the final resolution of the loss. By definition, an object has the qualities of something essential for the psychic function of the individual. Hence, object loss may be compared to a wound and mourning to wound healing. Like wound healing, successful mourning involves an orderly sequence and an irreducible interval of time, interference with which may distort the process of healing and lead to pathological consequences. And, like wound healing, pre-existing and previous conditions will influence or change the course of the process and sometimes prevent it altogether.

The Stage of Shock and Disbelief

The first response upon learning of an unexpected death is one of shock and disbelief. The reality simply cannot be accepted. The survivor may respond with a refusal to accept or comprehend the perceived datum, often crying out, "No!", "It can't be!", "I don't believe it!", "It isn't so!"; or he may throw himself on the body, attempting to find signs of life or to bring the dead back to life. This reaction may then be followed by a stunned, numbed feeling in which the grief-stricken person blunts or blocks out the data of his sense organs and does not permit himself any thoughts or feelings which acknowledge the reality of the death. He may try desperately, but in an automatic fashion, to carry on his ordinary activities, as if nothing had happened, or he may sit motionless and dazed, unable to move. At such times the victim seems out of contact and it may be difficult to gain his attention. This phase may last a few minutes or hours or even days, alternating with flashes of despair and anguish as the reality of the loss briefly penetrates into consciousness.

Sometimes the initial response is overtly an intellectual acceptance of the reality of the loss and an immediate initiation of apparently appropriate activity, such as making arrangements, comforting others, etc. But it is only by not permitting access to consciousness of the full emotional impact of the loss that this can take place. In such an instance the loss is recognized but its painful character is denied or at least muted. The activity, while appropriate, serves to aid this denial of affect.

In general, distinctive of this initial phase are the attempts to protect oneself against the effects of the overwhelming stress by raising the threshold against its recognition or against the painful feeling evoked thereby. Denial is the most prominent psychological mechanism operating at such times. Although such responses are more usual when the death is sudden and unexpected, they may also be observed when the death has been anticipated. In general, however, when death is anticipated there is more opportunity to work through the initial awareness of the fact of death, and the shock phase is less prominent or absent.

The Stage of Developing Awareness of the Loss

Within a short time the reality of the death and its meaning as a loss begin more and more to penetrate consciousness in the form of an acute and increasing awareness of the pain and anguish of the loss, the feeling of something missing or lost, often felt as a painful emptiness in the chest or epigastrium. The affect experienced is primarily acute sadness, with which may be admixed some anxiety, helplessness or hopelessness. The environment seems frustrating and empty since it no longer includes the loved person. Aggression may be felt as anger toward persons or circumstances held to be responsible for the death, including the mourner himself, who may hold himself responsible and feel guilt.

Crying, with tears, is typical of this phase. It is during this period that the greatest degree of anguish or despair, within the limits imposed by cultural patterns, is experienced and expressed. Some cultures demand loud and public lamentation, whereas others expect restraint and avoidance of public display of grief. Familiarity with such cultural patterns is necessary in evaluating the appropriateness of a grief response. Regardless of such factors, the wish and need to cry is strong and crying seems to fulfill an important homeostatic function in the work of mourning. In general, crying seems to involve both an acknowledgement of the loss and the regression to a more helpless and childlike status evoked thereby. In the latter sense crying is a communication. The grief-stricken person who cries is the recipient of certain kinds of support and help from the group, although this varies greatly in different cultures. Grief is one situation in which the tears of an adult are generally accepted and understood and the person who is able to cry still feels self-respect and worthfulness and that he is deserving of help.

Some persons suffering a loss want to cry or feel that they should cry, yet are unable to. This type of inhibition of crying must be distinguished from not crying simply because the person who died is not seriously missed, in which case there is no inclination or need to cry, and from the voluntary suppression of crying because of an environmental or cultural demand, in which case the person either "cries inwardly" or waits until he is alone and unobserved before crying. Inability to cry, however, is a more serious matter. It is most likely to occur when the relationship with the dead person had been highly ambivalent and when the survivor is experiencing a good deal of guilt and shame. Such a person may feel very distressed that he is not able to cry or that he does not even feel like crying. His ambivalence, usually not acknowledged consciously, is often expressed in his concern that others will regard him as hard-hearted, against which possibility he protests his devotion to the deceased. When the predominant affect is hopelessness there is the additional element of withdrawal and detachment, with apathy toward the event. Inability to cry under the circumstances of a serious loss is a harbinger of later difficulties, as will be discussed.

Restitution—the Work of Mourning

The institutionalization of the mourning experience in terms of the various rites and rituals of the funeral help to initiate the recovery processes. First, it involves a gathering together of family and friends who mutually share the loss, although not all to the same degree. At the same time there is acknowledgment of the need for support of the more stricken survivors whose regression is accepted. In this setting overt or conscious expression of aggression is reduced to a minimum. Many of the rituals of the funeral serve the important function of emphasizing clearly and unequivocally the reality of the death, the denial of which cannot be allowed to go on if recovery from the loss is to take place. The viewing of the body, the lowering of the casket, and the various rituals characteristic of different religious beliefs allow for no ambiguity. Further, this experience takes place in a group, permitting ordinarily guarded feelings to be shared and expressed more readily. In addition, individual religious and spiritual beliefs offer recourse in various ways to the help and support of a more powerful, beneficent figure or provide the basis for the expectation of some kind of reunion after death. The funeral ceremony also initiates the process of identification with the lost person through the various rituals which symbolize an identity between the mourner and the dead (e.g., sack cloth and ashes). In primitive societies this acting out of the identification is more vivid and literal. In many cultures the funeral ceremony includes a feast or some sort of wake in which is symbolically expressed a triumph over death, a denial of the fear of death or of the dead, an attempt to return to life and living, expressed through primitive fantasies of oral incorporation.

For the mourner, however, the main work of grief goes on intrapsychically, the institutionalization mainly providing support and sustenance during this period. As the reality of the death becomes accepted, the resolution of the loss involves a number of steps which proceed haltingly and interruptedly. First, the mourner attempts to deal with the painful void, the awareness of the object loss, which is felt also as a defect in the psychic self. He cannot yet accept a new object to replace the lost object, although he may passively and transiently accept a more dependent relation with old objects. In this phase he may be more aware of his own body, experiencing various bodily sensations or pains, in contrast to the earlier period when he may have been quite numb even to great physical hardship. Often such a pain or discomfort is identical with a symptom experienced in the past by the dead person, sometimes during the terminal illness. Suffering like the dead relative involves a partial identification. The mourner suffers in place of the dead person and by so doing not only maintains a tie with the deceased, but also appeases some of his own guilt for any aggressive impulses toward the dead. Under normal circumstances such symptoms are brief, if they occur at all, but in some cases they constitute a prominent feature of the response to the loss and as such are pathological. (See Chapters XXVII and XXXII.)

For some time the mourner's thoughts are almost exclusively occupied with thoughts of the lost object, first with more emphasis on the personal experience of the loss, later with more emphasis on the object lost. He finds it necessary to bring up, to think over and to talk about memories of the dead person, a process which goes on slowly and painfully, with great sadness, until there has been erected in the mind an image of the dead person almost devoid of negative or undesirable features. Such a process of idealization, however, requires that all negative and hostile feelings toward the lost object be repressed, and such repression may lead to fluctuating guilty, remorseful and even fearful feelings, with regrets for past acts or fantasies of hostility, inconsiderateness or unkindness, some of which may be exaggerated. Sometimes there may be a haunting preoccupation with feelings of responsibility for the death. The various primitive concepts of the dead coming back to haunt or retaliate have their origin in such guilty feelings. As the idealization of the dead person proceeds, though, two important changes are being achieved. The lost object is more and more detached from the self by being enshrined in the form of an intellectual memory, often buttressed by external memorials of various sorts. In addition, the mourner consciously and unconsciously begins to take for himself certain admired qualities and attributes of the dead person through the mechanism of identification. This may appear in his adoption of certain mannerisms of and in his acknowledged wish to be like the lost person or to carry on his ideals and good deeds. When guilt is present there is a greater tendency for the mourner to take on undesirable traits or even symptoms of the deceased or to exaggerate the need to fulfill the wishes of the deceased. Such identification with negative features is a potential source of later psychopathology in the survivor.

Many months are required for this process and as it is accomplished the survivor's preoccupation with the dead person progressively lessens. Now, reminders of the dead person less often and less intensely evoke feelings of sadness and more ambivalent memories can be tolerated with less guilt. As the ties are progressively loosened, the earlier yearnings to be with the dead person, even in death, begin more and more to be replaced by a turning to life and a wish to live. Now, the identification with the ideals, wishes and aspirations of the lost object provide an impetus to continue in life, often expressed as a wish "to be what he would have wanted me to be" or "to carry on for him." When successful, this represents a developmental process, an actual growth experience, which may sometimes even contribute significantly to a characterological change in the mourner, as when a son settles down and assumes responsibilities which he had evaded prior to his father's death. As already stated, the end result of a stress may be a salutary one.

As the psychic dependence on the lost object diminishes, the mourner's interest in new objects begins to return. Early in the mourning process this may take the form of interest in and concern with other mourners who have lost the same object, described by Greene[7] as the use of a vicarious object. In this process the mourner temporarily relinquishes his preoccupation with himself and the dead person and instead feels sorry for and takes care of the other mourner: "I feel so sorry for my son who lost his mother." This allows him to reinvest in his other objects and at the same time to gain some comfort by identifying with the person whom he now comforts and cares for. It also provides some respite from the painful, though necessary, task of dwelling on the loss and the lost object. In family units different members may facilitate each other's work of mourning by alternating in such roles. Eventually, however, the mourner's interest in persons and matters not concerned with the loss and with mourning begins to revive and with this there develops an inclination to replace the lost object with new objects. At first, to be acceptable, the new object sought may have to be as much as possible like the old object, or the mourner may endow him with the qualities of the old object, still a more or less vicarious rather than realistic way of relating to the new object. Finally, however, this tendency attenuates and the new object choices are more realistically achieved. During all this period the mourner imposes on himself a ban against pleasure and enjoyment. The final resolution of the grief is marked by a progressive relinquishing of such restrictions.

The successful work of mourning takes anywhere from six to

twelve months and the complete resolution of the grief is indicated by the ability to remember comfortably and realistically both the pleasures and disappointments of the lost relationship. When successful, the survivor becomes capable of carrying on with his life and with new relationships, often having profited from the positive identification with the lost person. Many factors influence what the eventual outcome will be, including (a) the importance of the lost object as a source of support —the more dependent the relationship, the more difficult will be the task of resolving it; (b) the degree of ambivalence toward the object; (c) the age of the lost object—the loss of a child generally has a more profound effect than the loss of an aged parent; (d) the age of the mourner; (e) the number and nature of other object relationships; (f) the number and nature of previous losses and grief experiences; (g) the degree of preparation for the loss—with an aged or sick person some of the grief work may go on before the death; (h) the physical and psychological health of the mourner at the time of the loss, a factor important in determining his capacity to deal with the loss at the time it occurs.

Unsuccessful or Unresolved Grief

Unsuccessful or unresolved grief may take a number of forms, some of which constitute psychopathological entities which will be described in more detail later (Chapter XXXI).

DENIAL OF THE DEATH. This is an exaggeration or prolongation of what is often normally felt and constitutes a psychotic response which largely rejects reality. The person refuses to acknowledge the death and continues to act and speak as if the deceased is still alive. The reaction may also include a denial of the painful affects and their replacement by inappropriate pleasure and good spirits. Ophelias's response to her father's murder in *Hamlet* is a good literary example of this.

DENIAL OF THE LOSS OR OF THE AFFECT. The death is acknowledged, but its significance is denied intellectually or affectively; i.e., the survivor may say that the death did not affect him, that it represented no loss, or that he just did not or could not feel anything, although he acknowledges that he knows he should have felt sad. In the presence of such denial mechanisms the work of mourning does not take place or takes place incompletely. A psychotic depression, manic reaction or some other illness, including organic disease, may follow some months later or on an anniversary of symbolic importance for the lost relationship.

THE USE OF A VICARIOUS OBJECT. The survivor may minimize the effect of the loss, which instead is projected onto another mutual mourner, for whom he may feel sorry. In addition, the other mourner is taken as a replacement object who is unrealistically expected to fulfill the role of the lost object. If this is done at the expense of the work of grief, a depressive response may develop at some later date, as when the vicarious object disappoints or leaves (Greene[7]). Following this, the survivor may fall ill.

PROLONGED UNRESOLVED GRIEF. For a variety of reasons, some persons never completely dissipate the sense of loss of and their dependence on the lost object, and they remain in a prolonged, even permanent state of unresolved grief. They continue actively to miss the dead person, feeling sadness or crying at every memory or reminder, even years later. Mentioning the person readily evokes tears. Sometimes this failure of resolution takes the form of anniversary reactions; feelings of loss, sadness, helplessness, hopelessness, or other symptoms arise on anniversaries of meaningful experiences with the lost object, such as holidays, birthdays or the anniversary of the death. Occasionally, some persons may even go to the extreme of attempting to preserve all the possessions of the dead person exactly as they were or to shut out all matters that do not pertain to the deceased.

Along with the clergyman, the physician is the person most frequently involved in comforting and helping the bereaved. Because there is much evidence to indicate that maintenance of health is dependent on successful resolution of grief, the doctor properly assumes responsibility for aiding the work of mourning as well as for recognizing those instances in which difficulties or failures in the work of grief may forewarn of more serious developments at a later time.

PSYCHOLOGICAL RESPONSES TO EXTERNAL DANGER AND DISASTER

By and large, the external dangers with which modern man is confronted involve major disruptions in the social and cultural organizations in which he lives or personal threats or personal dangers of one sort or another. Political and economic upheavals or man-made and natural disasters either suddenly or gradually disrupt or threaten to disrupt the whole social fabric in which one has grown accustomed to operate and to live. Significant under such circumstances are the changes in role or status in various social groups, the interference in the continuity of family life, the loss of home and other possessions, the disruption of the means of communication, the disorganization of social and governmental agencies. The study of the impact of such major alterations in social structure affords some insight into how the consistency and structure of social and family institutions contribute to the stability and effective function of the mental apparatus and the adjustment of the individual. Sudden loss of social and physical landmarks or serious alterations in the configuration and organization of the social and group structures impose a major adaptive task upon the individual, whose behavior and psychological function reflect the effort to maintain adjustment, to survive and to reconstitute.

Natural Disasters

Studies of civil disasters, such as tornadoes, floods and explosions, reveal consistent patterns of behavior which are instructive in illustrating the nature of the psychological devices used under such circumstances. Naturally, there are differences in such patterns depending on the person as well as on the nature of the disaster. Disasters differ in respect to: (a) whether there is a period of *warning* and if so, how long; (b) the presence and duration of *threat*, or the situation of actually imminent danger; (c) the duration of the *impact*, during which the person has to "hold on," brief with a tornado as compared to a flood; (d) the nature of the opportunity to examine the situation and make decisions on action (the *inventory* stage); (e) the type of *rescue* operations possible.

The phases of response to disaster have been categorized as follows (Wolfenstein[17]):

THE THREAT.   When the threat of danger is remote, warnings tend to be ignored and the danger denied. During peacetime it is difficult to arouse interest in civil defense. On the other hand, persons who already are latently anxious about their own destructive impulses may be excessively alarmist and disturbed even in response to very remote threats. As a threat becomes more immediate, however, many people still continue to use denial. Some simply refuse to acknowledge that the danger is real and may even accuse the authorities of exaggerating, while others may acknowledge the danger verbally but still not take the necessary protective action even when the opportunities are available. Especially if the danger has not previously been experienced, the predominant feeling is that it really won't happen here, or "I won't be injured," reflecting the strong sense of personal and community invulnerability which may persist even when the danger is intellectually accepted. Efforts of the authorities to get people to respond to the threat are often ignored or met with scepticism by the very persons who later blame them for not giving warning.

THE IMPACT.   At the time of impact there is a strong tendency to feel that the blow is being directed primarily at oneself, that one is at the center of the disaster, a striking contrast to the earlier feeling of invulnerability. The victim is often surprised to find other areas damaged and other persons injured. The discovery that the damage is widespread has the secondary impact of a concern that hoped for sources of help may not be available. On the other hand, the fact that the disaster victim shares this experience with a group makes him less inclined to blame himself, which the victim of a solitary accident often does.

THE "SHOCK" PHASE.   Immediately after a disaster it is common to find the victims stunned, dazed and apathetic. There is a reduction in the capacity of the victims to perceive or respond to what is going on around them and often a remarkable lack of expression of affect or pain, even in the presence of grievous losses or serious wounds. There is also a sense of unreality—"It didn't happen," "It's only a dream"—which only gradually is replaced by a realization of and a response to what is going on. Some victims remain in unconscious or dissociated "zombie-like" states for prolonged periods, even without manifest brain or other physical injury. There may be a profound inhibition of activity, the person remaining motionless or initiating movement only slowly and with difficulty. The victim may simply sit or stand motionless, wander aimlessly or putter about at inconsequential tasks. He may be partially or completely incapable of responding to rescue efforts, or he may be extremely docile and subdued. At first, the affects are missing, sporadic or inadequate. When they can be recognized and reported, they include those associated with fear, abandonment, being lost, occasionally utter helplessness, less often hopelessness. This "shock" phase may last for minutes or hours and shows many characteristics of the primitive depression-withdrawal reaction (Chapter XIV), an attempt to insulate and protect against the magnitude of the stress, which is too enormous to handle all at once.

RESCUE AND RECOVERY.   In this period one sees a gradual return of activity and responsiveness. The victims begin to participate in the rescue operations, although in a docile and often uninvolved way. They are often extraordinarily grateful for any assistance, but also altruistic, insisting that others be cared for first. Human contacts of all sorts assume enormous importance. There may be a phase of relative euphoria and elation, with feelings of relief at having been spared and tremendous feelings of community and fellowship, social and other barriers often temporarily breaking down. At the same time hostility and resentment may be directed toward outsiders, including the relief organization, who are seen as cold and unfeeling. From time to time this relative euphoria, with its accompanying more or less altruistic or brotherly overactivity, is interrupted by feelings of loss, sadness, guilt, shame, helplessness or hopelessness, as the victim periodically allows himself to appreciate the reality of the loss of loved ones or possessions or failures of performance during the disaster. Often there are fleeting or sustained periods of free-floating anxiety, in which the person has difficulty in sleeping and has recurring dreams of terror.

Following the catastrophic event, people are apt to find themselves living it over again in memory. Some try to avoid this, even to the extent of amnesia, or at least not wanting to see or hear any reminders. Others are absorbed by the memories and talk constantly of the experience. This remembering and reiterating, although painful, constitutes a means whereby the person is able to shift from passivity to activity. The account and the memory become progressively revised, with omissions, embellishments and transformations, so that the survivor comes to picture himself as less helpless, less overwhelmed, less afraid than he really was. Humor may be introduced to add a light touch to a grim incident. The sense of abandonment and loss is assuaged by being able to relive the experience with sympathetic listeners.

The subsequent recovery depends as much upon the way in which the social structure is reorganized as upon developmental factors characteristic of the individual. There is much evidence that the shared nature of the experience in the long run considerably aids the process of recovery. Since there are many mutually shared losses, the technique of dealing with a loss by the use of a vicarious object is widespread. In general, provided the social structure is reconstituted, failure to recover from a traumatic experience is usually indicative of pre-existing psychological difficulties. Most disaster victims re-establish the pre-existing state of health and show few residua of the experience.

Such observations on reactions to disaster serve to emphasize the deep sense of personal invulnerability and the strong need of most people to maintain undisturbed their familiar environment and their psychic objects, as represented by other persons, home, job, possessions, community, etc. So powerful are these influences that many are incapable of contemplating the real possibility of danger and therefore fail to prepare themselves psychologically and materially. The stunning impact of the disaster reflects the incapacity of the unprepared mental apparatus to cope with such a magnitude of change in the environment, with its loss of valued objects, destruction of familiar landmarks, and threat of or actual bodily injury. It also vividly illustrates the degree to which one normally is dependent on input from a familiar environment for the maintenance of psychic stability. Ordinarily, change is necessary and stimulating, but there is an abruptness and magnitude of change which results in disorganization, revealed in the victim's loss of previously well-developed capabilities and in the degree of his helpless dependence. At the same time, one also notes the tendency to lose control over previously well-controlled impulses, especially aggression. Striking are the altruistic and object-relating activities that mark the beginning of recovery. In general, the fact that losses were shared by a community facilitates the work of mourning.

Psychological Reactions in Military Combat

Military combat also constitutes a complex social laboratory situation in which reactions to stress have been observed. Here one deals with a selected population, all young males, operating in a unique social milieu and under different ethical standards, separated from their families, homes and normal activities, and exposed to real danger. The sequence of events marking breakdown during combat provides another set of data on patterns of reaction during severe and often prolonged psychological stress. A wealth of data are to be found in the various publications on military psychiatry, especially of the Special Commission of Civilian Psychiatrists on "Combat Exhaustion" (Bartemeier, et al.[1]) of which the following is a summary. The factors involved in determining the vulnerability to breakdown of any individual soldier will not be discussed here, other than to emphasize the constructive and integrative influence on the stability of the soldier of the close-knit combat group of which he is a member. Disruption or disorganization of the group and/or of its leadership constitutes one of the most important factors in accelerating individual breakdown. Once initiated, the patterns of behavior show considerable consistency among large numbers of persons.

INCIPIENT STAGE. The first indications of breakdown are irritability and sleep disturbances. The irritability is manifest externally by over-reaction to minor irritations, in appropriate anger and tears at slight provocation. "Startle reactions" and hypervigilance are prominent. The soldier has difficulty falling asleep and remaining asleep.

STAGE OF PARTIAL DISORGANIZATION. With persistence of the stress a variety of additional manifestations appear. They include (a) general psychomotor retardation, with difficulty or slowness in concentration, action and response; (b) a tendency to become seclusive, morose and silent, or to talk, smoke and drink excessively; (c) a tendency to discard belongings with the complaint that they are becoming too heavy, too much to carry; (d) a loss of interest in comrades, military activity, food and even letters from home; (e) an increased apprehensiveness; (f) an increased dependence on comrades and reluctance to accept responsibility; (g) a tendency to be confused and to show an impairment of judgment; (h) various somatic symptoms, such as sweating, palpitation, tremor, vomiting and diarrhea.

STAGE OF COMPLETE DISORGANIZATION. If the soldier is not removed from the scene of combat, all of the above symptoms may suddenly become much worse; he may become unstable, erratic, confused, defiant, savagely irritable. He may run about aimlessly, oblivious of danger, stare into space, break into uncontrollable sobbing and screaming, babble like a baby, become ataxic and tremulous, and occasionally collapse.

Such combat reactions show certain differences from those noted as the result of sudden civilian disasters. Perhaps most important is that the breakdown is preceded by a long period of preparation for the stress of combat and then a rapid or gradual wearing down or destruction of the defenses that had been built up. There is a progressive loss of control over one's own behavior, the victim seeming to become more and more in danger of being overwhelmed by internal forces. It is of theoretical significance in the light of earlier discussions of the primal affects (Chapter XIV) that the reaction includes manifestations of both primitive anxiety and depression-withdrawal, the latter becoming more prominent as stress persists. Perhaps a more significant influence in the combat situation than in other stress situations, however, is the quantity of aggression which is released. This appears in the form of attacks of rage, blind hate, etc., and contributes to the prominence of guilt and the consequences thereof. Aggression directed toward buddies, officers or the group jeopardizes the group structure and impairs its value to the individual.

Deprivation and Isolation

Loss of personal liberty, imprisonment, solitary confinement, being cast adrift or lost, all constitute highly stressful experiences, information about which has been obtained from studies of persons who have been confined in prisons, detention camps or concentration camps, or who have been the victims of marine accidents, etc. Experimental situations involving varying degrees of sensory isolation and motor restriction also provide a further source of information about such reactions. Roughly speaking, all these situations involve not only separation from familiar surroundings and objects and real danger to health and life, but also a severe restriction of the quantity and variety of sensory experience as well as of the range of motor activity. The victims are subjected to an exceedingly monotonous and limited environment and have little opportunity for exercise, much less for action. In situations of imprisonment they are also completely at the mercy of their captors and subject to great anxiety on that score alone. The person lost at sea or in the Arctic is helpless before nature but has a much greater possibility of maintaining his self-actional identity.

Concentrating mainly on those aspects of the reaction that have to do with sensory and motor restrictions, and ignoring responses more related to danger and separation from objects, we gain further evidence to indicate the need for sensory input and motor activity for psychic adjustment. In solitary confinement, the hunger for human contact is so great that prisoners even come to welcome interrogation by their captors. Notable in all of these situations is difficulty in maintaining contact with reality, the emergence of vivid imagery, occasionally having the quality of visual or auditory hallucinations, the tendency to misinterpret environmental stimuli, including those from the body, and a decrease in the capacity to carry on logical, coherent, rational thinking. It would appear that logical, reality-oriented thinking is dependent on some type of sustained input from the real environment. Otherwise, internally derived psychic processes, not necessarily related to reality, come to occupy more and more of mental life (as is true of dreaming during ordinary sleep). Some persons successfully struggle against this loss of control and weakening of ego autonomy by systematically reviewing past intellectual experiences, such as books read or trips made; by inventing or elaborating mental exercises within the confines of the situation, such as analyzing or counting features of the cell; by improvising games or exercises with pebbles, sand and bits of food; and by investing in the activity of other living creatures, such as insects or rats. Such efforts, which serve to compensate for the real poverty of the environment, often are of great value in enabling the victim to survive and further indicate the role of psychic nutriment in maintaining mental control and contact with reality. Persons who innately do not have the capacity to do this or for whom the circumstances of their imprisonment render it difficult or impossible are more likely to break down. Profound degrees of apathy, depression and withdrawal, interrupted by bursts óf disorganized panic, are then the consequence, and, if allowed to go on, this state may terminate in death. Such a prisoner relinquishes interest in everything, including food, gives up hope and loses his will to live. Beyond a certain point it is no longer possible to make contact with him and death soon ensues, sometimes through an intercurrent infection.

The relative consistency of these responses to external circumstances over which the individual has little or no control provides valuable insight into the mode and range of function of the mental apparatus. They are, so to speak, "experiments of nature," revealing the more or less characteristic psychological and behavioral mechanisms whereby the organism reacts to and overcomes stress and reestablishes a dynamic steady state. The deviations from these more consistent patterns usually constitute the reactions of individuals with significant abnormalities of psychological development and structure which render them less able to respond with and to utilize these mechanisms effectively. This inability may include absence of, as well as exaggeration of, one device or another. The person who is unable to utilize some degree of denial may be as badly off as the person who uses denial excessively. Deviations from these patterns are in the direction of increasing pathology, analogous to the comparison between a wound with uncomplicated healing and a wound which becomes infected, with abscess formation or dehiscence.

REFERENCES

1. Bartemeier, L., Kubie, L. S., Menninger, K., Romano, J. and Whitehorn, J. C.: Combat Fatigue. J. Nerv. & Ment. Dis., *104*:358, 1946.
2. Cohen, E. A.: Human Behavior in the Concentration Camp. New York, W. W. Norton & Co., 1953.
3. Engel, G. L.: Is Grief a Disease? A Challenge for Medical Research. Psychosom. Med., *23*:18, 1961.
4. Freud, A. and Burlingham, D.: War and Children. New York, International Universities Press, 1944.
5. Freud, S.: Mourning and Melancholia. *In:* Complete Works of Freud, Standard Edition, vol. XIV. London, The Hogarth Press, 1957, p. 237.
6. Goldberger, L. and Holt, R. R.: Experimental Interference with Reality Contact (Perceptual Isolation). J. Nerv. & Ment. Dis., *127*:99, 1958.
7. Greene, W. A.: Role of a Vicarious Object in the Adaptation to Loss. I. Use of a Vicarious Object as a Means of Adjustment to Separation from a Significant Person. Psychosom. Med., *20*:344, 1958.
8. Grinker, R. and Spiegel, J. P.: Men under Stress. Philadelphia, The Blakiston Co., 1945.
9. Hinkle, L. E. and Wolff, H. G.: Communist Interrogation and Indoctrination of "Enemies of the State". A.M.A. Arch. Neurol. & Psychiat., *76*:115, 1956.
10. Jacobson, E.: Observations on the Psychological Effect of Imprisonment on Female Political Prisoners. *In:* Eissler, K. R.: Searchlights on Delinquency. New York, International Universities Press, 1949, p. 341.
11. Kinkead, E.: In Every War but One. New York, W. W. Norton & Co., 1959.
12. Lindemann, E.: Symptomatology and Management of Acute Grief. Am. J. Psychiat., *101*:141, 1944.
13. Marris, P.: Widows and Their Families. London, Routledge and Kegan Paul, 1958.
14. Meerloo, J. A. M.: Mental Danger, Stress, and Fear. J. Nerv. & Ment. Dis., *123*:513, 1956.
15. Roheim, G.: Psychoanalysis and Anthropology. Culture, Personality, and the Unconscious. New York, International Universities Press, 1950.
16. Solomon, P., Kubzanksy, P., Leiderman, P. H., Mendelson, J., Trumbull, R. and Wexler, D. (eds.): Sensory Deprivation. Cambridge, Mass., Harvard University Press, 1961.
17. Wolfenstein, M.: Disaster. Chicago, The Free Press of Glencoe, 1957.
18. Wretmark, G.: A Study in Grief Reactions. Acta psychiat. et neurol. scandinav., *136*:292, 1959.

CHAPTER XXVII

PSYCHOLOGICAL STRESS

In Chapter XXVI consideration was given to certain categories of environmental events which constitute psychological stresses of major magnitude. The nature of these events is such that no possible question can be raised as to their potentially stressful character for most people. Yet it remains a striking fact that not only are such extreme conditions less stressful for some individuals than for others, but there are even those for whom they are not stressful at all. Indeed, some persons deliberately seek out situations of challenge and hardship and others achieve their greatest heights of fulfillment and satisfaction under just such arduous and dangerous conditions. Clearly, the stressfulness of an event cannot be estimated simply from its external features. It is necessary to know something of the meaning of the event for the individual in terms of his past experiences and development and in terms of his current psychological resources and vulnerabilities. A natural disaster may threaten one man with injury or loss, provide a second man with an opportunity to demonstrate his manliness, and present a third man with the occasion to expiate guilt through pain and suffering. For the second man, failure to master the situation may induce shame, and for the third man to escape without injury or loss may only increase his feelings of guilt. Evidently, the stressfulness of an event for any single individual is a highly personal matter, determined in the final analysis by intrapsychic factors.

THE SIGNIFICANCE OF UNRESOLVED
INTRAPSYCHIC CONFLICT

Actually, everyday experience and clinical observation establish that the types of environmental circumstances which prove stressful psychologically for most people are a far cry from the dramatic events described in the last chapter. Often enough the setting or event seems so trivial to the observer as to defy comprehension. But more careful study usually reveals that what seemed trivial by general consensus nonetheless had grave implications for the particular individual. In most instances the more obvious external event simply provides a clue indicating a possibility of stress, but the stress itself, to be understood, must be defined in intrapsychic terms. In Chapter XXV we categorized psychological stress in terms of (1) loss or threat of loss of psychic objects, (2) injury or threat of injury, and (3) frustration of drives and drive derivatives or threats thereof. Such a classification acknowledges that in the final analysis the stress is defined not in terms of the manifest external event, but in terms of what is experienced intrapsychically. This in turn is determined by the nature of past experience and especially what has been stressful in the past and what traces thereof persist in the form of unresolved intrapsychic conflict.

In earlier chapters attention was given to how the mental apparatus functions to mediate between the various contradictory influences that impinge on the individual from within and from without, reconciling them so as to assure satisfaction of needs within the reality of the physical and social environment. Full development includes the acquisition and maintenance of a psychic sense of the self, an identity which is derived from past experience and past object relationships. Each individual is thus irrevocably tied to his past in the psychological sense that his evaluation of the present takes place in terms of the internalized record of all past conflicts, successes, failures, relationships, goals and standards. Further, the past has a dynamic influence in that it also motivates behavior. But for the most part this influence takes place at an unconscious level of mental functioning. This influence of the past on the present reflects for each individual the whole development of the regulatory and defensive functions of ego, that is, to maintain identity and the intactness of the psychic self, to assure biological needs, to fulfill certain social roles, and in so doing to overcome obstacles and resolve conflicts. This internalized record of the past also includes all past conflicts and unfinished business as well as the apparently solved or settled conflicts for which solutions are available. All the conflicts of life in one way or another involve past efforts to avoid object loss, injury, or drive frustration and to establish and maintain one's psychic integrity and identity. Therefore, all past conflicts and their solutions provide the background for how the world will be experienced and what will constitute stress at any time. Virtually no event can take place which does not in some way touch upon the past; even that which is completely new evokes reflections from one's previous experiences with the completely new. Past conflicts, solved or unsolved, are inevitably touched on by and related to the present, and present conflicts are inevitably influenced by and related to past conflicts.

The many layers and ramifications of past conflicts and their relations to current situations render it virtually impossible to predict the outcome of an event unless one also has knowledge of its potential to revive old conflicts or to provoke new derivatives thereof. For example, a man involved in a minor auto accident in which neither injury nor damage is suffered may have no disturbance, other than the flash of apprehension at the moment of the accident, once he is satisfied that no damage has occurred. Another man, under the same circumstance, may experience intense and prolonged anxiety, with many fearful fantasies as to what might have happened to himself or to others, or he may even imagine that the consequences were or will be much more serious than actually is the case. Still another person may be provoked into an unreasonable burst of rage at the other driver, at his wife if she was with him, or at no one in particular. A fourth man may feel overcome with guilt, whether or not he was responsible for the accident, and may indulge in inappropriate atonement and self-punishment. A fifth may be overwhelmed by feelings of shame and inadequacy, unjustifiably blaming himself for incompetence. A totally inappropriate sense of relief may be felt by still another man, who considers his "narrow escape" grounds for celebration. Even sudden death may occur, as indicated by the recent report in the press of an elderly man who collapsed and died while being questioned by the police after an insignificant accident; at the time of the accident he was on the way to visit the grave of his wife, who had died three days earlier. All of these situations are characterized by the fact that the person is unable to settle the matter on the basis of the reality of no damage or injury, but instead experiences the incident in terms of intrapsychic conflicts and unfinished business which are peculiar to him. The anxious man may have been frightened at the implications of aggression in the accident, perhaps reminding him of earlier conflict situations in which he had felt threatened by the aggression of others. The angry man may have failed to resolve his own aggression toward other figures, past or present, and the accident released a flood of apparently justified rage unconsciously meant for the other figure. Similarly, the guilt-stricken man may have been suffering from conflict over some fantasied or actual expression of aggression in the past and experienced the accident as proof of guilt. The man feeling shame and inadequacy may have experienced it as confirming an earlier, conflict-determined self-depreciation. The celebrant may have felt his narrow escape to be a magical sign indicating forgiveness or expiation for some unresolved guilt, justifying celebration. For the man who died, the accident may have been the last straw. (See Chapter XXXIII.) In all such examples, past unresolved conflicts over aggression render the person incapable of responding to the trivial accident with the realistic judgment that no damage and no injury to oneself or to anyone else has taken place.

The nature of life and living renders intrapsychic conflict inevitable and therefore multiplies enormously the number and variety of circumstances which might be experienced as stresses. The inevitability of intrapsychic conflict stems from the fact that not all aims, needs and modes of action are mutually compatible. Actually, it is one of the functions of the psychic apparatus—specifically, the ego—to order, regulate and relate these unavoidable incompatibilities. The primary function of the mental apparatus, to interpose a delay between the stimulus of drive and the action necessary to satisfy it, in itself makes it inevitable that conflict will be characteristic of psychic functioning, for the necessity to delay a satisfaction already establishes the need for a hierarchy of values. One activity, gratification or object must be given up for another, and this cannot be done without conflict. As mind matures, these hierarchies of values become crystallized in the form of unconscious and conscious aims, wishes, aspirations, goals, ideals, hopes and fears (structures; see Chapter XXII). These are the mental representatives of what originally existed in the form of biological needs on the one hand and the demands of a physical and social environment on the other, the incompatibilities among which necessitated their hierarchal arrangement in terms of values. Always something must be given up, modified, substituted for or delayed in order that something else higher in the value system at the moment not be jeopardized. Success in such endeavors is marked by contentment, pride, confidence and a sense of personal intactness, integrity and control. Failure is marked by some unpleasant affect, such as anxiety, shame, guilt, disgust, etc., a decrement of the sense of the self as intact, secure and good. As already discussed, these commonly mark the transition between health and disease (Chapter XXV).

The variety of intrapsychic conflicts to which man is subject is legion and reflects the basic nature of life and of psychic development as already described, as well as of the unique background of each individual. To illustrate, one intense wish may be in conflict with another, as when a wish to be loved is countered by a hostile wish toward the same object. A current ideal may be in conflict with a persistent earlier wish, as when the desire to be independent conflicts with a continuing desire to be helped or taken care of. A self-oriented need may conflict with an object or socially determined expectation, as when an impulse to flee a danger is countered by society's expectation that one help others or that one stand up and "take it." A developing biological capacity may lead to conflict, as when awareness of reproductive maturity arouses fears of childbirth established in childhood. One aspect of a drive may conflict with another, as when a wish to bear a child conflicts with fears or taboos concerning the act of intercourse. The intensity of a need or impulse may lead to conflict by threatening to override other dangers, as when a hungry or angry man risks his physical safety to satisfy that need. The internalization, through introjection and identification, of conflicting attitudes and standards of different objects, as those between disagreeing parents, may be a source of intrapsychic conflict. Thus, satisfying mother's expectations may threaten to jeopardize the relationship with father, and vice versa. Intrapsychic standards (ego ideal) may be in conflict, as when the ideal image of oneself as the successful man conflicts with one's image as the kind, considerate man. Conflict between past and present is inevitable, as when there is persistence of object-directed attitudes and wishes which had been rejected in the past, such as the taboo sexual or aggressive impulses toward parents and siblings, or internal standards derived from the past may be in conflict with current expectations of oneself or of society.

All of these intrapsychic conflicts involve in final analysis the three categories of psychological stress, as earlier defined. The acting on a need or wish, even at the level of fantasy, may bring with it a fear of disapproval, rejection or even injury at the hands of an object. The situation is psychically experienced as conflict because the person's past attempts to reconcile and satisfy object-directed needs and to avoid injury appear to justify such an evaluation of danger, even though in current reality no such danger exists or more effective means of coping with it are available. By the same token, external events also tend to be interpreted in terms of past experiences, as illustrated in the hypothetical reactions to an accident cited earlier. Thus, one may suffer or be threatened with the real loss of an object or else the loss or threat of loss may only be the product of fantasy, a psychological conviction that the relationship is disturbed and that one is no longer loved or loving, a feeling arising from past and current intrapsychic conflict. The same holds true for the threat of injury, which may actually exist in the environment or which may be the product of conflict-determined fantasy. It is an irony of life that such fantasies commonly lead to behaviors that tend to convert the fantasy to reality and appear to confirm the fear. Thus, the person who is suffering from object loss in fantasy may actually behave in such a way as to disturb seriously his relationships and thereby lose part or all of the gratifications of the object relationship. In respect to both object loss and injury, whether real, threatened or fantasied, some frustration of drives is inevitably involved. Even when the threat of loss or injury originates in the external environment, it is inevitable that the nature of the frustration imposed will be colored as well by the individual's past experiences with loss and injury.

From such considerations it is apparent that there can be no such thing as *a* psychological stress in an absolute or isolated sense, since everything that is stressful for the individual inevitably lights up a life-long heritage of previous stresses. When we speak of stress in terms of object loss, injury or frustration of drives, it is mainly to emphasize one aspect of the experience, either because it is more prominent or in order to focus attention on the consequences of that particular aspect of the stress. Further, psychological, behavioral and physiological conse-quences of object loss, injury and drive frustration are not identical, though they are related. (See Chapters XXX through XXXIII.) For these reasons it is useful now to explore in more detail the three cate-gories of psychological stress according to the types of circumstances and events which may potentially prove stressful. Familiarity with each circumstance is helpful in identifying when an individual may be exposed to stress, though, as repeatedly emphasized, none of the circumstances to be described is necessarily stressful.

LOSS AND THREAT OF LOSS OF OBJECTS

Object loss may be classified as having already taken place or as merely being threatened, and either loss or threat of loss may occur in reality or in fantasy (psychic loss). *A real loss or threat of loss* refers to such changes in the status of an external object as to render it actually unavailable or inaccessible currently or in the immediate future. When the object has already been lost and therefore no longer has a real existence in the environment, the survivor is deprived of the interactions with the object that are essential to maintain and reinforce its psychic representations, the stability of which is thereby undermined. As a result, the contributions made by the psychic object representation to the regulatory and defensive functions of ego and to the intactness of the psychic self are jeopardized or lost. "I need" and "I miss" are ways of verbalizing this awareness of the dependence on objects and the feeling of inadequacy of the psychic self following object loss. When the loss has not yet occurred but real grounds exist for the anticipation that it will or might take place, as with an illness, military conscription, chil-dren growing up and leaving home, an impending political change, etc., the object is still available in the environment, but the anticipation of its loss or of separation from it requires that the consequences of the loss be dealt with before it actually takes place.

In *fantasied (psychic) loss or separation* or threat thereof, the person experiences a sense of loss or anticipation of loss which has no true basis in reality. Such a fantasy is generally the consequence of intrapsychic conflict and may include a misinterpretation or exaggeration of environmental events so as to mean loss or separation when in actual reality there has been none. (How the object can be missing psychologically although still present in reality was discussed in Chapter XXII.) For example, a person experiencing conscious or unconscious guilt or a person who has had tenuous and unsatisfactory relationships in the past may feel himself to be unloved or unwanted. In the guilt-ridden person this is an intrapsychic process of self-depreciation, a harsh, rejecting judgment of the self, whereas in the deprived person it may be a more accurate appraisal of what life really has been like in the past. In either case, however, the result may be the misinterpretation that people really do not care for him. In terms of the *psychic* reality of such persons, there is a real poverty of gratifying object relationships. In such a prevailing psychological climate, such feelings of being unloved and unwanted are readily provoked by minor or ordinary expressions of indifference or irritation on the part of other persons.

Thus the designations "real" and "fantasied" (or "psychic") as applied to object loss refer to two extremes of a continuum. The real loss of an object in the external environment is stressful not only in terms of its current value but also in terms of past successes or failures with that object or similar objects. Similarly, a fantasied (psychic) object loss, although based primarily on intrapsychic conflict, nonetheless often occurs in relation to some current situation that bears some resemblance to past traumatic circumstances.

In the final analysis, what counts in both instances is how the object loss is experienced intrapsychically and the resulting consequences to the over-all psychological adjustment, including especially the degree to which the psychic sense and image of the self are damaged, disrupted or interfered with. The affects of giving up—that is, helplessness and hopelessness—mark the greatest degree of disruption of psychic self. (See Chapter XVIII.)

Classification of Object Losses

Although we acknowledge that the significance of object loss for any individual can be evaluated only in terms of that person's intrapsychic experience of the loss, it is nonetheless useful and necessary for clinical purposes to classify the variety of losses and separations to which man is prone and the circumstances under which they occur. To a large extent this has already been done in the first part of this book and especially in Chapters XIX and XX, where are discussed the varieties of losses and separations experienced in the course of the normative development of the adult man and woman. The types of object loss described in those chapters represent the ordinary and more familiar varieties of losses to which anyone may be exposed, and they will not be discussed further. In addition, however, there are a number of less obvious circumstances which may also be experienced as object loss. These too need be made more explicit, as follows:

LOSS OF PARTS OF THE BODY OR FUNCTIONS THEREOF. Loss of or damage to parts of the body, as with amputation, paralysis, blindness, decline in physical attractiveness or strength, menopause, impotence, decline in intellectual capacity or any physical illness may be experienced psychically as an object loss. Such losses are especially significant when they interfere with one's occupational or social status or impair valued skills or talents. Their impact as losses is especially serious when they involve emotionally invested parts of the body, such as the face, the breasts or the genitals. Occasionally a long-standing physical defect acquires such positive emotional meaning or confers such social advantage upon the disabled or crippled person that it achieves the status of an object for him. Under such circumstances the correction of the defect may be experienced paradoxically as a loss and hence may be stressful. This is one reason why some patients resist corrective surgery or fall ill after the defect has been corrected. In evaluating a physical illness in terms of its significance as object loss, it is necessary to balance the meaning for the individual of the physical changes against the advantages gained through being sick or disabled. Not infrequently relationships with other objects are improved or new objects are gained during illness, more than compensating for the physical loss.

LOSS OF MEMBERSHIP OR STATUS IN SOCIAL, POLITICAL, PROFESSIONAL, MILITARY OR RELIGIOUS GROUPS. Membership and status in groups in which certain beliefs and values are shared constitute an important stabilizing influence for personal psychic adjustment and provide many gratifications which stem from the interpersonal relationships within the group and the shared beliefs, goals, ideals and activities of the group. Threats to or disruption of the group, whether originating within or outside the group, may be felt as a serious loss, depending upon the degree to which the group had come to provide support and to gratify personal psychological needs. This may be true even among groups which may be considered by some standards deviant or peculiar. Indeed, some persons with deviant psychological needs or patterns of behavior aggregate in groups in which such needs or behaviors are accepted or shared because of the support that the group provides these individuals.

THREAT TO OR DISRUPTION OF LARGER, MORE ABSTRACT SOCIAL ORGANIZATIONS. Even when they are only abstractions, the stability of large social organizations and their representatives obviously has real and practical meaning for the lives and destinies of individuals. Hence, changes in or threats to one's country or political system and its leaders may have psychological implications far beyond the actual impact on the everyday life of the individual. The death of a president or other leader commonly evokes feelings of loss and outpourings of grief even among persons for whom there has never actually been any personal relationship. Upon such personally remote leaders or institutions may be projected many unrealistic expectations and conflicts of childhood.

FAILURES OF PLANS OR VENTURES. When one has invested much energy and effort in a plan or program, whether business, profession, family, hobby, etc., and has anticipated or enjoyed material or psychological reward therefrom, its failure may be a serious blow. The frustration of secret hopes or aspirations, occasionally quite unrealistic, may be a source of loss and disappointment not readily acknowledged and hence not easily recognized. The frustration of the wish to have a child is an important and common example.

DISILLUSIONMENT WITH OBJECTS. Real failures in performance or departures from ideals by objects, leading to disillusionment, are often tantamount to object loss, especially when the object has been much admired and looked up to and has been a model for ego ideal formation. Under such circumstances the basis upon which certain personal standards and aspirations were established and the concept of self are also jeopardized.

CHANGES IN WAY OF LIFE AND LIVING. People readily become involved in certain patterns and conditions of living, to which they grow accustomed and in which they establish a satisfying modus vivendi. Thereafter, to give up this way of life may mean giving up something that has become familiar and comfortable. This may be the case even in situations which at the outset were disagreeable or unpleasant, but in which the individual eventually not only adjusted but may even have prospered. After achieving a successful adjustment to a difficult situation, he may then feel unprepared to return to his former way of life or to begin a new one. Thus, to cease to be a patient, a disabled person, a prisoner, a farmer struggling against recurring drought, etc., may for some involve more loss than gain. (See also Chapter XXIII.) Similarly, individuals may become so accustomed to a life of excitement, of pressure, of uncertainty, of monotony, of consistency, that any change is felt as a loss.

LOSS OF HOME, HOUSE, PERSONAL POSSESSIONS, VALUED GIFTS AND MEMENTOS. These are heavily invested with memories and all that one puts into them in the course of acquisition or construction. Their loss generally involves far more than the actual material value or ease of replaceability, especially when they have provided continuity and stability of living for a long time and when they evoke many past memories of earlier objects. Many people, especially the elderly, cling to old and worn-out furniture or clothing, or they remain in poor quarters in a declining neighborhood, rather than exchange them for something newer or move to better surroundings.

LOSS OF JOB, PROFESSION, OCCUPATION. As the means whereby one earns a livelihood and enjoys status as a contributing member of society, these have obvious meaning as objects. Loss of job, unemployment and reduction in job status and income are important categories of loss with special significance in terms of self-esteem and role in the family. Enforced retirement may be felt as loss when the position has been a gratifying one and there appear to be no other means available for achieving comparable gratification in the future.

LOSS OF PETS. Pets are far more important as objects than generally appreciated. The pet fills the unique role of an unambivalent object to which can also be ascribed many qualities felt desirable by the owner. Most pets are uniquely loyal and rarely run away, at least so prevailing fantasy holds. For certain persons, especially the elderly and the socially isolated, a pet can be the most important living object and its loss profoundly felt.

Patterns of Object Relationships Predisposing to Object Loss

In addition to categories of objects, it is also helpful to identify certain patterns of interpersonal relationships which particularly predispose to object loss by virtue of the limitations they impose on object relating. In Chapter XVII are described the characteristics of the object relations of the mature adult. Now we shall discuss types of immature interpersonal object relationships which have their origin in failures or difficulties in earlier patterns of development and object relating. There is considerable overlap among these categories since they describe not entities but qualities of object relating, more than one of which may characterize an individual.

TRANSFERENCE OBJECT RELATIONSHIP. All object relationships to some degree involve transference—the tendency unconsciously to attribute to current objects the qualities, attitudes and modes of relating characteristic of childhood objects (parents, siblings, etc.). The immature person and the person under stress tend to relate excessively in terms of transference, sometimes to the extent of behaving as if all the determinants of the old relationship, including conflicts, expectations and gratifications, still operate unchanged in the new relationship. This is an unconscious process and is especially productive of conflict, actual and intrapsychic, because of the taboos and restrictions inherent in the earlier relationships. Examples are persons who seek in vain an ideal mate, the unattainable "ideal" being based unconsciously on the image of a parent or on some other taboo object to whom the person has remained attached in an ambivalent manner; or persons who, because they have not detached sexual aims from parental objects, attempt to dissociate tenderness from sexual feelings, and hence cannot find both love and sexual gratification with the same individual; or persons who compulsively repeat the family triangle, being attracted only to individuals who are unavailable; or persons who continue to act out aggressive, angry feelings displaced from parents or siblings onto current objects; and many others.

The genesis of transference relationships is highly individual and accounts for a large proportion of the fantasied object losses and separations that mar life. By imposing on the current relationships unresolved conflicts and unfulfilled wishes of the past, they introduce elements into the relationship which are not readily accessible to conscious understanding or handling. Periodic breakdown of communication, conflict and disappointment are the inevitable consequences of such a situation.

ANACLICTIC OBJECT RELATIONSHIP. This designates object-relating patterns characterized by a basically dependent attitude, in which the person expects the object to support, supply, gratify and respond and in which the object is not perceived as having needs and sensitivities of its own. This is reminiscent of the object relationship of infancy. Individuals requiring this kind of relationship are highly vulnerable to object loss, not only because of their great dependence on external supplies and their poverty of internal resources, but also because there are few persons available who are capable of maintaining for very long such a thankless role as an object. Such dependent individuals commonly expect the same support from society as they do from other persons.

NARCISSISTIC OBJECT RELATIONSHIP. In this type of relationship, the self is taken as the model of the desirable object, a tendency especially likely to develop if the objects of childhood were consistently frustrating. Under such circumstances the child may tend to turn more to himself for gratification and to base his later object choice on his own qualities as he sees them. In real life one is unlikely to find many other persons who fulfill these special requirements and hence the supply of satisfactory narcissistic objects is bound to be limited. Further, since such narcissistic persons are prone to project their own qualities onto the other persons not so endowed, they are frequently disappointed. Then a previously satisfactory object becomes unsatisfactory.

SYMBIOTIC OBJECT RELATIONSHIPS. In this type of relationship two persons relate in a tightly knit, integrated, complementary manner, each one fulfilling certain specific needs and functions of the other. In the symbiotic relationship the patterns of relating are very explicitly defined and the mutual dependence is extreme. To a much greater degree than exists ordinarily in human relationships, each individual relinquishes (if he has ever adequately developed) certain modes of functioning, which are delegated to and taken over by the symbiotic partner. Commonly, each partner not only gratifies vicariously certain needs of the other but also supports the other's ego defenses. Such symbiosis is especially likely to originate in an early relationship with a mother who binds the child to her for her own needs and security. The symbiotic object is therefore most likely to be the mother or a reasonable facsimile thereof. A person demanding such relationship is highly vulnerable to the loss of the symbiotic object because he depends inordinately on complementarity with the other person for his own sense of wholeness. The survivor not only is crippled by the loss but has very little possibility of finding a replacement.

AMBIVALENT OBJECT RELATIONSHIPS. All relationships are inherently ambivalent, since there is no possibility in nature that the needs of two persons will always be confluent. There are some individuals whose early life experiences have been so marked by conflict with objects that the pattern of their subsequent relationships includes to a high degree alternating attitudes of love and hate. This may reflect actual inconsistency on the part of childhood objects. For such persons psychic object representations are more sharply delineated into both "good" and "bad" and readily shift from one to the other. Hence they are hyperalert for indications that the external object is changing from a "good" to a "bad" object, a change which more often takes place in fantasy than in reality. Persons with such highly ambivalent psychic object representations are likely to be very cautious in regulating distance from objects. Although they yearn for closeness, they fear it, for the "good" gratifying object may become "bad" and frustrating, in which case they may feel smothered or entrapped. Hence they are characteristically cautious, distrustful and suspicious of objects. They provide the curious paradox of not only resisting closeness or intimacy in a relationship but even responding to such overtures by breaking off the relationship lest it turn out badly. The need to keep the now threatening object at a distance constitutes a self-imposed object loss, for in the process the "good" must be given up with the "bad." Individuals with such basically ambivalent object-relations have great difficulty in maintaining satisfactory relationships and are constantly exposed to object loss in spite of seemingly favorable environmental conditions. They must remain in control of themselves and of their objects if they are to succeed in regulating the optimal (safe) distance from objects.

A similar problem in object relating may be found among persons who have not achieved clear and stable differentiation between self and objects. Such persons find closeness threatening to their weak, unstable sense of self (identity).

SADO-MASOCHISTIC OBJECT RELATIONSHIP. This is one of a number of complementary forms of object relating in which two people relate on the basis of complementary needs. The sadistic person, who derives gratification from inflicting pain, suffering and humiliation, finds a masochistic partner who derives his gratification from suffering. The masochist seeks pain and suffering in order to alleviate feelings of guilt, and only after so doing is he able to experience gratification. This type of relationship provides another paradox in that the very conditions which ordinarily would be considered incompatible for a gratifying relationship are precisely those which make the relationship possible. The masochist suffers a loss if the cruel partner reforms, and the sadist is frustrated if the masochist absolves his guilt and is no longer willing to suffer. Such pairs are frequently, but not exclusively, marital partners. Not infrequently this involves a transference repetition of relationships with sadistic and/or masochistic parents.

PARTIAL OBJECT RELATIONSHIPS. Because of the persistence of childhood conflicts, especially sexual conflicts, certain persons relate mainly in terms of certain attributes of the other person. A part symbolically represents the whole of an earlier relationship. This is another variant of a transference relationship. (See also primary vs. secondary models of cognition, Chapter XXII.) The relationship is predicated on an overdetermined value of some feature, such as hair, facial configuration or clothing (fetishes), or on the fantasied absence of existing features, notably the genitals, or the fantasied presence of absent features, such as the unconscious fantasy of a penis in the woman or breasts in the man. These peculiar qualifications mark highly abnormal requirements for object relating and hence predispose to object loss.

VICARIOUS OBJECTS. These are objects through whom one lives out needs of one's own or who take the place of lost objects through projecting onto them the qualities of the lost object. (See Chapter XXVI.) The vicarious object sooner or later disappoints because he proves unable or unwilling to fulfill the role ascribed to him. And the person who is chosen as a vicarious object is also doomed to disappointment since his relationship is based on a false premise; he has not been taken as an object for his own qualities but for qualities falsely ascribed to him. This is a less stable situation than the more usual transference relationship in which the object is chosen because he does share certain characteristics of the missing object. Hence he may find the other person withdrawing when he no longer is useful or necessary as a vicarious object.

These defective patterns of object relating represent only some of many varieties encountered in clinical practice. However, they suffice to illustrate how the particular conditions under which object relationships evolved in the course of development serve to circumscribe and limit later capacities for relationships and hence render one more vulnerable to object loss, in fantasy as well as in reality.

INJURY AND THREAT OF INJURY

As a source of psychic stress threat of injury is more important than actual injury, and, at least in clinical practice, the threat is more often symbolic than real. The developmental processes whereby this takes place are highly complex and have already been touched upon earlier. Through a host of experiences in which the biological system of defense against injury is activated, the individual develops his own catalogue of situations to be avoided, some because they truly are dangerous and some because they have been so experienced by him in the past. In the course of development the experiences which come to mean danger include, first, mounting drive pressures when needs were unfulfilled, second, excessive sensory stimulation, culminating in pain, then the communicated anxiety of objects, and, finally, the communicated verbal warnings and threats of objects, in that order. Connected with each of these are a host of psychological associations, including specific perceptions as well as symbols, which serve thereafter as the psychic stimuli warning against a return of the original traumatic situations. Henceforth, such associations act as threats of injury, especially when the past traumatic situation was not successfully mastered.

Accordingly, in contrast to object losses, which we were able to categorize in terms of fairly explicit events, the variety of circumstances which are experienced as threats of injury are far more individual and subtle and hence much less susceptible to definition in terms of recognized environmental situations. With the exception of the obvious external danger situations, universally experienced as threatening to produce or actually producing bodily injury, the great bulk of situations which evoke defensive patterns against injury are merely symbolic threats, learned in the course of development, highly individual and defying precise characterization. To these, as well as to the universal dangers, the psychological and physiological response is "as if" their consequence would indeed be a bodily injury. (See Chapter XXXII.)

As symbolic threats, most of these are highly individual. Nonetheless, a number of situations are commonly experienced by many as threatening, mainly because they are reminiscent or symbolic of ubiquitous traumatic states. These include: (a) new situations or unfamiliar places, especially when these also involve separation from familiar persons; (b) new responsibilities in work, family, community, etc., in which concern about failure and consequent disapproval also plays a role; (c) examinations, exhibitions, contests, performances, etc., in which one's abilities are publicly scrutinized and one's standing, reputation and future may hang on the result; (d) various ceremonies, such as graduation, Bar Mitzvah, etc., which have the quality of initiation rites, symbolically marking a transition from one developmental phase to another; (e) situations of rivalry or competition, especially with older, stronger or authority figures; (f) contact with others who are frightened, in danger, mutilated, disfigured, injured, dying or dead, including dramatic portrayals thereof on stage, screen, etc.; (g) intense sensory input, especially when sudden and unexpected, such as loud noises, flashes of light, etc., or great reduction in sensory input, as in dark, silent, isolated places; (h) unusual or unexpected bodily sensations, including pain, as may occur during illness, which may be experienced as more threatening than the actual underlying body processes or the danger thereof justify; (i) omens, magic, the uncanny, the occult, superstitions and other phenomena that are part of the social, cultural and religious belief systems of a people whereby certain dangers, some real, some fantasied, some from the past and some of the present, are ritualized and institutionalized—the breaking of a taboo among primitive people is among the most threatening situations known to man. (See also Chapters XXXII and XXXIII.)

In addition to such situations, which are generally accepted and understood by most people as commonly being threatening, there are other situations which are perceived as dangerous only by a few individuals, their dangerous aspects being totally incomprehensible to others and often even to the person so responding. These are the phobic situations, in which no real danger exists, yet the person responds as if facing an imminent and overwhelming threat. Here the origin of the danger is internal, evolving from intrapsychic conflict, the impulses experienced as dangerous remaining unconscious but being projected to the environment in a symbolic form. The phobic object or situation represents in condensed symbolic terms the internal danger and its history. Typical phobias include those of heights, crowds, elevators, enclosed spaces, unfamiliar places, darkness, animals, insects, etc., and are highly specific for each individual. Other types of idiosyncratic danger situations include certain foods or medicines, the ingestion of which is conceived of as dangerous; things which may penetrate the body through eyes, nose, respiratory tract, mouth, anus, genitals, pores of the skin, etc.; situations in which the environment and people in it are felt not to be under control; X-rays, light waves, radio waves, cosmic radiation and other physical phenomena which may be regarded as having a dangerous influence. Such unrealistic fears of injury all are indicative of psychiatric disease.

FRUSTRATION OF DRIVES AND DRIVE DERIVATIVES
AND THREATS THEREOF

The satisfaction of drives requires suitable objects in the external environment; therefore, in the final analysis, frustration of a drive implies unavailability of a suitable object, either because the object does not exist in reality or because internal psychodynamic processes or external environmental conditions render the object inaccessible. (See Chapter XXII.) But the need for an object originates internally and, as was discussed in earlier chapters (see particularly Chapter II), is mediated through a central nervous system organization concerned with the needs of the individual for survival, growth and continuation of the species. The pressure of the drive, therefore, builds up within the organism in response to biological and mental influences and only secondarily in response to environmental changes. An unfulfilled need must be present before the environment can act as a stimulus. The man who has just indulged himself to the full with food, drink or sexual activity is not easily tempted.

As psychic stresses, such needs as those for oxygen, food and water require little discussion. These belong in the category of imperative needs and, whether acute or chronic, the underlying drives mobilize behavioral and psychological responses specifically directed toward alleviating the distress. For the most part the pressure of the need saturates psychic experience to the exclusion of other considerations, making it difficult for the sufferer to attend to anything else. Observations of starving people confirm this all-pervasive preoccupation with food and means of securing food. Sexual interests as well as previous social and personal standards, goals and aspirations are abandoned in the single-minded quest for food. Similarly, the patient suffering air hunger is quite incapable of attending to other needs without tremendous effort or help from the outside.

Frustration of genital sexual drives by purely externally imposed restraints, as when the sexual partner is absent, ill or inaccessible, constitutes a less pressing stress for the otherwise sexually mature individual. Most persons can tolerate abstinence for considerable periods of time, and many gain some relief through masturbation and fantasy, provided there is no conflict about such means. Nonetheless, such externally imposed sexual abstinence eventually does constitute a psychic stress, especially when the withdrawal of the sexual partner is not understandable or is a rejection. Eventually it tends to activate latent sexual drives and intrapsychic conflicts and thereby to induce further stress unless a satisfactory solution, free of conflict, can be achieved.

Far more important as psychic stresses in every day life are the drives which are frustrated by intrapsychic conflict and/or the inability to cope with ordinary life situations. These stresses stem either from (a) the persistence from childhood of drives and their derivatives in the form of unconscious wishes and fantasies which had not successfully undergone the developmental transformations appropriate for adulthood or from (b) the inhibition of more age-appropriate drives by the persistence of childhood conflicts. Under such conditions drive-seeking discharge evokes memory traces of past consequences, either threatened object loss or threatened injury. Thus the psychic stress of such drive frustration includes both the unpleasant tension of the dammed-up drive itself and the fantasied consequences in terms of object loss and/or injury.

A full catalogue of the varieties of frustrated drives to which man is heir is hardly possible in these pages. The following are intended primarily to illustrate the principle under consideration. Such drive activity which fails of satisfaction makes up, for the most part, the reservoir of unconscious forces which exert their influence on behavior and mentation. They remain unconscious for the very fact that they cannot, because of internal taboos or inhibitions, be expressed or gratified. Derivatives may reach consciousness in a highly distorted or disguised manner in the form of dreams, parapraxes, fantasies, wishes, fragments of behavior, obsessions, delusions, hallucinations, illusions, bodily symptoms, etc., all of which go to make up the symptoms of psychological illness as well as being an occasional part of every day mental activity. As examples, we mention the following: (a) the wish to continue to experience the modalities and character of object relating typical of infancy or early childhood, a wish generally incompatible with the physical and social status of the adult; (b) oral wishes, sucking, biting, swallowing, directed in fantasy toward human objects, not food alone; (c) anal wishes, to soil, to defile, to mess, etc., persisting from childhood; (d) sexual wishes directed toward taboo objects; (e) aggressive, destructive, rivalrous impulses originally directed toward parents or siblings and unresolved; (f) wishes to bore or penetrate or be penetrated derived from the phallic phase of development.

What is common to all such drive frustration situations is that the underlying complex, whether active or latent, not only is readily stimulated by environmental influences, because of the very fact that the drive is unsatisfied, but also is generally incapable of being satisfied, because it gives rise to intrapsychic conflict and/or is unacceptable to the environment or to the self. Further, the presence of such complexes not only predisposes to fantasies of object loss and/or injury but also renders the individual more vulnerable to both real object loss and threat of injury. Some reference to such interrelationships is found in Chapter XXV.

CHAPTER XXVIII

PSYCHIATRIC DISEASE: I. PREDISPOSITION AND PATHOGENESIS

Psychiatric disease is manifested by disturbances in thinking, feeling, relating, behavior and social adjustment. It may also include somatic manifestations, discussion of which, however, will be reserved for later chapters (XXXII and XXXIII). These disturbances represent patterns of response to psychological stresses and/or physical stresses directly affecting the central nervous system. Before delineating psychiatric diseases in terms of phenomenology and clinical syndromes, we shall first consider some of the predisposing factors.

As already indicated in Chapters XXVI and XXVII, the character of these reaction patterns is determined more by the nature of previous development and experience than it is by either the specific character or the magnitude of current stresses. In general, it is difficult to predict the nature of the response to a psychic stress, the same stress being capable of yielding very different responses in different persons and even in the same person at different times. This is in contrast to the relative specificity of response to different physical stresses, as to micro-organisms, radiant energy, mechanical trauma, and so forth. Hence in respect to psychiatric illness, it is more the psychological status and potential of the individual than the nature of the stress which determine the vulnerability to and the character of the eventual psychological disturbance.

Predisposition to and pathogenesis of psychiatric disorders are thus embedded in the whole developmental matrix of the past and simply are not accessible to categorization into discrete, more or less independent variables. Past environmental, biological and psychological events have significance mainly in terms of the traces they have left behind in the mental apparatus and the influence of these traces on subsequent responses, behavior and development. The fundamental characteristic of the mind, that is, to take in and to be changed by what impinges on it, whether from the internal or external environment, and the more or less intrinsic biological developmental timetable of the underlying drive structures render inescapable a developmental perspective in understanding pathogenesis. In a sense, then, the discussion that follows is a reconsideration of some of the developmental processes which were presented in the first half of this book but now with reference to the etiology and pathogenesis of psychiatric disorder. This is another way of emphasizing again that health and disease are relative concepts. What we are dealing with in relation to psychiatric illness includes many of the same influences that are involved in normative development, but to which for one reason or another some individuals fail to make a successful adjustment or because of which they fail to progress to the next developmental sequence.

The factors predisposing to psychiatric illness may be considered under three headings, biological, psychological and social.

BIOLOGICAL FACTORS

The primacy of the biological to the psychological in the phylogeny and ontogeny of mental development is a basic thesis of this work and has been fully discussed in previous chapters. From this perspective alone, it is obvious that the various biological, genic, congenital and environmental factors which determine individual differences in the development, structure, function and organization of the central nervous system must constitute relevant factors in the predisposition to psychiatric disease, at least to the extent that they are concerned in the development of the mental apparatus. Though this is a logical proposition, the fact remains that at present there is still virtually no explicit information implicating specific biological processes in the genesis of most varieties of psychiatric disorder, with the exception of such conditions as mental deficiency, the organic brain syndromes and the epilepsies. The paucity of such established relationships should be grounds for neither discouragement nor surprise. It simply reflects the fact that present knowledge and methods of studying the brain have not yet reached the stage where more than the most limited inferences can be drawn about relationships between behavior and psychological processes on the one hand and chemical, electrical or physiological events in the brain on the other. Such poverty of knowledge justifies neither a purely psychogenic theory of psychiatric disease nor the exaggeration of the importance of trivial biological findings, the meaning and relation of which to psychological processes remain obscure or dubious.

The problem involved in tracing the connection between biological factors early in life and subsequent behavior is a formidable one, not only because such influences are remote, but also because so little is known about the transition from the biological to the psychological. Further, it is difficult to identify what aspect of early experience operates through biological mechanisms and what through psychological mechanisms. Some idea of the complexities of this problem may be obtained by reference to an experiment in which early life deprivation of mothering in monkeys had profound consequences on adult sexual adjustment. Harlow separated infant Rhesus monkeys from their mothers at birth and raised them with cloth models of the mothers.[4] They had no other monkey or human relationship. These infants came to relate to the so-called cloth mother surrogates, clinging to them and running to them for comfort when threatened. Upon reaching adulthood the social, sexual and maternal behavior of these animals differed from that of other laboratory-reared animals in a number of respects. Upon attaining sexual maturity these animals exhibited no sexual interest in each other or in sexually active adults. Further, they proved incapable of copulation, the males being impotent and the females frigid. Although the females could be impregnated by vigorous normal males and could carry the pregnancy to term, they subsequently manifested little maternal behavior toward their young. Apparently, then, monkeys raised without a reciprocal relationship with another living being during infancy, though provided with opportunities for sucking, clinging and body contact, fail to achieve the capacity for normal adult sexual and maternal behavior. Evidently some kind of mutual exchange between the infant and the mother or some other monkey is necessary if the specific responsivity and behavior needed for adult courtship, mating and maternal behavior are to evolve successfully.

Is this consequence in the monkey a result of some permanent alteration or failure in development of the nervous system organization underlying the sexual act or is it traceable to a purely psychological mechanism such as inhibition or conflict? No answer is possible, but a more general question is suggested. To what extent do the original biological characteristics of the individual define and circumscribe his psychological potential and to what extent does subsequent psychological experience alter or modify biological potential? To generalize to humans from the monkey observations, individuals may differ at birth in their biological potential for full sexual maturity, but this in turn may be influenced by the nature of early relationships. If poverty of human contact in early life can in man as well as in monkey result in a failure of maturation of sexual behavior (and there is some evidence to support this), then we are perhaps identifying remote influences on the development of the central nervous system organization necessary for such behavior, that is, on a drive system, which ordinarily does not mature for some years (see Chapter XVI). In such a case the failure of development of or damage to a drive system would have preceded its contribution to psychological processes and hence would also be expected to have psychological consequences and be reflected in psychological processes as well as in manifest behavior. It might result in an adult who has little or no genital sexual drive and consequently little interest in or aptitude for heterosexual matters. Such a person might also be impotent (or frigid). This would represent a psychological defect resulting from a developmental failure consequent to deficiency of certain experiences necessary for sexual development. It is to be contrasted to the situation in which sexual development does take place but its expression is thwarted by psychological influences, i.e., conflict. Such a person might also be impotent (or frigid) and consciously might even evince little interest in heterosexual activity, yet the genital sexual drive is obviously active, as evidenced by the nature of his unconscious mental activity.

The essence of the issue at hand is that structure, as represented in the organic givens of the central nervous system, circumscribe and determine the range of initial behavior, but experience influences subsequent development of structure. What was designated in Chapter XXII as psychic structure must be a borderland to organic structure. The point has not yet been reached where it can be stated where one ends and the other begins.

Hence, though it is not possible to identify how specific chemical or physiological processes are concerned in the predisposition to and pathogenesis of psychological disorders, attention can still be drawn to a number of ways in which variations or defects in certain biological systems might be involved. For example, children certainly differ in their range and capacity of perception, in their preference for one modality of perception as compared to others, in their activity patterns, in their cognitive styles, in their capacities for and techniques of learning and problem solving, in their intrinsic vigor or energy, and in many other ways not easily defined. We can presume that some of these differences are based on intrinsic biological determinants. Such biologically determined features in themselves or in relation to more or less incompatible environmental conditions may be important as modes of relating or reacting to the environment and therefore may be remote determinants of maladjustment. The biological determinants may be nonspecific, as when a child with unusual intellectual capacities is the exception in a family of marginal capacities. Or more specific biological determinants of mental mechanisms may be involved, predisposing to the choice of one psychic device over another in response to the same conflict or developmental task. It is conceivable, for example, that biologically determined characteristics of the brain play a role in the predilection of one person for the more expressive, affective responses that characterize the hysterical as compared to another's tendency toward the cognitive, overintellectualizing responses that mark the obsessive-compulsive. These are perhaps styles of mental activity which in some cases may be based more on biological givens than on learning, a view in keeping with the manifest differences in the "personalities" of infants even within the first months of life.

Such biological individuality may be taken as a limiting factor circumscribing the range of psychological developments possible in any one individual. Thus, given the same initial psychological capacities but different life circumstances, one person may develop into a warm, expressive, artistic, creative, well adjusted adult while another may become blatantly hysterical; or one may become a well-controlled, careful, thoughtful intellectual, while another becomes an obsessive-compulsive neurotic. Although this can only be a speculation at the present, it is still one which must be kept in mind until it is proved wrong.

Such intrinsic psychobiological characteristics present early in life may also be important in predisposing to certain later developments because of incompatibilities that may develop between mother and infant. For example, the mother-infant relation may be disturbed if the mother is eager to suckle and the baby is a weak sucker; if the mother wishes a quiet baby and the baby is very active; if the mother wants a babe in arms but the baby stands and walks early. In the same sense the child with insatiable sucking needs or with premature and vigorous penile erections may be exposed to different experiences and stresses than the child not so endowed. Similarly, the child with unusual or precocious sensitivity of one or another sense modality may require modes of relating with the parent which are distinctive and which may not be identified by the mother. Thus, some babies are so sensitive to noise, light or tactile stimulation that such a stimulus readily becomes unpleasant and a source of distress. This may not be recognized by the mother, for whom the stimulus is not distressing.

Intrinsic characteristics of the central nervous system are not the only biological factors which may influence psychological development. A great number of processes operating elsewhere in the body also have the potential to influence brain and psychic development because of how they or their effects are perceived and/or how they affect drive systems. Most evident are the consequences of obvious disorders in infancy and early childhood which affect systems or organs that are especially concerned with survival, growth, the relationship with the mother or drive discharge. Among these may be cited respiratory difficulties, such as asthma or croup; mouth lesions, such as hare-lip or cleft palate; intestinal malabsorption, as in the celiac syndrome; intestinal hypermotility, as in so-called infant colic; lower bowel disturbances, such as constipation, diarrhea or spasm; skin disorders, interfering with or intensifying the need for skin stimulation; motor disabilities, interfering with holding, clinging, grasping, locomotion, etc.; sensory defects, such as blindness and deafness; endocrine abnormalities, involving sexual differentiation or growth and development; metabolic errors, involving metabolism and storage of carbohydrates, fats or protein, and leading to alterations in nutritional needs, to damaging by-products, or to changes in appetite, and many others. Such remote influences on psychic development are not necessarily restricted to manifest disease states. Indeed, there is evidence to support the view that individuals differ in respect to the degree to which different bodily systems affect psychic development. This difference is sometimes apparent in the particular body system through which the individual preferentially experiences pleasure or which he uses for relating activities, be it visual, auditory, olfactory, oral, anal, cutaneous, muscular, respiratory, etc. Obviously, psychological development is also affected by one's appearance, physical attractiveness, strength, the presence of physical defects, and a host of other biologically determined physical characteristics which are involved in how one relates to others and how one sees oneself. (See also Chapter XXXIII.)

Biological factors may also be more proximately involved in the pathogenesis of psychiatric disorders, as when the brain itself is the target of some physical stress. These will be discussed further in Chapters XXX and XXXI.

With the exception of the last category, it is clear that these biological differences are remote at best; therefore, their true relationship to subsequent psychopathological developments is not easily established. For the most part existing evidence is meagre. Nonetheless, it is important that such possibilities be kept in mind as we explore further other factors concerned in pathogenesis.

PSYCHOLOGICAL FACTORS

Many of the psychological determinants of psychiatric disease can be inferred from the material on development covered in the first part of this book and from the discussions of psychological stress and intrapsychic conflict (Chapters XXVI and XXVII). Though the first part of the book emphasizes the normative aspects of development, there are nonetheless many references to pathogenic consequences (Chapters VII, IX, X, XII and XVI). These will not be repeated here. The following considerations serve mainly to emphasize certain developmental processes and certain concepts having particular importance for the understanding of the psychogenesis of psychiatric disease.

Unresolved Intrapsychic Conflicts

The significance of unresolved intrapsychic conflicts as determinants of psychological stress was considered at length in Chapter XXVII. In a broader sense, this ongoing dynamically active influence of the past, in terms of unfulfilled, persistent drives and all the derivative motivations and attendant conflicts, constitutes a reservoir of potentially pathogenic intrapsychic influences determining illness. In general, it is the activation of old unresolved conflicts which constitutes the greatest obstacle to coping successfully with current demands, whether they arise from bodily changes or environmental pressures. The nature of the unresolved conflict and its psychological relevance to the current setting are of importance in determining both the choice of psychological devices to deal with the current situations and their appropriateness in that setting. The reader is referred to Chapter XXVII.

The Repetition-Compulsion

When there have been failures to achieve certain gratifications or to overcome certain dangers earlier in life there is a strong tendency for the mental complex associated with the drive not satisfied or the danger not overcome to continue to operate within the mental apparatus as an active, motivating influence. This leads to the phenomenon referred to by Freud as the *repetition-compulsion*, an unconscious tendency to displace to the present the earlier failure and to persist in the attempt to overcome it even though the consequences continue to prove unrewarding or painful. This appears in the recurring anxiety dreams of the accident victim, who dreams repetitively of the frightening experience, each time awakening in terror. It is also illustrated by the person who has the tendency to repeat relationship patterns that have already proved to be fruitless, such as the man who dissolves one unhappy marriage only to select a similar woman as his second wife. In such behavior we observe a persistence of the wish to enjoy the gratification or overcome the danger and the paradox that the individual appears not to learn from experience and not to be deterred by pain or defeat. The latter characteristic identifies the behavior as pathological, especially when the person knows consciously and in advance that the consequences of his act will be unrewarding, and yet in spite of this knowledge still doggedly pursues a course doomed to failure.

Underlying the repetition-compulsion are two dynamic forces. The first is the persistence of an unconscious wish, strong either because it was never adequately gratified or because it was excessively gratified. which continues to press for satisfaction even though the satisfying activity is no longer (or perhaps never was) permissible. This also reflects the everpresent tendency to overcome an obstacle. At the same time the persistence of such a wish evokes a counteracting disapproval from superego, out of which may evolve a compromise, namely that some measure of gratification of the wish is permissible, provided a price is paid in the form of punishment. This becomes an important mechanism in symptom formation, for unconsciously (and consciously at times) there is considerable willingness on the part of humans to pay a price in order to reap a reward. In actuality the price proves to be pain, disability, frustration, failure, humiliation, feelings of guilt or shame, etc., which, once suffered, may serve to elicit feelings of self-justification, namely, that the forbidden aim is now earned. In this manner superego influences paradoxically may keep alive a hope that the unsatisfied wish may be gratified after all; therefore, guilt may be regarded as the second force underlying the repetition-compulsion.

The repetition-compulsion plays an important role in the pathogenesis of psychological disorders, for it constitutes a resistance against overcoming unresolved conflicts and it militates against learning from experience. In the hierarchy of motivations that influence human behavior there always are some which follow the principle of the repetition-compulsion and it is these which constitute the points of lowered resistance to the vicissitudes of life. Especially when one meets a frustration in the environment the tendency is toward reactivation of these complexes and a fruitless repetition of past attempts to gain satisfaction or avoid distress. Sometimes such motivations are reawakened by relatively unimportant or merely symbolic influences, as, for example, the anniversary date of an earlier traumatic experience. The fact that all past unresolved conflicts and the wishes underlying them have the capacity to be so reactivated by current stimuli places the repetition-compulsion in a central position in the psychogenesis of psychiatric illness.

Traumatic Experience vs. Traumatic Events

The importance of major traumatic events in early life for the psychogenesis of disease should not be underestimated, but far more significant are traumatic situations or experiences sustained over an extended period of time. These may be subtle or they may be flagrant, but by imposing a continuing demand on the developing child they are more likely to produce psychological deformation. The most important source of such chronic stress is in early relationships. For example, we may contrast the potentially traumatic consequences to a child of the death of a parent with the effects of a more sustained disturbance in the relationship. In the case of loss by death many factors are involved in determining how serious the consequences will be for later development and health. These may include the nature of the relationship with the lost person, the number and adequacy of concurrent relationships, the age at which the loss occurred, the stability of the family group, the nature of the replacements and support available after the separation, the basic resources of the child, and many others. When conditions are favorable, some individuals may weather such experiences relatively unscathed. But the outcome is much less promising when the child's major developmental experience takes place in the framework of a persistently disturbed relationship. This is especially likely to be the case when the needs and modes of behavior of the child and those of the parent are to a high degree mutually incompatible, or when the needs of the parent place the child in conflict with other persons or with the social environment. Under such circumstances the child's success in coping with and maintaining a satisfactory relation with the parent may be accomplished through psychological developments which may not prove effective or useful under different circumstances and hence may predispose him to failures of adjustment later in life.

Important in bringing about such consequences are the processes whereby the child avoids unpleasant and sustains pleasant affect communication from the parent. As discussed in Chapters XIV, XVIII and XXVII, the child to a considerable extent gears his behavior to the affective quality of the parents' expression and behavior. He is made uncomfortable by the parents' unpleasure affects and is pleased and gratified by their manifestations of contentment and pleasure. For example, a parent with the morbid anxiety of a phobia is likely to communicate to the child the conditions under which he feels anxious. To avoid being exposed to the parents' anxiety, the child may feel compelled either to avoid the parent's phobic situation and thereby protect the parent from anxiety or to plunge into it in order to gratify the parent's wish to be reassured that he or the child is really not afraid. Phobic parents not infrequently force their children to do what the parents themselves fear to do. In either case the child's psychological adjustment involves developing techniques of keeping the parent from being anxious, and also, in order to avoid anxiety on his own part, he is prone to incorporate the conflict of the parent and thereby make it his own. Making it his own helps him to avoid being a threat to the parent, for he now "knows" unconsciously what is dangerous to the parent and defends himself accordingly. Similar developments may ensue in response to other affects of the parent, such as guilt, shame, helplessness, hopelessness, etc., each of which is likely to be communicated nonverbally to the child, who in turn becomes enmeshed in repeating behavior intended to alleviate the parent's distress and in avoiding behavior which might intensify it. When he succeeds in alleviating an unpleasant affect of the parent and thereby rendering him comfortable, the particular behavior of the child which appeared to bring about this result is likely to be reinforced. Such processes entrench patterns of behavior and personality traits which, although useful at the time, may prove inappropriate and ineffective later in life.

The consequences of all this in terms of later disposition to illness are manifold. The following are some examples. (a) The child may adopt the same ego defense mechanisms and patterns of behavior as the parent, as illustrated in the phobic and counterphobic patterns mentioned above. (b) He may attempt to adjust to the misinterpretations of reality of his psychotic or severely neurotic parent as if the parent's perceptions of the environment were accurate. If he does this, his own reality testing may become defective. (c) The child may be forced to submit to the acting out by the parent of hostile or disguised sexual wishes which actually represent attempts on the part of the parent to settle unresolved problems with his own parent rather than being appropriate responses to the child's actual behavior. In such cases the parent unconsciously confuses the child with his own parent, a reenactment of the childhood fantasy, "When I get big, you'll get small and then I'll get even." (d) He may be encouraged unconsciously by the parent to act out forbidden wishes and impulses of the parent, who unwittingly derives vicarious pleasure therefrom, at the same time punishing the child for so behaving. (e) The child may incorporate into his own psychic structure the unconscious conflicts of the parent and thereby protect himself from the discomfort of provoking distress in the parent by unwittingly activating the parent's conflict. He "knows" unconsciously what to avoid. (f) The child may be forced by the parent to act as an intermediary in dealing with the spouse, the grandparents or others. In this way, then, he has to adjust to their conflicts with each other and yet somehow keep the peace and satisfy everyone. (g) Unable to alleviate the parent's unpleasant affects, the child may come to see himself as bad, incompetent, unloved or unlovable, or he may be obliged to withdraw and detach himself, suffering thereby certain untoward consequences of separation. (h) The child may develop exaggerated resistance and hostility to the parent in order to keep him at a distance, thereby protecting himself from the effects of the parent's discomfort or threatening behavior. (i) He may withdraw from the one parent whom he cannot gratify and align himself with the other, who is more satisfying, with consequent disturbance in his own maturation and sexual identity.

Such developments may have grave consequences for successful maturation and health, since they interfere seriously with the child's developing capacity to evaluate reality and achieve identity. To a very considerable degree the circumstances of childhood, regardless how bizarre they may be, are felt by the child to be the "norm" against which later reality is tested. For example, a child whose mother's compulsive concern about bowel function results in the regular administration of enemas may feel this to be the natural state of affairs and he may be surprised to learn that other children are not so treated. It is, therefore, only with difficulty that such primary determinants of pleasure and pain are relinquished, especially when they had been reinforced by prolonged and repeated experience. The child's long dependence on the parents is the crucial factor which makes inescapable such efforts at adjustment to the parental needs, wishes, fantasies, conflicts, hostilities and modes of behavior. These processes play a critical role in the transmission of illness and illness potential from generation to generation. They constitute formidable factors militating against the smooth and successful resolution of the normal developmental crises of the formative years, greatly increasing the likelihood that the unresolved problems of the parents' childhood will remain unresolved in the child.

The Patterns of Childhood Object Relationships

The significance of particular patterns of object relating as determinants of vulnerability to object loss was discussed in Chapter XXVII. In part these define another aspect of the material discussed in the preceding section.

Predisposition to Anxiety and/or Depression

Early life experience may prematurely or excessively mobilize the emergency systems underlying anxiety or depression-withdrawal, resulting in an enhanced readiness to respond with either of these two patterns.[1, 3] This may result in a generalization of the evocative stimuli to include a wide range of input only remotely and symbolically related to the original trauma. Thus, even though the original situations in which the anxiety or depression-withdrawal reaction had been stimulated no longer exist, the person may subsequently respond explosively and indiscriminately to a great variety of configurations historically associated with the original traumatic situation. Very likely there are critical periods in life during which such predispositions are established. The mechanism of conditioning may be of importance in such developments.

Sexuality and Aggression

The implication of sexual factors and of aggression in the genesis of conflict has already been fully discussed in earlier sections. They are noted here again for completeness, and with the reminder that the sexual and/or aggressive impulses, both of the child toward others and of others, especially the parents, toward the child, may play an important role in the genesis of illness. The eventual disposition of sexual and aggressive drives is an important determinant of the reservoir of unresolved intrapsychic conflict and of the range and nature of later object relations.

Predisposition to Guilt and Shame

Internal and environmental factors which aggravate the readiness to experience guilt and/or shame and which limit the capacity to develop standards appropriate for adulthood and its social setting are potent influences in the development of illness (Chapters XIII, XIV, XVII and XVIII).

SOCIAL FACTORS

Social and cultural factors constitute the third category of influences concerned in the predisposition to and pathogenesis of psychiatric disorders. Given the same biological and psychological conditions, differing social conditions may have very different consequences in terms of future illness. Thus, one set of social circumstances may intensify or entrench whereas another may neutralize the pathogenic significance of certain biological or psychological factors. Such effects might operate directly on the developing child or adolescent or they may be mediated through the family and its members. In adulthood the influence of society is more directly on the individual. The fact that in the final analysis these influences operate via the mental apparatus of the individual, that is to say, are internalized and become psychological forces operating within, does not relieve us of the necessity of examining them in their primary social context. In certain situations it is more difficult for the individual to escape from unfavorable social conditions than to avoid unsatisfactory interpersonal relations.

Value Systems

The values of the society and of the various groups with which the individual and the family are related will be of importance in determining what is regarded as right or wrong, good or bad. These values include moral and ethical standards as well as standards of performance, achievement, activity, behavior, dress, etc. Such values and standards constitute points of reference, deviation from which creates strain. Thus, the culture that values strength and aggressiveness imposes a psychological burden on the individual who for biological or psychological reasons does not have or cannot develop these attributes. He realistically runs the risk of not being regarded as an acceptable object by other persons who share these values, and his own sense of self-esteem may be damaged. Other problems may arise when the parents or family stem from groups with value systems differing from those of the dominant group. In extremely authoritarian or autocratic cultures, where individual freedom is rigidly curtailed by political or religious dictation, certain persons can be caught in an intolerable conflict between opposing values, while others may be relieved not to have to assume responsibility for their own standards and behavior; they merely conform. Either of these situations may predispose to breakdown, the first when the social setting does not change, the second when it does. Conflicting values may also be found among various subcultures in a society, so that being brought up with one set of values may ill-prepare one for successful adjustment in another setting, and in that sense may constitute a predisposing factor to later breakdown.

Value systems are also involved in prejudices, including racial, religious and other minority biases. The member of such a minority group is likely to be subjected to unusually intense hostile and rejecting forces during his upbringing and to be confronted with contradictions concerning his evaluation of himself and of his family. Hostility to the parents, to his own group or to the dominant group, attempts to be accepted or assimilated by the dominant group and to disown one's own group, all make for confusion in identity, intensify intrapsychic conflict, and generally generate further frustration and disappointment. Changing one's name in an attempt to dissociate oneself from the parents' heritage, for example, frequently comes to be a source of gnawing guilt. It is not uncommon for the member of a persecuted minority to have a depreciated self-image, to feel insecure and to lack self-confidence, all conditions rendering him more vulnerable to other stress. He may also identify with his persecutors without thereby gaining acceptance by either group.

Assumptive Beliefs

These are the assumptions made by a group or society to explain natural and social phenomena and which therefore order life, customs and manners. They include the rational, scientific, supernatural, magical, divine, etc. Such assumptions form an important condition for group membership and acceptance, as do the values of the group. Societies differ in their tolerance of differing beliefs and therefore in the variety of groups to which a person might belong. The child's development and education take place within the framework of the assumptions of his particular society, which may prepare him well or ill for future situations. This may be illustrated by the contrasts between a society which believes man is master of his fate and one which believes that he is helpless before nature; or one which believes government is to serve man and one which holds that man is to serve government; or one which believes death is the end, a permanent separation, and one which regards death as a reunion with one's loved ones. Clearly the nature of such belief systems influences what is perceived as stress in one society as compared to another.

Roles and Opportunities

The opportunities available to an individual and the varied roles he might fulfill provide a range of conditions for growth, development and self-fulfillment, limited in some societies, rich in others. Eventually the child learns his place and potential. Where opportunities are limited or restricted, some persons may suffer frustration and discouragement, and deviant, asocial or antisocial tendencies may be encouraged. Furthermore, when the variety of roles is limited there is less opportunity for persons with potential for breakdown to find a social setting supportive in maintaining compensation. Conversely, when opportunities are abundant and the individual is expected to make his own place in society, some persons may feel or actually are incapable of so doing and may suffer accordingly. Highly structured societies of great stability, in which roles are well defined by long tradition, provide still another set of variables determining which individuals remain healthy and which ones break down.

Social Conditions

The actual social conditions under which the child lives and is brought up may serve to accentuate or to suppress certain psychological qualities or problems. Poverty, overcrowding, violence, promiscuity, social isolation, discrimination, segregation, poor housing, and so forth, are obvious conditions adaptation to which serves in most persons to stunt development and perpetuate unresolved conflicts and ungratified needs. It is the rare person who not only successfully weathers such unfavorable circumstances but even profits from them. Experience indicates that the most effective buffer against such damaging social conditions is the well-knit family group, but it is difficult for a family to remain intact and effective under such circumstances.

Social conditions which ostensibly are highly favorable may also have pathogenic significance. Settings of great wealth and social prestige, etc., may for some people accentuate hedonism, self-indulgence, snobbery, materialism, and other tendencies which interfere with identity formation and the achievement of a satisfying role in society, whereas for others they may provide a wider range of opportunity for development, fulfillment and social usefulness.

Family

The role of the family in normative development has been discussed in Chapter XXI. As the social unit within which the child develops, the disturbed family becomes a potent influence in predisposing to later psychopathology. In the section Traumatic Experience vs. Traumatic Events, emphasis was placed on the impact on the developing child of psychological disturbances of one or the other parent. It is also necessary to consider how such disturbances involving individual family members may affect the function of the family. In Chapter XXI we discussed the family as a small group, the structure and function of which play an essential role in the personality development of the individual. It was also pointed out that the actions of any of its members affect all members, who must find and maintain reciprocally interrelating roles with all other members. For the child this involves dealing not only with individuals in terms of mutual needs but also with the family as a group in terms of what is necessary to maintain the family intact and effective.

A variety of processes may threaten or disrupt the structure of the family and interfere with its effectiveness as a setting for the child's development. These failures of family function all may have important consequences in disposing the child to later difficulty. They represent conditions in which the child is subjected to and must adjust to unusual pressure and deforming conditions within the family. Under such circumstances he has to learn ways of surviving with the least amount of discomfort, but often this is accomplished at the cost of a serious restriction in his capacity to function and relate in settings outside the family. Indeed, so dependent may he become on the highly specific requirements engendered by his particular family setting that other environments seem strange, alien and inhospitable, and other persons are found to be difficult if not impossible to relate to. Further, the pathological conditions of the family and the behavior of its members may inordinately influence the patterns and modes of thinking and behaving of the developing child. This extrabiological transmission of familial characteristics is a major factor in the perpetuation of psychopathological traits.[8, 9]

* * * * * *

This catalogue of the biological, psychological and social factors involved in the predisposition to and pathogenesis of psychiatric disease is by no means complete. Enough examples in each category are given to demonstrate the multi-faceted determinants of psychological breakdown. Exclusive theories which place all emphasis on one component to the exclusion of the others or reductionistic theories which attempt to convert the social and psychological into the biological, or the social and biological into the psychological, are patently untenable. So, too, are the neo-Darwinian theories which put the biological and psychological in conflict with society. Man is a social animal and his social and interpersonal needs are in the service also of assuring biological needs, including survival of the species.

REFERENCES

1. Engel, G. L. and Reichsman, F.: Spontaneous and Experimentally Induced Depressions in an Infant with a Gastric Fistula. A Contribution to the Problem of Depression. J. Am. Psychoanalyt. A., *4:*428, 1956.
2. Freud, S.: Beyond the Pleasure Principle (1920). *In:* Standard Edition of the Complete Psychological Works of Sigmund Freud, vol. XVIII. London, The Hogarth Press, 1955.
3. Greenacre, P.: The Predisposition to Anxiety. Psychoanalyt. Quart., *10:*610, 1941.
4. Harlow, H.: The Heterosexual Affectional System in Monkeys. Am. Psychologist, Jan. 1962.
5. Hilgard, J. R. and Newman, M. F.: Evidence for Functional Genesis in Mental Illness: Schizophrenia, Depressive Psychosis, and Psychoneurosis. J. Nerv. & Ment. Dis., *132:*3, 1961.
6. Johnson, A. and Szurek, S.: Etiology of Antisocial Behavior in Delinquents and Psychopaths. J.A.M.A., *154:*814, 1954.
7. Kardiner, A. and Ovesy, L.: The Mark of Oppression. New York, W. W. Norton & Co., 1951.
8. Lidz, T.: Schizophrenia and the Family. Psychiatry, *21:*21, 1958.
9. Lidz, T.: The Intrafamilial Environment of the Schizophrenic Patient. *In:* Masserman, J. (ed.): Individual and Family Dynamics. New York, Grune & Stratton, 1959.
10. Mirsky, I. A., Miller, R. E. and Murphy, J. U.: The Communication of Affect in Rhesus Monkeys. I. An Experimental Method. J. Am. Psychoanalyt. A., *6:*433, 1958.

CHAPTER XXIX

PSYCHIATRIC DISEASE: II. PHENOMENOLOGY

The varieties of psychiatric illness are highly diverse and do not fit easily into discrete diagnostic categories because they represent complex and changing patterns of response to psychological stresses and/or to those physical stresses that directly affect the brain. In the over-all clinical picture of the disorder, we note the attempts to resolve conflict, to avoid pain or injury, to assure gratification of needs, to regulate and secure object relations, and to maintain the intactness and integrity of the psychic and biological self in a physical, interpersonal and social environment. For the most part, the psychological devices utilized are the same as those utilized in the ordinary adjustments of everyday life, but for one reason or another these prove inadequate. Such disturbances cannot be expected to show the consistency that we customarily find among many organic processes in which the course is more determined by the reaction rates of biological processes, as, for example, those determining the speed of wound healing, antibody formation or the renal clearance of a toxic substance. Hence, diagnostic categories among the psychiatric disorders are much more difficult to establish, and natural histories cannot be as readily delineated. Therefore, we shall first give attention in general terms to the phenomenology of psychiatric disease, without attempting to fit the phenomena into diagnostic categories. Later we shall examine some of the factors responsible for the grouping or association of some of these phenomena into syndromes, and then we shall consider the problem of nosology and classification— what names to use and how to relate one syndrome to another (Chapters XXX and XXXI).

As discussed in Chapter XXIV, the identification of any disease

321

state is a relative matter. It involves an awareness by the ill person of a deviation from what he considers to be his "normal," "healthy" or "happy" state (the development of symptoms) and/or the appreciation by an observer, physician or other, of a deviation from what *he* considers to be a "normal," "healthy" state (the development of signs). Hence, *recognition* of illness by either party is dependent upon his personal concept of illness, whether determined by personal experience, special training or the social-cultural setting.* Although individuals may differ appreciably in respect to the degree and character of the disturbance they are willing to regard as illness in themselves or in others, there is no difficulty in identifying and categorizing in general terms those phenomena which commonly, but not necessarily, characterize psychological illness. It is important not to lose sight of the fact that even the most disturbed, bizarre behavior may still serve a useful purpose for an individual, whether it be to reduce suffering or to enable him to cope with something that appears more difficult. But this generally takes place at the expense of some new defect, disability or compromise with reality. A phobia, for example, replaces an unknown inner danger with a "known" external danger which can be avoided; an hallucination may overcome the pain of a loss, as when one sees the dead alive again. In both examples, however, the person's adjustment and effective functioning are compromised in the process of avoiding distress.

---

* The reader is referred to Chapters XXIII, XXIV and XXV for a discussion of the contrast between the concept of disease as a natural phenomenon and the concept of disease in the institutional context of what conditions are cared for by physicians. The latter judgments, though progressively codified by medicine, nonetheless differ from time to time, place to place, group to group, and person to person. In the present chapters we shall have to concentrate on what patients and observers, trained and untrained, currently and in the social setting of the western world, commonly consider to be evidences of psychological disorder. At the same time, this does not relieve us of the scientific responsibility to recognize that distinctions between disease and health based on such considerations are artificial and fluid and that the further understanding of health and disease demands an approach not restricted by how the physician sees his own role and function and what society expects of him. In Chapter XXIV we used grief as an example of a natural phenomenon which is not ordinarily conceptualized as disease, but which, nonetheless, involves processes indistinguishable from and continuous with those occurring in other conditions commonly accepted under the rubric, "disease." This example is relevant because it serves to emphasize the special difficulties encountered when dealing with disorders manifest predominantly in psychological, behavioral and social rather than somatic terms. And when, in addition, moral and ethical considerations are involved, as with asocial, antisocial, criminal and deviant behavior, the matter is further confused by legitimate questions as to whether such processes are to be viewed as the health problems of an individual or as problems for society. For contrasting views, see Szasz.[4]

The phenomenology of psychiatric disease will now be considered under a number of headings.

AFFECTS

The inner experiencing and the behavioral expression of affect are cardinal phenomena of disease, as they are of psychic life in general (see Chapters XIV, XVIII, XXV, XXX and XXXIII). This is inherent in the function of affects as communications of need, distress and difficulty to the self and to the environment. Most obvious as expressions of illness are the signal-scanning affects of unpleasure, i.e., anxiety, shame, guilt, disgust, sadness, helplessness and hopelessness. As the indicators of failures of psychological homeostasis, they constitute the main source of suffering by the psychologically sick person. Much of the phenomenology of disease is understandable in terms of these unpleasant feelings and the attempts to terminate, attenuate or avoid them.

In general, the affective components of psychological disease include the following: (a) Signal-scanning affects of unpleasure may occur in episodes or in the form of sustained unpleasant moods. (b) Signal-scanning affects of pleasure may occur inappropriately in degree or setting, as when euphoria, laughing or giggling, or exaggerated good spirits are manifested out of context with the social setting or psychic reality (cf. especially hypomania and mania). (c) There may be inadequate control of drive-discharge affects, aggressive or libidinal, which may be expressed too intensely, at inappropriate times and under inappropriate circumstances or which may be directed toward inappropriate (displaced) objects. (d) Affects may be excessively controlled, as when they are either not experienced or not expressed, even when it is appropriate to do so. Excessive control may result in behavior that is expressionless, cold, intellectualized or inhibited, and/or in the inner experience of "no feeling," coldness, detachment, etc. These represent efforts to avoid unpleasant feelings or to avert unpleasant responses from the environment. (e) Affect experience and expression may be dissociated from cognitive expression. As a result there may be anything ranging from such commonplace behavior as smiling to cover up anger to the bizarre behavior of complete dissociation, in which words and feelings no longer bear any relation to each other.

OVERT BEHAVIOR

Here we refer to what the person does and how he acts. Psychologically sick behavior may be impulsive, unpredictable and uncontrolled, or inhibited, mechanical and restricted. It may be compulsive, repetitious or stereotyped. It may be inappropriately aggressive, hostile, destructive and murderous, or self-destructive and suicidal. It may be hypererotic, hypoerotic or perversely erotic. It may be asocial, antisocial or negativistic. It may be excessively dependent and clinging or excessively self-indulgent and independent. It may be overactive and gregarious or withdrawn, seclusive, isolated and detached. It may be marked by irritability, distractability, agitation, disorganization and confusion, or it may be eccentric, manneristic or bizarre. It may be defective or overly exacting in respect to moral and ethical standards. It may be overly conforming, passive, submissive or excessively rebellious, contentious and defiant. It may include disturbances in speech (mute, blocked, perseverative, excessive, etc.), in appetite (increased, decreased or perverse), in sleep (insomnia, hypersomnia, nightmares, etc.), and in control over certain body functions (incontinence, eneuresis, impotence, frigidity, tics, paralyses, incoordination, tremors, etc.). It may include alterations in consciousness and awareness (startle, hypervigilance, distractability, inattention, dazed behavior, twilight states fainting, convulsions, stupor, coma, etc.).

Many of such behaviors occur appropriately in response to specific life situations and cannot in themselves be regarded as signs of illness, whereas others obviously are in themselves abnormal. As criteria for the diagnosis of illness, they must be evaluated in the context of the total situation as to the appropriateness of the behavior for the particular person under the particular circumstances at the time. The values, standards and expectations of the observer and of society constitute additional limiting and defining variables. Both quantitative and qualitative considerations apply. As a general rule of thumb, behavior which is not reasonably understandable in terms of the real situation and which appears to be beyond the individual's capacity to control or modify in relation to changing circumstances or in response to correction of misunderstanding is likely to be indicative of illness. The validity of such an evaluation is strengthened when it is established that the person who manifests such behavior is unaware of the nature or implications of his behavior or of the fact that his behavior is inappropriate or unusual.

It is also necessary to emphasize, however, that not all psychological illness is manifest by obviously disturbed behavior. It is possible to suffer psychological illness and yet maintain behavior that for the most part is indistinguishable from behavior generally regarded as normal. Many persons suffer intensely from painful, disagreeable or unpleasant feelings or thoughts and yet are so successful in maintaining an acceptable behavioral facade that few appreciate their suffering and illness.

MENTAL PROCESSES

Disturbances in mental processes may be subjectively experienced (*symptoms*), in which case the sufferer may or may not tell someone, or they may be revealed in the content of speech (*signs*). They involve either alteration in the control over the content of thought or disturbances in the quality and form of thinking, especially as it bears on integrative functions, the correct appraisal of reality, apperception and the cognitive functions involved in learning. The psychologically sick person finds it difficult or impossible to control his mental processes and bend them to the service of reality testing and adjustment. Illogical, irrational or inappropriate thoughts or ideas enter his mind and either he cannot control them or he does not recognize their irrational quality. He has difficulty in regulating and controlling successfully the mental processes necessary for the accurate appraisal of the data of his senses, the interpretation of reality, the establishment of logical connections, the integration of past and present, or the differentiation between what is fantasy or mental and what is concrete and real, what is inside or what is outside. Mental processes, so to speak, no longer have the degree of autonomy and freedom from internal and external influences which differentiates the mature mental apparatus from the immature. The hard-won autonomy of ego is compromised or lost.

Disturbances Involving Thought and Thinking

These include a variety of disturbances whereby the control over thought is impaired or thinking processes per se become disordered or defective:

COMPULSIONS. Compulsions involve impelling thoughts which demand the performance of certain rituals or the execution of certain repetitive acts, usually with the associated feeling that by so doing something bad will be warded off (e.g., hand washing, counting, touching, walking on cracks, etc.). Distress is felt if the act is not carried out, yet relief of the distress is shortlived if the act is performed, for the commanding thought soon reappears and the act or ritual must be repeated again and again. Compulsions have a magical quality and may be compared to superstitions.

OBSESSIONS. Obsessions are repetitive thoughts or fantasies, often of sexual, sadistic, destructive, obscene, disgusting or blasphemous character, which intrude into consciousness against the will. Though they are experienced as alien or absurd, the patient feels powerless to prevent them and often is horrified, ashamed or guilt-stricken by them.

OBSESSIVE PREOCCUPATION AND FANTASY. These involve the inability to interrupt or terminate preoccupation with some painful, difficult, unpleasant, frightening or shocking experience or situation of the past. Such preoccupation may absorb the person's attention and distract him from other activities. Pleasant but unrealistic or inappropriate fantasies or reveries may also dominate mental activity and interfere with more reality-related thinking and activity.

RUMINATIONS.   Ruminations are repetitive or continuous speculations, often circular, generally about abstract or trivial matters, which also interfere with other thought processes and activities.

DOUBTING AND INDECISION.   These may take the form of excessively time-consuming uncertainties, often about relatively minor and ordinary matters, such as what to wear, what to eat, where to go, what to do next, etc.

INHIBITION OF THINKING.   The process of thinking itself may be inhibited or one may feel that it is. In either event, thoughts come or appear to come slowly and with great resistance and are likely to be limited in scope, imagination and affective color.

PHOBIC THOUGHTS.   These are irrational fears or concerns that have no basis in reality yet are persistent and not dissipated by logic, even when the sufferer knows them to be irrational. They include such fears as of crowds, darkness, heights, bacteria, insects, disease, dirt, injury, etc., usually referred to oneself, but sometimes to others as well. They are always associated with anxiety.

DELUSIONS.   Delusions are false beliefs or ideas which cannot be changed by reason and are not part of generally accepted belief systems. They may include ideas of persecution, grandeur, guilt, poverty; ideas of influence, that one is being controlled, influenced or manipulated by outside forces or people; ideas of reference, that events or processes in the environment, such as radio or TV programs, car horns or street lights, have special meaning or are personal messages.

DISSOCIATION.   Dissociation of thought refers to various departures from logical thinking, as when the proper relationships between ideas are disrupted, contradictions between ideas are tolerated, words are used incorrectly or their meaning is changed, and symbolic, abstract and concrete meanings are confused one with the other. These include processes that were designated as "primary process thinking" in Chapters XIV and XXII. They are also sometimes grouped under the heading "primary thought disorder."[1] Dissociation of thought results in incoherence, circumstantiality, flight of ideas, blocking, perseveration, incomprehensible and bizarre stream of speech, neologisms (new idiosyncratic words), "word salad" (meaningless combinations of words and phrases), and "clang associations" (words strung together on the basis of similar sound). The capacity to utilize abstract concepts is interfered with and words tend to be used in their more concrete, literal sense.

Disorders of Perception and Apperception

These include disturbances in the processes whereby stimuli from the external environment and from within the body are received and interpreted, as follows: (a) There may be hypersensitivity, hyposensitivity or insensitivity of any of the modalities of sensation, such as blindness, hyperacusis, anesthesia, etc. (see also Chapter XXXII). (b) *Illusions* are misinterpretations of sensory data, as when a bed post is mistaken for a person, a distant sound for a human voice, an itch for a crawling insect or a strange place for a familiar one. (c) *Hallucinations* are sensory perceptions of external events experienced without the corresponding input from the environment. They are actually the projection of mental images to the outside as if real. They may include sounds, voices speaking to or about one, visual images, odors, tastes, tactile sensations, etc. (d) *Depersonalization* is a more complex derangement in the perception of oneself and one's body and includes feelings of unreality, estrangement, loss of or changes in the sense of identity, amnesia, multiple personalities, changes and distortions of the body image, and dream-like states. (e) *Derealization* involves complex distortions of the environment and of spatial and temporal relations, so that the environment seems changed, strange, distorted, different, strangely familiar (déja vu), or unfamiliar.

Disorders of Intellectual Function

These involve particularly the functions concerned with knowledge and learning and include: (a) reduced attention and ability to concentrate; (b) defects in the ability to establish orientation as to time, place and person; (c) defects or selective gaps in recent and remote memory, retention, recall and the ability to learn; (d) deficiencies in quantity and quality of general knowledge and information; (e) defects in judgment and comprehension.

In general, these various disorders of mental functioning either evolve from mental mechanisms serving adaptive functions or they are the direct or indirect consequences of disturbances in brain function. For example, depersonalization phenomena or hallucinations may occur in response to purely psychological stress, as during certain intense affects, hypnosis or sensory deprivation. Or they may occur with lesions or upon electrical stimulation of the temporal lobe and in response to certain chemical agents. Similarly, defects in memory, retention and recall may be psychologically mediated, as with repression or denial, or they may be the consequence of metabolic deficiency or damage to brain structures that are concerned with the processes whereby memory is laid down or mobilized (delirium or dementia).

OBJECT RELATIONSHIPS

Psychiatric illness commonly is marked by disturbances in human relationships, which to varying degrees are unsatisfying, conflictful or unrealistically perceived. Patients may have or may feel that they have difficulty making or holding friends, that they do not get along with people, that they do not understand or are not understood by others, that they cannot relate to or converse with others. Occasionally a patient may inappropriately feel the opposite, that he has innumerable friends and is universally admired and loved. Patients may variously feel excluded, estranged, despised, misunderstood, put upon, taken advantage of, cheated, or that others are untrustworthy, unreliable, provocative, demanding, acquisitive, hostile, seductive, inconsiderate, disinterested, neglectful, jealous or envious. They in turn may be seen by others (as well as by themselves) as quarrelsome, inconsiderate, provocative, seductive, demanding, clinging, dependent, shy, awkward, suspicious, detached or inaccessible. They may consciously or unconsciously be preoccupied with sexual problems, which color all their relationships and result in unsatisfactory sexual and marital experiences. They may have special problems in relating with certain figures, as with parents, the spouse, siblings, children, authority figures, peers, inferiors, etc., or there may be restrictions in the type of person with whom they are or are not able to relate effectively, as male, female, older, younger, more aggressive, more passive, sexually inhibited, seductive, and so on. Some of these patterns of relating were discussed in Chapter XXVII.

DISTURBANCES IN IDENTITY AND SELF CONCEPTS

Some of these difficulties have already been mentioned in terms of depersonalization phenomena and others can be inferred from the defects in object relating discussed in the preceding section. Additional manifestations include (a) feelings of inferiority, superiority, childishness, weakness, incompetence, impotence, etc.; (b) confusion in sexual identity—the man who feels himself to be feminine or inadequately masculine or paternal, the woman who feels herself to be masculine or inadequately feminine or maternal, the person who has bisexual feelings or attitudes, or perverse sexual identity; (c) borrowed or "as if" identities, as seen in persons who feel little or no sense of personal identity or individuality and who try to imitate and be like other persons; (d) weak or fluid self concepts, leading to confusion between self and objects and to mental uncertainty as to whether thoughts, ideas, feelings and even parts of the body are one's own or someone else's; (e) identity defusion, where the various life experiences, object relations and roles contributing to identity formation have not yet been consolidated, resulting in feelings and behavior indicative of confusion about one's identity and a tendency to shift rapidly from one position to another. Such disturbances in identity and self concepts usually exist more at an unconscious than at a conscious level of mental operation.

* * * * * *

Somatic manifestations will be discussed in Chapters XXXII and XXXIII.

* * * * * *

This catalogue of signs and symptoms is meant only to provide a sampling of the varieties of phenomena characteristic of what generally falls under the heading of psychiatric illness. It is by no means complete and provides no information about the clinical characteristics of the illness of any one individual. Nor does it indicate that certain phenomena commonly tend to group together with sufficient consistency as to justify their being considered as discrete syndromes or symptom complexes. It is now our task to investigate some of the unifying dynamic, genetic and etiological factors which are responsible for such grouping into syndromes and then to consider these from the point of view of nosology and classification.

REFERENCES

1. Bleuler, E. P.: Dementia Praecox or the Group of Schizophrenias. Translated by J. Zinkin. New York, International Universities Press, 1950.
2. Engel, G. L.: Is Grief a Disease? A Challenge for Medical Research. Psychosom. Med., 23:18, 1961.
3. Menninger, K.: The Course of Illness. Bull. Menninger Clin., 25:225, 1961.
4. Szasz, T.: The Myth of Mental Illness. New York, Paul B. Hoeber, Inc., 1961.

CHAPTER XXX

PSYCHIATRIC DISEASE: III. FACTORS UNDERLYING SYNDROME FORMATION

Before coming to grips with the difficult problem of nosology as applied to psychiatric disorders, it is useful first to identify some of the factors which determine that certain signs and symptoms commonly group together, that others occur together rarely or even appear to be mutually incompatible, and that some individuals consistently manifest certain patterns of illness and never manifest certain other patterns. These are the unifying influences responsible for syndrome or symptom-complex formation and it is to such groupings of clinical phenomena that diagnostic labels are applied.

These unifying factors include the following.

THE NATURE OF THE STRESS

The nonspecificity of the stress was emphasized in Chapter XXVII, but this does not mean that there are not certain types of responses characteristic of each category of psychological stress or that there are no differences between the reactions to psychological stress as compared to physical stress directly affecting the brain.

Psychological Stress

Although there are obvious interrelationships among the three categories of psychological stress—object loss, threat of injury and drive frustration (see Chapters XXV and XXVII)—each one nonetheless is responsible for certain distinctive responses. Thus, object loss characteristically evokes grief and mourning and the withdrawal-conservation patterns. It is conducive to the affects of sadness, helplessness and hopelessness and to behavior and mental processes which have the function to minimize, to overcome or to prevent the loss and/or the consequences thereof (Chapters XVIII, XXV, XXVI, and XXVII). Further, a current loss or threat of loss is likely to reactivate the psychological and behavioral reactions associated with previous losses, especially those which had occurred in childhood and those in which the work of grief had been unsuccessful. Accordingly, object loss, whether actual or threatened, real or fantasied, commonly and characteristically is responsible for a variety of depressive phenomena. These may dominate the illness or merely contribute to the clinical picture.

In contrast, threat of injury is more likely to activate flight-fight responses and to be associated with the affects of fear, anxiety and reactive rage and with ego processes and behavior designed to ward off injury or damage. Here, too, the role of earlier experiences with injury or threat of injury is important.

The physiological concomitants of the flight-fight patterns and of the withdrawal-conservation patterns are probably different. (See Chapter XXXIII.)

Drive frustration, whether originating from rising internal pressures or provoked by external restraints or stimulation, will lead to various direct, displaced or disguised expressions of the drive seeking discharge and the inhibition thereof. When intrapsychic conflict is the main factor blocking expression of drives, the affects of anxiety, guilt, shame and disgust are especially likely to be provoked. When the frustrated wish is a sexual one this quality is likely to appear in the manifest or disguised sexual character of behavior, in conscious or disguised sexual feelings, in the sexual content of thought, fantasies, delusions or hallucinations, in the nature of object relations, and so forth. Again, the predispositions established during early life, especially those concerned with the persistence of pregenital aims or with failure to attain or resolve the Oedipus complex, serve to entrench certain conflicts and to perpetuate the devices utilized in the past for their expression and control.

When the underlying drive activity involves aggression, irrespective of its determinants, one may again expect the clinical picture to include direct and/or disguised expressions of destructiveness, hostility, rage or hate, which sometimes may be turned on the self in the form of self-destructive or suicidal activities.

Physical Stresses Affecting the Brain

Physical stresses may affect higher brain centers diffusely or may affect particular anatomical or functional units of the brain. In either case the nature of the brain function so affected confers characteristic features upon the resultant clinical syndrome. Such features are sufficiently distinctive as to constitute reliable diagnostic criteria which identify the resulting syndromes as being based on organic brain disease.

Stresses which diffusely damage or which interfere with the over-all metabolism of the cortex, whether reversibly or irreversibly, characteristically produce deficits in the level of awareness and in intellectual functions. Awareness is reduced and often fluctuates, and the capacity for attention, orientation, learning, memory, recall, abstract thinking, calculation and motor skills is impaired. This is true irrespective of the nature of the stress, be it hypoxia, hypoglycemia, trauma, degenerative change, an infectious process, a neoplasm, etc. More individual and varied are the behavioral and psychological *consequences* of the intellectual defect and the decrement in higher control over thought and behavior which accompanies such a defect. The decrement in intellectual ability in itself is commonly experienced as stressful, the patient often being painfully aware of his lessened ability to comprehend and cope with the environment or with his impulses. Hence the clinical picture also includes reactions to or defenses against loss and/or threat of injury, as well as behavior and mental processes indicative of the lessening of higher controls. These aspects of the clinical picture, in contrast to the more consistent and less personal intellectual defects, are more determined by the individual's past psychological development and the particular circumstances existing at the time the brain damage is taking place. Thus, one patient may be excited, anxious or depressed, aware of his defect and his incapacity to cope with it; another may be calm, composed, successfully compensating for or adjusting to the defect; one may be preoccupied with sexual fantasies, another with some aspect of his work; one disoriented patient may believe himself to be at a bar, another at home. There is wide variability in such manifestations, but the defects in attention and intellectual functions remain highly consistent, differing only in degree. They reflect the presence of the diffuse organic brain damage, whether due to primary brain disease or failure of metabolic support consequent to physiological or biochemical malfunction elsewhere in the body. The terms *delirium* and *dementia* are applied to the reversible and irreversible syndromes, respectively.

When such structural or metabolic defects have been present since infancy, or when the development of the brain itself has been incomplete, the main defect is in the capacity to learn, leading to the various syndromes of mental deficiency, or oligophrenia.

When physical stress affects particularly the temporal lobes or their associations, a variety of distinctive phenomena result, including syndromes of depersonalization or derealization; simple or complex hallucinations in the auditory, visual, olfactory or gustatory sphere; aphasia, alexia or apraxia; intense feelings of anxiety, emptiness, depression or anger, which typically begin and end abruptly; or bursts of rage or excitement. Any of these may occur with or without concurrent disturbance in consciousness. Again, the character of such reactions is not based on the specific nature of the agent or lesion affecting the temporal lobes. What differentiates these patterns from similar responses to psychological stress is their tendency to be abruptly episodic, beginning or ending suddenly, with relative well-being between episodes, that is, having the ictal characteristics of a convulsive disorder (epilepsy). They may also be associated with localizing neurological signs.

Certain chemicals or drugs affect certain parts or functions of the brain and yield distinctive syndromes. For example, the so-called hallucinogens or psychotoxic drugs, such as mescaline and LSD-25 (lysergic acid diethylamide) may produce states of depersonalization and derealization, with vivid hallucinations, usually visual. Stimulating drugs, like amphetamine and quinacrine, produce hyperalertness, vigilance, push of activity and thought, and sleeplessness. These drugs and chemicals most likely elicit such responses through their specific chemical affinity for certain structural or functional components of the central nervous system.

AFFECTS

A review of the material on affects will clarify how particular affects may contribute to the characteristics of a syndrome. (See Chapters XIV and XVIII.) Anxiety, shame, guilt, disgust, sadness, helplessness, hopelessness and rage, in particular, because of the dynamic factors involved in their differentiation, each include a particular cluster of drive, ego and self-object processes and behavioral features which serve to lend characteristic features to illness patterns. When illness is marked by overt manifestation of such affects there is a tendency to categorize the illness in terms of the predominant affect, e.g., anxiety reactions, depressive reactions, guilt neurosis, affective disorders, etc. Inappropriate pleasure reactions, such as certain types of elations, euphoria, hypomania and mania, also are included in this category. Closer examination reveals that these most often represent phases of psychological decompensation in response to stress. When some degree of compensation is reachieved, the affect may become less manifest, the conflict or stress underlying it coming to be handled by more effective ego mechanisms of defense and regulation. This general concept has already been amply discussed in the earlier chapters and will not be elaborated further here other than to point out that the ego mechanisms evoked in the course of specific affects also tend to fall into particular groupings and hence to contribute a more or less consistent patterning of psychological and behavioral responses. Thus, even though manifest anxiety, guilt or hopelessness, as the case may be, is no longer present, the reactions to cope with it still may contribute to a more or less consistent syndrome. Some of these will be discussed later in another context. (See Superego and Ego Ideal, p. 336.)

The physiological concomitants of the affects also demonstrate some specificity. (See Chapter XXXIII.)

EGO FUNCTIONS AND CHARACTER STRUCTURE

The patterning of ego defenses constitutes an important unifying factor in determining the disease picture. Thus, one type of clinical picture is found when there is excessive or sweeping repression (e.g., hysteria) and another when there is weakness of repression (e.g., certain adolescent turmoils, schizophrenia). Excessive and inappropriate use of projection to deal with sexual and aggressive impulses contributes to a syndrome characterized by morbid suspicion, jealousy, delusions and hallucinations, e.g., paranoia. Some types of ego defense, such as repression, displacement, isolation, undoing and reaction formation, are more conducive to effective reality testing, whereas others, such as denial and projection, may interfere with reality testing. Preponderance of one or the other group will accordingly lead to quite different clinical pictures, reality testing being fairly well maintained in one and impaired in the other.

Still unanswered is the critical question as to what determines the choice of a particular ego mechanism. As discussed in Chapter XXVIII, it is probable that both biological and experiential factors contribute to the predisposition of an individual to use certain ego mechanisms in preference to others. Certainly relevant is the level of psychological development achieved. The types of stress and conflict to which the individual had been subjected during early development are undoubtedly relevant determinants, but as already emphasized, these factors alone cannot account for the pattern of ego development. Nonetheless, whether it is a biological influence, difficult life circumstances or inadequate objects, alone or in combination, the person who remains at a generally immature level of psychological development may also be expected to use ego defenses and regulatory devices characteristic of earlier childhood. For this reason, familiarity with the sequences of ego development in childhood, as outlined in the first part of this book, is essential for an understanding of the patterning of ego mechanisms of defense and control in illness. Similarly, when conflicts cluster about some early developmental period and remain unresolved, the ego mechanisms that had previously been utilized to deal with the early conflict tend to persist into adulthood to be utilized again when the old conflict is reactivated. Thus, when a sexual conflict of the oedipal period is dealt with by massive repression, the tendency is for repression to be intensified when the sexual pressures of biological or environmental reality are encountered in adolescence and early adulthood. Or if a child in the latency period had excessively utilized magic gestures, isolation, undoing and reaction formation to deal with his aggressive or sexual impulses, he is very likely to retain this pattern in adulthood in the form of a distinctive character structure, if not in the form of actual illness.

Character structure, the more or less characteristic and lasting structuring of ego whereby the forces from both internal and external environments have been mediated in the course of development, provides for each person a basic background on which illness patterns develop. Character structure also figures importantly in determining the form that an illness may take. (See also Chapter XXXI.) To a significant degree it is possible to make fairly reliable inferences on the basis of an individual's pre-illness character structure as to what illness patterns he might be prone to. For example, the person whose character structure leads him to be rigid, controlled, pedantic, overly scrupulous, cold, emotionally unexpressive, overconcerned with details, indecisive, anxious to satisfy everyone and overly cautious has a greater potential to develop one or more of the following syndromes: an obsessive-compulsive neurosis, marked by rituals, obsessive doubting, obsessive thoughts, and compulsions; a psychotic depression, with severe feelings of guilt, shame, self-blame, self-recrimination, delusions of poverty or badness, and suicidal inclinations; recurring headache or other pain syndromes; spastic colon, with alternating and stubborn constipation and diarrhea. The same individual under different circumstances may manifest first one of these syndromes, then another. Dynamically, the common denominator in all these syndromes is the presence of conflict and morbid guilt and shame concerning especially aggression and anal-soiling impulses. The various syndromes represent different ways of maintaining tight control over the underlying aggressive impulses, and they include different responses to the guilt and shame evoked thereby. It must be emphasized that this particular conflict does not necessarily result in these particular characterological developments. But when it does, the tendency to develop one of the above syndromes is increased. On the other hand, the person with such a character structure is unlikely to manifest reactions such as alcohol addiction, sexual perversion, fugue states or delinquent, antisocial behavior, in all of which conditions control over impulses is relinquished to a greater degree than these people are capable of.

From the above comment we might generalize to say that specific conflict is but one of many factors which contribute to character formation. The latter, the outward indications of patterns of ego functions typical of the individual, is a better indicator of potential future illness patterns than is the nature of the intrapsychic conflict. The conflict, however, may play a more specific role in determining the circumstances under which the illness may be precipitated. Further, the conflicts of the past, persistent in the mental apparatus in the form of unconscious fantasies and wishes, contribute to the picture of the illness, at least in terms of how the direct or disguised attempts to gratify the frustrated wish may be manifest and what type of defense has been utilized in the past to cope with such wishes. Thus, if an oral wish continues to be active in the unconscious mind, one can be certain to find some expression of it in behavior, gestures, mannerisms, content of speech, appetite or eating patterns, dreams, fantasies, etc. However, the multiplicity and variety of such unconscious wishes and fantasies blocked by conflict are such that great variability may be anticipated in how such influences may be manifested by one individual as compared to another.

SUPEREGO AND EGO IDEAL

Some indication of the role of superego and ego ideal in symptom formation is to be found in the earlier discussions of guilt and shame (Chapter XVIII). As mental agencies concerned with concepts of right and wrong and with goals and ideals, superego and ego ideal functions play a highly significant part in determining the form that illness might take.

Superego function may be too exacting, harsh and punitive, in which case the patient not only may suffer from inordinate feelings of guilt but may also excessively utilize techniques of self-punishment and atonement to alleviate or avoid feelings of guilt. This results in a variety of illness patterns in which the struggle with guilt feelings is predominant. They include such reactions as (a) depressions characterized by intense feelings of self-abasement, self-depreciation, guilt, worthlessness and a strong need to be punished, sometimes carried out by means of self-injury or suicide; (b) masochistic patterns, characterized by martyrdom, by a predilection for painful, disagreeable, humiliating and defeating situations, a proneness to accidents, injury or surgery, and an intolerance of success and good fortune; (c) perversion masochism, in which sexual pleasure is possible only at the price of pain inflicted by the sex partner; (d) obsessive-compulsive neurosis, sometimes called "guilt neurosis," in which guilt leads to exaggerated magical techniques of doing and undoing, isolation and reaction formation as means of coping with forbidden impulses; (f) "psychogenic" pain, the suffering of pain as an experience primarily psychological or secondarily solicited from the environment in the form of injuries, operations, etc., in which the pain serves to attentuate guilt and permit some small measure of success and gratification. (See also Chapter XXXII.)

The common denominator of all such syndromes in which superego development leads to excessive guilt is the pervasive need for punishment and atonement and the consequent tendency to manifest preferentially behavior which elicits punishment from the environment. This leads to the apparent paradox that for these persons success, reward, recognition and good fortune may act as stresses precipitating increase in symptoms, whereas difficulty and hardship may actually permit them to enjoy better health and more success.[5, 6] By the same token, attempts at gratification of drives intensify guilt and thereby limit the capacity to maintain satisfying object relationships. For this reason, guilt greatly increases the susceptibility to object loss while increasing the capacity to tolerate injury.

Defective superego function may also contribute to syndrome formation through types of parent-child relationships in which a parent unconsciously encourages his child to act out behavior forbidden to himself by his own superego standards. (See also Chapter XXVIII.) Developmentally it results in a specific defect in superego formation in the sense that it sanctions indulgence by the child in certain behavior or activity ordinarily forbidden. The term *superego lacunae* has been applied to this process whereby specific superego defects are induced in a child.[11] The resultant encouragement to act out in some way brings the person into conflict with society, and the attempt to control the impulse induces an intrapsychic conflict. As discussed in Chapter XXVIII, this pattern is encouraged by its object-relating advantages. The operation of this psychodynamic mechanism constitutes another type of unifying influence on symptom formation, namely, the tendency to act out certain impulses in spite of—or even because of—the threat of punishment. (See also the repetition-compulsion, Chapter XXVIII.)

Still another type of defective superego function is one in which this controlling function is weak or ineffective, permitting the acting out of self-indulgent, aggressive or other behavior that has little regard for the well-being of others. Such relative lack of social consciousness and responsibility may also come about through a sense of guilt and the expectation of retaliation or punishment from society. In the latter case, superego is not "weak"; it is harsh, but inadequate. It permits certain indulgence and acting out, provided punishment is exacted subsequently or in advance. (See also Chapter XXXI.)

Defects in ego-ideal function, responsible for feelings of inferiority or superiority, shame or pride, also contribute to certain psychopathological constellations. Having excessively high expectations for oneself in regard to behavior, performance or personal appearance in itself increases the likelihood of failure, with resulting feelings of shame and inferiority. Such self-depreciatory feelings contribute to patterns of depression, withdrawal and insecurity, limit the range and number of object relationships, and predispose to giving up and the affect of hopelessness. There is often resort to the use of drugs, alcohol or narcotics and other artificial props to restore self-esteem magically, and when these fail, suicide may be the last resort. As will be discussed further, the sequence through giving up and hopelessness may eventuate in many types of illness, including organic processes (Chapter XXXIII).

The environmental models upon which ego ideal and superego are based may also contribute to disease pictures. This constitutes an indirect reflection of the influence of the goals, standards, mores and customs of the social group or subgroup in which the person is brought up and lives. The role of such factors is most apparent in cross-cultural studies, through which one can appreciate the variations in the manifestations of disease resulting from the influence on the individual of the particular cultural setting in which he grew up. (See also Social Factors, p. 340.)

OBJECT AND SELF CONCEPTS AND OBJECT RELATIONS

Certain manifestations of illness reflect different levels of differentiation of psychic self from psychic objects. These have already been referred to in Chapters XXVII and XXVIII. When the boundaries between psychic self and psychic object are poorly defined or are fluid, the consequent patterns of thought and behavior indicate a confusion in the interpretation of what originates from within and what derives from the environment. This may be responsible for and may contribute to the formation of syndromes marked by delusions, illusions, hallucinations, ideas of reference, ideas of influence, depersonalization and derealization.

For each developmental level of psychic object and psychic self one may expect to encounter patterns of thinking, behavior and object relating consistent with that level. Some of these may be inferred from the developmental material covered in Part I of this book and further examples may be found in the patterns of object relationships listed in Chapter XXVII. When the capacity to differentiate psychic self and psychic objects is poorly developed, the clinical pictures that evolve are quite different from those occurring when this intrapsychic capacity is adequate but the person has a limited capacity to relate satisfactorily to objects because of intrapsychic conflicts that generate guilt or shame. The first situation yields much more disorganized patterns and greater disruption of the facilities of reality testing, usually manifested clinically by one of the psychotic syndromes.

Narcissism is sometimes used as a unifying concept to categorize some of these phenomena. In a general sense, the term refers to the disposition of love (or libido) directed to the self. In its healthiest sense, it takes the form of degrees and qualities of self-esteem, self-respect and self-confidence that are in keeping with reality and are not achieved at the expense of objects or society (Chapters XIV, XVII and XVIII). As compared to this more or less ideal state, varying degrees and qualities of narcissism can be defined in terms of the extent to and manner in which an individual orients his life and behavior in terms of himself and his self-interest and the degree to which he fails to take account of the needs, aspirations and conditions of others. In respect to syndromes, a high degree of narcissism may be expressed in such diverse forms as the person with a self-indulgent, hedonistic character disorder who wants what he wants when he wants it; the complaining, dependent, hypochondriacal person who is largely preoccupied with his own body sensations; the severely depressed person whose guilt leads him to an exaggerated appraisal of himself as uniquely bad, "the worst criminal in the world"; the manic or hypomanic person who fantasies a totally unwarranted sense of power, competence, wealth and importance; the paranoid psychotic who believes all aggressive or sexual impulses are directed at him. In general, the more narcissistic an individual, the less aware is he of others and the less accessible he is to their influence and to the influence of environment.

THE NATURE OF INTRAPSYCHIC CONFLICT

Any particular intrapsychic conflict may be dealt with psychologically in a great variety of ways and therefore, per se, does not contribute specifically to the clinical picture of psychiatric disturbances. More relevant to syndrome formation are such factors in the conflict as the levels of fixation or regression concerned in the genesis of the conflict, the nature of the drive contributing to the conflict, the predisposition to anxiety, depression, guilt or shame, the degree of differentiation of self-object, and the nature of object relations. These all have already been discussed to some extent in other contexts (Chapter XXVIII). There are differences, for example, in the form of expression of conflicts depending on whether they derive from aggressive impulses originating in the oral, anal or phallic phases of psychosexual development. The reader is also referred to the earlier chapters on development for a fuller discussion of these specific modes. The significance of intrapsychic conflict for character formation was discussed earlier in this chapter.

SOCIAL FACTORS

Reference already has been made to how social factors early in life may influence syndrome formation through their role in superego and ego ideal development. Social factors may also have direct impact because of the actual demands, expectations and requirements imposed by society upon the individual and the current conditions under which he can maintain status and a role in society. Thus, the value systems of a society will significantly influence what kinds of behavior lead to acceptance, help or support from at least some segments of society and what kinds of behavior lead to rejection, isolation or punishment. Accordingly, the manifestations of illness are to some extent influenced by how society responds and in what manner this response helps one to deal with intrapsychic conflict and its derivatives. For example, where guilt invokes a need for punishment, the particular behavior manifested is likely to be that which will elicit punitive reactions from the social group in which the individual is living. Where the need is for support and help, the patient is likely to present himself in a help-soliciting role which is socially recognized or acceptable. Failure to do so either reflects the unconscious need for punishment or an ignorance of the mores of the group.

The behavior expected of a patient in relation to the role ascribed to the physician in any particular society is another variable determining how the patient presents himself. The same patient coming to a psychiatrist may report different complaints and difficulties than he would if describing his illness to a surgeon or internist. Many types of social and group structure and organization in a complex society serve to mold behavior so as simultaneously to satisfy some need of the individual and at the same time conform to the group values and expectations. Changing conditions in the course of history have an enormous influence on the outward manifestations of illness and indeed on whether a particular behavioral or psychological complex is regarded as illness at all. For example, the clinical picture of hysteria, which to a large degree involves expressing feelings in an exaggerated way, has varied widely in different eras and different settings in accordance with changing modes and customs as to how one is expected to emote and relate. Drama and literature well illustrate the dominant patterns of hysteria through the ages.

* * * * * *

Undoubtedly other unifying factors underlying syndrome formation could be cited, and many remain to be discovered. The examples given suffice to demonstrate how various influences in the course of development yield particular complexes of behavior having sufficient consistency and uniqueness to justify categorization into clinical syndromes. At the same time, these do not represent static entities, but rather dynamic patterns of behavior, constantly in flux as circumstances change. This is a far cry from the older perspective of disease entities having more or less independent existence. Such a dynamic view, however, does not preclude the possibility that invariant elements do exist, perhaps at a cellular or biochemical level, and that these determine the occurrence and character of certain clinical phenomena. Should this be so, they would have the status of a necessary, but not sufficient condition, just as the tubercle bacillus is a necessary but not sufficient condition for tuberculosis. As discussed in Chapter XXIII, the immediate effects of the viable tubercle bacillus account for only a few, not all the clinical manifestations of tuberculosis.

REFERENCES

1. Cattell, J. P.: The Influence of Mescaline on Psychodynamic Material. J. Nerv. & Ment. Dis., *119*:233, 1954.
2. Connel, P.: Amphetamine Psychosis. Maudsley Monograph No. 5. London, Chapman and Hall, 1958.
3. Engel, G. L., Romano, J. and Ferris, E. B.: The Effect of Quinacrine on the Central Nervous System. Arch. Neurol. & Psychiat., *58*:337, 1947.
4. Engel, G. L. and Romano, J.: Delirium, a Syndrome of Cerebral Insufficiency. J. Chron. Dis., *9*:260, 1959.
5. Engel, G. L.: Psychogenic Pain and the Pain-Prone Patient, Am. J. Med., *26*:899, 1959.
6. Engel, G. L.: Pain, Success and Guilt. Psychosom. Med., *24*:37, 1962.

7. Freud, S.: On Narcissism (1914). *In:* Standard Edition of the Complete Psychological Works of Sigmund Freud, vol. XIV. London, The Hogarth Press, 1957, p. 67.
8. Freud, S.: Criminals from a Sense of Guilt (1915). *In:* Standard Edition of the Complete Psychological Works of Sigmund Freud, vol. XIV. London, The Hogarth Press, 1957, p. 332.
9. Freud, S.: Those Wrecked by Success (1916). *In:* Standard Edition of the Complete Psychological Works of Sigmund Freud, vol. XIV. London, The Hogarth Press, 1957, p. 316.
10. Hoch, P. H.: Pharmacologically Induced Psychoses. *In:* Arieti, S. (ed.): American Handbook of Psychiatry, vol. 2. New York, Basic Books, 1959, p. 1697.
11. Johnson, A. and Szurek, S. A.: Etiology of Antisocial Behavior in Delinquents and Psychopaths. J.A.M.A., *154:*814, 1954.
12. Lindemann, E. and Clarke, L. D.: Modification in Ego Structure and Personality Reactions under the Influence of the Effects of Drugs. Am. J. Psychiat., *108:*561, 1952.
13. Menninger, K.: Man against Himself. New York, Harcourt, Brace & Co., 1938.
14. Opler, M. K.: Culture and Mental Health. New York, The Macmillan Co., 1959.
15. Penfield, H. and Jasper, H.: Epilepsy and the Functional Anatomy of the Human Brain. Boston, Little, Brown & Co., 1954.

CHAPTER XXXI

PSYCHIATRIC DISEASE: IV. NOSOLOGICAL CATEGORIES

In the last chapter we indicated some of the unifying influences in syndrome formation. We shall now consider some of the syndromes and the various ways in which they may be categorized. It will be noted that these categories are not necessarily mutually exclusive, some representing different ways of grouping the same clinical phenomena. Further, more than one category of disturbance may be observed in the same patient at the same time or at different times. This is to be expected since the categories constitute convenient ways of designating complex patterns of psychological and behavioral responses to stress rather than independent entities, a point which deserves repeated emphasis.

These various categories will be delineated in phenomenological and in genetic-dynamic terms. It should be pointed out that the latter method constitutes a formulation in terms of a particular theory of personality (psychoanalytic theory), and within this framework provides an explanation of the disorders. It does not represent a complete etiological statement, the latter not being possible since our knowledge of etiological determinants remains fragmentary. Nonetheless, such formulations, incomplete as they may be, have considerable heuristic value and provide one basis for the differentiation among the various patterns of illness.

NEUROSIS AND PSYCHOSIS

Neurosis and psychosis provide the closest approximation to a polarity in the categorization of psychiatric disorders and hence may

343

usefully be differentiated through contrast. They constitute two contrasting modes of response to stress which, at least at their extremes, may readily be differentiated. However, as we shall see, some phenomena commonly noted in the psychotic may also occasionally be seen in the neurotic, and vice versa. Further, both the neurotic and the psychotic are also capable of behavior and mental processes that are entirely normal and appropriate so that at certain times or under certain circumstances the degree of illness may be inapparent. The diagnosis of neurosis or psychosis is based on the over-all pattern, not on the presence or absence of one or another quality of behavior or thought processes. It is in keeping with these facts that we speak in terms of differentiating the neurotic person from the psychotic person rather than neurosis from psychosis.

The Phenomenological Differentiation

1. The *neurotic* person generally regards himself as ill, though he often interprets his illness as physical rather than psychological. He may speak of himself as being upset, nervous, jittery, tense, anxious, depressed, fatigued or tired. Or he may suffer from fears, thoughts or impulses which he feels he cannot control, but which he recognizes as irrational or "silly." He may present with a wide variety of somatic symptoms, such as palpitation, blushing, sweating, anorexia, nausea, pain and many others (which will be discussed in Chapters XXXII and XXXIII). He commonly regards and physicians commonly interpret such symptoms as due to the presence of some organic pathological process. The *psychotic* person, in contrast, less commonly complains of being ill. Indeed, some may not regard themselves as ill at all, though upon recovery they may acknowledge their past state to have been illness. Thus, while the *psychotic* may feel badly or distressed and complain thereof, more typically he manifests deviant thought or behavior, often sufficiently gross to be obvious even to an untrained observer, though the psychotic does not himself necessarily recognize or acknowledge it to be unusual, inappropriate or disturbed. Instead he may believe or claim that it is the environment which is altered or other persons who are behaving improperly. The *psychotic*, like the neurotic, may also regard himself as physically ill and may even have similar symptoms, but generally they include a persistent, persecuting, delusional or bizarre quality which is different from how the neurotic or the person with a physical illness generally communicates his complaints.

2. The *neurotic* person makes a considerable effort to maintain behavior that is consonant with what society expects either of one who is psychologically healthy or of one who is physically sick, and to a considerable extent he succeeds in this effort. Hence, some neurotic patients may suffer with major symptoms and may even be considerably

restricted in their activity and yet not appear to the casual observer to be overtly sick or disturbed. The *psychotic* person, on the other hand, either makes much less effort or has less capability to maintain socially acceptable behavior. Hence, his disturbances in thinking and behavior are more likely to be blatantly obvious to others, who are conscious of his bizarre mannerisms, the illogicality of his thought and speech, his defective judgment, the presence of hallucinations, delusions or illusions, the display of affects that are inappropriate in intensity or quality, and other types of irrational behavior or thought.

3. The interpersonal relationships of the *neurotic* person may range through dependent, clinging, demanding, exacting, hostile, quarrelsome, provocative, querulous, seductive, ingratiating, inhibited, and in various ways may be difficult, but in general these ways of relating are exaggerations of qualities of relating that occur from time to time among healthy persons. Compared to the healthy person, however, the neurotic is much less able to regulate his pattern of relating. The *psychotic* person, on the other hand, not only has great difficulty in relating at all, but also he is difficult to relate to. His relating patterns may be marked by detachment and withdrawal, cold aloofness and inaccessibility, intense and inappropriate erotic or hostile behavior, infantile clinging and dependent behavior, and sometimes by bizarre, nonverbal expressive behavior. The person attempting to relate to the psychotic also finds it difficult to establish and maintain a relationship, the patient at times appearing to be peculiarly remote, strange, inaccessible, incomprehensible and unpredictable. In part the obstacle to relating stems from a difficulty in understanding the communications of the psychotic.

4. In work and social adjustment the *neurotic* is much more capable of effective performance than is the psychotic. Even when neurotic symptoms are disabling to a high degree, as with severe phobias, compulsive rituals or depression, the neurotic may still succeed in carrying on some range of ordinary activity, and he remains painfully aware of his failure to live up to society's expectation. It is mainly when his disturbance is manifest or experienced predominantly in physical terms, such as palpitation, weakness, headaches, vomiting, etc., permitting the illusion of a physical illness, that the neurotic can with more ease relinquish an active work and social role. Here society's attitudes towards the physically, as compared to the psychologically, sick person contribute to this difference. The *psychotic* person, in contrast, not only is less effective in work and social relations, but he is to varying degrees less aware of his failures in these areas. In this respect his evaluation of his own performance and his judgment are likely to be seriously defective. In terms of social roles and group participation, the *neurotic* shows a greater inclination to align himself with healthy and with other neurotic individuals in more conventional social roles and groups. The

psychotic, provided he does not totally isolate himself, either relates imperfectly or peripherally with such groups or gravitates toward fringe, eccentric or asocial roles and groups, such as among hoboes, wanderers, faddists and various borderline bohemian, religious or political sects. For the psychotic these may constitute protective or supportive social environments which may reinforce psychological defenses, thereby making possible greater comfort and effectiveness.

Genetic-dynamic Differentiation

Although genetic (developmental) factors undoubtedly are of major importance in determining predisposition, our present state of knowledge does not permit any reliable differentiation between neurosis and psychosis on this basis. Both of these categories are marked by defects in psychological development, which, however, are more sweeping and involve greater defects in ego functions in the psychotic than in the neurotic. We presume these defects to be the product of both biological and extrabiological factors operating in the setting in which the child develops, but precise identification and evaluation of these factors are not yet possible. In any event, the consequence of such influences is a restriction in the capacity to deal with the vicissitudes of life and a persistent backlog of unresolved intrapsychic conflicts. The two categories tend to differentiate not so much on the basis of the nature of the unresolved conflicts as on the ego mechanisms used in the past and in the present to cope with such conflicts. Further, although this backlog of unresolved conflicts serves to render the ndividual especially vulnerable to certain types of life situations, and hence is important in determining what will constitute stress for each particular individual, the nature of the stress itself is of no value in differentiating neurosis from psychosis. In respect to these categories, the role of stress is entirely nonspecific.

Once the dynamic steady state is upset by some stress, both the potentially neurotic and the potentially psychotic are obliged to deal with the emergence of sexual and/or aggressive impulses which up to that point had been maintained under satisfactory control. For the most part, these impulses are derivative from infantile or childhood sources and are experienced as personally or socially unacceptable or dangerous. In the course of both neurosis and psychosis such impulses may be successfully kept from consciousness, they may become conscious but may be kept from expression or execution, or they may become overt and may have to be dealt with after the fact. What differentiates the psychotic from the neurotic are the psychological (ego) processes whereby these impulses are dealt with.

The *neurotic* pattern of response to the impulses that threaten to emerge is to attempt to control them through a variety of available mental mechanisms and at the same time to conform to the standards and the demands of the external environment and maintain object relations. To the degree that these mechanisms are successful, the neurotic manages not to know that he has hostile, sadistic, murderous, sexually perverse, incestuous or other socially or personally unacceptable impulses, or he vigorously repudiates them should they become conscious. Should they actually become conscious or achieve expression as conscious thoughts, uttered words or acts, the neurotic is likely to be overwhelmed by guilt, shame, disgust, anxiety or other unpleasure affects. In contrast, the *psychotic* distorts or changes his psychic apprehension of the external environment and/or detaches himself from it so as to achieve one of several ends. One aim is to eliminate those elements in the environment which might be seen as sources of danger or frustration. This is accomplished by denial and by various distortions of perception. Another aim is to render the environment one in which the feared or forbidden impulses cannot be acted out. This too is done by distortion or by withdrawal. A third is to disown feared internal impulses by projecting them onto the environment, thereby externalizing and objectifying them. All of these maneuvers involve major departures from effective reality testing. To the extent that he succeeds in this turning away from or psychically changing his perception of the external environment, the psychotic renders innocuous his hostile, murderous, sadistic, incestuous, perverse or other impulses in that they are not acted out. Under such circumstances they may be tolerated in the form of conscious fantasies. Should such devices fail and the impulses break through nonetheless, the psychotic remains relatively unaware of the social and moral implications of his behavior, for which he may find a justification in some delusional system.

Thus, we may say that the *neurotic* retains relatively intact the functioning of reality testing and he only reduces his contact with objects and with the external environment within the relatively circumscribed sphere of the conflict. The *psychotic*, on the other hand, to a large degree both relinquishes reality testing function and reduces contact with external objects, who are perceived as dangerous, threatening or ungratifying.

Both the neurotic and the psychotic utilize regression, but the the neurotic does so to a less sweeping and extreme degree than does the psychotic. This difference is evident in the utilization of less primitive defense mechanisms of ego by the neurotic. Thus, the *neurotic* makes greater use of repression, displacement, identification, rationalization, isolation and undoing, all of which interfere less with reality appraisal while at the same time being more effective in controlling and keeping out of consciousness unwanted and feared psychic productions. The *psychotic* may also use these mechanisms, but he uses incorporation, introjection, denial and projection to a greater extent than does the neurotic. By the same token, the mode of thinking of the *neurotic* in general follows the rules of *secondary thought process*, with due regard for logical relationships. Hence, judgment and the interpretation of reality remain intact, except in the area of the conflict, in which some defect may be present. The thinking of the *psychotic*, on the other hand, is more characteristic of *primary process thinking*, marked by condensation, symbolization, tolerance of contradictions and disregard for the restrictions and requirements of temporal, spatial, causal and other logical relationships. (See Chapters XIV, XVII and XXII.) Here, incidentally, we may see a reappearance of some of the misapprehensions of the environment characteristic of the infant before objectification is achieved. (See Chapter VIII.)

The difference in degree of regression is also evident in the nature of the object relations and the character of intrapsychic object and self representations. In general, the *neurotic* has been more successful in establishing an identity than has the psychotic (Chapters XVI and XVII). Further, in the *neurotic* relatively clear distinction is maintained between psychic self and psychic object, but object choice is limited by the persistence of unresolved conflict with early (childhood) objects. The neurotic is therefore attracted to external objects who unconsciously are perceived in the same terms as were the childhood objects and with whom he becomes enmeshed in a repetition of the same unresolved conflicts as existed with the earlier objects (*transference*). The *psychotic* also is involved in conflictful transference relationships, but, in contrast to the neurotic, he has been less successful in achieving a clear delineation between psychic self and psychic objects, the boundaries between which are fluid or even at times nonexistent. Hence, external objects not only are confused with childhood objects but also are inadequately differentiated from the self. This constitutes another deficiency in reality testing. In addition, such confusion of psychic objects with psychic self is responsible for the uncertainty of the psychotic as to whether thoughts and feelings originate from the environment or from within his mind and for the delusions of bodily change that occur so commonly in the psychotic. Such gross disturbances in the intrapsychic representation of self and object are also reflected in the great difficulty experienced by the psychotic in establishing relationships with environmental objects, whom he confuses with earlier objects as well as with the self. The difficulty in maintaining boundaries between self and object is responsible for a fear of close personal relationships, in which the psychotic may find it difficult to maintain his tenuous identity and may experience a feeling of being overwhelmed, engulfed or swallowed up by the external object. At times, the psychotic literally is unable to establish whether thoughts, fantasies or actions are his own or those of an external object. Similarly, he has difficulty appreciating the individuality and needs of the other person, since these are perceived primarily in terms of his own intrapsychic experience of the moment. On the other hand, the psychotic may be more perceptive of certain unconscious motivations of others, a phenomenon which may be due to a greater sensitivity to nonverbal expression; some psychotics react more to how the other person behaves than to what he says and therefore accurately sense ambivalent attitudes.

The neurotic and the psychotic differ also in their manifestations and expressions of drive activity. In the *neurotic* they are more organized, restrained and object-directed. Even when his drives are derived from relatively primitive, infantile sources, they are kept from the conscious awareness of the neurotic, being disguised and changed so as to render them more acceptable to the self and to the environment. In general, naked drive activity is inhibited and is replaced by substitute mental processes or acts, in the form of obsessions, compulsions, phobias, conversion symptoms (Chapter XXXII), etc., which include both the disguised drive and the psychic process inhibiting its overt expression. The *psychotic*, on the other hand, is more prone to exhibit drive activity in a relatively primitive, archaic and undisguised form, though usually in a sporadic, disorganized and ineffectual manner. It may occasionally take the form of violent acts or crude sexual behavior, but more often it is manifest in the content of verbal expression (fantasy) or in activities which are largely self-directed (narcissistic) and which to only a small degree constitute effective interactions with environmental objects. Indeed, one major impairment of the psychotic is his inability effectively to consummate drive activity with objects.

Affects per se do not differentiate the neurotic from the psychotic. Any type of affective expression may be experienced and manifested. In general, the intensity of the signal-scanning affects of unpleasure correlates with the relative success (in maintaining psychological compensation, a dynamic steady state) of ego mechanisms or of supporting factors in the environment. (See also Chapters XIV, XVIII, XXXII and XXXIII.) The more effective such influences, whether consonant with neurotic or psychotic patterns, the less intense is the experience and expression of unpleasure affects. On the other hand, as mentioned under phenomonological considerations, the affective expression of the *psychotic* is more likely to be, or to appear to an observer to be, inappropriate in intensity, quality and timing than is that of the *neurotic*. In part this reflects the fact that affect expression, like other behavior, is more divorced from the conditions of external reality in the psychotic than in the neurotic, and therefore it makes less "sense" to the observer, who is operating on different logical premises than is the psychotic.

Such basic distinctions between the neurotic and the psychotic hold true regardless of whether the provoking stress is psychological or whether it is physical, affecting the brain. If it is physical, we assume that interference with brain function somehow alters the effectiveness of the ego processes of control and defense whereby intrapsychic conflict is being handled. This weakening of ego, organically produced, reduces the ability of the person to deal effectively with previously controlled impulses, which may then be responded to by devices either neurotic or psychotic in character.

The various subcategories of neurosis and psychosis will not be discussed here. The reader is referred to the standard texts of clinical psychiatry for descriptions of the neurotic syndromes of conversion hysteria, anxiety hysteria, obsessive-compulsive neurosis, hypo-chondriasis, depression, traumatic neurosis and mixed neurosis, and for descriptions of the psychotic syndromes of schizophrenia, paranoia, hysterical psychosis, depression, mania and hypomania, delirium, dementia and other organic states. Some of the interrelationships between neurotic, psychotic and other patterns are discussed further in the balance of this chapter and in Chapters XXXII and XXXIII.

CHARACTER DISORDER

Character disorder refers to aspects of psychiatric illness which in certain respects overlap the other categories, since some type of charac-terological defect is present in or antedates the development of most psychiatric disorders. As discussed earlier, a person's character structure defines his more or less consistent, habitual ways of thinking, feeling and behaving (Chapter XXX). In genetic-dynamic terms it describes the set of attitudes and mechanisms habitually adopted by the person's ego to deal with instinctual forces, to assure satisfaction, to reconcile conflicts and to achieve adjustment within a particular interpersonal and social environment. It is the more stable and cohesive part of the personality and that part of the personality which allows an individual to be characterized in adjectival terms. When a person is exposed to stress his defensive and adjustive set is put under strain. If the stress and the latent intrapsychic conflicts activated thereby cannot be coped with within the framework of his established character structure, the essential cohesiveness of this structure is disrupted, resulting in an exaggeration of some of the already present defense mechanisms or the recruitment of new ones. Commonly the predisposition to psychiatric illness is already evident in the premorbid character structure. In any case, when pre-existing character structure no longer effectively serves its function, some illness (neurosis, psychosis, perversion, addiction, an organic process, etc.) may eventuate.

The character structure of a particular person is not easily defined; certainly it is difficult to draw the line between a character disorder and the wide range of character, temperament and personality that underlie the individuality of human beings. In general, *character disorder* is marked not only by a greater degree of rigidity and inflexibility of the mental mechanisms but also by their lesser over-all effectiveness in maintaining adjustment and assuring further development. This may reflect the magnitude and nature of the unresolved intrapsychic conflicts and the range of psychological devices available to cope with them during the critical years of childhood. Since the self-image includes character structure in an over-all sense, a person generally sees the behavioral devices making up his character as "natural," as part of his immutable self. He may or may not be satisfied or pleased with his own character, but he experiences it as syntonic, as belonging. This is no less true of character disorder than of character structure in general. Hence, although among character disorders are included a wide range of character structures which either limit an individual's range of adjustment and growth and/or involve him in various types of antisocial, asocial or dysocial acting out behavior, the underlying structure is not experienced by him as alien.

There is no simple classification of character disorders. Some include ego patterns that in general correspond to those found in particular neuroses or psychoses and hence are called *neurotic* or *psychotic character disorders*. These differ from the corresponding neurosis or psychosis in that they represent relatively more successful modes of adjustment for the individual, at least in terms of his comfort. In contrast to neurosis or psychosis, they do not include symptoms and hence are not so much experienced as a source of suffering by the patient, other than to the degree that he is dissatisfied with his performance or its consequences. Under stress the neurotic or psychotic character may decompensate, in which case more frankly neurotic or psychotic symptoms may emerge. Other types of character disorder are distinguished by characteristic ways of seeking or achieving drive satisfaction, of object relating and of dealing with the external environment. Some can be described only in terms of an exaggeration of certain traits, such as angry, bitter, misanthropic, jealous, passive, greedy, stubborn, etc. In general, character disorders are not viewed by the environment as pathological, but rather as encompassing the range of character types typical of the human race. People generally deal with them in terms of value judgments. The concept of character disorder and its relations to other categories of psychopathology can best be clarified by presenting some of the better defined types.

Neurotic character disorder and its relation to *neurosis* may be illustrated by contrasting the *obsessive-compulsive character** with the

---

* Also called anal character. (See Chapter IX.)

obsessive-compulsive neurosis. The former is marked by traits of meticulousness, scrupulousness, indecisiveness, neatness, orderliness, punctuality, over-intellectualization and inhibition of emotional expression. These traits are *ego-syntonic,* meaning that they are felt by the person to be natural and appropriate, if not actually desirable. To others the obsessive-compulsive character seems to be a cautious, conscientious, precise, dependable, unusually hard-working person who, however, is reserved and emotionally restricted in his human relations. In many spheres of activity these obviously are highly desirable traits, and indeed it is not uncommon for the obsessive-compulsive character to gravitate to occupational roles in which such traits are valued and useful. What differentiates the obsessive-compulsive character from a more mature character is the rigidity of these patterns. The more mature person has the capability to behave in this manner, but he is not obliged to. He can be precise, punctual, thorough, well-controlled and neat when the occasion demands that he be, and he can make the judgment as to when this is the appropriate behavior. The obsessive-compulsive person, in contrast, is not free to behave differently, and he feels discomfort if he is not able to maintain such standards. This is well illustrated by the housewife who has to keep her house spotlessly clean, not because it is socially, esthetically or hygienically desirable to do so, but because she feels uncomfortable if she does not. She does not gain pleasure and satisfaction from having a neat, clean house, but rather suffers distress when it is not so. Further, her never-ending battle against dirt and disorder takes precedence over other matters; she cannot play or indulge herself until all her work is complete, even if it means staying up late at night.

Among persons with the obsessive-compulsive character, we find an exaggerated, unconscious concern about aggressive and sexual impulses, which are dealt with by reaction-formation and the application of vigorous control of themselves and of the environment. Dirt and disorder are experienced as symbols of these forbidden and feared impulses and are dealt with accordingly. As long as such people are able to keep rein over their own impulses and over the environment by such controlling behavior (which incidentally also has the asset of being socially acceptable and reasonably effective) and can do so without significant discomfort, they remain in the category of *character disorder.* But should for one reason or another these devices prove inadequate, they may be replaced by true compulsive rituals, such as repetitive handwashing, counting or checking the gas jet or water faucet. Such behavior not only interferes seriously with living but also is recognized to be irrational. In addition, such a person may now to his great distress find himself powerless to prevent the intrusion into consciousness of crude, sadistic, obscene, blasphemous or other objectionable ideas or fantasies (obsessions), or he may be assailed by obsessive doubting of a paralyzing degree. His condition has now evolved into an *obsessive-compulsive neurosis*, in which the compulsions, obsessions, haunting indecision, and the unpleasant feelings associated therewith, as well as the sense of a relative loss of control (decrease in ego autonomy) all are experienced as *ego-alien*. The patient now is aware of being ill or disturbed. Relatively speaking, the manifest neurosis is a less successful level of adjustment than is the underlying character disorder. (See also Chapter XXX.)

Essentially the same principles hold in respect to the relationship of the *psychotic character disorders* to the manifest psychoses. A *paranoid character* is consistently aloof, hypersensitive, suspicious, vigilant, hypercritical, blaming of others and given to viewing the environment as hostile and unfriendly. Under stress such a person may develop a full-blown *paranoid psychosis*, marked by frank delusions of persecution, hallucinations, ideas of reference and other disorders in thinking. As a paranoid character, he may be viewed by his associates as eccentric, cranky and difficult to get along with, but as a paranoid psychotic he more likely will be regarded as mentally disturbed.

Another group of character disorders clusters about particular conflict situations and characteristic attempts at their solution, but they do not necessarily correspond to any particular neurosis or psychosis. These are illustrated by such disorders as the *masochistic character*, in which a person deals with his own aggression and the guilt evoked thereby by means of an exaggerated need to suffer and hence a typically passive, long-suffering, martyred attitude, inviting his counterpart, the person with a *sadistic character* to utilize him as an object of aggression. The masochist invites hardship, suffering, defeat and humiliation, tends to be prone to accident, illness and surgery, and commonly suffers pain as a psychogenic symptom. In brief, his over-all behavior and mode of adjustment are to an overriding degree determined by his need to control aggression and expiate guilt. The behavior of the complementary sadist is circumscribed by an intense need to discharge aggression, which for him takes priority over other human needs. Some individuals oscillate between these two poles and are called *sadomasochistic*. Many other character traits determined by persistent unresolved childhood conflicts may be identified. Some of these correspond to the affects of partial and fused drives, discussed briefly in Chapter XVIII.

Still another type of character disorder, marked by a more distinct tendency to act out against the environment, is variously designated as an *impulsive, acting out, psychopathic* or *sociopathic character disorder*. With this character structure there is a tendency to deal with all problems, whether they derive from intrapsychic conflict or from the environment, as though they are located in the external environment and can be solved by acting against and changing the environment (the *allo-plastic* solution). Disorders of this type are characterized by a relative lack of control over drive, an inability to delay satisfaction and a disregard for the needs and standards of the objects through whom gratification is sought. Thus, these individuals give the appearance of being impulsive, hedonistic, asocial, antisocial and without conscience. They are often involved in behavior which borders on criminality or actually is criminal. Their apparent freedom to indulge themselves is deceptive, for to a large degree this behavior proves to be unrewarding. Their short-term ("pleasure principle") perspective and/or their unconscious sense of guilt repeatedly leads them into situations in which they are hurt or punished. There is some evidence that a biologically determined hyperactivity or hypermotility, a tendency to interact vigorously with environment, is a predisposing factor for this kind of development. Under favorable circumstances such tendencies are perhaps successfully channelled into more socially acceptable and useful activities, even though they may have been manifested as quasi-delinquent behavior in childhood and early adolescence. But when life circumstances are such that major intrapsychic conflicts derived from infancy and childhood remain unresolved, this active tendency is reflected in a preference for vigorous and violent outwardly directed activities as means of satisfying the persistent unresolved needs of infancy and early childhood. Though these efforts fail, the operation of the repetition compulsion perpetuates the pattern.

Thus, the impulsive (psychopathic, sociopathic) person deals essentially with the same types of unresolved conflicts that are found in the neurotic or psychotic, but utilizes an alloplastic rather than autoplastic approach. Intolerant of frustration or deprivation, he tries to force the environment to satisfy his needs and to relieve his distress. In this respect his behavior is reminiscent of that of the small child who brooks no delay and makes obvious that he wants what he wants when he wants it. This type of person typically functions better in (and therefore seeks) social situations in which such behavior is more acceptable or even desirable. But by the same token, when external circumstances successfully block acting out, he may decompensate psychologically and become more disorganized, psychotic, depressed, suicidal or even physically sick.

In contrast to the impulsive, acting out people are those who are inhibited and hypoactive, individuals who either have failed to develop some of the more mature ways of interrelating with the environment or who for various reasons have had to inhibit excessively expression of impulses. Such persons may appear inhibited in their sexual and social relations; they seem to lack initiative and zest for living, are easily fatigued or give up in the face of obstacles, are followers rather than leaders.

The reader is referred to a clinical text for descriptions of other varieties of character disorder.

SEXUAL PERVERSIONS AND SEXUAL DISORDERS

This phenomenological behavioral category includes all varieties of deviant sexual behavior, such as homosexuality, exhibitionism, transvestitism, pederasty, voyeurism, sodomy, fetishism, sadism, masochism and oral, anal and other pregenital perversions, as well as certain other sexual disorders such as promiscuity, impotence and frigidity.

As types of behavior, the sexually perverse activities may occur sporadically among otherwise healthy people, neurotics, psychotics and those with character disorders, or they may represent preferred or compelling modes of sexual behavior dominating the way of life of the individual. All such patterns of sexual behavior have their origin in the modes of sexual expression and experience common to infancy and childhood, prior to the development of mature genital sexuality, which were discussed in Part I of this book. To varying degrees and in various forms such polymorphously perverse sexuality persists in everyone in the form of unconscious fantasy and drive structures and of course constitutes a major part of the drive component of a person's residual unresolved intrapsychic conflicts. The psychic attempts to cope unconsciously with such impulses make up a considerable part of the phenomena of neurosis, psychosis and character disorder. At times in any of these conditions the defenses against the perverse impulses may for one reason or another be evaded or overcome, whereupon the perverse impulse erupts as a conscious fantasy or is acted upon. Such an event is almost always followed by intense shame, guilt, anxiety or other unpleasant affect and by intensification of old or by development of new neurotic or psychotic defenses. These, then, are examples of sexual perversion resulting from temporary failure of pre-existing neurotic, psychotic or characterological modes of adjustment. For such people the sexual perverse fantasies or acts are felt to be ego-alien, or at least are ambivalently regarded.

Among another group, the deviant sexual behavior is experienced as desirable and appropriate, even when it is known to be socially disapproved. Some of these persons may also manifest other traits characteristic of neurosis, psychosis or character disorder, but the particular perverse sexual behavior indulged in is not included among the drive activities that the ego has decreed must be repressed, altered or avoided. On the contrary, the perverse sexual activity is used both as a means of defense, whereby other dangerous impulses can be replaced, and as a means of object relating, whereby some type of sexual gratification and object relationship can be achieved. This combination of successful defense and drive gratification confers upon the sexual perversion its compelling quality, even in the face of social disapproval. It not only averts something psychically conceived as dangerous or disagreeable, but at the same time it affords pleasure in its own right. Hence, in contrast to the neurotic symptom or to the episodic perverse act, it is felt as *ego syntonic.*

Clinically this type of sexual perversion is characterized by an impelling need and preference for sexual activity which is pregenital in aim and/or is performed with homosexual, immature or nonhuman objects. Social disapproval is either ignored or rationalized or is regarded as a risk worth taking. At worst it is seen as a lesser risk than that which is being struggled with intrapsychically. For example, homosexual activity not only may constitute a means of object relating and sexual gratification, but also may serve as a means of avoiding castration anxiety, an unconscious residue of childhood fears of the dangerous castrating (or castrated) women or the rivalrous father. The homosexual man finds it safer to avoid women, who may castrate or who may remind him of a penisless (castrated) state, or he finds it safer to submit passively and sexually to a man than to compete with him heterosexually.

The problems posed by this type of compelling and preferred sexual perversion are of course much determined by the prevailing attitudes of the culture in which the so-called sexual deviant operates and lives.

Other sexual disorders, such as impotence, premature ejaculation, frigidity, dyspareunia, compulsive masturbation and promiscuity, to mention a few, are symptoms and not syndromes. They too may be observed in all categories of psychological illness as well as in persons who in other respects are not readily classified in any such category. They may be traced to inhibition of genital sexual drives by unresolved conflict or to an epigenetic failure of genital sexual maturity caused by inadequate stimulation during the critical periods of libido development. The latter view has found some support in experiments with animals. (See reference to Harlow in Chapter XXVIII.)

ADDICTION

The syndromes of addiction to drugs and to alcohol comprise another behavioral, phenomenological category of disturbed behavior. Habitual use of alcohol or drugs for longer or shorter periods may be found in any of the diagnostic categories already described. The basic feature common to all cases of addiction is the ability of the chemical agent to relieve, at least temporarily, emotional distress, whether this relief results from the pharmacological action of the substance, the psychological significance of taking or receiving it or the support provided by the social structure countenancing the use of the substance, or any combination of these. A secondary feature common to addiction is the fact that many of the chemical substances used produce physical dependence and/or organic damage of varying degrees. In general, the person who utilizes alcohol or a drug as a crutch to relieve discomfort, to facilitate social relations or to achieve some degree of oblivion from a painful reality does so in spite of (but sometimes because of) knowledge of its ultimate harmful effects. Further, he comes to depend on it and cannot do without it. Unusually intolerant of discomfort to begin with, he responds to the return of distress as the drug action wears off or as the unpleasant withdrawal symptoms of physical dependence develop by taking more of the agent and thereby contributes to the establishment of a vicious cycle.

Typically, the potentially addictive person betrays an exaggerated need to be dependent upon the environment for supplies. He has a limited capacity for gratifying object relationships and a low tolerance for frustration or discomfort. These are partly, but not completely, *oral character traits*. Such underlying traits may also be found among certain neurotic, psychotic or characterological disorders, such as hysteria, some depressions, hypomania, dependent characters, etc., and it is among such disorders that addiction is most commonly found. On the other hand, there are other conditions in which addiction is uncommon, such as the obsessive-compulsive character or neurosis, in which a person fears the loss of control, and certain phobic and paranoid states, in which patients fear to be poisoned or rendered helpless to enemies.

The consistency with which certain psychological features occur among addiction-prone individuals also accounts for the fair degree of consistency of the clinical syndromes which commonly develop in those who have been chronically addicted, notably the alcoholics. The clinical features of such syndromes as delirium tremens, Korsakoff psychosis, alcoholic hallucinosis and alcoholic deterioration are determined both by the operation of certain psychological features common to those who are prone to alcoholism and by the direct effects of alcohol on the brain itself.

AFFECTIVE DISORDERS

The predominance of certain affects in the clinical picture of certain syndromes has naturally led to their being designated affective disorders. In general, these syndromes cluster about the two primary affects of unpleasure, anxiety and depression-withdrawal, and their derivatives.

With better understanding of the role of anxiety as an affect, the tendency to use the word "anxiety" as an adjective in the designation of syndromes has considerably diminished. For example, one does not often any longer hear such a diagnosis as "anxiety hysteria," though as a convenient descriptive term it still has some heuristic value. Instead, anxiety is more generally recognized as a relatively nonspecific reflection of the failure of defenses, an indication of a phase of psychological decompensation. It ranges from anxiety reactions in response to such everyday experiences as examinations, new or unknown situations, ordinary dangers, etc. (which reflect anticipation of a danger or the risk of possible decompensation in the future rather than actual decompensation), to the decompensation of a previously well compensated but pathological state. Thus, diffuse, generalized anxiety may emerge during the development or course of neurosis or psychosis when the mental mechanisms characteristic of the neurotic or psychotic state have not yet achieved or are failing to maintain an adequate adjustment. Similarly, anxiety may emerge when the processes underlying a character disorder, a sexual perversion or the use of drug prove ineffective, or when an organic process affecting the brain weakens ego defense mechanisms. Accordingly, the presence of generalized anxiety or the occurrence of anxiety attacks is indicative not of any one clinical entity but rather of a failure of the processes maintaining adjustment, whatever they may be. Diffuse (or "free-floating") anxiety may usher in, or appear during the course of, a psychosis as well as a neurosis. It may also be the first indication of the development of an organic disease in the brain, or anywhere else in the body for that matter. It may anticipate and exaggerate an impending threat, such as surgery, an examination, a new job, etc., or it may occur in the course of any other type of psychological abnormality.

Because the psychopathological disorders constitute attempts at adjustment of a lesser order of effectiveness, it is logical to anticipate that they will include a much greater readiness for anxiety. Indeed, chronic, low-grade anxiety is often in the background, and is being kept in control by neurotic, psychotic, characterological or other devices which reduce but do not eliminate this constant undercurrent. The clinical diagnosis is based on the over-all pattern, not on the presence and magnitude of anxiety, which is mainly an index of how effective this pattern is in achieving adjustment and/or comfort for the individual. (See also Chapters XXXII and XXXIII.)

The experience of anxiety may at times be linked to very explicit situations, either external circumstances or fantasies. This is most typically illustrated by the *phobia,* in which through the ego mechanisms of projection and displacement an internal danger (an unconscious fantasy) is externalized and located in the environment as a specific danger situation to be avoided. To the extent that the person is able to avoid that danger situation, whether it be crowds, a closed space, an animal, etc., he is able to keep at a low level or even eliminate anxiety, though at the price of an appreciable restriction of function, activity and gratification. The *compulsive ritual,* through the ego mechanisms of isolation and undoing, may also serve to reduce anxiety, as illustrated by the patient who is conscious of emerging anxiety when he does not carry out a ritual or who feels that he is warding off some external danger, as from dirt, germs or poison, when performing the ritual. Although both the phobia and the compulsive ritual more commonly are manifestations of neurosis, they may also be found in psychosis. The differentiation rests in part on the appraisal of this symptom by the patient. The neurotic, even though he feels obliged to respect the requirements of the phobia or compulsion, nonetheless recognizes that it is unrealistic. He refers to it as "silly" or "irrational," and wishes to be relieved of the necessity to give in to it. The psychotic, in contrast, sees the external danger as real and considers his attempts to avoid or counteract it as appropriate.

The syndromes of *depression* reflect the ubiquity and the variety of expression of the affective responses to loss, actual or threatened, real or fantasied. As another basic type of psychological response, depressive symptoms, like anxiety, occur through the whole range of psychological disorders, as well as being part of everyday experience in response to the vicissitudes of life. Occasionally they so dominate the clinical picture as to constitute its identifying feature. Depression includes the complex of feelings associated with object loss and with giving up, as described in the discussions of depression-withdrawal, sadness, helplessness and hopelessness in Chapters XIV and XVIII. Depressive symptoms, therefore, are more common when developmental factors and current circumstances have lowered the capacity to cope with object loss. As with anxiety, the presence and intensity of such affects reflect the effectiveness of psychic and psychosocial processes, in this case in maintaining satisfactory object relations, avoiding object loss and regulating the intrapsychic relationship of psychic objects and psychic self. Again, the basic disorder may be neurotic, psychotic, characterological or organic, or it may not fit clearly into any of these categories. In this sense, depressive manifestations may constitute symptoms of any of the nosological categories of psychological disorder. They reflect the greater susceptibility to object loss of the persons involved. They also commonly occur as part of the symptoms of any organic illness, often manifest in such terms as fatigue, exhaustion, lack of energy, etc.

Because so many factors (in the course of development) can interfere with satisfying object relations, many persons are especially prone to be deficient in their object-relating capacities and hence to be vulnerable to depression of major proportions, the nature of which is determined by the various factors involved in ego and superego development. At one end of the spectrum are the depressions characterized mainly by loneliness, sadness and helplessness, in which there is felt a great dependence on external objects as sources of supply. At the other end are the depressions marked by shame, guilt and hopelessness, in which restrictive influences of ego ideal and superego sharply limit object relationships to particular types of individuals. (See Chapters XVIII and XXVII.) The lonely, sad and helpless people are vulnerable to object loss because their needs from and demands on external objects are too great and therefore are not readily fulfilled. Those who feel shame, guilt and hopelessness are also vulnerable to object loss because their demands on and requirement of themselves are too great and therefore they readily judge themselves to be inadequate or bad and consequently unworthy to receive what they need from objects. Such depression-prone conditions may take the form of neurosis, psychosis or character disorder, and attempts may be made to alleviate or ward off depression by the use of drugs or alcohol, by acting out or by deviant sexual behavior. They may also culminate in other physical illness. (See Chapters XXXII, XXXIII.) The criteria already advanced are necessary to differentiate depressions which develop along these lines.

Sometimes the defense against loss and depression involves a denial of the feelings of depression, if not a denial of the loss as well. Under such circumstances the pattern of reaction is marked by the apparent opposite of depression. The patient claims and manifests high good spirits, great optimism, overactivity, euphoria, invulnerability and grandiosity; he feels that he loves and is loved by everyone, that he is wealthy, powerful and influential, and that he has endless resources, which he squanders with reckless abandon. Such a pattern only thinly hides the underlying depression, with which it may abruptly be replaced. Such patterns, called hypomania or mania, depending on their degree, are usually clearly psychotic. Occasionally they may recur cyclically, alternating with depression, the so-called manic-depressive psychosis.

Anxiety and the affects of depression may both occur in the same illness, mixed or in rapid alternation. This is to be expected if affects do indeed reflect the changing economy of mental functioning. Thus, a patient who is fundamentally anxious may at the same time be retarded and depressed, and a depressed patient may be anxious or agitated.

THE ORGANIC BRAIN SYNDROMES

These have already been discussed in Chapters XXIX and XXX, to which the reader is referred. As previously emphasized, any type of pathological process affecting brain structure or metabolism is capable of producing an organic syndrome, but the psychological and behavioral characteristics of the syndrome are relatively independent of the nature of the organic process. The latter, however, may be expected to yield other clinical or laboratory data which serve to identify its nature, be it an infectious agent, a neoplasm, a vascular process, a toxic agent, or whatever.

When cerebral metabolism is interfered with transiently, the resulting syndrome, *delirium*, may be thought of as cerebral insufficiency in the same sense that we speak of transient, reversible disturbances in the metabolic competence of other organs, such as renal insufficiency, hepatic insufficiency or myocardial insufficiency. When structural damage takes place and neurons are destroyed, the resulting syndrome is largely irreversible, because of the low potential for regeneration of the nervous system. Such irreversible or progressive syndromes are called *dementia*. It should be emphasized that the irreversibility of the cellular damage does not mean that certain function previously served by the damaged neurons cannot be taken over by other units of the brain organization.

Delirium, dementia, temporal lobe syndromes and drug effects regularly produce certain psychological and behavioral consequences, as described in Chapter XXX, in the course of which any of the other nosological categories discussed in this chapter may be recognized. The patient with an organic syndrome may develop or intensify neurotic or psychotic patterns, may intensify certain character traits and weaken others, may engage in one or another perverse sexual act, may come to lean on alcohol or certain drugs, or may experience intensification of certain affects, such as anxiety, shame, guilt, helplessness, hopelessness, euphoria, rage, etc. All this, however, is but another way of saying that the organic processes affecting the brain have consequences which act as psychological stresses as well as directly damaging ego functions, opening up thereby the possibility of any type of psychological illness in the wake of the organic process.

Mental deficiency, presumably based on biological defects interfering with the development of the capacity to learn, may also be associated with any other type of psychiatric disorder.

* * * * * *

This catalogue provides only a rough classificatory scheme into which patterns of psychiatric illness may be fit. Many reaction patterns not only do not fit comfortably into any one category, but also shift, often rapidly, from one to another. More often than not, a single diagnosis is not possible. But this fluidity should not be grounds for discouragement. It is, after all, only in keeping with the fact that these are patterns of reaction to and attempts to maintain adjustment during stress. Indeed, considering the tremendous variability of the life circumstances, past and present, from individual to individual, it should perhaps occasion surprise that any consistent clinical syndromes can be identified. Some of the factors contributing to syndromes and categories were discussed in Chapter XXX. That relative consistency can be demonstrated, and the clinical evidence that no one individual is capable of every type of response, are strong evidence that there are indeed common factors underlying the tendency to develop one kind of pattern as compared to another. Some of these factors are perhaps biological, others extrabiological, and their identification is a pressing research task of psychiatry.

Further, it must be emphasized that there is a continuity between the relatively successful everyday response to stress and those responses which are traditionally designated as illness. From the institutional (rather than the scientific) perspective, the point at which an individual becomes a "patient" is determined by whatever it is in his social setting and background which leads him or his associates to think of "illness" and "medical care." This will vary greatly at different times and under different circumstances. Yet the awareness of stress, the development of an unpleasure affect, the appearance of "distress" signals, or the initiation of mental mechanisms or behavior to alleviate stress or an unpleasure affect, all are initial indications of a changing dynamic steady state not basically different whether the ultimate outcome is or is not successful or whether it falls into the conventional category of a "disease." This view has already been discussed in reference to grief (Chapter XXIV). Such behaviors as seeking out human contacts for help or succorance, avoiding human contacts that may be demanding or a source of conflict, seeking distraction or reassurance, or attempting to think it out, laugh it off, cry it out, walk it off, work it off or sleep it off—all are techniques of dealing with stress that are not ordinarily considered as expressions of illness, yet if they are persistent or in other ways are ineffective, they may merge into reactions commonly designated as neurosis, psychosis, etc. Some writers go so far as to question the usefulness of the traditional terms and to suggest instead a hierarchical classification based on the progressive degrees of failure of the regulatory and integrative functions of ego in response to stress (cf. Menninger[11]).

REFERENCES

1. Alexander, F. and Ross, H. (eds.): Dynamic Psychiatry. Chicago, University of Chicago Press, 1952.
2. Arieti, S. (ed.): American Handbook of Psychiatry. New York, Basic Books, 1959, vols. 1 and 2.
3. Bleuler, E. P.: Dementia Praecox or the Group of Schizophrenias. Translated by J. Zinkin. New York, International Universities Press, 1950.
4. Bleuler, E. P.: Textbook of Psychiatry. Translated by A. A. Brill. New York, The Macmillan Co., 1924; New York, Dover Publications, 1951.
5. Engel, G. L. and Romano, J.: Delirium, a Syndrome of Cerebral Insufficiency. J. Chron. Dis., 9:260, 1959.
6. Ewalt, J. R., Strecker, E. A. and Ebaugh, F. G.: Practical Clinical Psychiatry. 8th ed. New York, McGraw-Hill Book Co., 1957.
7. Fenichel, O.: The Psychoanalytic Theory of Neurosis. New York, W. W. Norton & Co., 1945.
8. Freud, S.: Inhibitions, Symptoms, and Anxiety (1915). In: Standard Edition of the Complete Psychological Works of Sigmund Freud, vol. XX. London, The Hogarth Press, 1959. p. 77.
9. Henderson, D., Gillespie, R. D. and Batchelor, I. R. C.: A Textbook of Psychiatry for Students and Practitioners. 8th ed. New York, Oxford University Press, 1956.
10. Hollender, M.: Ambulatory Schizophrenia. J. Chron. Dis., 9:249, 1959.
11. Menninger, K.: Psychological Aspects of the Organism under Stress. J. Am. Psychoanalyt. A., 2:67, 280, 1954.
12. Michaels, J.: Disorders of Character. Springfield, Illinois, Charles C Thomas, 1955.
13. Noyes, A. P. and Kolb, L. C.: Modern Clinical Psychiatry. 5th ed. Philadelphia, W. B. Saunders Co., 1958.
14. Wikler, A.: Opiate Addiction: Psychological and Neurophysiological Aspects in Relation to Clinical Problems. Springfield, Illinois, Charles C Thomas, 1952.

CHAPTER XXXII

SOMATIC CONSEQUENCES OF PSYCHOLOGICAL STRESS: I. COMPENSATED STATES; CONVERSION REACTIONS; PAIN

In the preceding chapters psychiatric disorders were presented in terms of disturbances in thinking, feeling, behavior and social relationships evoked by psychological stresses and/or by physical processes affecting the brain. The various factors predisposing to such derangements were considered mainly in terms of their effects on psychological and behavioral processes. Reference was made to somatic disturbances which may also be a part of such disorders, but full discussion of this aspect was deferred, not because somatic processes are uncommon or unimportant, but because the understanding of the genesis of the various somatic responses to psychological stress requires a perspective broader than the framework of psychiatric disease alone.

Ideally, the functions of the mental apparatus and central nervous system are not only to integrate and order mental and bodily activities so as to assure smooth and harmonious physiological function and the satisfaction of biological needs, but also to buffer the body against stress. This buffering action is achieved through the psychological and neural processing of the input from the body and from the external environment, sparing the body from the necessity to respond instantly to environmental changes and providing it with a system of warning signals intended to assure its integrity and well-being by anticipating dangerous situations. The mental apparatus may be regarded as optimally fulfilling its function when this biological end is achieved within the framework of effective, satisfying and productive psychological and social adjustment as well. Such a state is marked by general feelings of well-being, such as contentment, satisfaction, vigor, confidence, self-assurance, joy, etc. (i.e., the signal-scanning affects of pleasure, Chapter XVIII), and by smooth, integrated and appropriate psychosomatic interrelationships. Under such conditions, somatic processes, such as circulation, respiration, secretory and motor activity of the gut, secretion of hormones, the tone and movement of striated muscles, to mention but a few, are regulated and change according to the actual physical and metabolic needs of the body. The regulation of the internal milieu is achieved within a wide margin of safety, cellular repair and growth are adequately supported, and the neuromuscular system smoothly executes the requirements for action or change in position. No signals or warnings indicating the need for emergency defense or action of the body arise within the mental apparatus and therefore such biological emergency systems are not mobilized.

Such an ideal state of harmonious somatic function is maintained as long as no physical stress intervenes and as long as the mental apparatus copes with psychological stress in such a way that bodily defense mechanisms are not invoked and physiological functions continue to be adequately supported. But such success of the mental apparatus in resolving psychological stress without evoking somatic emergency systems is not necessarily accomplished without some deviation in psychological and social function or adjustment. Indeed, the mental mechanisms used and the behavior generated may not only be maladaptive, but may also satisfy the criteria for psychiatric disease, as outlined in Chapter XXXI. To the extent that this is the case, these represent psychopathological modes of adjustment without somatic involvement. For example, the person who responds by denial to the psychological stress of a death, simply behaving as if no death had occurred, even to the extent of hallucinating the dead person as being alive, succeeds in averting the entire sequence of psychological and somatic changes that ordinarily mark such an event. (See Chapters XXVI, XXVII and XXXIII.) Similarly, if a realistic external danger is successfully denied, the emergency bodily responses to protect against injury and to prepare for action will not take place. (See Chapter XXXIII.) This may place the person in jeopardy, and hence be a poor adjustment, but it "saves" him from psychological distress and from the associated emergency somatic response. (See Chapter XXXIII.) The phobic patient may be comfortable and free from anxiety as long as he respects the self-imposed limitations of the phobia, and the obsessive-compulsive person may feel well and function adequately within the restrictions imposed by his rigid defenses of isolation, undoing, reaction formation and intellectualizing. Certain types of atoning or self-effacing behavior may reduce shame and guilt, thereby minimizing the somatic changes ordinarily accompanying these unpleasant affects.

All such conditions, however, involving as they do compromise solutions, seriously curtail the range and scope of the individual's function and activity and, accordingly, his capacity to cope with further increments of stress. In addition, the very nature of these psychopathological adjustments serve to render stressful much that would ordinarily not be so. Hence, for many reasons the effectiveness of such devices in protecting the body against stress is decidedly limited. Once adjustment fails, whether it be the more encompassing adjustment of the healthy person or the marginal, compromise adjustment of the psychologically sick person, various emergency somatic processes to cope with stress are invariably mobilized. These include the biochemical and physiological components of the affects, that is, the bodily part of the reaction to the perception of a danger of injury, depletion or failure of need gratification. (See also Chapters VII, XIV, XVIII, XXV and XXXIII.) In essence, they indicate that psychological stress is no longer being adequately contained at the mental level and is being communicated to the body. This may be called a state of *psychological decompensation*, whether the preceding state had been one of health or psychiatric disease.

The concepts of psychological compensation and decompensation define two major pathways determining somatic changes or symptoms in response to psychological stress. In the psychologically compensated state psychological stress is effectively dealt with intrapsychically and/or by behavioral processes; therefore the various biological defense systems, local as well as general, are not activated. But it can happen that the mental mechanisms and behavior utilized to achieve this nonetheless result either in the body being in some way subjected to physical stress or in the body being utilized psychologically in such a way as to simulate somatic disability (the conversion reactions).

In the psychologically decompensated state, on the other hand, whether developing in a previously healthy person or in a person who has been sick psychiatrically or in any other way, psychological stress acts to mobilize biological systems for the defense and protection of the body. The somatic reactions characterizing the decompensated states will be discussed in Chapter XXXIII.

In clinical practice there is considerable overlap between these two categories. In the face of chronic or recurring stresses, psychological compensation, a relative state at best, is not easily maintained. Hence it is usual to see transitions between relatively compensated and decompensated states as circumstances and the adequacy of ego defenses and controls changes. Further, as has already been emphasized, a successful reaction to one stress often is accomplished at the cost of compromising defenses against another stress or of exposure to new stresses. Therefore, in respect to the resulting somatic patterns, it is not at all uncommon to see more than one pattern at the same time. This will be considered further in Chapter XXXIII. Nonetheless, for purposes of clarity it is useful to deal with each of these categories as if they were indeed independent.

SOMATIC PHENOMENA IN COMPENSATED STATES

Psychological Compensation Which is Somatically Maladaptive

There are many ways in which psychological or behavioral devices which provide or are intended to provide psychological compensation and to afford some peace of mind lead to somatic changes because of ill-serving somatic needs. In some instances the devices used incidentally expose the body to damage and in some instances pain or injury is solicited for psychological ends. These include the use of alcohol or narcotics, self-inflicted injuries or mutilations, deliberate or unconscious suicide attempts, and the many situations in which the body is mortified to relieve or avert mental pain and suffering and to alleviate guilt. Especially important among the latter are certain unconsciously motivated accidents and the soliciting of surgery, as well as deliberate exposure to physical dangers or disregard of elemental needs. In any such situation the body is unnecessarily exposed to physical stresses and may be damaged accordingly.

Injury may also be suffered in situations in which the operation of a physiological system serving a biological need is diverted to serve purely psychological ends. Under such circumstances the requirements for physiological homeostasis are inadequately served. Thus, for example, appetite or eating may be used as a means of dealing with psychological needs and thereby become divorced from its primary nutritional function. Under such conditions persons may undereat, overeat or have bizarre food requirements unrelated to the nutritional patterns of hunger or satiety.[7a] Derangements in appetite or eating thus may serve such psychological ends as to compensate for feelings of loss or loneliness, to cope with oral aggressive or oral sadistic impulses, or to mediate oral sexual ideas. The more effective the eating behavior is in coping with the underlying psychological stress and in achieving psychological compensation, the greater is the likelihood that such untoward consequences as starvation, nutritional deficiency or obesity will ensue. Similar results may ensue from such misuse of other physiological systems.

Somatic systems may also be abused, as when certain false concepts of the body and its functions are used as means of dealing with psychological stress. Thus, psychological feelings of inner badness may be dealt with literally by the excessive use of cathartics and enemas, sometimes leading to severe electrolyte depletion. Sexual or aggressive feelings, regarded as dirty, may be combated by compulsive hand washing, sometimes resulting in a dermatitis of the hands.

Finally, coping with psychological stress may so distract one that other stresses or needs are overlooked. This may become particularly serious in the psychotic, whose failure of reality testing and detachment from objects render him poorly equipped to cope with the vicissitudes of the environment. The catatonic schizophrenic, mute, motionless, barely responsive, becomes largely dependent on others to meet his most elemental needs.

Somatic damage or disease developing under such circumstances may be regarded as remote, often fortuitous, consequences of psychological or behavioral processes which are inadequate to secure the body against injury. Such disorders may not be regarded as psychogenic in origin, even though psychological processes have played a role in the eventual outcome. Thus, although there is a major psychogenic component in the etiology of alcoholism, cirrhosis of the liver is more directly a complication of the ingestion of alcohol, psychological factors being only remote influences. This is in contrast to the conversion reactions, which are truly psychogenic and which we shall now discuss.

Conversion Reactions

Conversion reactions comprise a major category of psychogenic somatic disturbances. They represent a psychological means of dealing with stress which makes use of the fact that it is possible to express ideas symbolically through body activities or sensations. The gesture is a familiar example of how a body movement may be used to communicate an idea or a wish and to relieve tension. The conversion reaction, however, typically occurs when the wish, idea or fantasy in question not only cannot be consciously expressed but cannot even be consciously acknowledged. Under such circumstances the idea may achieve expression in the form of a body activity or sensation which symbolically represents the idea in question and yet at the same time effectively prevents it from being acted upon. As a means of dealing with psychological stress and resolving intrapsychic conflict, such symbolic use of the body replaces both action and conscious cognition, both of which are felt as threatening. By this means psychological compensation is maintained but at the expense of some abnormal utilization of the body part selected for this purpose. The result is a somatic symptom based on psychological misuse of the body part, not on disease of the part so involved. Physical examination, therefore, demonstrates no organic defect.

Conversion reactions may occur under a wide variety of stressful circumstances and in persons of the most varied psychological characteristics, from the essentially healthy to the psychotic. They are most common in and characteristic of hysteria, a condition in which there is a predilection toward use of the body for expression of feelings, wishes and ideas, but it is not correct to equate the conversion reaction with hysteria, as has been customary in the past.

The use of the body as a means of expression and communication is already well known to us as one aspect of affects; indeed, this is the primary mode whereby the infant communicates needs and dangers internally and to the environment. (See Chapters XIV, XVIII and XXII.) Such bodily affect patterns are phylogenetically determined and hence are common to the species. Ontogenetically, affective expression in bodily terms precedes cognitive development. It is only in the course of further maturation of the mental apparatus that affects achieve psychic representation and attain the status of intrapsychic warning and monitoring systems, indicating the status of self and objects. The conversion process becomes possible only after such a level of cognitive development has been reached, namely, after drives and affects have come to be represented in the form of wishes, ideas or fantasies (derivative drives, Chapter XXII). As long as they are not blocked by intrapsychic conflict, such derivative drives are accessible to consciousness in the cognitive form of wishes, ideas or fantasies which may be expressed as spoken words or in action. But if they are blocked, an alternative mode of expression, the conversion reaction, is still possible. In this process the forbidden wish is kept out of consciousness but at the same time is translated ("converted"), not into words, but into some bodily activity or sensation which suitably represents it in a symbolic form. It is a token gesture, so to speak, which substitutes for the real thing. It symbolically represents not only the forbidden or feared wish but also the counter idea, that is, both the "I wish to . . ." and the "but I shouldn't." In this manner both conscious awareness and action are blocked and the conscience is appeased. If the conversion is successful, both expression and discharge are achieved in a token fashion, psychological compensation is maintained, and no generalized unpleasure affect reaction takes place.

A useful analogy for the understanding of the conversion reaction is the game of charades. In this game one is asked to translate a verbal (cognitive) message into bodily terms, as pantomime, gestures or other movements. These are meant symbolically to represent the cognitive content that the player has in mind. His first effort is to contrive some body activity which has this particular meaning to him (comparable to the communication to the self), and he hopes this will have the same meaning to the other players (the "objects"). The players, however, whose information is limited to the manifest behavior, may have difficulty in resolving the ambiguity of the communication, since in the game there are only a limited number of bodily actions available to express a great variety of ideas.

In this analogy to the conversion reaction, the message being communicated in the game corresponds to the unconscious wish or fantasy which cannot be expressed or acted on, and the charade corresponds to the conversion manifestation. The conversion reaction differs from the game of charades, however, in that neither the sender nor the person for whom the message is meant (the object) consciously knows its real meaning. Thus, the person with a conversion reaction manifests or experiences some bodily reaction, the real meaning of which is not consciously known to him, though unconsciously it satisfies a need and avoids a conflict by substituting a symbolic gesture or sensation for a desired but forbidden or feared thought or action. The net result is a physical symptom which to varying degrees is disabling and which thereby also effectively precludes entertaining or acting on the forbidden wish. This is generally experienced by the subject and is communicated to others as some indication of physical illness, since it is always manifest in physical terms. Being physically ill also confers certain advantages and provides certain gratifications through the responses elicited from others, responses which to some degree compensate for the disability and for the failure to fulfill the wish ("secondary gain").

The variety of wishes or fantasies which may be so exhibited runs the gamut of the many ways in which needs may be experienced or have been expressed in the course of development (see Chapters IV–XIII), limited only by their capability of being represented in some bodily form. Erotic and aggressive motives are prominent because these are the elements in object relating which are most commonly involved in conflict, most urgently demand control, and most readily are expressed in bodily terms. However, any motive which meets the disapproval of the self or of the environment may be so dealt with.

In Table 1 are summarized common conversion reactions. It will be noted that these involve a great variety of body parts and functions, all of which share the quality that they are accessible to voluntary control (motor) or awareness (sensation), or that they had been involved in some way in object relating activities in the course of development, or that they are capable of being imagined in the form of some concepts of the body image or a function thereof (including concepts of how the mind as an organ functions). Each conversion manifestation character-

Table 1. Common Conversion Manifestations

Motor

- Paralysis or weakness
- Seizures, generalized or localized
- Tics, tremors and other abnormal movements
- Abnormal postures: torticollis, camptocormia, pseudocontractures, stiffness
- Gait disturbances, astasia-abasia
- Aphonia, dysphonia, hoarseness, mutism
- Blepharospasm, ptosis, ocular palsy

Sensory

- Pain in any location
- Anesthesia, hypesthesia, dysesthesia
- Blindness, tubular vision
- Deafness
- Sensations of heat or cold

Upper Gastrointestinal Tract

- Globus hystericus, dysphagia
- Nausea, vomiting
- Anorexia, hyperphagia, bulimia
- Polydipsia
- Abdominal bloating

Lower Gastrointestinal Tract

- Incontinence
- Constipation
- Diarrhea

Respiratory

- Hyperventilation, dyspnea, sighing
- Cough
- Breath holding
- Yawning

Cardiovascular

- Heart consciousness

Urinary Tract

- Urgency, frequency, dysuria
- Incontinence
- Retention

Genital

- Vaginal or penile anesthesia
- Dyspareunia
- Pseudocyesis
- Certain forms of impotence and frigidity

Skin

- Blushing, blanching
- Hemorrhagic stigmata

Consciousness and Mental Functions

- Fainting
- Narcolepsy (sleep attacks)
- Amnesias
- Fugues
- "Weakness," "fatigue," "lack of energy" as "paralysis of will"
- Multiple personality
- Pseudodementia (Ganser)

istically is overdetermined; that is, multiple factors are involved in determining the choice of the particular bodily expression used. The expression which proves to be the most satisfactory psychologically is the one which can most economically symbolize these multiple determinants.

We may best illustrate conversion by an example. A variety of early life experiences may combine to make looking or being seen a conflict-ridden area. These experiences may have involved such elements as curiosity about sexual differences or parental sexual activities, impulses to exhibit the body or genitals, exposure to exciting but frightening sights, aggressive looking or spying, fears of being seen or caught in some forbidden activity, and many other motives. When the person experiences a psychological stress which activates such buried wishes, anxiety, shame, guilt or some other painful affect may develop. On the other hand, no such affect may develop, but instead sudden blindness, a conversion reaction, may occur. In such a case the disturbing wish or fear, namely, to look or be looked at, to see or be seen, has been effectively disposed of and is expressed by the idea, "I cannot see." This forms the basis for the conversion symptom, blindness. Such blindness is psychological, not organic. It involves an inhibition of the process of seeing at the psychological (unconscious) level of not seeing what one feels one should not see. Pupillary and other visual reflexes and EEG are unaffected, indicating that visual stimuli do indeed reach the brain, including the visual cortex; but these are not psychologically processed into conscious visual experience. The person so struck blind not only is unable to see but also at the same time communicates to others, "I am not looking." In this is contained the leading motivation, "I wish to look," which now is blocked and remains unconscious.* Thus, he simultaneously expresses the wish symbolically yet makes it impossible for the wish to be acted upon. For all practical purposes he is blind. He behaves as a blind person is expected to and the environment treats him accordingly.

Now it must be emphasized in this example, as well as in general, that the psychological factors determining the choice of a symptom, in this instance blindness, cannot be derived from the symptom alone. Like the game of charades, only a limited number of body activities are available to express many different ideas. Indeed, the conversion symptom consistently condenses many different, though usually related, motives from the past.

The development of a conversion reaction generally involves the

---

* The wish to be seen, as well as the wish to look, may also be symbolically expressed through blindness. The small child readily believes that when he does not see, he cannot be seen, as anyone who has played hide-and-seek with a baby will know.

following sequences and elements. A derivative drive in the form of an unconscious wish or fantasy is activated from within or by an external stimulus, as by a specific provocation, a danger or a threatened loss. For reasons rooted in the past or in current circumstances, the drive cannot be acted upon or be permitted access to consciousness and therefore must remain unconscious (repressed). But implicit in the blocked drive is the need for an object-relating activity, gratification of which is now doubly jeopardized. On the one hand, to act on the unconscious wish may lead to repudiation by the object (in reality and/or intrapsychically), while on the other, not to act on it means giving up the gratification implicit in the object relationship. Instead of giving up the unsatisfactory wish and seeking a new solution, the repetition compulsion (see Chapter XXVIII) dictates a compromise, namely, to substitute for the unconscious wish a token gesture which in bodily terms represents simultaneously the wish *and* the blocking of its fulfillment in reality. This is the conversion reaction.

What determines which body activity will satisfactorily serve these ends? The conversion symptom always has its sources in the history of the individual's past object relationships and in the types of bodily activities or experiences which had been involved in the gratifications and conflicts that marked these relationships. Such determinants may contribute to the form of the conversion symptom in one or more of the following ways:

1. The conversion symptom actually is a suitable translation into "body language" of the wish and/or the defense against the wish (e.g., "I can't see," "I can't swallow it," "My heart aches for. . .," "I am hurt" (pain), etc.).

2. It corresponds with the memory trace (not necessarily conscious) of a previous body experience (often a physical symptom) which existed at a time in the recent or distant past when the wished for object relationship was relatively gratifying. In such cases the body experience, whether it was a touch, a caress, a blow, a pain, shortness of breath, weakness, stiffness of a limb, unconsciousness, vomiting, or whatever, may have been an important medium through which the desired object relationship was secured. It is as if the revival of the past symptoms would re-create the conditions of the earlier object relationship. The old symptom is used to symbolize the longed-for gratification with which it was once associated, in fact or in fantasy. The term "somatic compliance" has been used to refer to this psychic reuse or perpetuation of a physical symptom or experience of the past as the determinant of the choice of the conversion symptom.

3. It corresponds either with the actual memory of or with a fantasy of a symptom experienced by the object. This involves *identification* with the object and may take the place of the actual relationship

(as when the object is no longer available, whether in reality or intra-psychically). Central for the phenomenon of conversion is that the identification includes assuming a symptom which the object had actually suffered or which the patient *believed* him to have suffered. Through sharing in this way the suffering or disability of the object the original relationship is recreated in fantasy. In this manner the conversion symptom may come to simulate any type of organically determined symptom, as breathlessness, pain, paralysis, fainting, convulsions, etc., which may have been manifested by an object. But how it is manifested by the patient as a conversion symptom often is determined more by what the patient believed (or wished) the object to have experienced than by what the object actually had experienced. Thus, if an asthmatic attack is conceived of as involving pain in the chest, then the corresponding conversion symptom commonly includes both breathlessness and chest pain. In any event, the symptom of the object is utilized to symbolize the forbidden gratification sought for in the relationship; through this means the relationship may be maintained in fantasy, if not in fact.

4. The conversion symptom may also correspond to a past or a current wish that the object suffer a bodily symptom. Thus, a wish that the object not see something may lead to the conversion symptom of blindness, or the impulse to hit the object may result in pain in the body part at which the blow was directed in fantasy. In short, the patient himself suffers what he intended the object to suffer (law of talion). A symbolic equivalent of the object-directed wish is exhibited, punishment is exacted, and the object relationship continues. The gesture, so to speak, substitutes for the real thing and makes it possible to maintain the relationship.

As a means of psychological adjustment, the conversion reaction generally is effective. Therefore, psychological compensation usually is maintained and emergency somatic defense systems are not mobilized. However, certain conversion reactions which are potentially disruptive of internal homeostasis may produce secondary physiological derangements. Thus, hyperventilation, whether it originates through identification with a dyspneic person or as a symbolic expression of sexual feelings ("panting"), is physiologically inappropriate in respect to actual respiratory needs. As a result of excessive ventilation, carbon dioxide is rapidly blown off, respiratory alkalosis develops, and with it develop secondary effects on the central and peripheral nervous systems, manifest in reduced consciousness, paresthesias or tetany. The patient with conversion hyperventilation is thus much more likely to complain of fainting, numbness and tingling, or muscle cramps than he is of over-breathing. Such symptoms represent not conversion reactions but additional examples of physiological maladjustments occurring in the course of maintaining relative psychological compensation (see p. 367). Vomiting, anorexia, bulimia and hyperphagia are examples of other conversion reactions which may have secondary pathophysiological consequences.

Hypochondriacal Symptoms and Somatic Delusions

The hypochondriacal symptom generally takes the form of an unpleasant bodily sensation, such as an itch, formication, "crawling," pulling, fullness or pain, or the persistent idea of the presence of an organic disease, such as cancer, tuberculosis or syphilis. The idea of a disease may also include symptoms related to the disease in question, as, for example, fullness, bloating, anorexia, etc., with the idea of stomach cancer. Hypochondriacal symptoms characteristically have an insistent, demanding, nagging, torturing and even persecuting quality and are a source of great distress to the patient, who pleads for relief. They involve especially the skin, abdomen, nose, rectum and genitals. At times hypochondriacal symptoms assume the quality of somatic delusions. Thus, the patient may experience or interpret the sensations to mean that something is growing inside, that his insides are rotting away, that a body part is changing shape, that bugs are crawling under the skin, etc.

The relationship between hypochondriacal symptoms and the conversion reaction is unclear. They may constitute exaggeration or misinterpretation of ordinary sensations originating in the periphery, but it is also possible that they merely represent conversion symptoms in individuals with the psychological defects characteristic of psychosis. (See Chapter XXXI.) The hypochondriacal complaint, in contrast to the conversion symptom, is more bizarre, less in keeping with concepts of reality, and more narcissistic. When it involves a delusional idea, somatic or persecutory, it is obviously a psychotic expression.

PAIN

Reference to pain as a conversion or hypochondriacal manifestation calls for a few words about pain as a psychological symptom. Pain belongs to the systems concerned with protection of the body against injury, and the experiencing of pain generally is regarded as indicating injury or damage of the part that hurts. It must also be recognized that for noxious stimulation of the peripheral end organ to result in pain not only must the pathways through the peripheral nerve and the neuraxis be intact but also this neural input must be processed psychologically. For this to be accomplished, consciousness and attention, among other higher neural functions, are required.

Further, since the identification and memory of situations and conditions under which pain is experienced constitute important elements for survival and effective function in the course of development, pain may be regarded as a psychological function of prime importance. Hence, though pain is invariably experienced in an anatomical location, it is a mistake to assume from peripheral reference that the pain so experienced is necessarily due to noxious stimulation of a sensitive end organ in that region. Indeed, it is quite possible for pain to be a purely psychic experience, without any concomitant peripheral source, just as may be true of other modalities of sensation, as in dreams and hallucinations.

To understand the circumstances which predispose to the suffering of pain as a purely psychic experience, it is useful first to consider the role of pain in psychological development.

1. As part of the system to protect the body from injury, pain warns of damage to or loss of parts of the body. It is, therefore, intimately concerned with learning about the environment and its dangers on the one hand, and about the body and its limitations on the other. We presume that what produces pain and where it is suffered are permanently registered in the central nervous system. Pain no doubt contributes to the development of a concept of the body image and is of importance in differentiating self from objects. That which hurts belongs to one's own body. Later we shall see how this contributes to the use of pain as a means of dealing with object loss.

2. Pain is much involved in the development of object relationships. In infancy, pain provokes crying, and this ordinarily elicits a comforting response from the mother or some other person. The sequence of pain—→crying—→being comforted by a loved person—→relief of pain can under certain conditions contribute to the attitude that suffering pain will arouse a loving response from the object or that pain can be relieved by the exhibition of love. (The mother "kisses" the pain away.) In this way a pleasurable element may be introduced. But it is not the pain that is pleasurable; it is the association of relief of pain with the reunion with a love object that is enjoyed. As we shall see, some individuals behave as if the pain is worth the price.

3. Early in childhood, pain and punishment become linked. (Indeed, in many languages the words pain and punishment stem from the same root.) This association establishes another parameter of communication between the child and adults, namely, that pain is inflicted when one is "bad." Accordingly, pain not only may come to constitute evidence that one really is "bad," thereby acquiring the capacity to

provoke feelings of guilt ("What did I do to deserve this pain?"), but it may also become an important medium whereby guilt is expiated. Children, as well as adults, may welcome, even solicit, pain as though it assures expiation and forgiveness and, hence, reunion with the loved one. Indeed, there are some children for whom reconciliations with an angry, punitive parent constitute the most intense and gratifying experiences in their lives. For them, to be "bad" and then to be punished may become a way of life. When pain serves in this manner to alleviate guilt and to re-establish a relationship, pleasure in a relative sense is again involved. To feel despised and abandoned is much worse than to suffer pain at the hands of the object who cares enough to punish, especially if the punishment also results in forgiveness and reconciliation.

4. Pain also early becomes very closely associated with aggression and power. The child quickly discovers that he can impose his will on others by inflicting or threatening to inflict pain, just as others have done to him. But he also learns that he may control his own aggression by threatening himself with pain. This provides an intrapsychic method of controlling aggression, for an act of aggression may be forestalled by experiencing pain instead. The person so operating may then either feel pain or expose himself to a painful injury.

5. Pain may also be associated with sexual development. We know that at the height of sexual excitement pain may be not only mutually inflicted but actually enjoyed. When this becomes the dominant feature of the sexual activity, we recognize it as the perversion called sado-masochism. There are also some persons who prefer to experience pain rather than have sexual experience, the latter existing only at the level of unconscious fantasy.

From such considerations it is easy to see that certain conditions early in life may predispose to excessive utilization of pain as a psychological means of adjustment. Certain individuals seem to experience pain with unusual intensity and frequency. With peripheral lesions they seem to suffer more pain than do most people, but also they commonly suffer pain without any demonstrable organic process. In such persons the presence or absence of a peripheral disorder is not well correlated with the presence or absence of pain; indeed it is not uncommon upon removal or cure of a painful lesion for the pain to persist or to recur, in the same site or elsewhere. For the most part, these people repeatedly or chronically suffer from one or another painful disability, sometimes with and sometimes without any recognizable peripheral change. Because of their extraordinary predilection to suffer pain, they have been designated as "pain-prone." They constitute a relatively homogeneous group in terms of the factors determining the choice of pain as the "preferred" symptom and the circumstances under which pain is likely to develop.

The Choice of Pain as Symptom: Pain as Punishment

Guilt, conscious or unconscious, is an invariable factor in the choice of pain as the symptom, as compared to the choice of other types of body sensations for which guilt is not invariant. Clinically we find either a long-term background of guilt and/or an immediate guilt-provoking situation. The clinical characteristics of the chronically guilt-ridden person are not difficult to recognize, if one appreciates the role of penitence, atonement, self-denial and self-depreciation as means of self-inflicted punishment to ease the feeling of guilt.

Many of these individuals are chronically depressive, pessimistic and gloomy people whose guilty, self-depreciating attitudes are readily apparent. They include the masochistic characters mentioned in Chapter XXXI. They are people who seem to have had no joy in or enthusiasm for life. Indeed, some seem to have suffered the most extraordinary number and variety of defeats, humiliations and other unpleasant experiences, not simply as consequences of the pain they suffer or just as a result of bad luck; rather, many of these difficult situations have either been solicited by the patient or simply were not avoided. Such persons drift into situations or submit to relationships in which they are hurt, beaten, defeated or humiliated, and, to our astonishment, seem not to learn from experience; for no sooner are they out of one difficulty than they are in another in spite of the most obvious warnings. At the same time, they conspicuously fail to exploit situations which should lead to success; indeed, when success is thrust upon them they may do badly. Unconsciously they feel that they do not deserve success or happiness and that they must pay a price for it. Many of these patients are unusually tolerant of pain inflicted upon them by nature or by the physician in the course of examination and treatment. In their medical histories we commonly discover an extraordinary number of injuries and operations and more than the usual number of painful illnesses and pains.

In the background of these patients we often find that aggression, suffering and pain played an important role in early family relationships. Quarreling between the parents, harsh punitive attitudes and actual physical punishment, painful illnesses, exposure to others suffering pain or to scenes of violence, the use of aggression or threats of aggression as means of control, a lack of warmth in human relationships—these are some of the childhood experiences common to these persons which no doubt contribute to their strong feeling of guilt and their tendency to use pain as a means of psychic regulation.

Precipitating Circumstances for the Pain Episode

FAILURE OF EXTERNAL CIRCUMSTANCES TO SATISFY THE UNCONSCIOUS NEED TO SUFFER. Some of these patients develop pain when

things go well for them. These individuals with an exaggerated need to suffer may remain relatively pain-free as long as external circumstances make life difficult. When the environment does not treat them harshly enough or they cannot get it to, it seems almost as if they must then inflict pain upon themselves.

REAL, THREATENED OR FANTASIED LOSS. Following the death or any other permanent loss of a loved person, the survivor may experience pain during the period of mourning and sometimes on anniversaries of the loss. The mourner may take a part of his own body as a love object to replace the lost person and by experiencing pain in this part, symbolically assure himself of its continued presence. Pain is especially likely to be the symptom if there is also a strong element of guilt, most often related to ambivalence toward the lost person.

Many episodes of pain occur in direct relationship to the loss of a loved person, but many more occur in relation to threatened losses, anticipated losses, anniversaries of losses or fantasied losses. Thus, we may find pain developing in relationship to the illness or impending departure of important family members or friends, especially when the patient responds with, or had previously experienced, aggressive feelings toward such persons. Or the patient may experience the loss or its anniversary as a painful reminder of guilt but actually suffer pain instead.

EVOCATION OF GUILT BY INTENSE AGGRESSIVE OR FORBIDDEN SEXUAL FEELINGS. When the expression of aggression is unacceptable or even when the threat or possibility that aggression might be expressed provokes guilt, pain may be experienced, sometimes without any aggression being expressed and sometimes remorsefully after it has been expressed. After the pain develops, the provoking situation may be forgotten or only vaguely remembered, or the patient may recall it remorsefully, consciously accepting the pain as a punishment and as a warning against future expressions of aggression. Some patients observe that their pains occur if they do not control themselves.

When the provoking situation involves sexual impulses, these, in contrast to the aggressive impulses, more often remain at an unconscious level and must be inferred. In general they involve situations which might normally be expected to be sexually exciting but are not so recognized by these patients, who instead experience pain, or more subtle situations in which the precipitating stimulus has special symbolic meaning to the individual, generally reminiscent of some childhood sexual conflict.

The location of the pain is determined by the factors considered earlier in respect to the choice of the conversion symptom (see p. 373).

REFERENCES

1. Alexander, F.: Fundamental Concepts of Psychosomatic Research. Psychogenesis, Conversion, Specificity. Psychosom. Med., 5:205, 1948.
1a. Barchilon, J. and Engel, G. L.: Dermatitis: An Hysterical Conversion Symptom in a Young Woman. Psychosom. Med., 14:295, 1952.
2. Breuer, J. and Freud, S.: Studies in Hysteria (1895). In: Standard Edition of the Complete Psychological Works of Sigmund Freud, vol. II. London, The Hogarth Press, 1955.
3. Deutsch, F. (ed.): On the Mysterious Leap from the Mind to the Body. New York, International Universities Press, 1959.
4. Engel, G. L.: Psychogenic Pain and the Pain-Prone Patient. Am. J. Med., 26:899, 1959.
5. Engel, G. L.: Guilt, Pain, and Success. Psychosom. Med., 24:37, 1962.
6. Engel, G. L., Ferris, E. B. and Logan, M.: Hyperventilation: Analysis of Clinical Symptomatology. Ann. Int. Med., 27:683, 1947.
7. Freud, S.: Fragment of an Analysis of a Case of Hysteria (1905). In: Standard Edition of the complete Psychological Works of Sigmund Freud, vol. VII. London, The Hogarth Press, 1953.
7a. Hamburger, W. W.: Appetite in Man. Am. J. Clin. Nutrition, 5:569, 1960.
8. Noordenbos, W.: Pain. Problems Pertaining to the Transmission of Nerve Impulses Which Give Rise to Pain. Amsterdam, Elsevier Publishing Company, 1959.
9. Rangell, L.: The Nature of Conversion. J. Am. Psychoanalyt. A. 7:632, 1959.
10. Romano, J. and Engel, G. L.: Studies of Syncope. III. Differentiation between Vasodepressor and Hysterical Fainting. Psychosom. Med., 7:3, 1945.
11. Seitz, P.: Experiments in the Substitution of Symptoms by Hypnosis. Psychosom. Med., 15:405, 1953.
12. Szasz, T.: Pain and Pleasure. New York, Basic Books, Inc., 1957.
13. Ziegler, F., Imboden, J. and Meyer, E.: Contemporary Conversion Symptomatology. Am. J. Psychiat., 116:901, 1960.

CHAPTER XXXIII

SOMATIC CONSEQUENCES OF PSYCHOLOGICAL STRESS: II. DECOMPENSATED STATES; SOMATOPSYCHIC-PSYCHOSOMATIC DISORDERS

In Chapter XXXII we defined psychological compensation as the state in which psychological stress is being successfully coped with through mental mechanisms and behavior, without the activation of emergency biological systems. The various ways in which somatic manifestations can come about under such circumstances were discussed. In the present chapter we shall be concerned with situations in which mental mechanisms do not suffice and biological systems are mobilized for the defense and protection of the body. It is as if, so to speak, the mental apparatus (the ego) now makes the judgment that what was apprehended as danger in psychological terms may indeed lead to physical stress and that emergency preparations are called for. In other words, the reaction to the signal that warns of injury becomes the same as the reaction to the injury itself; the mental abstractions of physical reality come to act like the physical reality itself. Thus, we are using the term "psychological decompensation" in the very limited sense of a failure to confine to the mental apparatus the handling of the psychological stress.

In respect to the production of somatic manifestations, such a differentiation between psychological compensation and decompensation defines not two independent states but two kinds of circumstances in which somatic changes may come about. Actually, both situations may be encountered in the same patient, occasionally even at the same time. This is a consequence of the multiplicity of stresses that may be operating at the same time and of the fact that it is entirely possible for one stress to be successfully contained by mental mechanisms while another is not. This means, for example, that a conversion reaction may effectively cope with one particular intrapsychic conflict, perhaps activated in the course of dealing with other stresses, without necessarily bearing on the over-all efforts at psychological adaptation. In such a case a conversion symptom may exist side by side with some other type of somatic response. It is not uncommon, for example, for a person with a duodenal ulcer which had become active during a period of psychological stress also to have pain as a conversion symptom, or for a person with the somatic patterns of the acute anxiety reaction simultaneously to manifest conversion symptoms. In such instances we presume the conversion symptoms to be accessory or secondary. Thus the conversion pain of the ulcer patient may be a means of dealing with feelings of guilt evoked by indulging in dependent or hostile behavior while ill; or the conversion symptom appearing during the decompensated state of the acute anxiety reaction may be an attempt to cope with an unconscious conflict uncovered in the course of regression.

The two situations may also exist side by side when the mental or behavioral reactions being utilized are proving inadequate. A conversion reaction may from time to time not successfully cope with the stress, in which case unpleasure affects break through and emergency somatic systems are activated. Under such circumstances the conversion symptom is not abandoned; indeed, it may even be intensified. For example, the patient who has been suffering pain as a conversion symptom to cope with feelings of guilt and has maintained a rather bland attitude toward the pain may under different circumstances find not only that the pain is growing more intense and unbearable but also that he is beginning to experience feelings of guilt, anxiety or depression as well. Now the pain no longer suffices as a means of intrapsychic regulation. Further, it is commonplace for certain behavioral devices to prove inadequate to the task of alleviating distress. For example, the patient who drinks to cope with feelings of anxiety, shame, guilt, inferiority or depression may repeatedly experience both the somatic reactions associated with those feelings as well as the direct and indirect consequences of alcohol ingestion, which only periodically and incompletely relieves the distress.

THE SOMATIC COMPONENTS OF AFFECTS

As discussed in earlier chapters, affects originate as biological emergency states serving to communicate needs and to prepare the body to tolerate stress (Chapters XIV, XVIII, XXII and XXV). These functions are mediated by central nervous system organizations which are already developed and operative at birth and are probably chiefly represented in the limbic system (MacLean[4]). Within the limbic system are found the neural organizations concerned with organized drive behaviors in relation to the external environment and with internal regulatory processes, the latter mediated via the autonomic outflow and the neuroendocrine system, especially the hypothalamus. Intimately related to this system is the reticular activating system (RAS) of the central gray matter and reticulum of the midbrain, which serves the important function of regulating the alertness of the organism through general as well as specific facilitatory and suppressor functions affecting almost every system of neural input and outflow. Through this medium the various exteroceptive, interoceptive and hormonal stimuli entering the nervous system can be effectively focused and screened to permit organization of necessary or appropriate behavior. The reciprocal feedback arrangements between the neocortical and the limbic systems and the reticular system provide the wherewithal whereby drive activities, perceptions from internal and external environemnts, and learned experience can be facilitated, integrated, suppressed or executed. With the development of the mental apparatus the control of these processes becomes a psychological function, and we have learned how this is handled economically through the signal functions of ego, that is, as affects become capable of functioning as intrapsychic warning signals. (See also John, E. R.,[3] for some neurophysiological correlates of such developments.) But should mental or behavioral patterns in response to the signal fail, not only do affects become felt but also the neural system discharging into the body may be activated, meaning in essence that bodily systems are being mobilized to assure needs and to cope with stresses that cannot be handled through intrapsychic processes and controlled behavior.

This, then, constitutes the most general and the most common avenue whereby somatic changes are brought about in response to psychological stress. On the psychological side this involves the experiencing of both signal-scanning affects of unpleasure and drive-discharge affects, felt as states of diffuse unpleasure, such as discomfort, distress or tension, or as their more definitive cognitive states, such as anxiety, fear, guilt, badness, shame, discouragement, anger, helplessness or hopelessness. What is felt includes not only such vague to precise mental content (the cognitive part), but also the awareness of physiological changes, such as palpitation, sweating, flushing, muscle tension or "butterflies in the stomach." As unpleasant mental states, such manifest affect reactions act as motivating influences to induce further mental activity and behavior to cope with the stress, to alleviate distress and to restore comfort. Until these purposes are accomplished (e.g., until compensation is achieved), the affect reaction also includes activation through the limbic system of the biological mechanisms concerned with defense against injury, preparation for activity and/or avoidance of exhaustion. The body, no longer buffered against the vicissitudes of the environment by an effectively operating mental apparatus, now is alerted to anticipate damage or exhaustion.

The differentiation of affects into the many shades of feeling known to man is a psychological, not a physiological, development, and with present knowledge there is little evidence to support the view that a specific physiological pattern corresponds to each affect quality. More in keeping with biological principles is the view that the somatic processes activated in the course of affect reactions are made up of basic biological defense and drive patterns which constitute final common pathways. What distinctive features may exist which more or less correspond to particular affects, such as nausea with disgust, blushing with embarrassment or shame, or palpitation with fear, may reflect the association of particular drive activities with such affects. (See Chapter XVIII.) It is even conceivable that some affect qualities have no distinctive somatic correlates.

Accordingly, we propose that the basic biological patterns be divided into the two main categories already considered in relation to the primal affects of unpleasure, namely, anxiety and depression-withdrawal (Chapter VII). The first category includes a variety of active modes of coping with stress which are designated the *flight-fight patterns* to indicate corresponding behavioral aspects (Cannon[11]). These involve not only the biochemical and physiological preparations for flight or fight but also internal changes anticipating bodily injury. The second category includes patterns of withdrawal from and insulation against environmental change, reduction of activity and husbanding of resources. These will be referred to as the *withdrawal-conservation patterns*. In addition, one might hypothesize an ultimate state of disorganization and exhaustion in which all defenses fail, culminating in death (Selye[7]).

Each of these will be discussed both in terms of the affective qualities as manifested psychologically and in terms of the physiological changes. Special somatic aspects of individual affects will also be discussed.

The Flight-Fight Patterns

This term defines a series of reactions, the origins of which are to be found in the primary biological pattern of activity underlying primal anxiety and rage (Chapter VII). It ranges from diffuse anxiety for no conscious reason, to anxiety with an apparent objective source in the environment, to flight from an external source of danger toward a haven of safety, to rage and attack directed at a threatening object. This spectrum extends from a state of threat in which there is uncertainty, to a threat against which defense or from which flight is planned or possible, to a threat to be eliminated by aggressive action.

Each of these states involves different behavioral and physiological sets. Thus, whether its source is in the internal or in the external environment, when the preparation to meet an uncertain danger cannot be organized or directed, there is a general alertness and vigilance, with increased awareness of environmental input that might signify danger. This probably involves selective activity of orienting and alerting systems so that perception and motility may be geared for rapid apprehension of stimuli and mediation of response. These are evident in the stare, the startle, the rapid movements and the trembling so characteristic of the acute anxiety reaction or fear state. (See also Chapter XXVI.)

As the source of the danger becomes objectified, whether accurately or not, the over-all behavioral response becomes one more oriented toward vigilance and activity to defend against or cope with the danger, whether by flight to safety or by attack. Now attention narrows to encompass mainly the threatening object and the means of coping with it, while other sensory input may be ignored. The soldier engaged in combat or fleeing from the enemy may be unaware of a wound and suffer no pain. Startle and tremor diminish as the more goal-directed preparations for motor activity take place. Deliberate flight and attack are the most highly organized and directed of such responses.

Physiological and biochemical changes reflect the changing conditions represented in these three points in the spectrum. In all three are observed as a major feature neuroendocrine changes concerned with both rapid and long-term preparation for tissue injury and its repair. This preparation includes activity of the limbic system and hypothalamus leading to activation particularly of the pituitary-adrenal cortical system and secretion of cortical hormones, the role of which in facilitating a wide range of metabolic processes involved in the long-term responses to injury is well known (Ingle,[20] F. Engel,[16] Selye[7]). Such neuroendocrine changes are relatively nonspecific, and are regulated by both neural and humoral feedback mechanisms. In addition, they exhibit an intrinsic diurnal rhythm which is apparently not significantly modifiable by stress.

Preparation for physical activity constitutes the second major feature. This includes the mobilization of substrate for energy, namely, free fatty acids from fat depots for muscle metabolism and glucose from hepatic glycogen for nervous system or muscle use. Such lipolysis is mainly stimulated by norepinephrine secreted in response to sympathetic outflow, while the glycogenolysis is mediated mainly through the action of epinephrine, secreted by the adrenal medulla. As long as the reaction is relatively undirected, as in diffuse anxiety, the predominant catechol amine secreted is epinephrine, whereas when the action to be taken becomes more defined, such as actual flight or attack, norepinephrine becomes the dominant catechol. The general circulatory changes show a pattern corresponding to the effects of the two catechol amines. During anxiety, with no clear solution, there is typically more rapid and active heart action, systolic pressure may rise, diastolic pressure may fall somewhat, and over-all peripheral resistance decreases. These are the circulatory responses more characteristic of epinephrine effect. When action becomes possible, either as flight or as attack, norepinephrine effects dominate, namely, rising systolic and diastolic pressures and increased peripheral resistance, while cardiac rate becomes more commensurate with the actual circulatory need. During both these situations there is an increase in muscle blood flow, mediated in part through the humoral effect of epinephrine and to a larger degree through a cholinergic sympathetic outflow to muscle arterioles from midbrain centers. Blood is redistributed in terms of the urgency of the need. The largest blood flow is to striated muscle, brain and heart; circulation to areas less essential under these conditions, such as the gastrointestinal tract, kidneys and skin, is reduced. Again, variations are found, depending on the degree to which activity, especially when directed, is imminent. Thus, as the affective state shifts from diffuse anxiety with no solution to organized flight or directed rage, blanching changes to flushing, perhaps anticipating the need to dissipate heat through increased cutaneous circulation. The extremities are typically cold and sweaty during diffuse anxiety, but become warm and dry as rage evolves. Gastric secretion and blood flow may rise during rage (see below).

Respiratory changes show a similar gradation. In the less organized phase, breathing tends to be irregular, with frequent sighing, but as action becomes imminent breathing becomes deeper and more regular, and there is an increase in total ventilation which may amount to a significant degree of overventilation, resulting in the blowing off of carbon dioxide and consequent respiratory alkalosis. Alkalosis has value for major exertion, for it not only shifts the oxygen dissociation curve of hemoglobin to yield greater O_2 uptake in the lungs and greater O_2 delivery in the muscles, but also it helps to compensate for the outpouring of acid metabolites during muscle activity. Further, it permits prolonged breath holding, sometimes a crucial factor in the use of the torso in sustained physical effort.

Variations in regional physiological patterns are perhaps more related to the drive aspect of the reaction. Thus, during acute diffuse anxiety and during the flight reaction the mouth is dry and the secretion, blood flow and motor activity of the stomach tend to be reduced, whereas in rage there is a tendency for salivary secretion and for the secretion, blood flow and motility of the stomach to increase, often markedly. Increased secretion may reflect an oral element in the aggression, an unconscious wish to bite, tear and consume. Clenching of the jaws and gnashing of the teeth are common accompaniments of rage. During extreme fear the sphincters may relax and the contents of bladder and rectum may be evacuated, changes which do not occur in rage.

The Withdrawal-Conservation Patterns

Knowledge of the physiological processes in these states is fragmentary at best. They are associated particularly with the affects attendant upon giving up, notably helplessness and hopelessness, whether these evolve through loss or through inability to cope with overwhelming threat of injury. Clinical observation leads us to believe that the physiological processes associated with the giving up states may be significantly different from those associated with states in which the person actively interacts with the environment in the attempt to re-establish a dynamic steady state. The postulated significance of the withdrawal patterns as conservative and energy-saving would lead to the expectation of physiological and biochemical changes consistent with that type of adaptive reorganization. So far these processes have been very incompletely studied. Among the random data available are the following:

1. There is reduced motor interaction with the environment, with decreased motor activity, lowered muscle tone and slumped posture—all indicative of disengagement from the external environment and disinclination to utilize the motor system for interaction with it. In a state of helplessness the person remains alert to possible help from the environment, but in hopelessness there is much greater detachment. In general the pattern involves an over-all reduction in activity and the physiological changes associated therewith. These may include increased sleep and a lowered threshold to hypnotic drugs.

2. Secretory and motor activity of the entire gastrointestinal tract is diminished. Virtual absence of gastric secretory activity, including response to histamine, has been described. The mucosa of stomach and colon becomes pale. Ingested food does not seem to be absorbed or handled metabolically in a normal fashion, weight loss on apparently good caloric intake being not uncommon.

3. Secretions of other mucous membranes may also be reduced.

4. There is one study indicating that the person who is not object-engaged does not respond to usual external stresses (e.g., threat of major surgery) with the same degree of activation of the pituitary-adrenal axis as do others.[32] This does not necessarily reflect a basic physiological difference; it may mean that threat of surgery does not constitute as great a psychological stress for such persons. The ordinary person shows a greater corticoid response to the anticipation of surgery than he does to the actual physical trauma of surgery.

Pending further investigation, the assumption that withdrawal-conservation states may be distinguished from the flight-fight patterns rests largely on clinical observations and theoretical assumptions. States of grief, loneliness, sadness, helplessness and hopelessness show many features radically different from those noted during anxiety, fear, rage and agitated guilt and shame.

Correlation with Affects

As already mentioned, strict correlation between the subjectively experienced affect qualities and physiological patterns is probably poor. Although what is felt in terms of differentiated affects has great variety (actually far beyond the descriptive names traditionally applied), the messages to the body call forth a far more limited repertoire of responses. More crucial, perhaps, are the degree to which the affect reflects object relating activities and the meaning of the message for the body, whether to prepare for injury or for exhaustion. These two aspects are of course closely interrelated and cannot be dealt with separately. Both will now be considered in terms of the affects.

ANXIETY. The range of physiological responses has already been discussed in terms of the awareness of the source of danger, the availability of a solution and of objects, and the direction and intensity of action planned or possible. More individual are some of the distinctive qualities of anxiety expression that have to do with the genesis and nature of the underlying conflicts, which in turn determine such specific reactions as nausea, vomiting, diarrhea, muscle cramps, etc., as well as various muscular postures of defense. These are discussed in Chapter XVIII.

SHAME AND GUILT. As indices of disapproval of the self, both shame and guilt, each for somewhat different psychodynamic reasons, may carry the implication of impending injury or damage. Hence, activation of the pituitary-adrenal cortical system is a common accompaniment of these affects, especially when they are being manifest in terms of great distress and suffering, as in the psychotically depressed person. Circulatory changes tend to correlate with the degree of activity, usually manifest as restlessness and agitation. On the other hand, when shame or guilt activates primarily ideas of abandonment, there may be a shift toward withdrawal-conservation patterns. In neither event, however, does there seem to be a specific physiological pattern characteristic of shame or guilt per se.

The more specific concomitants occasionally noted relate to the underlying drives or conflict. Thus, the blush of shame may relate to conflict over exhibitionistic impulses. The anorexia of guilt may relate to inhibition of oral aggressive (cannibalistic) impulses.

DISGUST. The physiological patterns of nausea and vomiting are the characteristic somatic reactions associated with disgust. This has already been discussed (Chapter XVIII).

SADNESS. No specific physiological data related to sadness are available. Both on the basis of clinical observation and on theoretical grounds it would seem not to involve the flight-fight patterns. Although behaviorally it does include some of the features of the withdrawal-conservation patterns, these are much less obvious than they usually are in the giving-up states. Tearfulness, sobbing, anorexia and sighing indicate somatic processes, but their nature remains to be elucidated.

HELPLESSNESS AND HOPELESSNESS. As the affects most indicative of giving up, these should be most closely related to the withdrawal conservation patterns, but data are not yet at hand. Helplessness differs from hopelessness in that belief in or hope for intervention or help from an object is retained and the person is more oriented to the environment, though relatively inactive.

ANGER, RAGE. The major physiological changes of anger and rage have already been described. The main variations relate not only to the intensity of the feeling but also to its direction. When anger is consciously controlled or consciously directed at oneself,* the magnitude of the bodily changes is not as great as when the feeling is outwardly directed. When rage is denied, the physiological changes may evolve, nonetheless. The general bodily reaction of rage involves especially the musculoskeletal system and its supporting systems, notably the circulation, but other systems may also be involved, depending on the mode of aggression. Thus, when the predominant aggressive fantasy is oral or anal there may be preferential activation of the upper or lower gastrointestinal tract, respectively. Also, individual muscle groups may be involved in relation to modes of attack or defense. The clamped jaw, the furrowed brow, the clenched fist, the rigid trunk, all are indicative of more chronic moods of anger, expressing both aggressive and guarding attitudes. Chronically elevated arterial blood pressure has been observed among animals exposed to prolonged and frustrated rage.

---

* Not to be confused with guilt. See Chapter XVIII.

SOMATIC DECOMPENSATION DURING
PSYCHOLOGICAL DECOMPENSATION

The physiological and biochemical processes associated with affects are all reversible and do not in themselves have pathological consequences in terms of tissue or organ damage, though they are responsible for some of the complaints of the person in the decompensated state, such as palpitation, dryness of the mouth, cold hands, etc. On the other hand, physiological decompensation or somatic damage may occur if other conditions prevail which in one way or another are incompatible with such biochemical or physiologcial processes. Some of these will now be considered in relationship to the two main reaction patterns.

Complications of the Flight-Fight Patterns

There are many ways in which physiological decompensation or somatic damage may take place in the course of the flight-fight patterns; what follows is intended to be illustrative rather than inclusive. In brief, such consequences result from the incompatiblity of simultaneous physiological or biochemical mechanisms or from the effects of the emergency reactions on already defective systems.

PHYSIOLOGICAL INCOMPATABILITIES. This category is well illustrated by *vasodepressor syncope*, the common faint, which typically occurs in settings of fear, especially when the fear must not be revealed. It may be provoked by any injury or threat of injury, when the general circulatory preparation for flight takes place but for some reason flight is impossible. The classic situation is one in which the individual is psychologically immobilized, as during a minor medical or dental procedure, pride preventing the acknowledgement of the fear and the social or other restraints of the external situation preventing actual flight or resistance. Under such circumstances the physiologically appropriate vasodilation in muscle in preparation for flight takes place, but simultaneously there is an inhibition of muscle action. In the erect position this may result in an acute peripheral circulatory inadequacy, for the necessary conditions for the return of blood to the right heart no longer pertain. The enlargement of the blood bed in muscle cannot be adequately compensated for either by heart action or by vasoconstriction elsewhere as long as the hydrostatic effects of gravity are not counteracted by the usual pumping action of muscle. Under such conditions the victim, so to speak, "bleeds" into his own muscles. As peripheral resistance declines, the systolic pressure falls and unless the head is lowered relative to the heart, the blood pressure becomes inadequate to maintain cerebral circulation and consciousness is lost. Thus, two physiologically incompatible reactions, the circulatory preparation for flight and the inhibition of motor activity, result in peripheral circulatory failure.

Another example of untoward consequences when the physiological preparation for physical exertion is not followed by physical activity is found in the metabolic complications of the preparatory overventilation and the consequent respiratory alkalosis which results from the excessive blowing off of carbon dioxide. This has already been discussed in relation to hyperventilation as a conversion symptom (Chapter XXXII).

DECOMPENSATION OR DISORDER OF ALREADY DEFECTIVE SYSTEMS. There are many circumstances in which the limited competence of a physiological system is seriously strained in the course of the physiological changes of an emergency reaction.

For example, the magnitude of the circulatory changes during the flight-fight patterns corresponds to that observed during moderate to strenuous physical exertion. Therefore, acute left ventricular failure with pulmonary edema may occur during acute anxiety or rage in the patient with compensated organic heart disease. Cardiac catheterization studies of patients with compensated heart disease reveal increased heart rate and a rapidly rising pulmonary arterial pressure during anxiety, indicating backward failure concomitant with the inability to increase cardiac output appropriate to the increased demand on the circulation. Similarly, the patient with coronary insufficiency may experience angina pectoris, a result of the inability to increase the blood supply of the heart commensurate with its greater activity. These are all conditions in which the circulatory preparations for activity characteristic of the flight-fight patterns impose a demand greater than the damaged cardiac system can accommodate to.*

In the presence of myocardial damage, epinephrine secretion and the associated shift in potassium ions may precipitate a paroxysmal arrhythmia.

In the diabetic, the mobilization of free fatty acids during the flight-fight reaction may elevate the level of blood ketones and thereby increase or provoke acidosis. Hyperglycemia and increased glycosuria may also occur in the diabetic under such conditions.

The nonspecific activation of the pituitary-adrenal cortex system characteristic of preparation for injury may in the predisposed individual facilitate adrenal cortical hyperplasia, resulting in so-called Cushing's syndrome. In the presence of certain genically determined defects in the biogenesis of adrenal steroids, disproportionate quantities of androgenically active compounds may be formed in response to the usual stress-invoked secretion of ACTH. In women with such biochemical defects hirsutism and menstrual disturbances may occur as untoward consequences of the otherwise normal neuroendocrine response to stress.

---

* It should not be overlooked that similar consequences may also ensue from the increased work of the heart demanded during sexual excitement and orgasm, pleasurable experiences.

Excessive sweating of hands and feet, a common accompaniment of the anxiety reaction, may predispose to fungus infections of the skin.

These selected examples suffice to illustrate how the physiological and biochemical processes of the emergency flight-fight patterns occurring in response to psychological stress may under certain conditions introduce an unexpected pathogenic element.

Complications of the Withdrawal-Conservation Patterns

In the absence of more than fragmentary information concerning physiological and biochemical processes in these states, speculations about their relationship to somatic complications are based mainly on empirical observations and inference. The assumption is required that what is experienced or expressed psychologically as "giving up" reflects or activates the physiological and behavioral states that we are subsuming under the heading *withdrawal-conservation* patterns. This implies that when "giving up" (experienced as "too much," "despair," "the end," "can't take it any more," "no use," "no hope," etc.) also includes the idea of abandonment of activity directed toward the external environment, the previously mentioned biological patterns of withdrawal and conservation may come into play. The psychological state of giving up in final analysis involves a loss of the sense of self as intact and in control. As the feeling of being unable to cope with something grows, the image of "I" seems less and less adequate or competent. This is the case regardless of the nature of the stress and of the sequence of affects that may precede such a state. In everyday life the stress which most frequently provokes giving up is object loss, real or threatened, but overwhelming threat of injury or any other psychic stress may also eventuate in such an outcome.

The following kinds of data may be cited as evidence for the potential pathogenic influence of such states:

1. Sudden death is known to occur in both man and animals in settings of overwhelming stress from which no escape is possible. Many species of animals, especially wild animals, die when physically restrained; this is familiar to those attempting to trap animals for zoos. Young, healthy soldiers in combat may die without injury and persons trapped in disasters may succumb when they give up hope. The breaking of taboos or the casting of spells among primitive peoples is alleged to result in rapid failure and death (so-called "voodoo death"). It has been shown that rats subjected to an impossible stress for which no solution is possible (swimming under a jet of water), die suddenly, not during the flight-fight pattern, but when they "give up" the struggle, a state which long precedes actual physical exhaustion. On the other hand, if the rats are removed from the stressful situation before the point of "giving up" and then are returned to the water, they are able to survive periods

of stress far longer than otherwise. Apparently they "learn" that it is not "hopeless" and do not so readily "give up" (Richter[50]). Curiously, clipping a rat's whiskers, presumably a source of sensory information, hastens "giving up" and shortens survival.

2. In folklore and in fact, a person may be said to "die of grief." Death may occur suddenly, the victim collapsing and dying upon hearing news of his loss; more commonly, the mourner goes into a decline and dies soon thereafter. The causes of death in such situations are not yet established, though in some instances it is clear that some pre-existing disease process was accelerated. Death is not to be ascribed to grief per se, but to changes, as yet unidentified, brought about in the course of the response to loss.

3. In settings of great social disorganization, in which familiar social supports and personal ties are disrupted, as in concentration camps, prison camps, disaster areas, etc., morbidity and mortality are alleged to be highest among those who give up hope. The exceptionally high mortality of American prisoners of war during the Korean War was ascribed more to the deliberate destruction by their captors of the prisoners' morale and group spirit than to physical conditions alone. Death commonly was preceded by a syndrome referred to as "give-up-itis." On the other hand, the maintenance of self-esteem, hope, purpose, firmly held religious or political convictions, and belief in his fellows enables a person to endure incredible burdens, as many heroic accounts attest. Autobiographical accounts of such persons reveal an extra-ordinary capacity for self-reliance and the ability for self-stimulation through mental activity and imagination.

4. Less dramatic but more important is the documentation that psychological "giving up," transient or sustained, commonly precedes the development or exacerbation of somatic illnesses. This, too, has been recorded in folklore through the ages and was commonly cited as a contributory factor in disease by the clinicians of past centuries. Because of the preoccupation with physical stresses and mechanisms of disease that has marked the past fifty years, such considerations have been largely ignored until recently. More systematic studies of patient populations with specific diseases (e.g., ulcerative colitis, thyrotoxicosis, tuberculosis, diabetes, asthma, leukemia, cancer, and many others) as well as of unselected patients admitted to the medical services of general hospitals reveal a consistently high incidence of such psychological states in the period immediately preceding the development of a manifest organic diseases. Such observations suggest that the biological changes concomitant with "giving up" may alter unfavorably the capacity to resist other physical stresses already present or to which the individual may be exposed while in this state.

The hypothesis derived from these data postulates that biological changes concomitant with "giving up" yield conditions which *facilitate* or *permit* pathological organic changes but in themselves are neither necessary nor sufficient to bring about such changes. Clinical observation leads to the impression that these conditions are more important for some pathological states than for others and, indeed, may even be necessary for some. However, until more is known about the nature of the basic biological states associated with the withdrawal-conservation patterns, nothing further can be said about mechanisms. It is reasonable to assume that such biological changes, whatever they may be, will be found to influence some pathological processes unfavorably, others favorably, and to be without influence on still others. In brief, there is no a priori reason to assume a uniformly harmful effect.

LOCAL SOMATIC DEFENSE REACTIONS

In addition to the more general biological defense patterns already described, there are also local defense patterns involving especially portals of entry into the body, such as the upper gastroenteric tract, respiratory passages, the lower bowel, the lower urinary tract, the skin and conjunctivae. All of these exhibit well-defined riddance reactions to cope with noxious agents, but such reactions may also be provoked by symbolic stimuli or by an anticipated danger of actual entry of the noxious agent. Physiologically the local reaction includes surface changes to dilute, wash away, neutralize or digest the noxious material, and motor activities to keep out or expel the noxious agent. The former include edema, vascular engorgement and hypersecretion and involve skin, conjunctivae and the mucous membranes of nasal and upper respiratory passages, bronchi, stomach and lower bowel. The latter include spasm, hyperperistalsis or reverse peristalsis of the smooth muscles of esophagus, stomach, bronchial tree, rectum and sigmoid. Thus, in response to certain symbolic psychological stresses some individuals may respond with such manifestations as engorgement and congestion of the nasal passages, nausea and vomiting, cardiospasm, pylorospasm, diarrhea, etc. Presumably the stress is symbolically experienced as calling for such local defense reactions, either because it is capable of being so represented or because it was in some way associated with a past situation when such reactions had been activated by some noxious agent. For example, an episode of nausea and vomiting caused by eating contaminated fish may be followed by nausea and vomiting upon eating any fish or even merely at the thought of eating fish.

As mechanisms, such reactions are closely related to the conversion reactions involving the same systems, and in some instances the two cannot be distinguished. (See Chapter XXXII.) The example of nausea and vomiting just cited does not, strictly speaking, constitute a conversion reaction as we have defined the conversion reaction. But were fish—the animal, the word or the idea—to be equated symbolically with an unconscious fantasy (e.g., a wish to take the penis in the mouth), then the reaction pattern more properly should be regarded as a conversion. Yet we have already learned how such an experience as the original food poisoning may provide the somatic substrate related to a simultaneous ideation and hence may constitute the basis for a later conversion reaction (somatic compliance). Accordingly, there are times when it is impossible to differentiate between a true conversion reaction and a local somatic defense reaction to a symbolic threat.

Such local reactions may also have implications in respect to altering resistance to other stresses. Thus, nasal congestion so produced may result in obstruction of paranasal sinuses or the eustachian tube, predisposing to sinusitis or otitis media. A change in the composition of mucous membrane secretions may alter unfavorably a balanced relationship with potentially pathogenic organisms in the nasopharynx. Experiments during hypnosis have demonstrated that anticipation of injury to the skin aggravates inflammation and increases local tissue damage in response to noxious stimulation. Proteolytic enzymes and a bradykinin-like polypeptide are implicated in such exaggerated reactions.

DISPLACED OR INCOMPLETE DRIVE PATTERNS

Some somatic reactions constitute not defenses but expressions of incomplete or substitute drive activities when the full expression of drive is blocked by conflict or by external restraints. For example, increased vaginal secretions (leukorrhea) may indicative be of sexual tensions. Increased secretory and motor activity of the stomach or of the bowel may reflect oral or anal drive activity. Psychosexual disturbances may interfere with the normal menstrual cycle and gestational processes; amenorrhea, dysmenorrhea, abnormal bleeding, sterility, spontaneous abortion, all have been noted under such circumstances.

Local patterns of muscle spasm in relation to suppressed or controlled rage have already been alluded to. These may lead to pain, as with tension headache (bitemporal with clenched jaws, bandlike with fronto-occipitalis contraction), low back pain, etc.

"Air swallowing" (with bloating and eructation) may occur when a strong need to discharge feelings by speech has to be suppressed.

Normally during speaking a small amount of air is taken into the esophagus at the beginning of inspiration and is used for phonation during the balance of inspiration. Some persons, especially when obliged to "hold their tongues," carry out some of the motor actions of speaking but block phonation. Under such circumstances the air is swallowed instead of being expelled. The result is the syndrome of aerophagia, in which the necessity to interrupt the motor act of speech in its final phase may be seen as blocking the use of speech for drive expression (usually anger, but this may also involve exhibiting oneself).

SOMATOPSYCHIC-PSYCHOSOMATIC PROCESSES

When certain organs or systems of the body are involved early in life in pathological processes, even though these are not necessarily manifest overtly as disease states, certain consequences for subsequent psychological development may ensue. Not only may such processes influence the development of particular psychological traits, but they may also determine a vulnerability to organic breakdown of the involved system or organ. In other words, certain organic defects, sometimes molecular (genic) in nature, if present prenatally or in infancy, may be responsible for subsequent psychological and somatic vulnerabilities. (See also Chapter XXVIII.) This consequence is especially likely when the organ or system in question is intimately related to or involved in development and in modes of expression and object relating.

This relationship is responsible for a certain measure of psychological specificity in these diseases, particularly in respect to character structure and the kinds of conflict situations in which the organic process may be activated. Among these disorders are those classically regarded as "psychosomatic," in which the concept of specificity was first developed (i.e., peptic ulcer, bronchial asthma, ulcerative colitis, rheumatoid arthritis, hypertension, neurodermatitis, hyperthyroidism) (Alexander[55]). Others, no doubt, may be added to this group.

Justifying this classification are two facts. First, clinical study of patients with these disorders reveals a certain consistency in the coexistence of particular psychological characteristics with each disease. Thus, given a patient with one of these disorders, it is possible to anticipate with considerable confidence the presence of certain psychological features. In terms of the life history, character structure and the nature of the settings in which the disease becomes manifest or exacerbates, patients with the same disease have many features in common. On the other hand, not all persons with such backgrounds and character traits have or will necessarily acquire that particular disease. Indeed, many persons psychologically indistinguishable apparently never have the organic disorder. This points to the second justification, namely, that an organic factor is necessary if the specific organic process is to develop. This factor may also play a role in psychological development, and hence may contribute to the consistency of the psychological features among those patients eventually manifesting the disease.

The relationship between the primary biological factor and psychological development has been best worked out in relation to peptic ulcer (Mirsky[57]). For this condition the biological feature is identifiable in the form of a high secretory capacity of the stomach, indicated by high plasma pepsinogen levels. Thus, patients with peptic ulcer show plasma pepsinogen levels in the high range. Further, persons with high plasma pepsinogen without ulcer have a high probability of having peptic ulcer under appropriate stress, whereas those with low or absent pepsinogen show a low probability of having peptic ulcer. A similar relation between high and low pepsinogen and susceptibility to gastric erosions under stress (restraint) has also been demonstrated in rats (Ader[54]). In addition, it is found that psychological features differentiate the population with high plasma pepsinogen from those with low pepsinogen. The psychological characteristics of the high pepsinogen population, whether or not they have or have had active peptic ulcer, correspond to those noted among the population with peptic ulcer, indicating that the gastric hypersecretory potential is a common denominator for both. The same consistency is found in the psychological characteristics of those persons with persistently low or absent pepsinogen (in some of whom, incidentally, pernicious anemia eventually occurs).

These conditions have been designated somatopsychic-psychosomatic on the basis of such data. In respect to peptic ulcer, it is postulated that the hypersecretory potential, which is demonstrable in early infancy, is a somatic given (perhaps genically determined), which has an influence on early psychological development, perhaps through elements involved in the nature of the mother-infant relationship. More intense oral needs may be a behavioral counterpart to the high secretory capacity of the stomach, as measured by pepsinogen. The significance of very high oral tension (or very low) as an element in the mother-child relationship and its consequence for the psychological development of the child have been discussed in earlier chapters and will not be developed further here (Chapters V, VI and VII). Suffice it to say that clinical study demonstrates both oral conflicts and hypersecretion to be important, if not necessary, components for the development of peptic ulcer. Thus, not only does the original somatic factor influence psychological development, but also this psychological development may define the life circumstances which may prove stressful psychologically and eventuate in activation of peptic ulcer. Under favorable life circumstances, the person with high pepsinogen may never be exposed to the particular conditions conducive to ulcer formation, whereas under less favorable conditions of development or of life, he may prove highly vulnerable. Thus, high pepsinogen defines the potentiality for an organic vulnerability (peptic ulcer), but factors in the course of development and in the current psychological and social setting will determine how this organic factor will influence psychological development as well as define the nature of the circumstances that might prove stressful. An infant with high pepsinogen (high oral tension?) may be so satisfactorily handled by the mother that oral gratifications are assured and later oral conflicts remain at a minimum. Such a person would be relatively protected against the kind of stress situations more likely to activate peptic ulcer and hence would be relatively resistant to ulcer formation in spite of high pepsinogen levels. Under less favorable circumstances psychological development would be more affected and the likelihood of ulcer formation correspondingly increased.

How many conditions are determined by this type of life-long interrelationship between early somatopsychic determinants and later psychic influences activating the specific somatic process is not known. The discovery of such biological indicators as plasma pepsinogen for peptic ulcer (and pernicious anemia) in other disease states may make it possible to identify the disease-vulnerable population before certain disorders become manifest and thereby to define more precisely the necessary and sufficient conditions for the active disease process.

REFERENCES

Somatic Components of Affects

Neurophysiology

1. Gastaut, H.: The Role of the Reticular Formation in Establishing Conditioned Reactions. *In* Jasper, H. H., et al. (eds.): Reticular Formation of the Brain. Boston, Little, Brown and Company, 1958.
2. Hess, W. R.: Functional Organization of the Diencephalon. New York, Grune and Stratton, 1957.
3. John, E. R. and Killam, K. F.: Electrophysiological Correlates of Differential Approach-Avoidance Conditioning in Cats. J. Nerv. Ment. Dis., *131*:183, 1960.
4. MacLean, P. D.: Contrasting Functions of Limbic and Neocortical Systems of the Brain and Their Relevance to Psychophysiological Aspects of Medicine. Am. J. Med., *25*:611, 1958.
5. Magoun, H. W.: The Waking Brain. Springfield, Illinois, Charles C Thomas, 1958.

6. Mason, J. W.: The Central Nervous System Regulation of ACTH Secretion. *In* Jasper, H. H. et al. (eds.): Reticular Formation of the Brain. Boston, Little, Brown and Company, 1958.
7. Selye, H.: The Concept of Stress in Experimental Physiology. *In* Tanner, J. M. (ed.): Stress and Psychiatric Disorder. Oxford, Blackwell Scientific Publications, 1960.

Flight-Fight Patterns
8. Basowitz, H., Persky, H., Korchin, S. J. and Grinker, R. R.: Anxiety and Stress. New York, McGraw Hill Book Co., 1955.
9. Board, F., Wadeson, R. and Persky, H.: Depressive Affect and Endocrine Functions. A.M.A. Arch. Neurol. & Psychiat., *78:*612, 1957.
10. Bogdonoff, M. D. and Estes, E. H.: Energy Dynamics and Acute States of Arousal in Man. Psychosom. Med., *23:*23, 1961.
11. Cannon, W. B.: Bodily Changes in Pain, Hunger, Fear, and Rage. New York, Appleton-Century Company, 1939.
12. Cardon, P. V. and Gordon, R. S.: Rapid Increase of Plasma Unesterified Fatty Acids in Man During Fear. J. Psychosom. Res., *4:*5, 1959.
13. Cohen, S. I., and Silverman, A. J.: Psychophysiological Investigations of Vascular Response Variability. J. Psychosom. Res., *3:*185, 1959.
14. Darwin, C.: The Expression of Emotions in Man and Animals (1872). New York, Philosophical Library, 1955.
15. Elmadjian, F., Hope, J. M. and Lamson, E. T.: Excretion of Epinephrine and Norepinephrine in Various Emotional States. J. Clin. Endocrinol., *17:*608, 1957.
16. Engel, F. L.: General Concepts of Adrenocortical Function in Relation to Response to Stress. Psychosom. Med., *15:*565, 1953.
17. Engel, F. L.: The Influence of the Endocrine Glands on Fatty Acid and Ketone Body Metabolism. A.M.A. Arch. Int. Med., *100:*18, 1957.
18. Fox, H. M., Murawski, B. J., Bartholomay, A. F. and Gifford, S.: Adrenal Steroid Excretion Patterns in Eighteen Healthy Subjects. Psychosom. Med., *23:*33, 1961.
19. Funkenstein, D. H., King, S. H. and Drolette, M. E.: Mastery of Stress. Cambridge, Harvard University Press, 1957.
20. Ingle, D.: The Role of the Adrenal Cortex in Homeostasis. J. Endocrinol., *8:*22, 1952.
21. Mason, J. W.: Psychological Influences on the Pituitary-Adrenal Cortical System. Recent Progr. Hormone Res., *XV:*345, 1959.
22. Mason, J. W., Mangan, G., Brady, J. V., Conrad, D. and Rioch, D. M.: Concurrent Plasma Epinephrine, Norepinephrine and 17-Hydroxy-corticosteroid Levels during Conditioned Emotional Disturbances in Monkeys. Psychosom. Med., *23:*344, 1961.
23. Mirsky, I. A.: Secretion of Antidiuretic Hormone in Response to Noxious Stimuli. A.M.A. Arch. Neurol. & Psychiat., *73:*135, 1955.
24. Mirsky, I. A.: Psychophysiological Basis of Anxiety. Psychosomatics, *1:*1, 1960.
25. Persky, H. et al.: Relation of Emotional Responses and Changes in Plasma Hydrocortisone Level After Stressful Interview. A.M.A. Arch. Neurol. & Psychiat., *79:*434, 1958.
26. Wolf, S. and Wolff, H. G.: Human Gastric Function. New York, Oxford University Press, 1943.

Withdrawal Conservation Patterns

27. Busfield, B., Wechsler, H. and Barman, W. J.: Studies of Salivation in Depression. A.M.A. Arch. Gen. Psychiat., *5:*462, 1961.
28. Darwin, C.: The Expression of Emotions in Man and Animals (1872). New York, Philosophical Library, 1955.
29. Engel, G. L., Reichsman, F. and Segal, H. L.: A Study of an Infant with a Gastric Fistula. I. Behavior and the Rate of Total HCl Secretion. Psychosom. Med., *18:*374, 1956.
30. Grace, W. J., Wolf, S. and Wolff, H. G.: The Human Colon. New York, Paul B. Hoeber, Inc., 1951.
31. Hess, W. R.: Functional Organization of the Diencephalon. New York, Grune and Stratton, 1957.
32. Price, D. B., Thaler, M. and Mason, J. W.: Studies of Preoperative Emotional States and Adrenal Cortical Activity in Cardiac and Pulmonary Surgery Patients. A.M.A. Arch. Neurol. & Psychiat., *77:*646, 1957.
33. Shagass, C.: Neurophysiologic Studies of Anxiety and Depression. Psychiatric Research Reports of the American Psychiatric Association, *8:*100, 1957.
34. Wolf, S. and Wolff, H. G.: Human Gastric Function. New York, Oxford University Press, 1943.

Somatic Decompensation, Local Defense Reactions

35. Bush, I. E. and Mahesh, V. B.: Adrenocortical Hyperfunction with Sudden Onset of Hirsutism. J. Endocrinol., *18:*1, 1959.
36. Cannon, W. B.: "Voodoo" Death. Psychosom. Med., *19:*182, 1957.
37. Chambers, W. and Reiser, M.: Emotional Stress in the Precipitation of Congestive Heart Failure. Psychosom. Med., *15:*38, 1953.
38. Chapman, L. F., Goodell, H. and Wolff, H. G.: Changes in Tissue Vulnerability Induced During Hypnotic Suggestion. J. Psychosom. Res., *4:*99, 1959.
39. Engel, G. L., Ferris, E. B. and Logan, M.: Hyperventilation: Analysis of Clinical Symptomatology. Ann. Int. Med., *27:*683, 1947.
40. Engel, G. L.: Biologic and Psychologic Features of the Ulcerative Colitis Patient. Gastroenterology, *40:*313, 1960.
41. Engel, G. L.: Is Grief a Disease? A Challenge for Medical Research. Psychosom. Med., *23:*18, 1961.
42. Engel, G. L.: Fainting. Physiologic and Psychologic Considerations. 2nd ed. Springfield, Illinois, Charles C Thomas, 1962.
43. Engel, G. L.: Humanism and Science in Medicine. *In* Brill, N. (ed.): Psychiatry in Medicine. Berkeley, University of California Press, 1962.
44. Hickam, J. B., Cargill, W. H. and Golden, A. C.: Cardiovascular Reactions to Emotional Stimuli. Effect on the Cardiac Output, A-V Oxygen Difference, Arterial Pressure, and Peripheral Resistance. J. Clin. Invest., *26:*1, 1947.
45. Hinkle, L. E. and Wolf, S.: A Summary of Experimental Evidence Relating Life Stress to Diabetes Mellitus. J. Mount Sinai Hosp. *19:*537, 1952.
46. Kaplan, S. M., Gottschalk, L. A. and Fleming, D. E.: Modification of Oropharyngeal Bacteria with Changes in Psychodynamic State. A.M.A. Arch. Neurol. & Psychiat., *78:*656, 1957.

47. Kowal, S. J.: Emotions as a Cause of Cancer. Psychoanalyt. Rev., *42*:217, 1955.
48. Liddell, H. S.: Experimental Neuroses in Animals. *In* Tanner, J. M. (ed.): Stress and Psychiatric Disorder. Oxford, Blackwell Scientific Publications, 1960.
49. Moore, A. U.: Conditioning and Stress in the Newborn Lamb. *In* Gannt, W. H. (ed.): Physiological Bases of Psychiatry. Springfield, Illinois, Charles C Thomas, 1958.
50. Richter, C. P.: The Phenomenon of Unexplained Sudden Death in Animals and Man. *In* Gannt, W. H. (ed.): Physiological Bases of Psychiatry. Springfield, Illinois, Charles C Thomas, 1958. (Also in Psychosom. Med., *19*:191, 1957.)
51. Rioch, D. M., Herbert, C. C. and Mead, N. A.: The Psychophysiology of Death. *In* Simon, A. (ed.): The Physiology of Emotions. Springfield, Illinois, Charles C Thomas, 1961.
52. Schmale, A. H.: Relationship of Separation and Depression to Disease. I. A Report on a Hospitalized Medical Population. Psychosom. Med., *20*:259, 1958.
53. Wolff, H. G.: Man's Nervous System and Disease. A.M.A. Arch. Neurol., *5*:235, 1961.

Somatopsychic-Psychosomatic Processes

54. Ader, R., Beels, C. C. and Tatum, R.: Blood Pepsinogen and Gastric Erosion in the Rat. Psychosom. Med., *22*:1, 1960.
55. Alexander, F.: Psychosomatic Medicine. New York, W. W. Norton and Co., 1950.
56. Engel, G. L.: Biologic and Psychologic Features of the Ulcerative Colitis Patient. Gastroenterology, *40*:313, 1960.
57. Mirsky, I. A.: Physiologic, Psychologic, and Social Determinants in the Etiology of Duodenal Ulcer. Am. J. Digest. Dis., *3*:285, 1958.

CHAPTER XXXIV

EPILOGUE: THE
FUTURE OF MEDICINE

The many ways in which somatic disturbances of varying types may come about in response to psychological stress, as presented in Chapters XXXII and XXXIII, should make it apparent that there is no duality between the so-called "psychiatric" and the "organic" diseases, in respect to either etiology or clinical expression. This makes more meaningful the often heard cliché that the physician's attention must be focused on the patient who is manifesting illness, not simply on the disease. Although there are important reasons why a particular disease process must be identified and elucidated as an entity, the ultimate goal must always be to analyze the process as part of the individual's experience of illness. This is more in keeping with the obvious clinical fact that the history of illness of a patient never is confined to the neat categories of disease described in our clinical texts. The designation of illnesses or of patients as medical, surgical, orthopedic, psychiatric, etc., reflects administrative convenience and medico-social convention, for which the main justification concerns techniques of treatment or examination, not the true condition of the patient. The student or physician who believes that a patient on the orthopedic service is fundamentally different from a patient on the psychiatric service will do well to explore thoroughly the histories of these two people, for it is possible for him to discover that it is the same patient manifesting two slightly different patterns of response to stress, responses that call for different methods of management, not necessarily different ways of viewing the patient.

An important common denominator underlying health and disease is psychological stress, which directly or indirectly determines not only

402

the individual's capacity to cope with other stresses but often his exposure to such stresses as well. If these influences are to be clarified, understood and brought under control, medicine must now turn its attention to the central mediating and controlling systems, the brain and the mind. In my judgment, the next great advance in medicine will evolve through the study of brain and behavior. This should parallel the "biochemical revolution" which is now in progress. But a warning is in order. The temptation no doubt will be to divorce brain from behavior, to pursue the reductionistic view that the study of brain by itself will be sufficient to solve the riddle of behavior and its relation to disease. Nothing could be more sterile. Without the painstaking study and analysis of behavior in psychological, interpersonal and social terms, we are ill-equipped to understand the function of the brain and, indeed, even to know what to study. As important as are the contributions of the basic scientists, the clinician must not underestimate the opportunities of his unique role, namely, to contribute through day-to-day observation to the understanding of the human being in health and illness. It is the natural history of health and disease, in the broadest sense, which provides the richest source of information as to what is relevant for study by the basic scientist. And it is the clinician who has the widest access to the life history, the trials and tribulations, the successes and triumphs, the losses and gains, and the whole developmental span of life of many human beings. The scientifically minded physician must now turn his attention to this rich source of information, through which his laboratory-oriented colleagues will be provided with meaningful leads for the elucidation of details and mechanisms. Nature determines which laboratory artifacts are relevant. But the physician must establish what is natural, in whatever terms the data are accessible, be they epidemiological, ecological, psychological, social or clinical.

AUTHOR INDEX

Abraham, K., 80
Ader, R., 397, 401
Ainsworth, M., 104
Alexander, F., x, 168, 188, 363, 380, 396, 401
Anshen, R. N., 220
Arieti, S., 342, 363
Aubry, S., xxxi

Bales, R. F., 220
Barchilon, J., 380
Barman, W. J., 400
Bartemeier, L., 287
Bartholomay, A. F., 399
Basowitz, H., 399
Batchelor, I. R. C., 363
Bateson, G., xxxi
Beels, C. C., 401
Benedek, T., x, 41, 42, 46, 47, 188, 191, 196, 199, 209
Benedict, R., 91, 96
Bernard, C., 11, 19
Bertalanffy, L., 9, 12, 19
Blauvelt, H., 19
Bleuler, E., 326, 329, 363
Board, F., 399

Bogdonoff, M., 399
Bornstein, B., 139
Boston, M., 104
Bowlby, J., 56, 104
Brady, J., 399
Brenner, C., 236
Breuer, J., 380
Bridger, W. H., 32, 36
Brill, A. A., 363
Brody, S., 42
Burlingham, D., 287
Busfield, B., 400
Bush, I. E., 400

Cannon, W. B., 12, 19, 27, 384, 399, 400
Cardon, P. V., 399
Cargill, W. H., 400
Cattell, J. P., 341
Chambers, W., 400
Chapman, L. F., 400
Clarke, L. D., 342
Cohen, E. A., 287
Cohen, S. I., 399
Colby, K. M., 232, 236
Connel, P., 341
Conrad, D., 399

405

SUBJECT INDEX

ABANDONMENT, affects associated with, in shock phase following natural disaster, 282
by internalized love object, fear of, in shame, 170
Abdomen, involvement in hypochondriacal symptoms, 375
Abortion, spontaneous, as expression of incomplete or substitute drive activity, 395
Abstinence, sexual, as psychic stress, 303
Accident(s), as self-punishment, 110
response to, in terms of unresolved intrapsychic conflict, 290
unconsciously motivated, as somatically maladaptive psychological compensation, 367
"Accommodation" (Piaget), 58, 59, 231, 258, 259
ACTH, stress-invoked secretion of, 391
Acting out, as attempt to alleviate or ward off depression, 360
as defense against infantile object ties, 147
as denial of reality in Oedipus complex, 107
as type of character disorder, 353
due to superego lacunae, 337
in gang behavior, 138
of parent's forbidden wish, 136

Action, primary model of, in psychoanalytic theory of behavior, 222
secondary model of, in psychoanalytic theory of behavior, 225
Activity, in primary sleep-waking cycle of newborn, 31 ff.
spontaneous, as common property of all organisms, 5
Adaptation(s), acquired, first (Piaget), in development of intelligence and reality sense in infant, 60
role in phenomenology of disease, 270
Addiction, anxiety in, 358
as category of psychiatric disease, 356
due to defect in ego ideal function, 338
to organic syndrome, 361
Adjustment, in work situation, as indicator of health or disease, 190
social, in latency period, 137
to environmental changes, as common property of all organisms, 6
Adolescence, 141–154
as disrupting experience for parents, 153
development of identity in, 151
ego in, 146
in boys, 143
in girls, 144
superego in, 150
Adrenal cortex, role in flight-fight patterns, 385

409

Anxiety, as response to psychological stress, 331
  to unresolved danger, 126
  as signal-scanning affect, 128
    in adulthood, 167
  biological anlage of, 55
  communicated to child, as determinant of psychiatric disease, 313
  correlation with physiological patterns, 388
  dreams of, as repetition-compulsion, 311
  drive aspect of, 126
  due to daydreams involving taboo areas, 132
    to discovery of parents' genitals, 88
    to erection, in childhood, 86
    to sexual taboos in latency period, 131
  ego aspect of, 125
  eighth month, 50, 69
  failure of mechanism of, depression-withdrawal as response to, 55
  feeling qualities and ideation accompanying, 167
  flight-fight patterns as behavioral aspects of, 384
  "free-floating," as sign of stress or disease, 168, 358
    following disaster, 282
  in autoeroticism, 86
  in infancy, 55
  in neurosis, 347
  in older men, 195
  in presence of strangers, 50, 69
  in response to deprivation and isolation, 285
    to specific symptoms of disease, 247
  interaction with other affects, 186
  kidding as means of dealing with, 143
  of objects, communicated as threat of injury, 301
  physiological decompensation associated with, 391
  predisposition to, as factor in psychogenesis of disease, 315
  role in psychic regulation, 127
  self-object aspect of, 126
  somatic components of, 382–387
  warning and flight response as components of, 55
Anxiety hysteria, 358
Anxiety syndromes, 358, 359
Apathy, following deprivation and isolation, 286
  following natural disaster, 282
  following real object loss, 276
Apperception, disorders of, as signs and symptoms of psychiatric disease, 327

Appetite, as example of secondary model of conation, 225, 226, 227
  as psychological representation of hunger, 114
  derangements of, for psychological compensation, 367
  increase of, in pregnancy, 204
"As if" identity, as manifestation of disturbance in identity and self concepts, 328
    as stage in development of identity in adolescence, 152
    in regressive ego pattern of adolescence, 148
Asceticism, as ego defense in adolescence, 149
"Assimilation" (Piaget), 58, 59, 64, 231, 258, 259
Assumptive beliefs, influence on predisposition to and pathogenesis of psychiatric disorders, 317–318
Atonement, as adaptive ego response to guilt feelings, 171
  as restitutive drive component of guilt, 172
  as underlying factor in ego defense by undoing, 134, 136
  excessive, due to defective superego function, illness patterns due to, 336
  role in undoing as ego defense, 134
Attention. See also Awareness.
  disorders involving, 327, 332
Authoritarianism, influence on predisposition to and pathogenesis of psychiatric disorders, 317
Autoeroticism, development of in second year of life, 74
  psychological and behavioral results of, 85
Autoimmune reactions, predisposing factors in, 260
Autonomous apparatuses, primary, 112
    in mental apparatus of newborn, 38
Autonomous ego, 116–118, 230
Autonomy, as function of psychic apparatus, 25
  finger sucking as early expression of, 44
  from internal and external pressures, as characteristic of effective mental apparatus, 25, 27, 113, 235, 325
  of ego, as characteristic of adult mental apparatus, 156
    secondary model of conation as indication of, 228
  of mental functioning, as product of ego development, 120
Avoidance behavior, learning of, 23
Avoidance conditioning, 126

Drive patterns, displaced or incomplete, in response to psychological stress, 395

Drive release, sudden, affects of, 186

Drugs, addiction to, as psychiatric disease, 356
syndromes due to, 333
use of, in attempt to alleviate or ward off depression, 360

Dynamic steady state, in newborn, 39
maintenance of, as function of central nervous system, 21

EGO, affects as functions of, 166
autonomous, 116–118, 230
at end of first year of life, 48
autonomy of, in adulthood, 156
secondary model of conation as indication of, 228
weakening effects of deprivation and isolation on, 286
conflict-free aspects of, 117
conflict-free sphere of. See *Ego, autonomous.*
defense mechanisms of, development in infancy, 48
defensive functions of, role in learning, 117
functions of, as factors underlying syndrome formation, 334
as internalized record of individual's past, 289
in latency period, 131
mental apparatus associated with, 27
in adulthood, 156–160, 166–188
in depression, 360
involvement in reproductive drive in woman, 200
of adolescent, 146
relation of drives to, 124
restriction of, in Oedipus complex, 107
role in consciousness and unconsciousness, 122
in development of mental apparatus, 116–120
in secondary process of mental activity, 123
signal and warning functions of, 118
warning function of, 55

Ego aspect, of anger and rage, 180
of anxiety, 125
of depression-withdrawal, 127
of disgust, 172
of guilt, 171
of helplessness and hopelessness, 176
of libidinal drive affects, 182
of sadness, 174

Ego aspect, of shame, 169

Ego controls, structure of, 227

Ego defense(s), 118–120
in adolescence, against infantile object ties and pregenital and genital impulses, 147
as stabilizing influences, 150
in adulthood, 157
individualization of, in latency period, 133
patterning of, as factor in syndrome formation, 334
structure of, 227

Ego functions, in character disorders, 350–355
in neurosis and psychosis, 346–350

Ego ideal, as internal motivating force of ego, 110
formation of, 109
function of, in latency period, 131
importance in latency period, 135
in depression, 360
in helplessness and hopelessness, 175
in pride, 177
role in development of mental apparatus, 121
in syndrome formation, 336

Embarrassment, as quality of shame, 169

Emergency system(s), as function of psychic apparatus, 26
of central nervous system, 22

Empathy, 185

Employment. See also *Work.*
loss of, as object loss, 297

Energy, conservation of, by ego functions, 120
by means of depression-withdrawal, 55
depression-withdrawal as indicator for, 127
in endogenous behavior patterns, 16
instinctual, 17
intake and utilization of, 12
psychic, in regulation of behavior, 232

Environment, attention to and awareness of, as functions of psychic apparatus, 24
changes in, adjustment to, as common property of all organisms, 6
external, response to changes in, as function of central nervous system, 22

Envy, affect quality of, 184

Epigenesis, 4
psychosocial concept of, 235

Eroticism, anal, in infancy, 76
pre-oedipal, 90
oral, in infancy, 76